MY YOUTH ROMANTIC COMEDY IS WRONG, AS I EXPECTED @COMIC

Original Story: Wataru Watari
Art: Naomichi Io
Character Design: Ponkan⑧
ORIGINAL COVER DESIGN/Hiroyuki KAWASOME (Graphio)

Translation: Jennifer Ward

Lettering: Bianca Pistillo

YAHARI ORE NO SEISHUN LOVE COME WA MACHIGATTEIRU.
@COMIC Vol. 7 by Wataru WATARI, Naomichi IO, PONKAN⑧
© 2013 Wataru WATARI, Naomichi IO, PONKAN⑧
All rights reserved.
Original Japanese edition published by SHOGAKUKAN.
English translation rights arranged with SHOGAKUKAN through Tuttle-Mori Agency, Inc., Tokyo.

English translation © 2017 by Yen Press, LLC

Yen Press
1290 Avenue of the Americas
New York, NY 10104

Visit us at yenpress.com
facebook.com/yenpress
twitter.com/yenpress
yenpress.tumblr.com
instagram.com/yenpress

First Yen Press Edition: December 2017

Yen Press is an imprint of Yen Press, LLC.
The Yen Press name and logo are trademarks of Yen Press, LLC.

D1517050

Library of Congress Control Number: 2016931004

ISBN: 978-0-316-51721-8

10 9 8 7 6 5 4 3 2 1

BVG

Printed in the United States of America

Page 125
Meguri is quoting a line from Chiba Ondou, a traditional-style song and dance that is the official dance of Chiba Prefecture. It's typical for every region in Japan to have a dance like this, which volunteers perform during local festivals.

Page 137
Pasela is the name of a karaoke parlor chain.

Page 140
Du-fu-fu is used in Japanese online culture as the stereotypical laugh of a disgusting *otaku*.

Page 144
Trolley Olley is a reference to a *Yu-Gi-Oh!* card, Express Train Trolley Olley.

Page 149
In Japanese, the character **Mr. Popo** in *Dragonball Z* speaks in a truncated, Tarzan-like manner.

192
Homoo, spelled with a dragged-out vowel, refers to a popular emoji of a fujoshi prowling around seeking BL: ┌（┌ ＾o＾）┐ホモォ

HxH normally refers to the *shounen* battle manga *Hunter x Hunter* by Yoshihiro Togashi, a manga with a particularly vibrant fujoshi fan base. In this case, it's also a reference to the idea of a romantic pairing between Hayato and Hachiman.

MY YOUTH R♥MANTIC COMEDY is WRØNG, AS I EXPECTED @comic

07

■ Original Story
Wataru Watari

■ Art
Naomichi Io

■ Character Design
Ponkan⑧

MY YOUTH ROMANTIC COMEDY IS WRONG, AS I EXPECTED @COMIC
CHARACTERS + STORY SO FAR

HACHIMAN HIKIGAYA
- LONER AND A TWISTED HUMAN BEING. FORCED TO JOIN THE SERVICE CLUB. ASPIRES TO BE A HOUSEHUSBAND.

YUKINO YUKINOSHITA
- PERFECT SUPERWOMAN WITH TOP GRADES AND FLAWLESS LOOKS, BUT HER PERSONALITY AND BOOBS ARE A LETDOWN. PRESIDENT OF THE SERVICE CLUB.

YUI YUIGAHAMA
- LIGHT-BROWN HAIR, MINISKIRT, LARGE-BOOBED SLUTTY TYPE. BUT SHE'S ACTUALLY A VIRGIN!? MEMBER OF THE SERVICE CLUB.

SHIZUKA HIRATSUKA
- GUIDANCE COUNSELOR. ATTEMPTING TO FIX HACHIMAN BY FORCING HIM INTO THE SERVICE CLUB.

SAIKA TOTSUKA
- THE SINGLE FLOWER BLOOMING IN THIS STORY. BUT...HAS A "PACKAGE."

HARUNO YUKINOSHITA
- YUKINO'S SISTER. UNIVERSITY UNDERGRADUATE. IS QUITE INTERESTED IN HACHIMAN.

MEGURI SHIROMEGURI
- THIRD-YEAR. THE PLEASANT AND GENTLE STUDENT COUNCIL PRESIDENT.

MINAMI SAGAMI
- HACHIMAN'S CLASSMATE AND A MEMBER OF THE GIRLS' B-GROUP.

KOMACHI HIKIGAYA
- HACHIMAN'S LITTLE SISTER. IN MIDDLE SCHOOL. EVERYTHING SHE DOES IS CALCULATED!?

HAYATO HAYAMA
- TOP RANKED IN THE SCHOOL CASTE. HANDSOME MEMBER OF THE SOCCER TEAM.

YUMIKO MIURA
- THE HIGH EMPRESS NONE CAN OPPOSE.

HINA EBINA
- A MEMBER OF MIURA'S CLIQUE, BUT A RAGING FUJOSHI ON THE INSIDE.

HACHIMAN HIKIGAYA, SECOND-YEAR AT SOUBU MUNICIPAL HIGH SCHOOL IN CHIBA CITY, IS A LONER. BUT EVER SINCE HE WAS FORCED INTO JOINING THE SERVICE CLUB, A MYSTERIOUS CLUB CAPTAINED BY THE MOST BEAUTIFUL GIRL IN SCHOOL, YUKINO YUKINOSHITA, HIS LONER LIFE HAS RAPIDLY BEEN VEERING OFF IN AN UNDESIRABLE DIRECTION. A NEW SEMESTER STARTS, AND THE SERVICE CLUB STARTS UP AGAIN. BUT THINGS ARE STILL FEELING WEIRD WITHIN THE CLUB, AND CULTURAL FESTIVAL SEASON IS COMING UP...

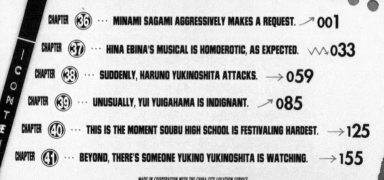

CONTENTS

MADE IN COOPERATION WITH THE CHIBA CITY LOCATION SERVICE

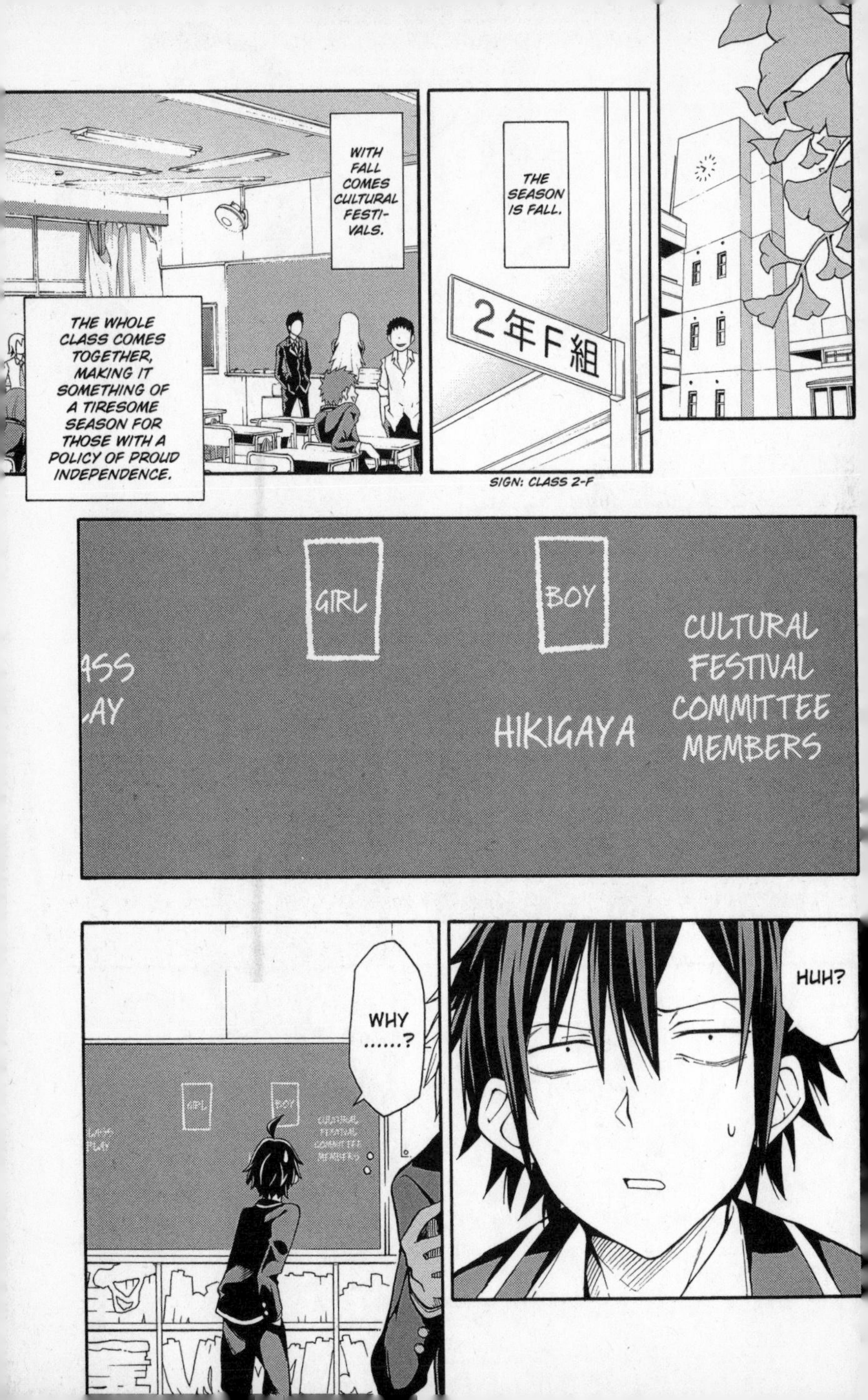
THE SEASON IS FALL.
2年F組
SIGN: CLASS 2-F
WITH FALL COMES CULTURAL FESTI-VALS.
THE WHOLE CLASS COMES TOGETHER, MAKING IT SOMETHING OF A TIRESOME SEASON FOR THOSE WITH A POLICY OF PROUD INDEPENDENCE.
CULTURAL FESTIVAL COMMITTEE MEMBERS
BOY
GIRL
HIKIGAYA
HUH?
WHY ......?

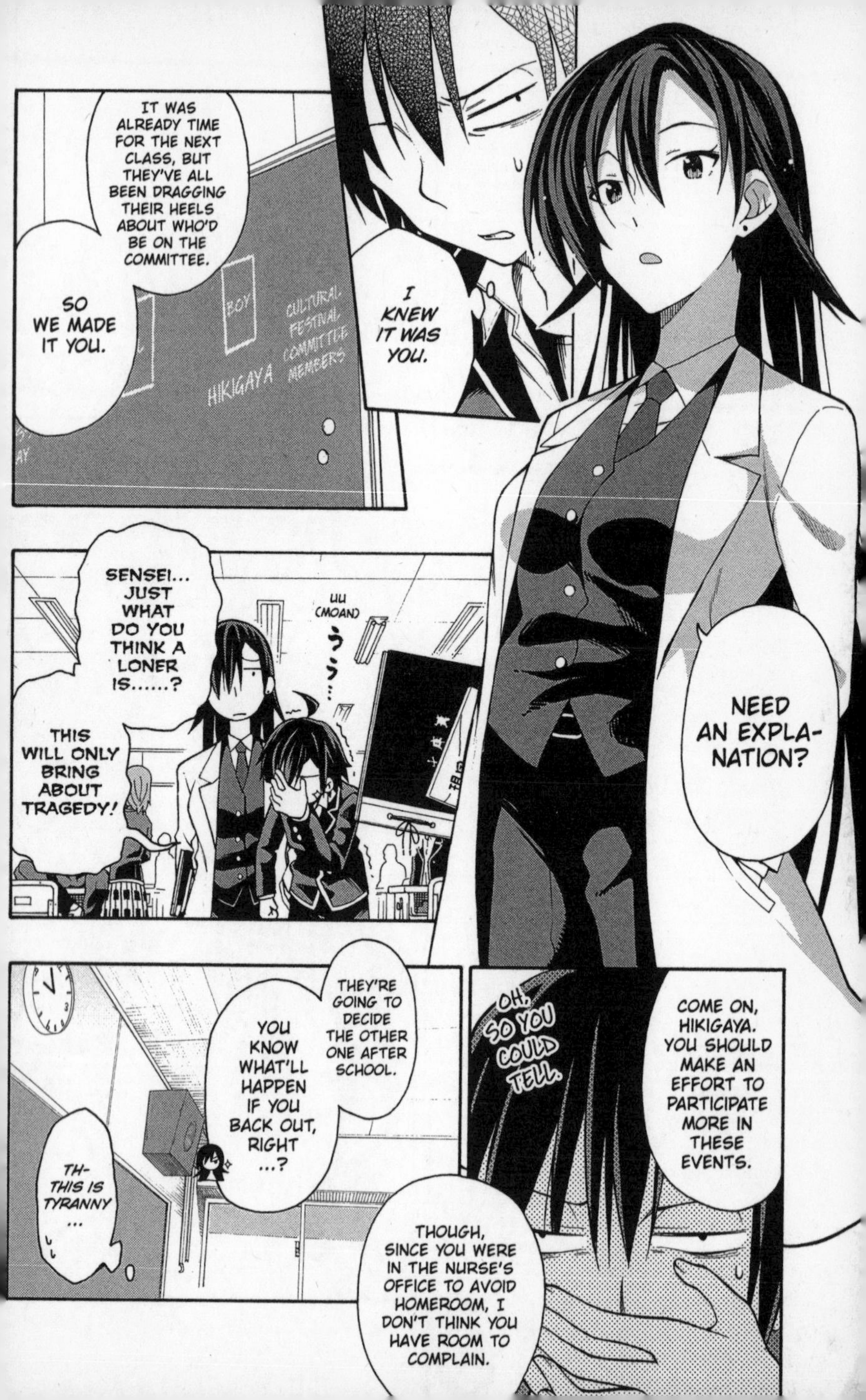
I KNEW IT WAS YOU.
NEED AN EXPLANATION?
IT WAS ALREADY TIME FOR THE NEXT CLASS, BUT THEY'VE ALL BEEN DRAGGING THEIR HEELS ABOUT WHO'D BE ON THE COMMITTEE.
SO WE MADE IT YOU.
BOY
CULTURAL FESTIVAL COMMITTEE MEMBERS
HIKIGAYA
SENSEI... JUST WHAT DO YOU THINK A LONER IS......?
THIS WILL ONLY BRING ABOUT TRAGEDY!
UU (MOAN)
うう…
OH. SO YOU COULD TELL.
COME ON, HIKIGAYA. YOU SHOULD MAKE AN EFFORT TO PARTICIPATE MORE IN THESE EVENTS.
THOUGH, SINCE YOU WERE IN THE NURSE'S OFFICE TO AVOID HOMEROOM, I DON'T THINK YOU HAVE ROOM TO COMPLAIN.
THEY'RE GOING TO DECIDE THE OTHER ONE AFTER SCHOOL.
YOU KNOW WHAT'LL HAPPEN IF YOU BACK OUT, RIGHT ...?
TH-THIS IS TYRANNY ...

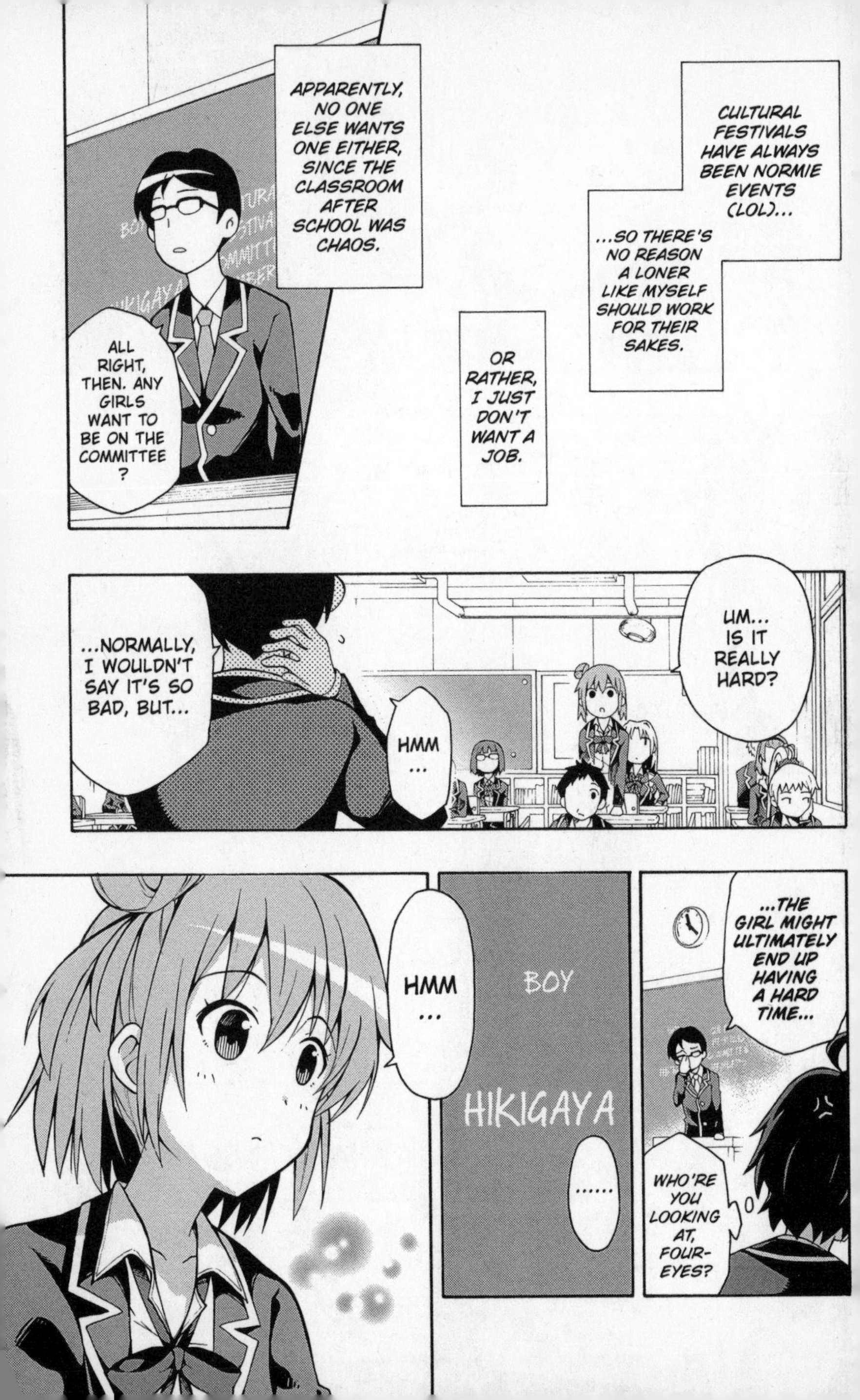
CULTURAL FESTIVALS HAVE ALWAYS BEEN NORMIE EVENTS (LOL)...
...SO THERE'S NO REASON A LONER LIKE MYSELF SHOULD WORK FOR THEIR SAKES.
OR RATHER, I JUST DON'T WANT A JOB.
APPARENTLY, NO ONE ELSE WANTS ONE EITHER, SINCE THE CLASSROOM AFTER SCHOOL WAS CHAOS.
ALL RIGHT, THEN. ANY GIRLS WANT TO BE ON THE COMMITTEE?
UM... IS IT REALLY HARD?
HMM...
...NORMALLY, I WOULDN'T SAY IT'S SO BAD, BUT...
...THE GIRL MIGHT ULTIMATELY END UP HAVING A HARD TIME...
WHO'RE YOU LOOKING AT, FOUR-EYES?
BOY
HIKIGAYA
......
HMM...

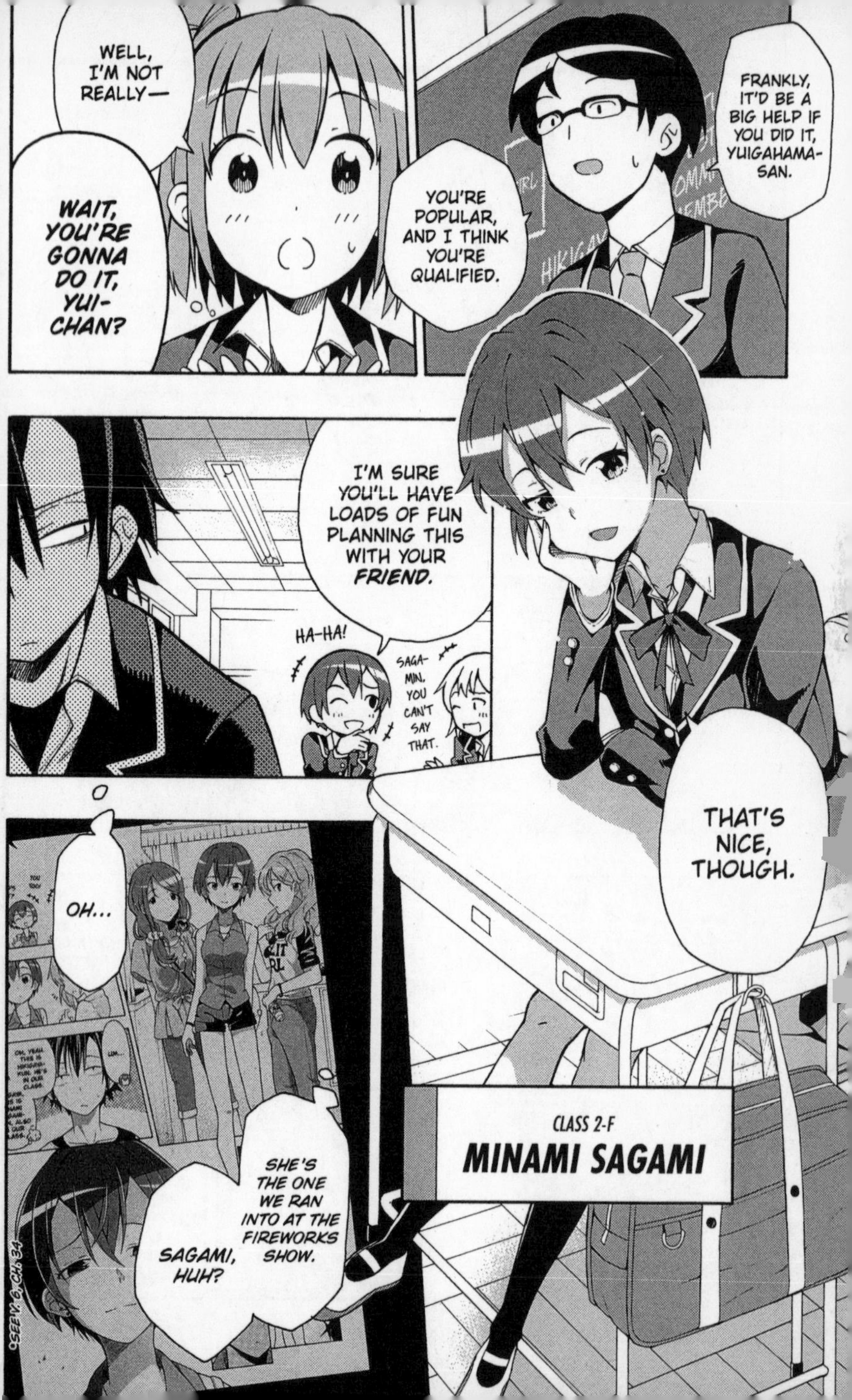
FRANKLY, IT'D BE A BIG HELP IF YOU DID IT, YUIGAHAMA-SAN.
YOU'RE POPULAR, AND I THINK YOU'RE QUALIFIED.
WELL, I'M NOT REALLY—
WAIT, YOU'RE GONNA DO IT, YUI-CHAN?
I'M SURE YOU'LL HAVE LOADS OF FUN PLANNING THIS WITH YOUR FRIEND.
HA-HA!
SAGA-MIN, YOU CAN'T SAY THAT.
THAT'S NICE, THOUGH.
CLASS 2-F
MINAMI SAGAMI
OH...
SHE'S THE ONE WE RAN INTO AT THE FIREWORKS SHOW.
SAGAMI, HUH?
*SEE V. 6, CH. 34

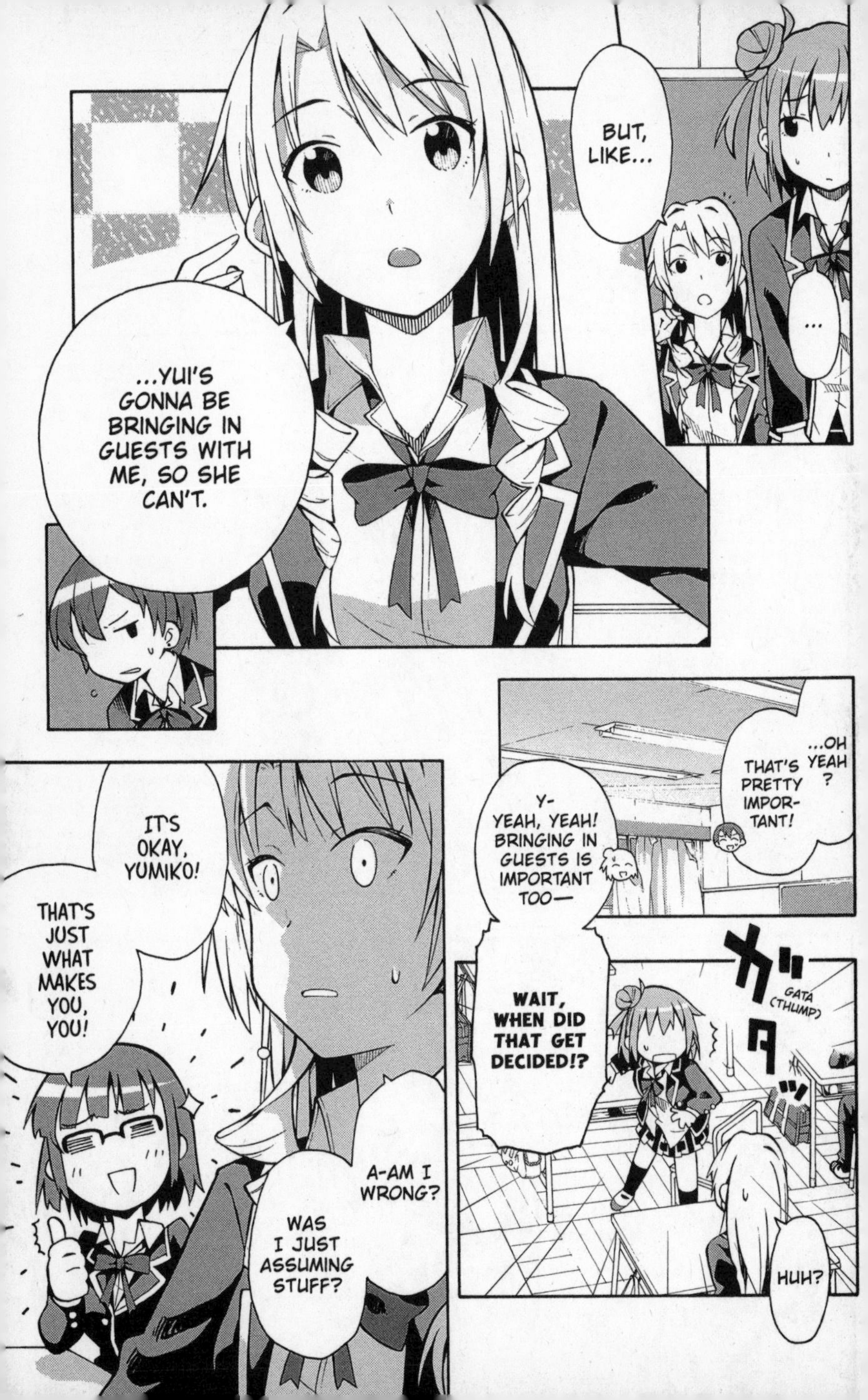
BUT, LIKE...
...YUI'S GONNA BE BRINGING IN GUESTS WITH ME, SO SHE CAN'T.
...
...OH YEAH?
THAT'S PRETTY IMPORTANT!
Y-YEAH, YEAH! BRINGING IN GUESTS IS IMPORTANT TOO—
GATA (THUMP)
WAIT, WHEN DID THAT GET DECIDED!?
HUH?
A-AM I WRONG?
WAS I JUST ASSUMING STUFF?
IT'S OKAY, YUMIKO!
THAT'S JUST WHAT MAKES YOU, YOU!

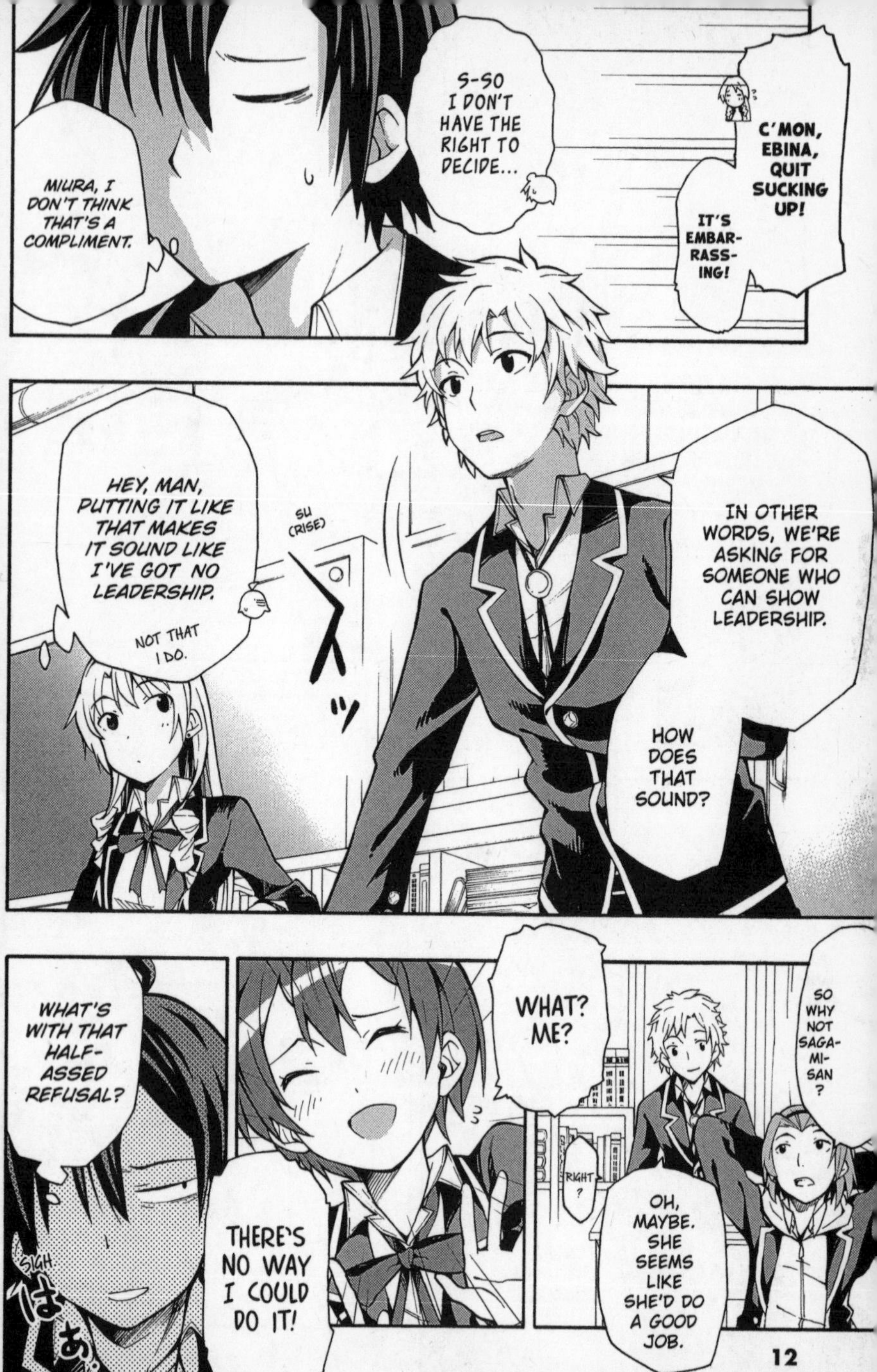
C'MON, EBINA, QUIT SUCKING UP!
IT'S EMBARRASSING!
S-SO I DON'T HAVE THE RIGHT TO DECIDE...
MIURA, I DON'T THINK THAT'S A COMPLIMENT.
IN OTHER WORDS, WE'RE ASKING FOR SOMEONE WHO CAN SHOW LEADERSHIP.
HOW DOES THAT SOUND?
SU (RISE)
HEY, MAN, PUTTING IT LIKE THAT MAKES IT SOUND LIKE I'VE GOT NO LEADERSHIP.
NOT THAT I DO.
SO WHY NOT SAGAMI-SAN?
OH, MAYBE. SHE SEEMS LIKE SHE'D DO A GOOD JOB.
RIGHT?
WHAT? ME?
THERE'S NO WAY I COULD DO IT!
WHAT'S WITH THAT HALF-ASSED REFUSAL?
SIGH

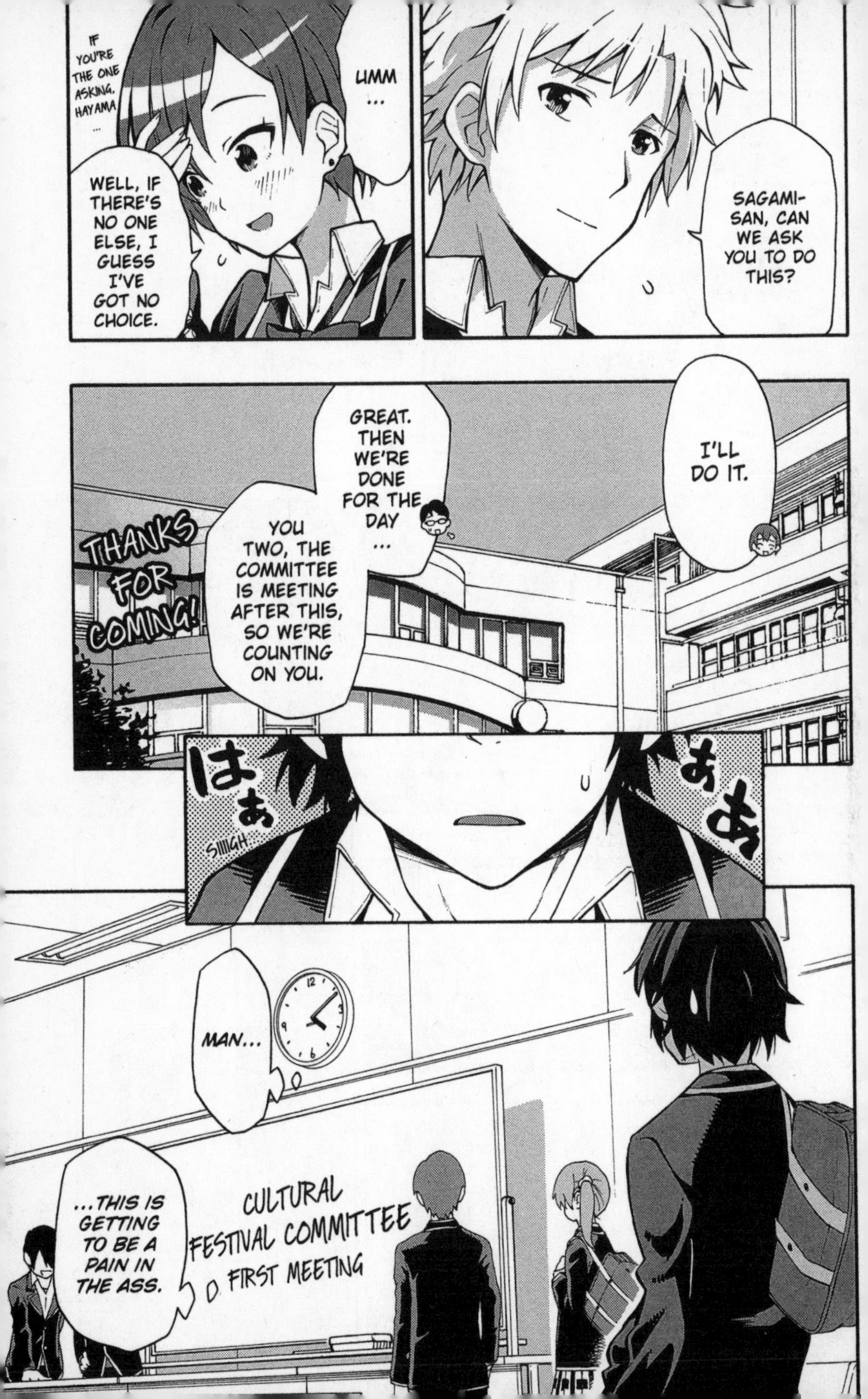
SAGAMI-SAN, CAN WE ASK YOU TO DO THIS?
UMM ...
IF YOU'RE THE ONE ASKING, HAYAMA ...
WELL, IF THERE'S NO ONE ELSE, I GUESS I'VE GOT NO CHOICE.
I'LL DO IT.
GREAT. THEN WE'RE DONE FOR THE DAY ...
YOU TWO, THE COMMITTEE IS MEETING AFTER THIS, SO WE'RE COUNTING ON YOU.
THANKS FOR COMING!
はぁぁぁ
SIIIGH
MAN...
...THIS IS GETTING TO BE A PAIN IN THE ASS.
CULTURAL FESTIVAL COMMITTEE FIRST MEETING

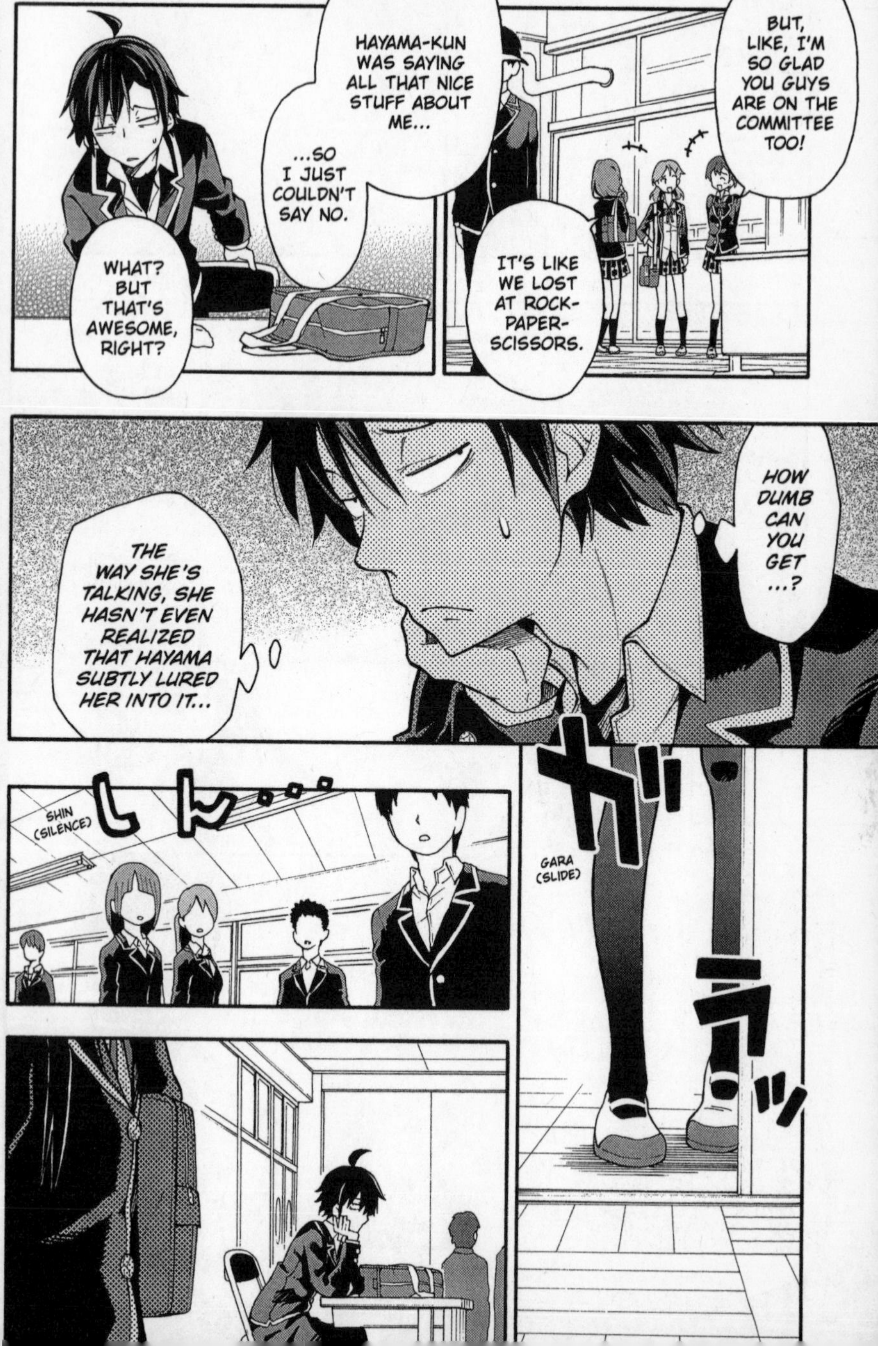
BUT, LIKE, I'M SO GLAD YOU GUYS ARE ON THE COMMITTEE TOO!
IT'S LIKE WE LOST AT ROCK-PAPER-SCISSORS.
HAYAMA-KUN WAS SAYING ALL THAT NICE STUFF ABOUT ME...
...SO I JUST COULDN'T SAY NO.
WHAT? BUT THAT'S AWESOME, RIGHT?
HOW DUMB CAN YOU GET...?
THE WAY SHE'S TALKING, SHE HASN'T EVEN REALIZED THAT HAYAMA SUBTLY LURED HER INTO IT...
GARA (SLIDE)
SHIN (SILENCE)

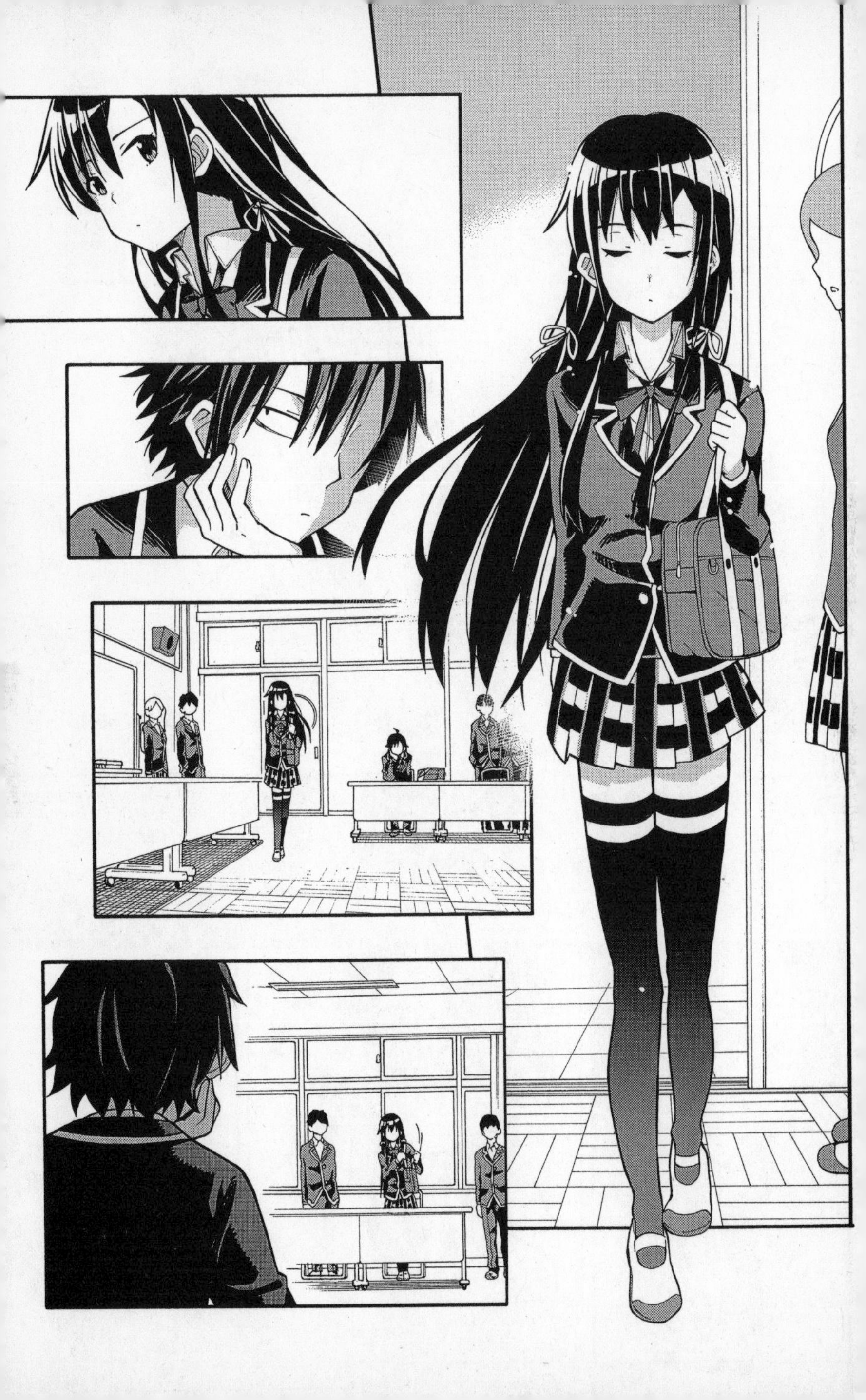

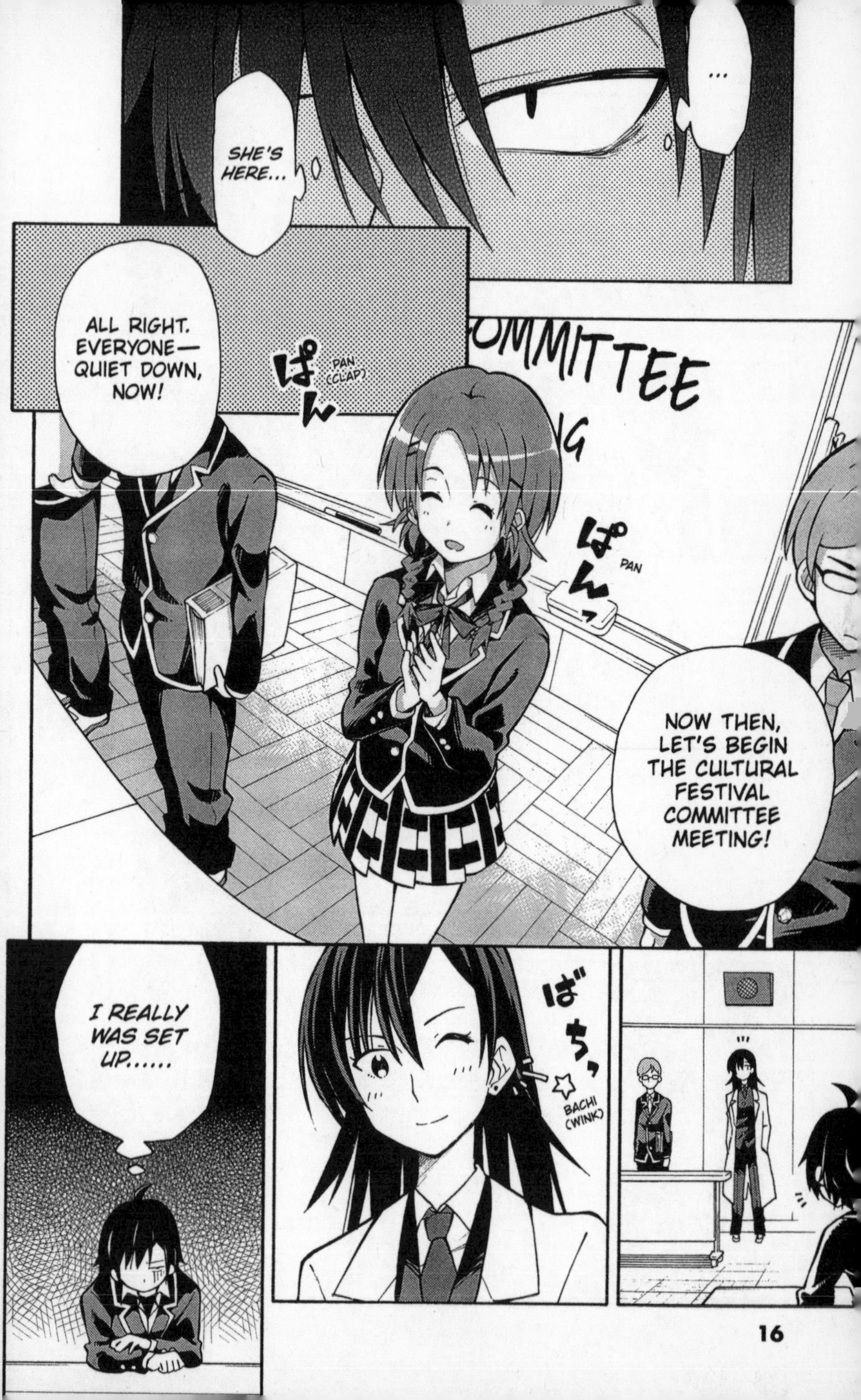
...
SHE'S HERE...
ALL RIGHT. EVERYONE— QUIET DOWN, NOW!
ぱん
PAN (CLAP)
OMMITTEE
G
ぱんっ
PAN
NOW THEN, LET'S BEGIN THE CULTURAL FESTIVAL COMMITTEE MEETING!
ばちっ
BACHI (WINK)
I REALLY WAS SET UP......

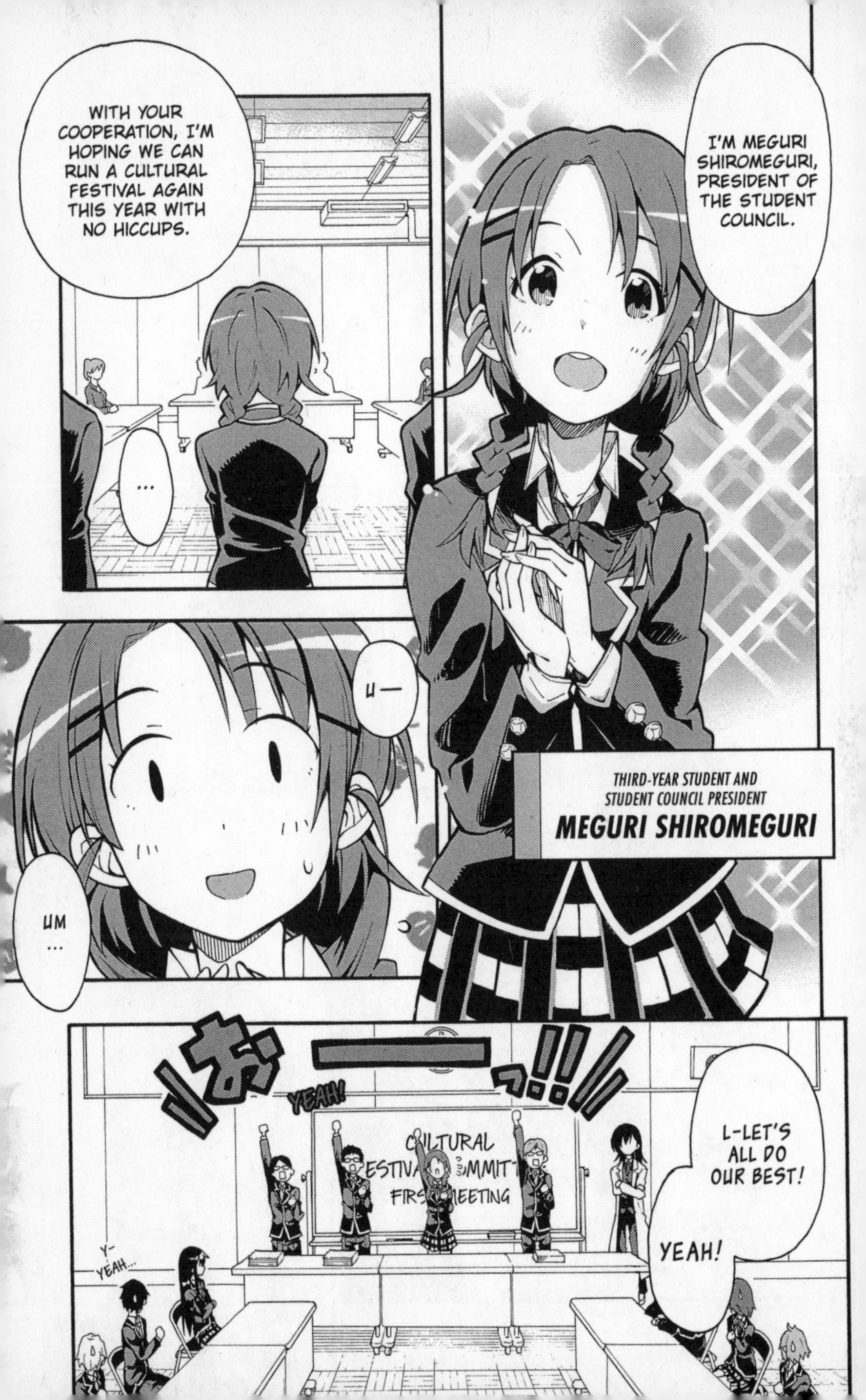
I'M MEGURI SHIROMEGURI, PRESIDENT OF THE STUDENT COUNCIL.
WITH YOUR COOPERATION, I'M HOPING WE CAN RUN A CULTURAL FESTIVAL AGAIN THIS YEAR WITH NO HICCUPS.
...
THIRD-YEAR STUDENT AND STUDENT COUNCIL PRESIDENT
MEGURI SHIROMEGURI
U—
UM ...
L-LET'S ALL DO OUR BEST!
YEAH!
おーーっ!!!
YEAH!
CULTURAL
Y-YEAH...

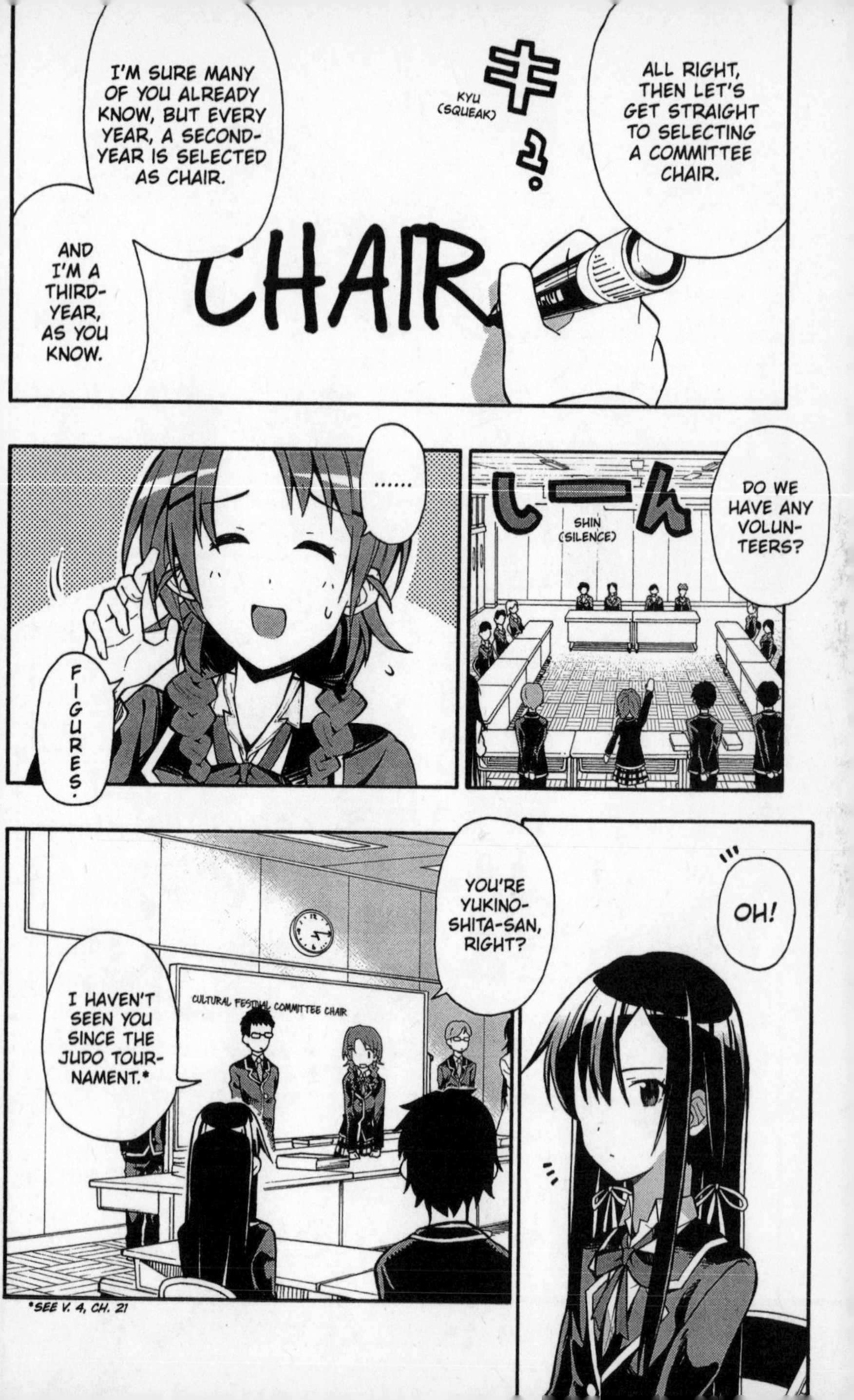
ALL RIGHT, THEN LET'S GET STRAIGHT TO SELECTING A COMMITTEE CHAIR.
KYU (SQUEAK)
CHAIR
I'M SURE MANY OF YOU ALREADY KNOW, BUT EVERY YEAR, A SECOND-YEAR IS SELECTED AS CHAIR.
AND I'M A THIRD-YEAR, AS YOU KNOW.
DO WE HAVE ANY VOLUNTEERS?
SHIN (SILENCE)
......
FIGURES.
OH!
YOU'RE YUKINOSHITA-SAN, RIGHT?
CULTURAL FESTIVAL COMMITTEE CHAIR
I HAVEN'T SEEN YOU SINCE THE JUDO TOURNAMENT.*

*SEE V. 4, CH. 21

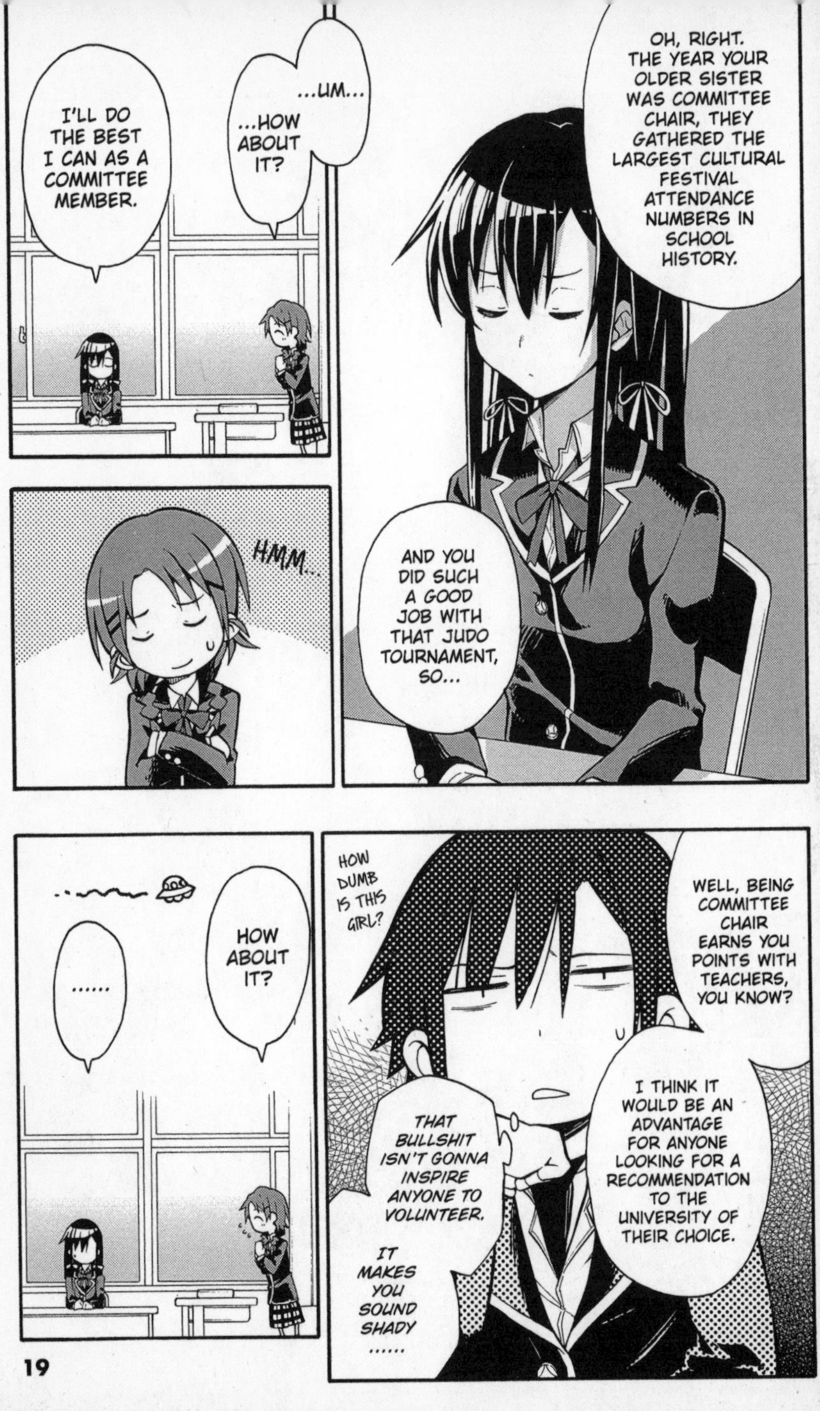
OH, RIGHT. THE YEAR YOUR OLDER SISTER WAS COMMITTEE CHAIR, THEY GATHERED THE LARGEST CULTURAL FESTIVAL ATTENDANCE NUMBERS IN SCHOOL HISTORY.
AND YOU DID SUCH A GOOD JOB WITH THAT JUDO TOURNAMENT, SO...
...UM... ...HOW ABOUT IT?
I'LL DO THE BEST I CAN AS A COMMITTEE MEMBER.
HMM...
HOW DUMB IS THIS GIRL?
WELL, BEING COMMITTEE CHAIR EARNS YOU POINTS WITH TEACHERS, YOU KNOW?
I THINK IT WOULD BE AN ADVANTAGE FOR ANYONE LOOKING FOR A RECOMMENDATION TO THE UNIVERSITY OF THEIR CHOICE.
THAT BULLSHIT ISN'T GONNA INSPIRE ANYONE TO VOLUNTEER.
IT MAKES YOU SOUND SHADY ......
HOW ABOUT IT?
......

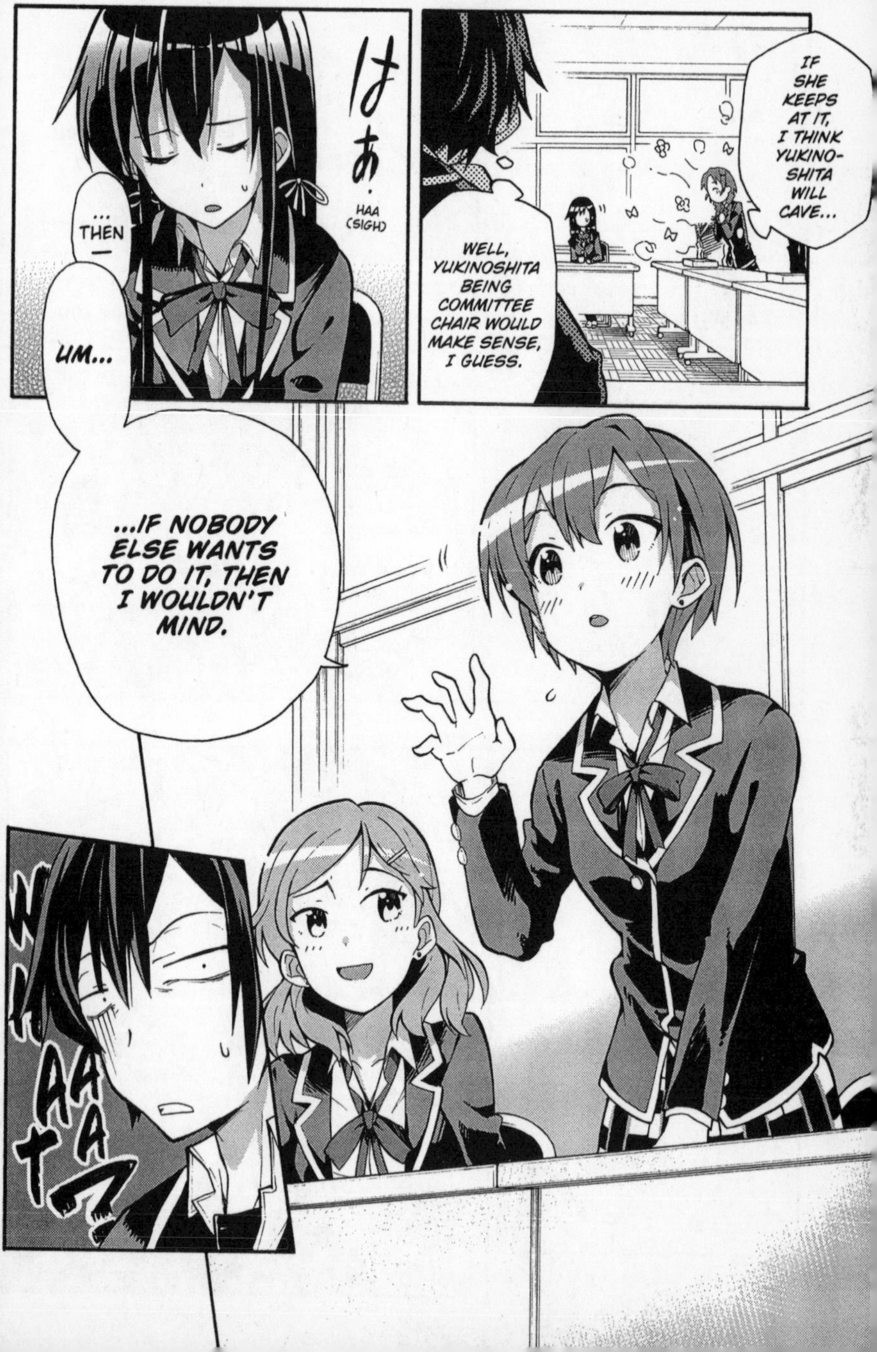
IF SHE KEEPS AT IT, I THINK YUKINOSHITA WILL CAVE...
WELL, YUKINOSHITA BEING COMMITTEE CHAIR WOULD MAKE SENSE, I GUESS.
はぁ
HAA (SIGH)
...THEN—
UM...
...IF NOBODY ELSE WANTS TO DO IT, THEN I WOULDN'T MIND.
WHAAAT?

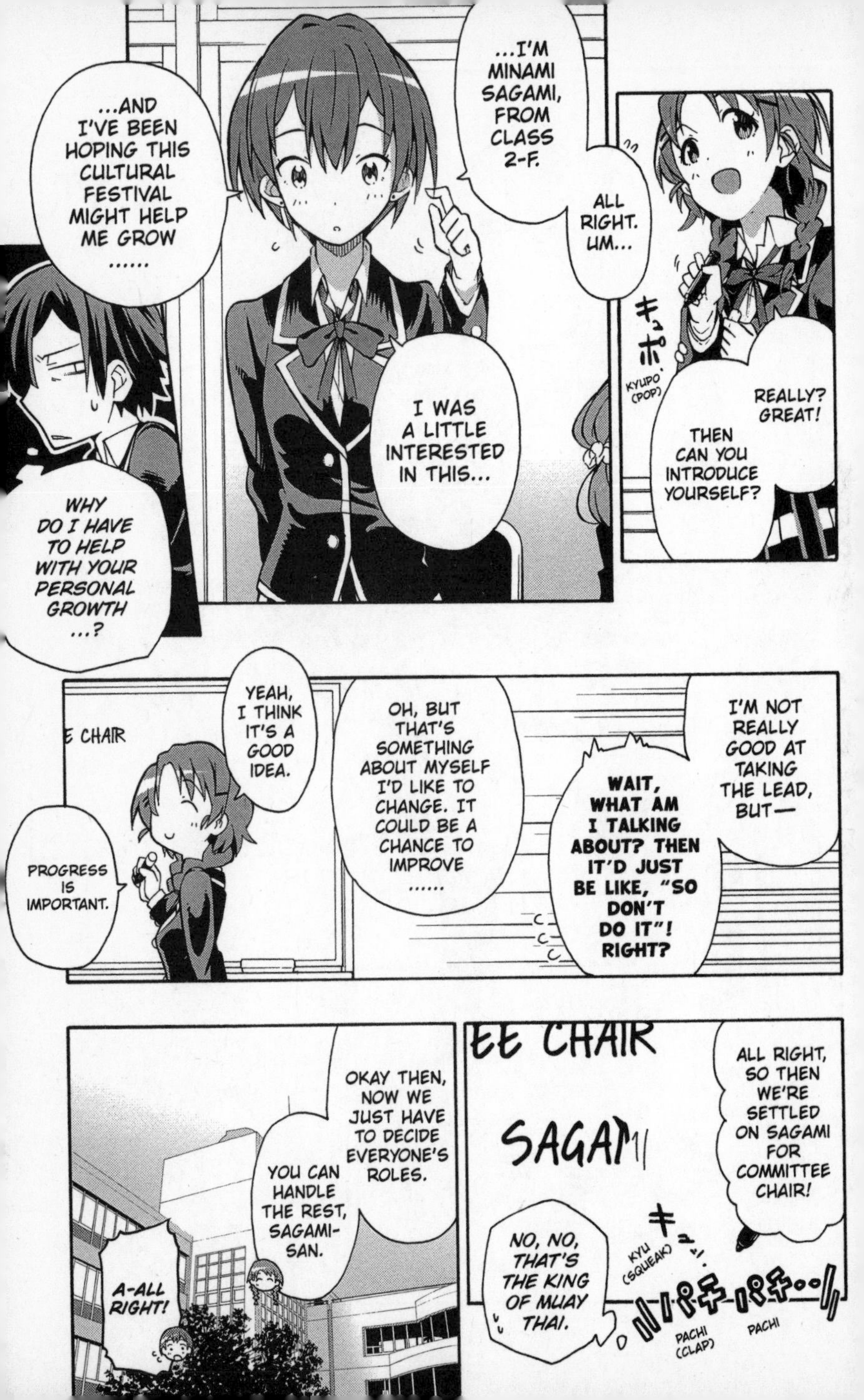

REALLY? GREAT!
THEN CAN YOU INTRODUCE YOURSELF?
KYUPO (POP)
ALL RIGHT. UM...
...I'M MINAMI SAGAMI, FROM CLASS 2-F.
I WAS A LITTLE INTERESTED IN THIS...
...AND I'VE BEEN HOPING THIS CULTURAL FESTIVAL MIGHT HELP ME GROW ......
WHY DO I HAVE TO HELP WITH YOUR PERSONAL GROWTH ...?
I'M NOT REALLY GOOD AT TAKING THE LEAD, BUT—
WAIT, WHAT AM I TALKING ABOUT? THEN IT'D JUST BE LIKE, "SO DON'T DO IT"! RIGHT?
OH, BUT THAT'S SOMETHING ABOUT MYSELF I'D LIKE TO CHANGE. IT COULD BE A CHANCE TO IMPROVE ......
YEAH, I THINK IT'S A GOOD IDEA.
E CHAIR
PROGRESS IS IMPORTANT.
EE CHAIR
SAGAM
ALL RIGHT, SO THEN WE'RE SETTLED ON SAGAMI FOR COMMITTEE CHAIR!
KYU (SQUEAK)
NO, NO, THAT'S THE KING OF MUAY THAI.
PACHI (CLAP)
PACHI
OKAY THEN, NOW WE JUST HAVE TO DECIDE EVERYONE'S ROLES.
YOU CAN HANDLE THE REST, SAGAMI-SAN.
A-ALL RIGHT!

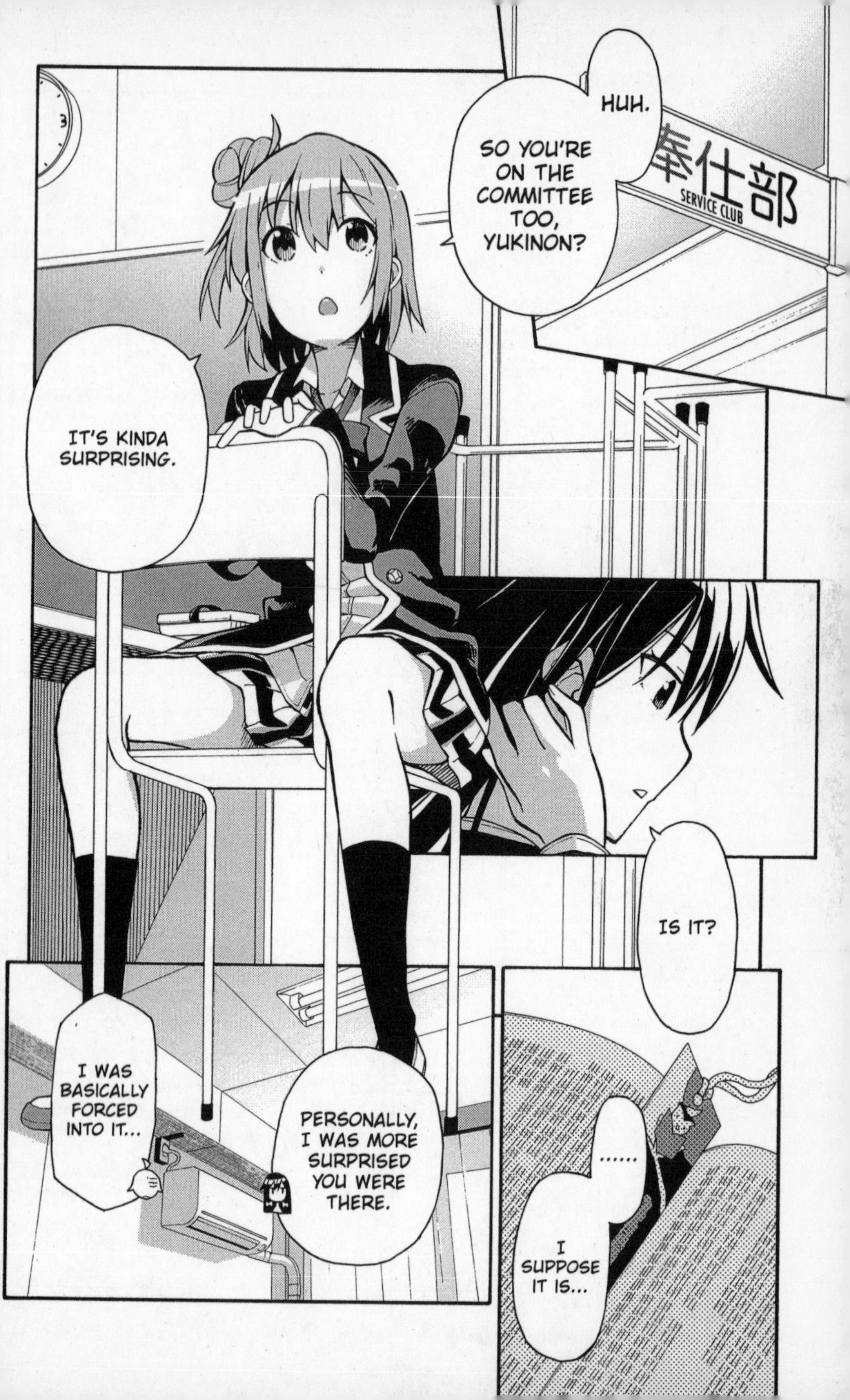
HUH.
SO YOU'RE ON THE COMMITTEE TOO, YUKINON?
奉仕部
SERVICE CLUB
IT'S KINDA SURPRISING.
IS IT?
......
I SUPPOSE IT IS...
PERSONALLY, I WAS MORE SURPRISED YOU WERE THERE.
I WAS BASICALLY FORCED INTO IT...

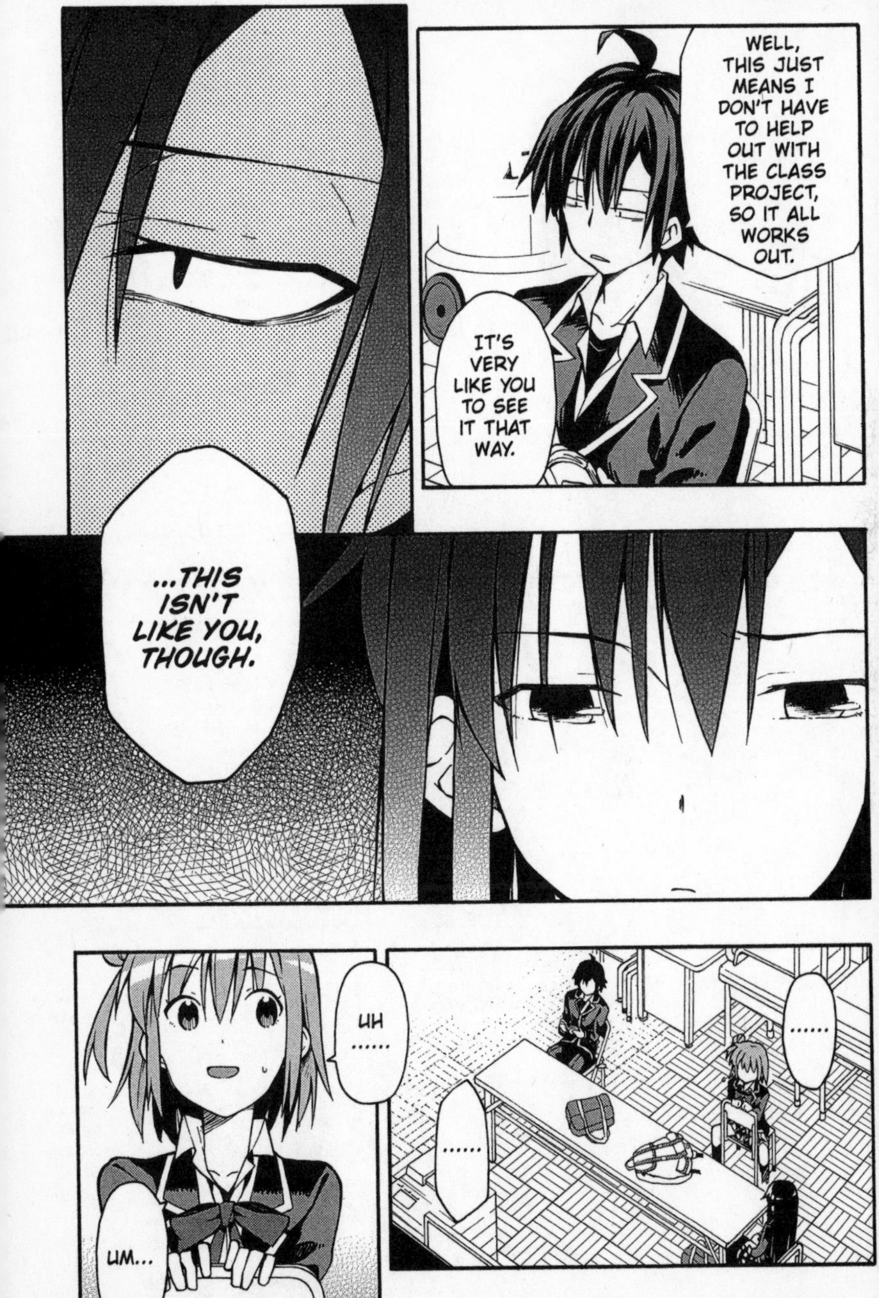
WELL, THIS JUST MEANS I DON'T HAVE TO HELP OUT WITH THE CLASS PROJECT, SO IT ALL WORKS OUT.
IT'S VERY LIKE YOU TO SEE IT THAT WAY.
...THIS ISN'T LIKE YOU, THOUGH.
......
......
UH ......
UM...

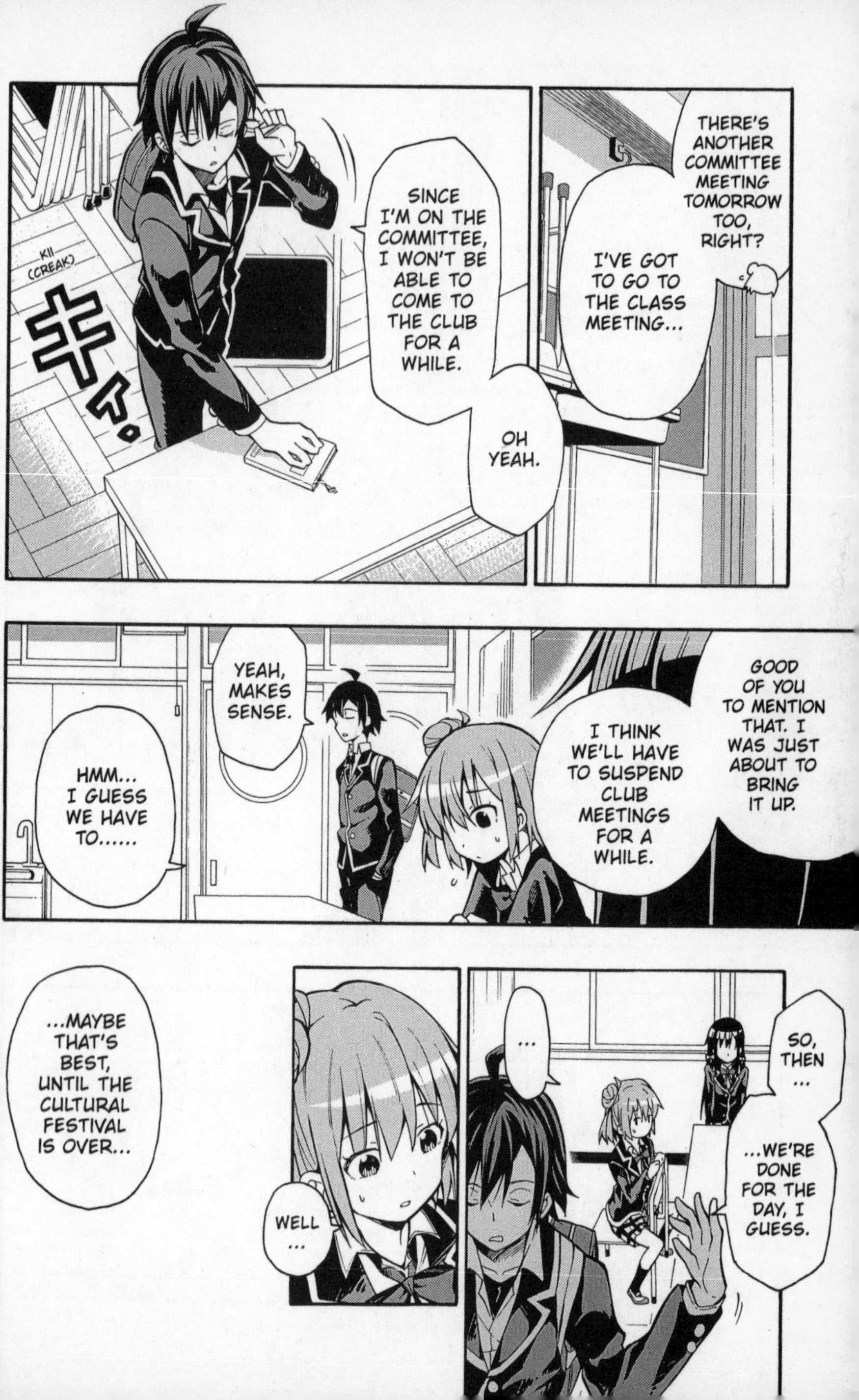
THERE'S ANOTHER COMMITTEE MEETING TOMORROW TOO, RIGHT?
I'VE GOT TO GO TO THE CLASS MEETING...
KII (CREAK)
キイ
SINCE I'M ON THE COMMITTEE, I WON'T BE ABLE TO COME TO THE CLUB FOR A WHILE.
OH YEAH.
GOOD OF YOU TO MENTION THAT. I WAS JUST ABOUT TO BRING IT UP.
I THINK WE'LL HAVE TO SUSPEND CLUB MEETINGS FOR A WHILE.
YEAH, MAKES SENSE.
HMM... I GUESS WE HAVE TO......
SO, THEN ...
...
...WE'RE DONE FOR THE DAY, I GUESS.
WELL ...
...MAYBE THAT'S BEST, UNTIL THE CULTURAL FESTIVAL IS OVER...

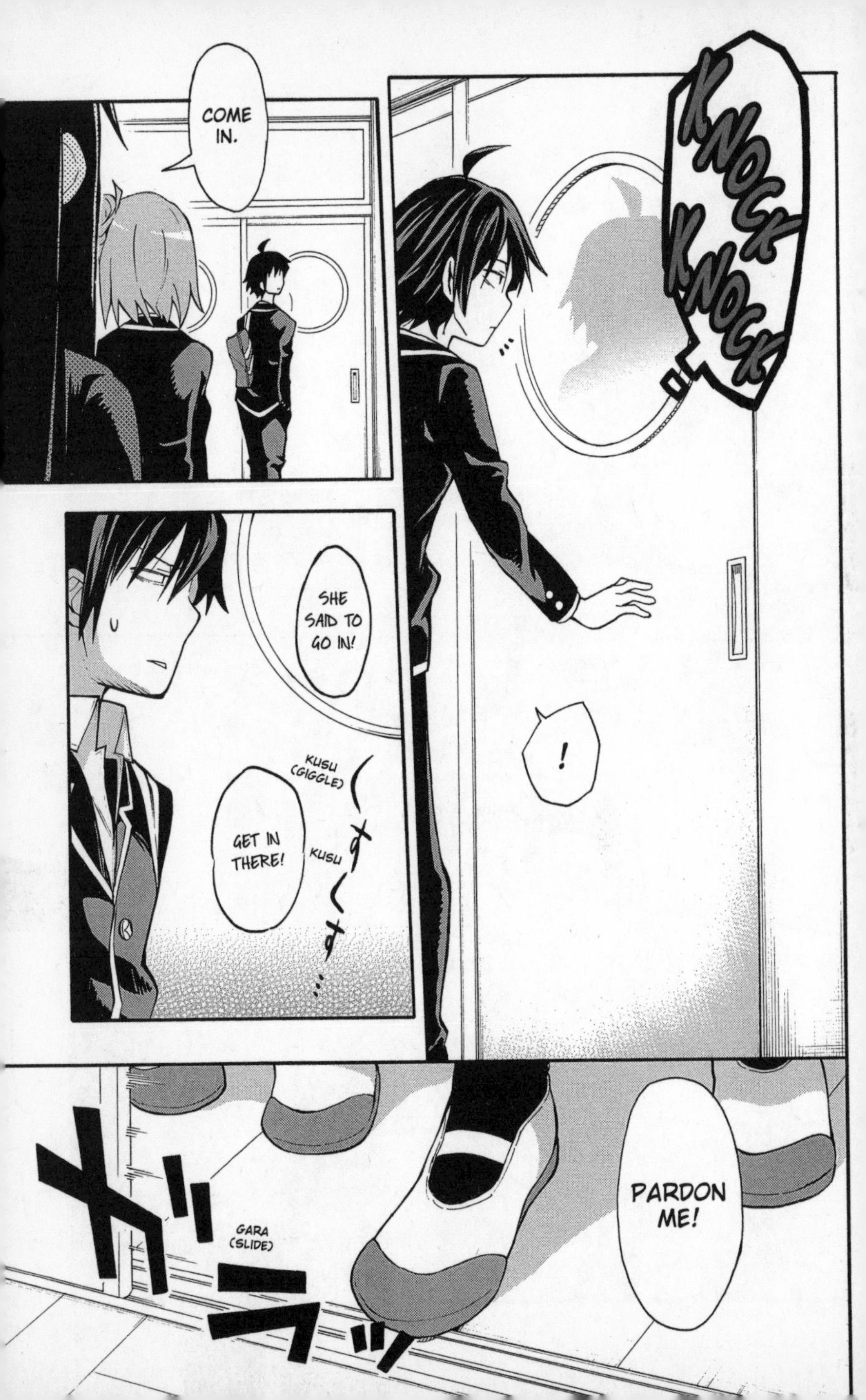
KNOCK KNOCK
...
!
COME IN.
SHE SAID TO GO IN!
KUSU (GIGGLE)
GET IN THERE!
KUSU
くすくす…
PARDON ME!
GARA (SLIDE)

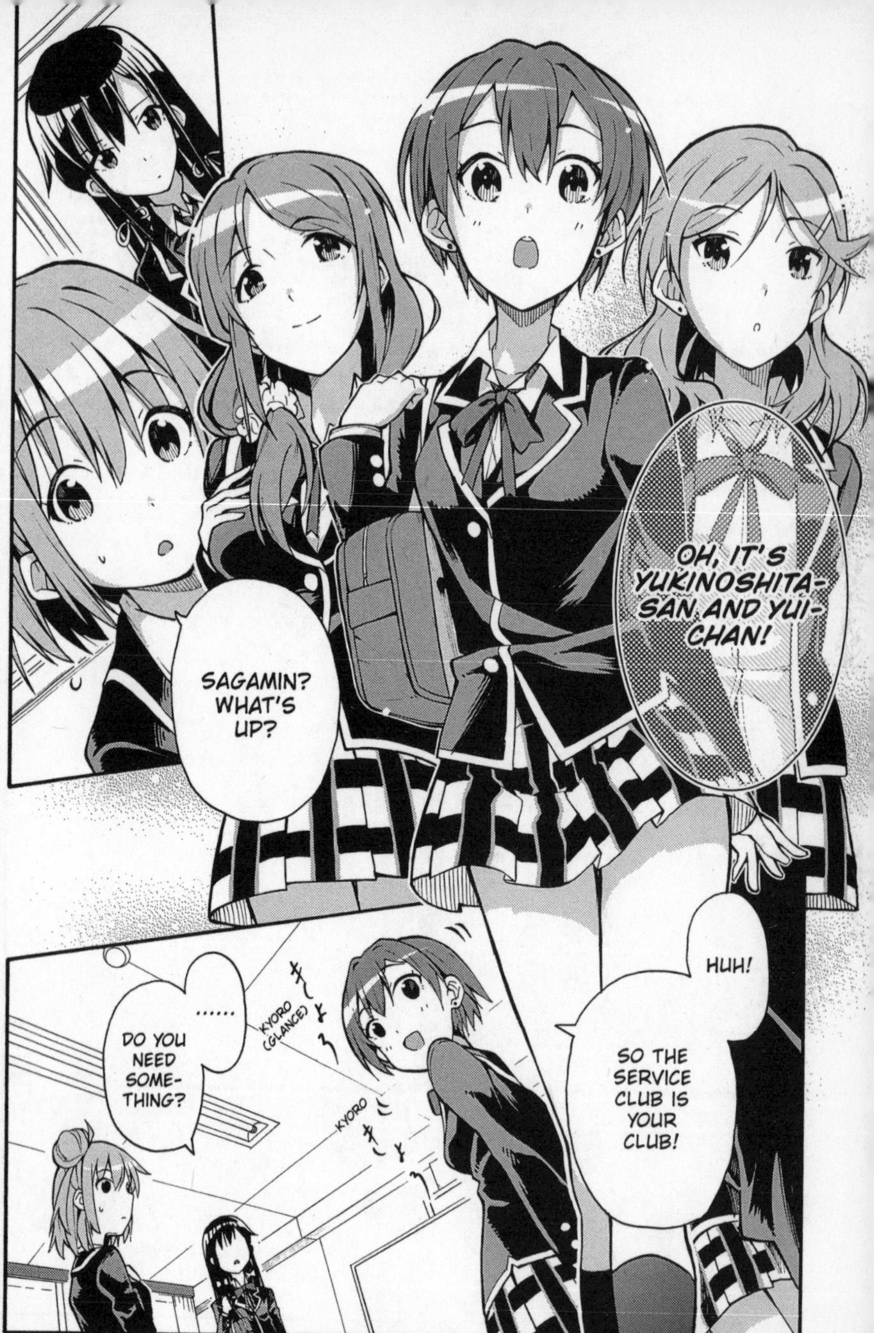
OH, IT'S YUKINOSHITA-SAN AND YUI-CHAN!
SAGAMIN? WHAT'S UP?
HUH!
SO THE SERVICE CLUB IS YOUR CLUB!
KYORO
KYORO (GLANCE)
......
DO YOU NEED SOME-THING?

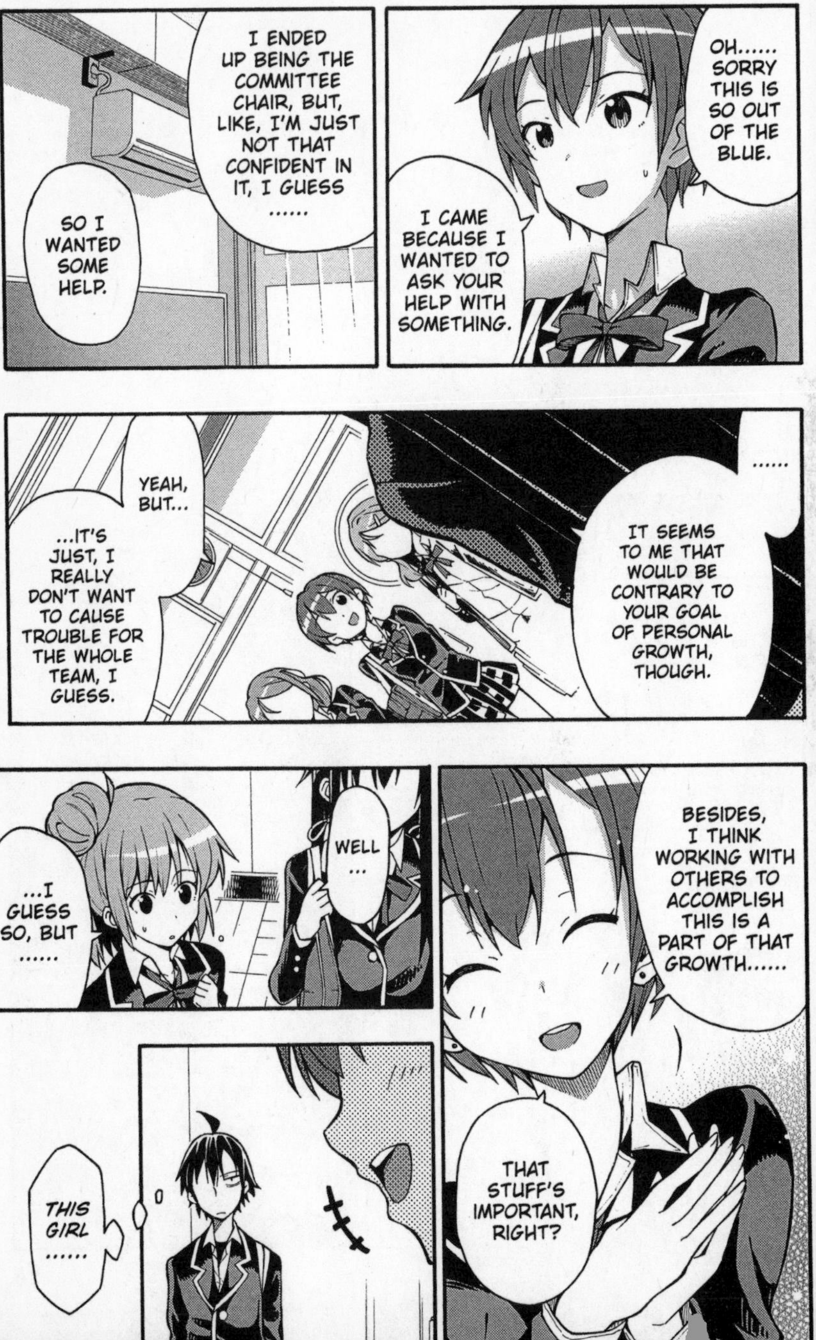
OH...... SORRY THIS IS SO OUT OF THE BLUE.
I CAME BECAUSE I WANTED TO ASK YOUR HELP WITH SOMETHING.
I ENDED UP BEING THE COMMITTEE CHAIR, BUT, LIKE, I'M JUST NOT THAT CONFIDENT IN IT, I GUESS ......
SO I WANTED SOME HELP.
......
IT SEEMS TO ME THAT WOULD BE CONTRARY TO YOUR GOAL OF PERSONAL GROWTH, THOUGH.
YEAH, BUT...
...IT'S JUST, I REALLY DON'T WANT TO CAUSE TROUBLE FOR THE WHOLE TEAM, I GUESS.
BESIDES, I THINK WORKING WITH OTHERS TO ACCOMPLISH THIS IS A PART OF THAT GROWTH......
THAT STUFF'S IMPORTANT, RIGHT?
WELL ...
...I GUESS SO, BUT ......
THIS GIRL ......

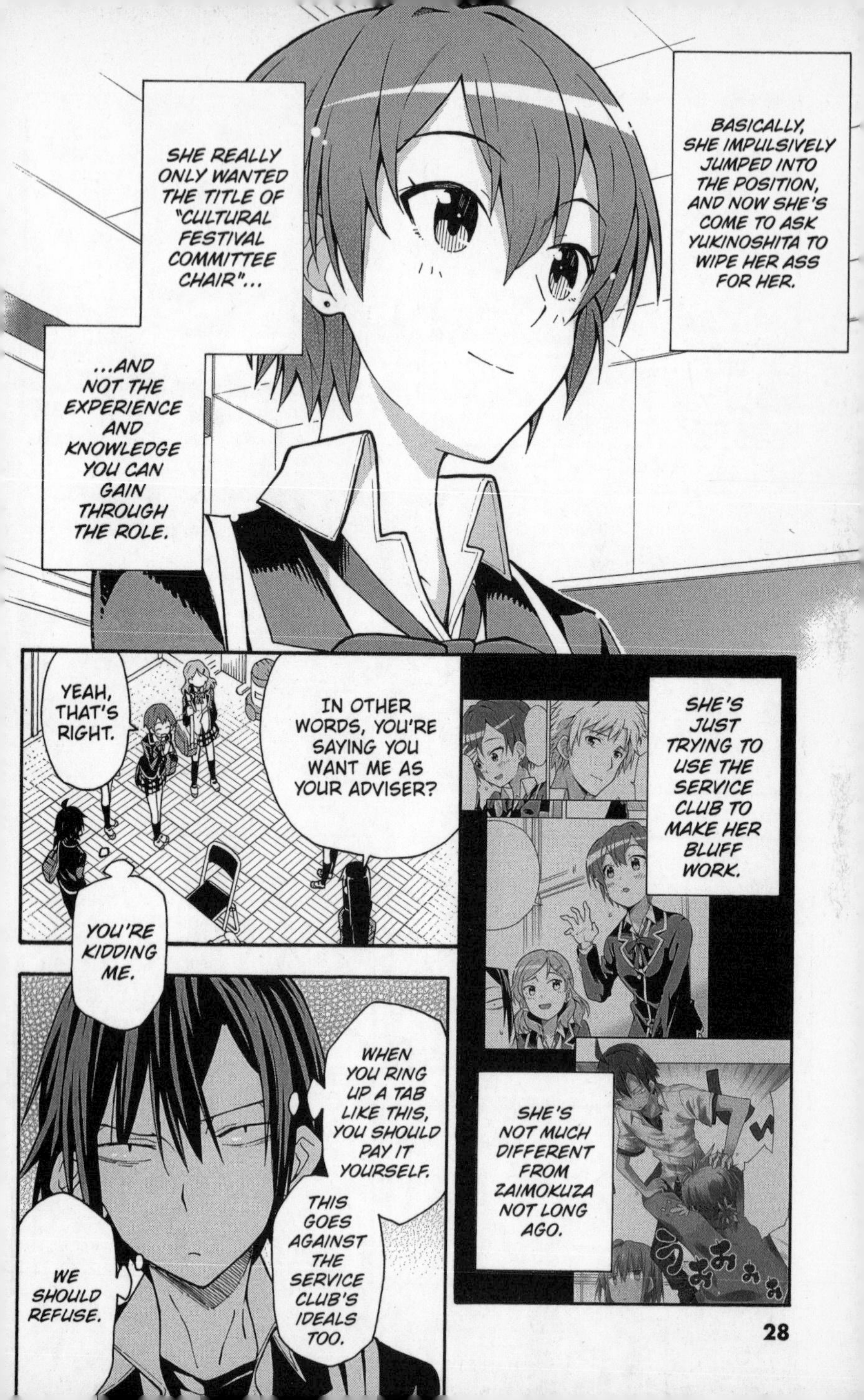
BASICALLY, SHE IMPULSIVELY JUMPED INTO THE POSITION, AND NOW SHE'S COME TO ASK YUKINOSHITA TO WIPE HER ASS FOR HER.
SHE REALLY ONLY WANTED THE TITLE OF "CULTURAL FESTIVAL COMMITTEE CHAIR"...
...AND NOT THE EXPERIENCE AND KNOWLEDGE YOU CAN GAIN THROUGH THE ROLE.
SHE'S JUST TRYING TO USE THE SERVICE CLUB TO MAKE HER BLUFF WORK.
SHE'S NOT MUCH DIFFERENT FROM ZAIMOKUZA NOT LONG AGO.
うおぉぉぉ
IN OTHER WORDS, YOU'RE SAYING YOU WANT ME AS YOUR ADVISER?
YEAH, THAT'S RIGHT.
YOU'RE KIDDING ME.
WHEN YOU RING UP A TAB LIKE THIS, YOU SHOULD PAY IT YOURSELF.
THIS GOES AGAINST THE SERVICE CLUB'S IDEALS TOO.
WE SHOULD REFUSE.

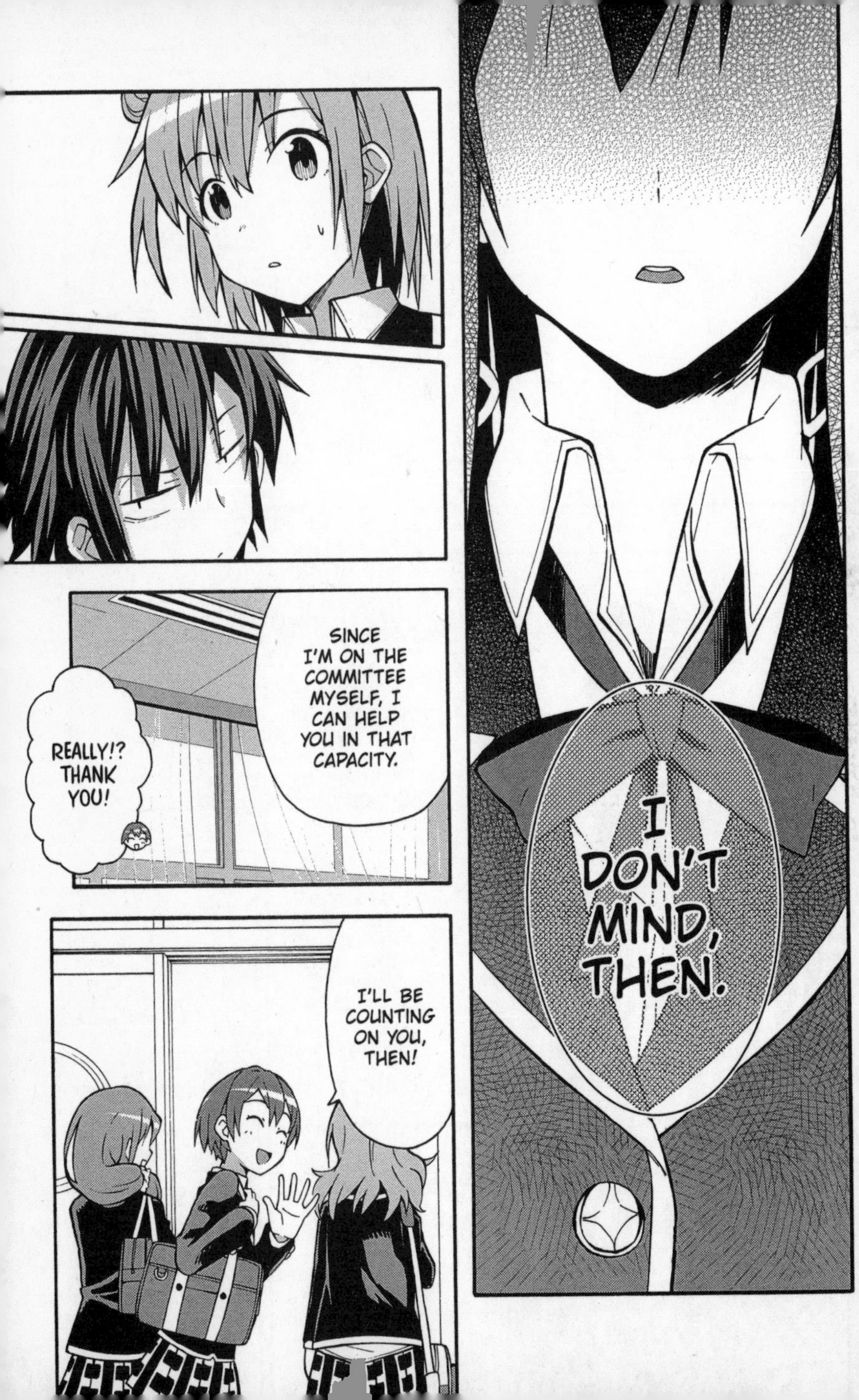
I DON'T MIND, THEN.
SINCE I'M ON THE COMMITTEE MYSELF, I CAN HELP YOU IN THAT CAPACITY.
REALLY!? THANK YOU!
I'LL BE COUNTING ON YOU, THEN!

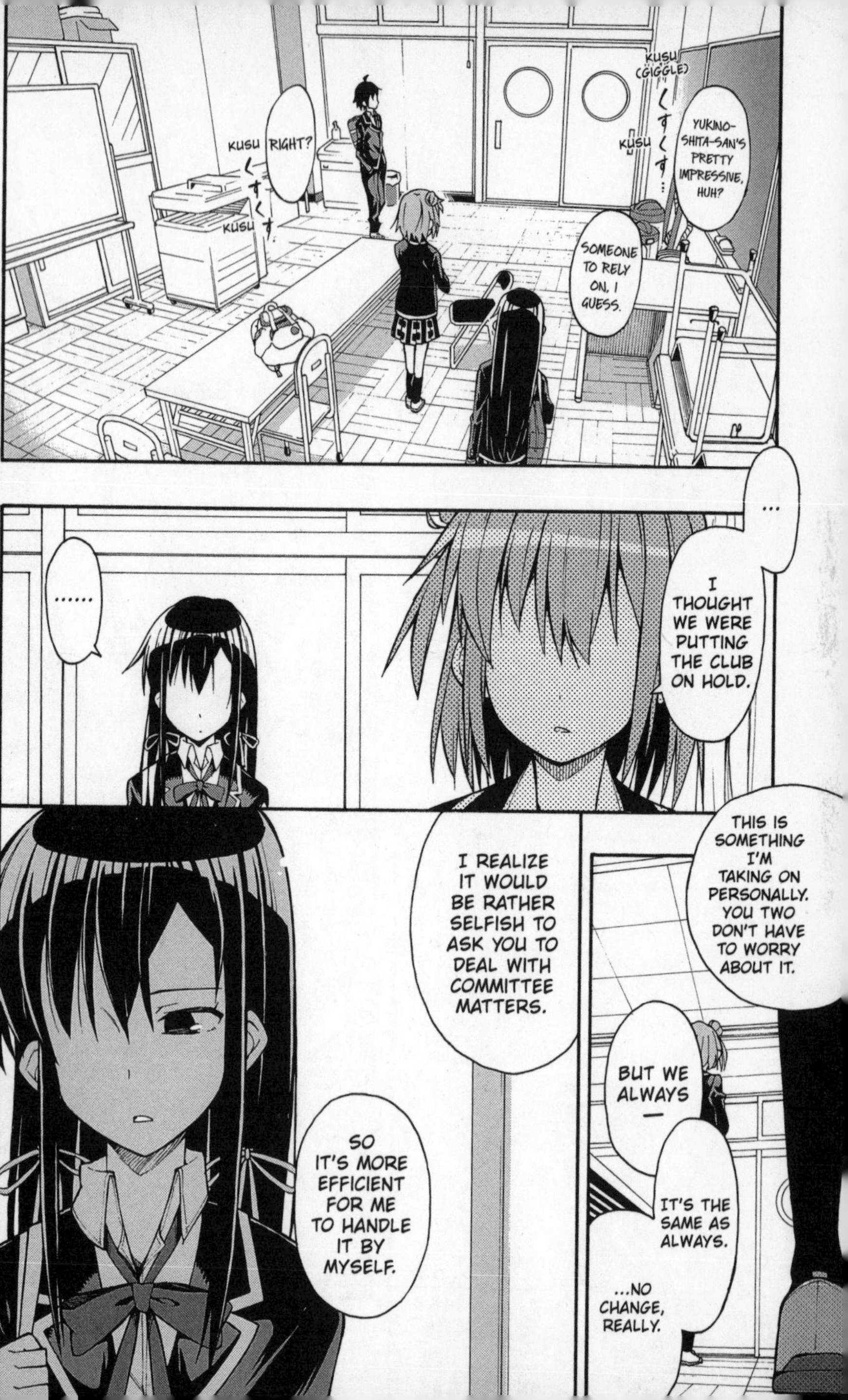
KUSU (GIGGLE)
くすくす…
KUSU
YUKINO-SHITA-SAN'S PRETTY IMPRESSIVE, HUH?
SOMEONE TO RELY ON, I GUESS.
RIGHT?
KUSU
くすくす
KUSU
...
I THOUGHT WE WERE PUTTING THE CLUB ON HOLD.
....
THIS IS SOMETHING I'M TAKING ON PERSONALLY. YOU TWO DON'T HAVE TO WORRY ABOUT IT.
BUT WE ALWAYS—
IT'S THE SAME AS ALWAYS.
...NO CHANGE, REALLY.
I REALIZE IT WOULD BE RATHER SELFISH TO ASK YOU TO DEAL WITH COMMITTEE MATTERS.
SO IT'S MORE EFFICIENT FOR ME TO HANDLE IT BY MYSELF.

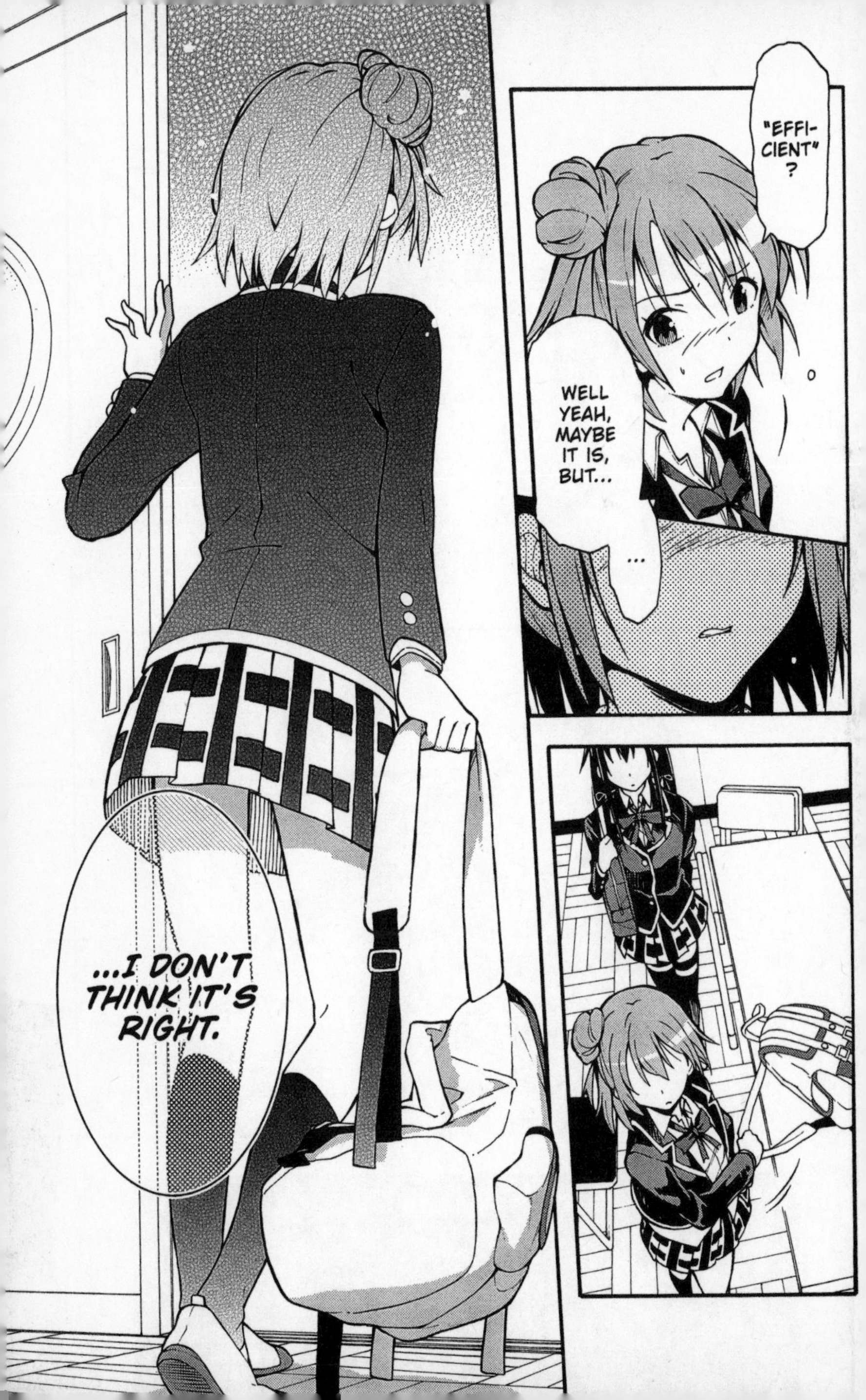
"EFFI-CIENT"?
WELL YEAH, MAYBE IT IS, BUT...
...
...I DON'T THINK IT'S RIGHT.

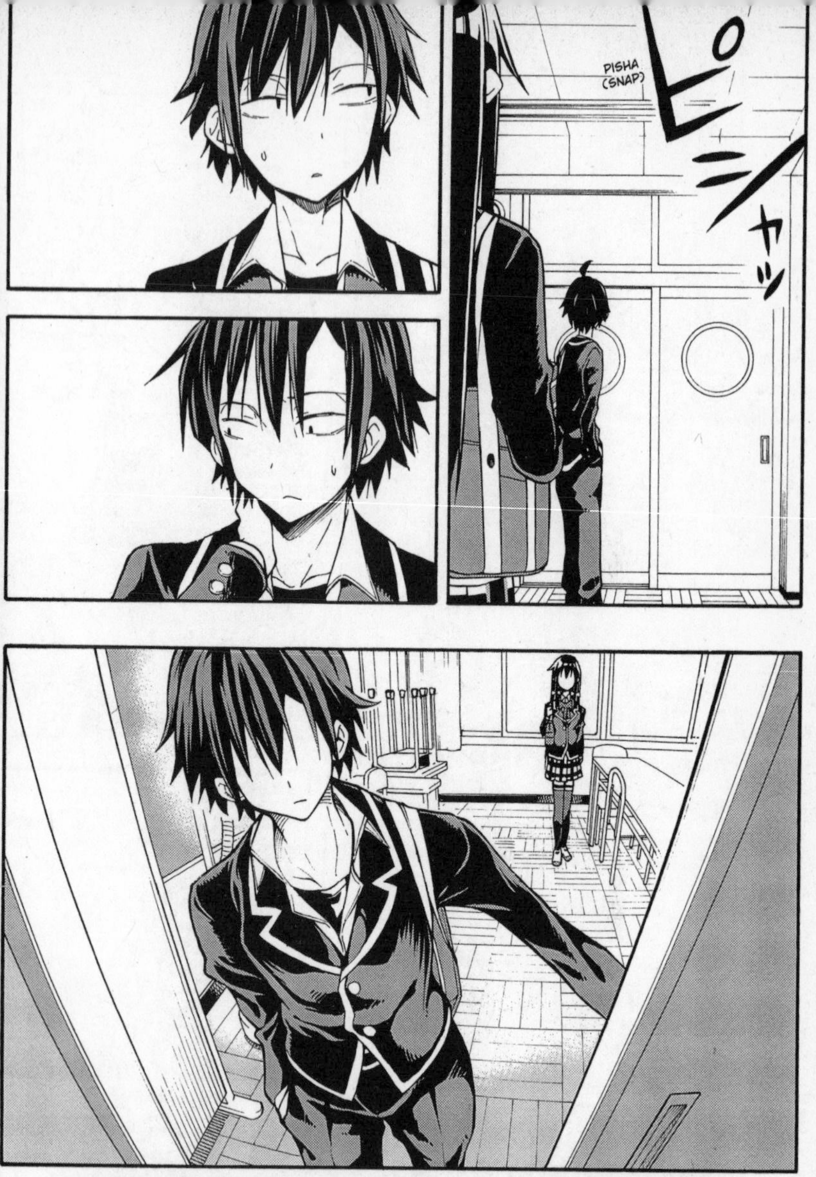
PISHA (SNAP)
ピシャッ

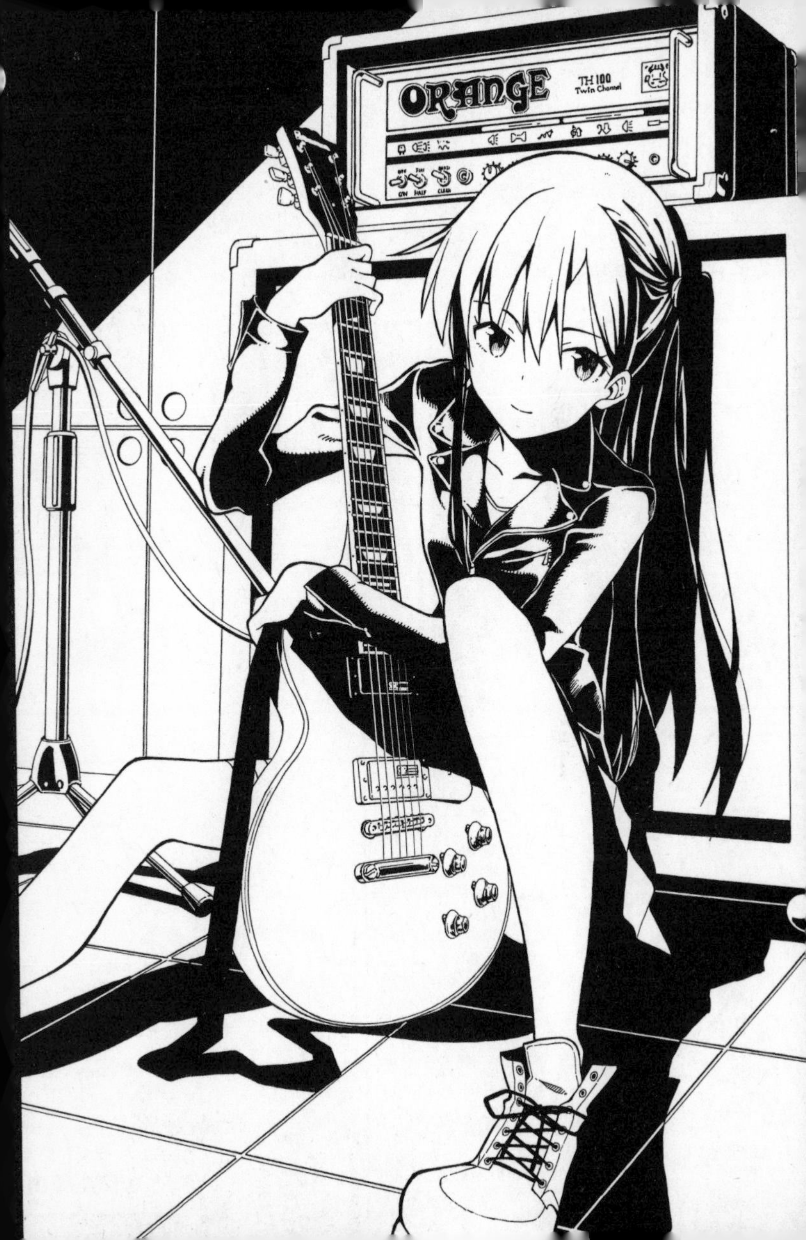
ORANGE
TH100
Twin Channel

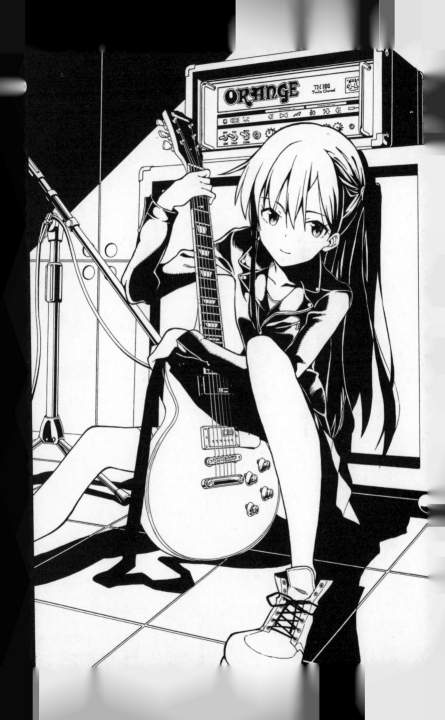

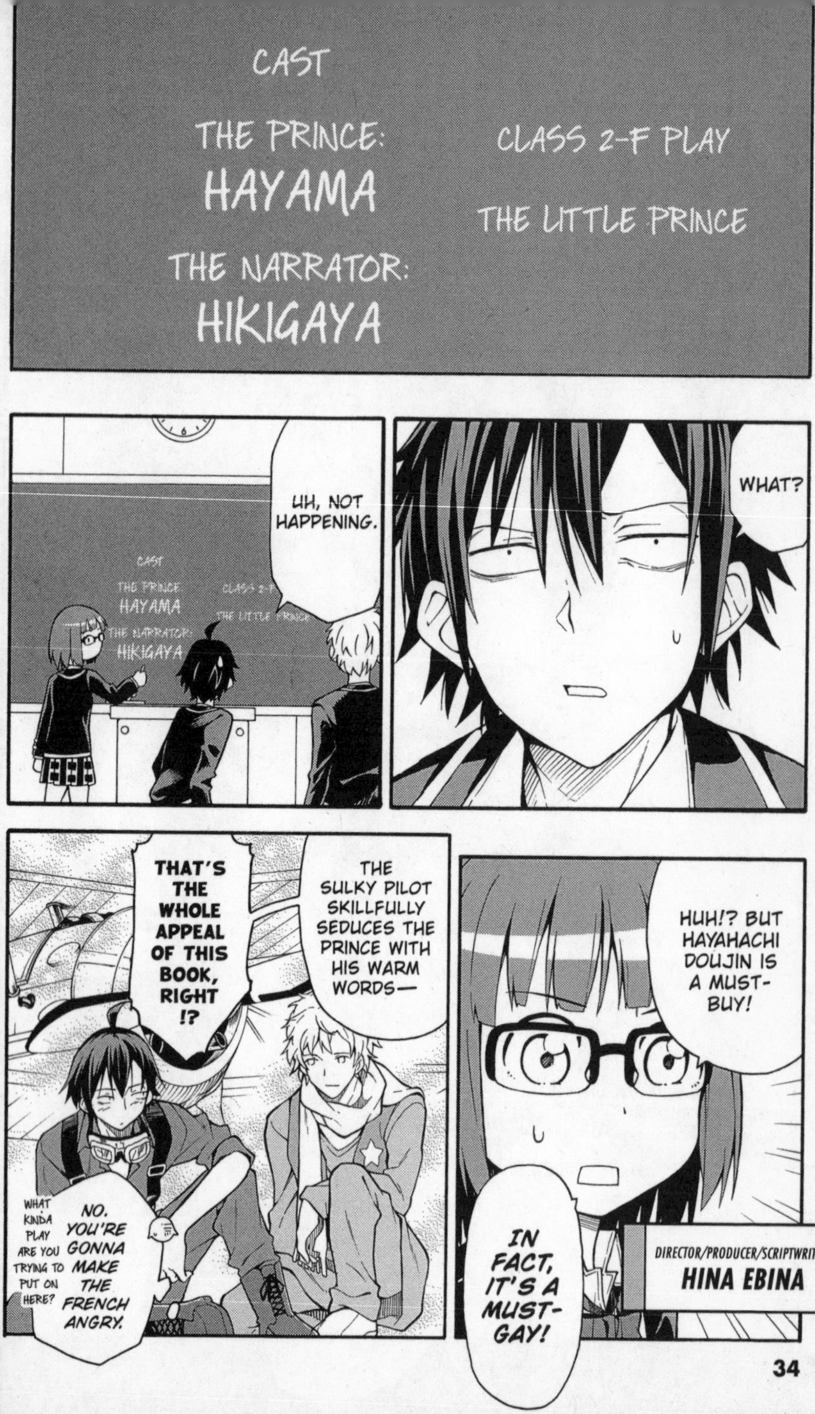
CAST
THE PRINCE:
HAYAMA
THE NARRATOR:
HIKIGAYA
CLASS 2-F PLAY
THE LITTLE PRINCE
WHAT?
UH, NOT HAPPENING.
HUH!? BUT HAYAHACHI DOUJIN IS A MUST-BUY!
IN FACT, IT'S A MUST-GAY!
DIRECTOR/PRODUCER/SCRIPTWRITER:
HINA EBINA
THE SULKY PILOT SKILLFULLY SEDUCES THE PRINCE WITH HIS WARM WORDS—
THAT'S THE WHOLE APPEAL OF THIS BOOK, RIGHT!?
NO. YOU'RE GONNA MAKE THE FRENCH ANGRY.
WHAT KINDA PLAY ARE YOU TRYING TO PUT ON HERE?

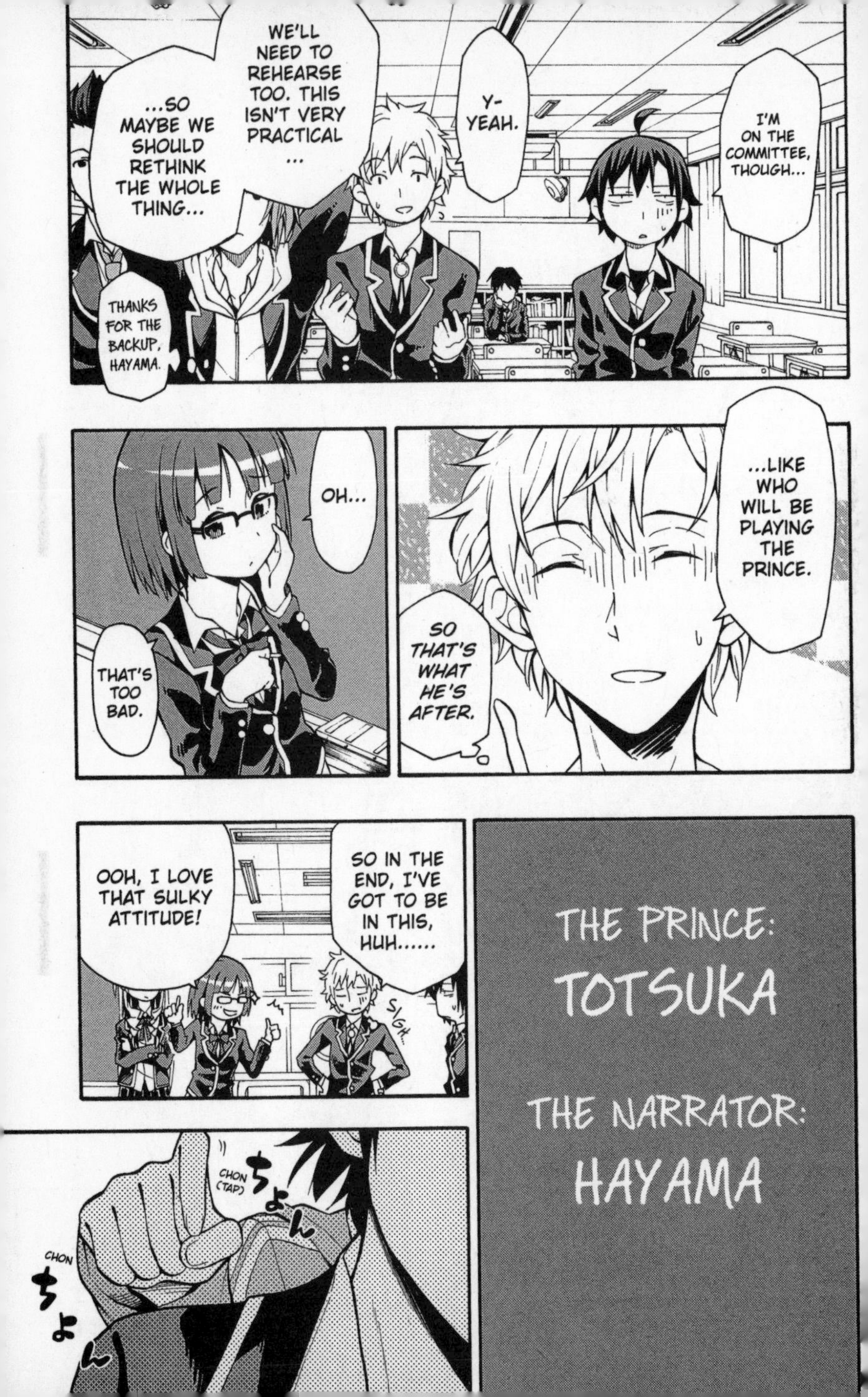
I'M ON THE COMMITTEE, THOUGH...
Y-YEAH.
WE'LL NEED TO REHEARSE TOO. THIS ISN'T VERY PRACTICAL...
...SO MAYBE WE SHOULD RETHINK THE WHOLE THING...
THANKS FOR THE BACKUP, HAYAMA.
...LIKE WHO WILL BE PLAYING THE PRINCE.
SO THAT'S WHAT HE'S AFTER.
OH...
THAT'S TOO BAD.
THE PRINCE: TOTSUKA
THE NARRATOR: HAYAMA
SO IN THE END, I'VE GOT TO BE IN THIS, HUH......
OOH, I LOVE THAT SULKY ATTITUDE!
SIGH...
CHON (TAP)
ちょん
CHON
ちょん

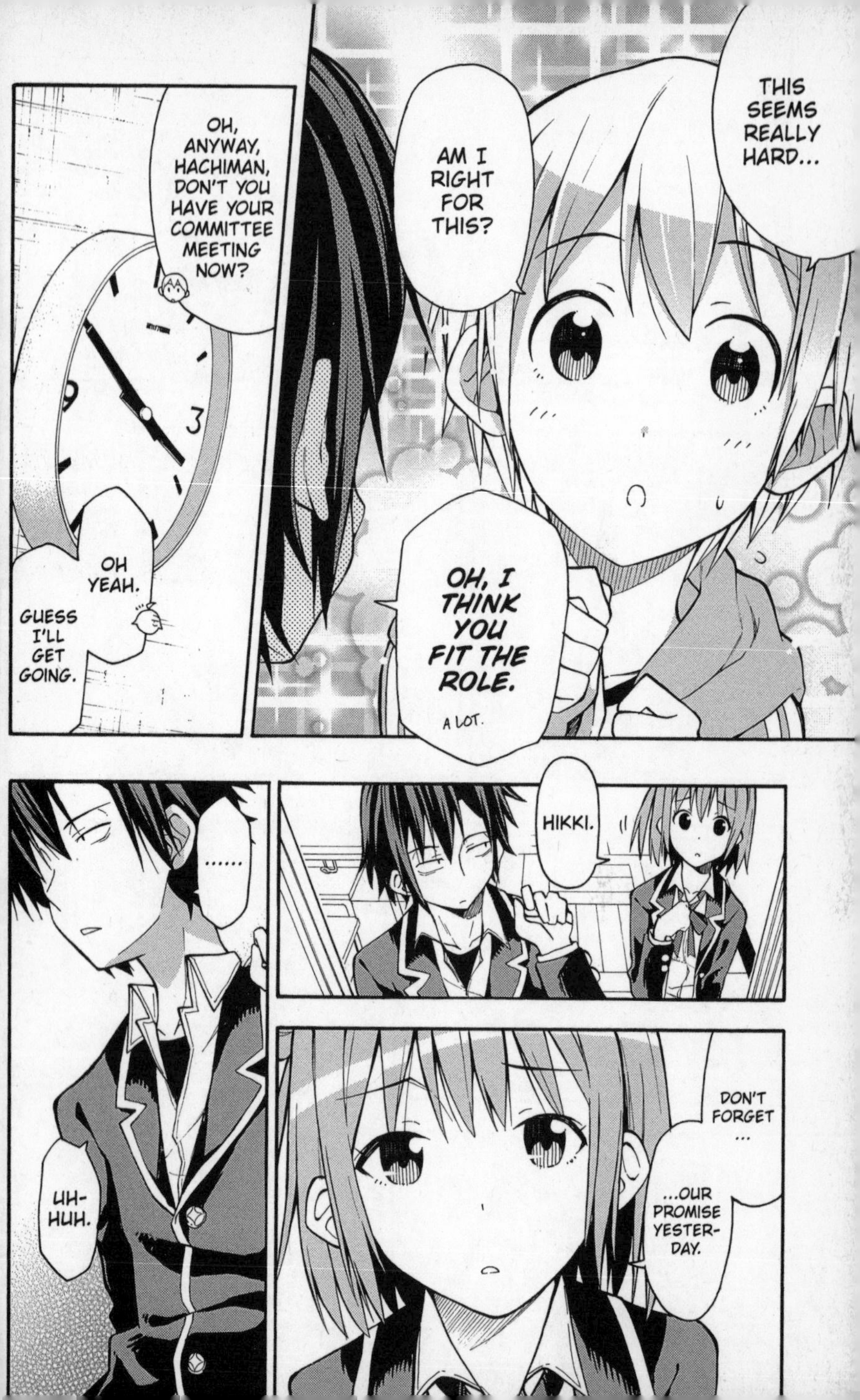
THIS SEEMS REALLY HARD...
AM I RIGHT FOR THIS?
OH, I THINK YOU FIT THE ROLE.
A LOT.
OH, ANYWAY, HACHIMAN, DON'T YOU HAVE YOUR COMMITTEE MEETING NOW?
OH YEAH.
GUESS I'LL GET GOING.
HIKKI.
DON'T FORGET...
...OUR PROMISE YESTER-DAY.
......
UH-HUH.

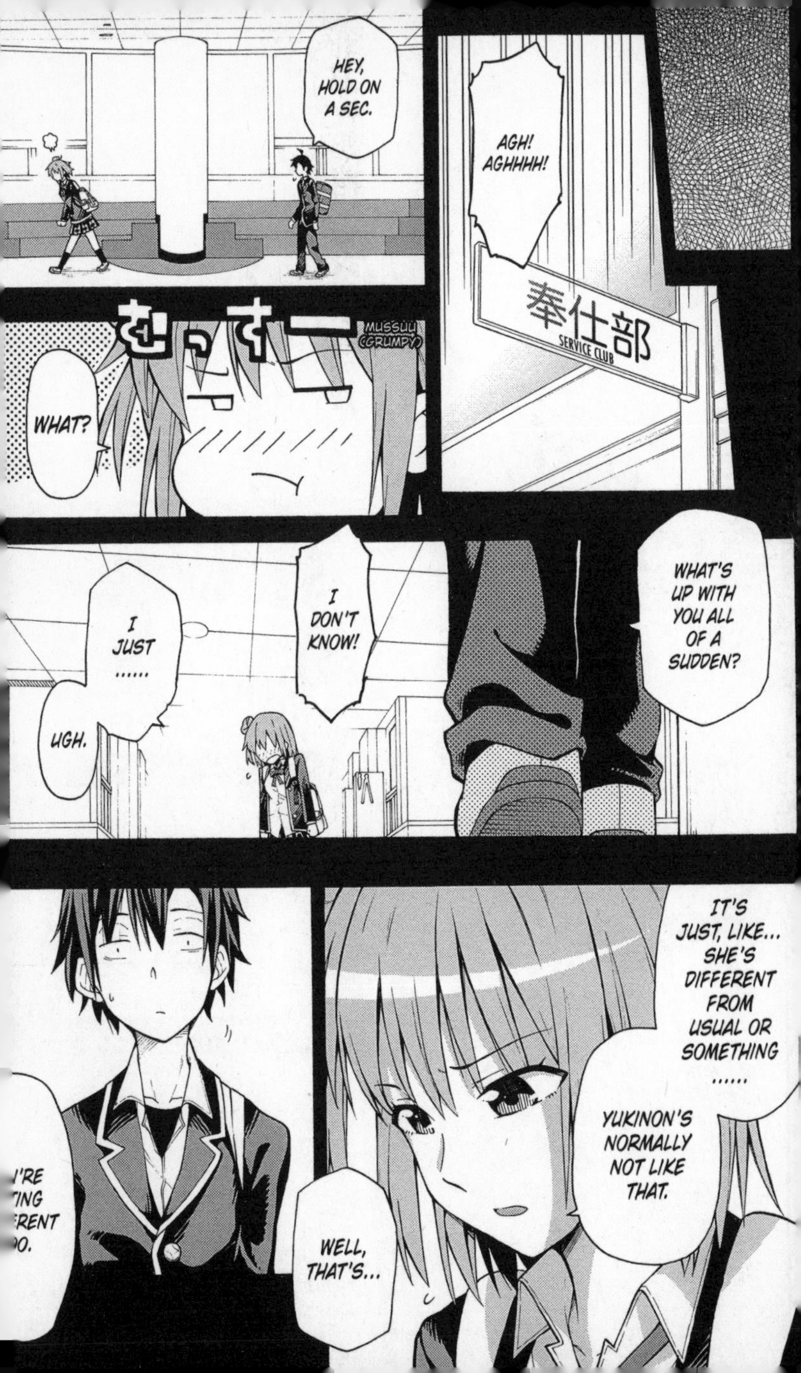
AGH! AGHHHH!
奉仕部
SERVICE CLUB
HEY, HOLD ON A SEC.
むっすー
MUSSUU (GRUMPY)
WHAT?
WHAT'S UP WITH YOU ALL OF A SUDDEN?
I DON'T KNOW!
I JUST ......
UGH.
IT'S JUST, LIKE... SHE'S DIFFERENT FROM USUAL OR SOMETHING ......
YUKINON'S NORMALLY NOT LIKE THAT.
WELL, THAT'S...

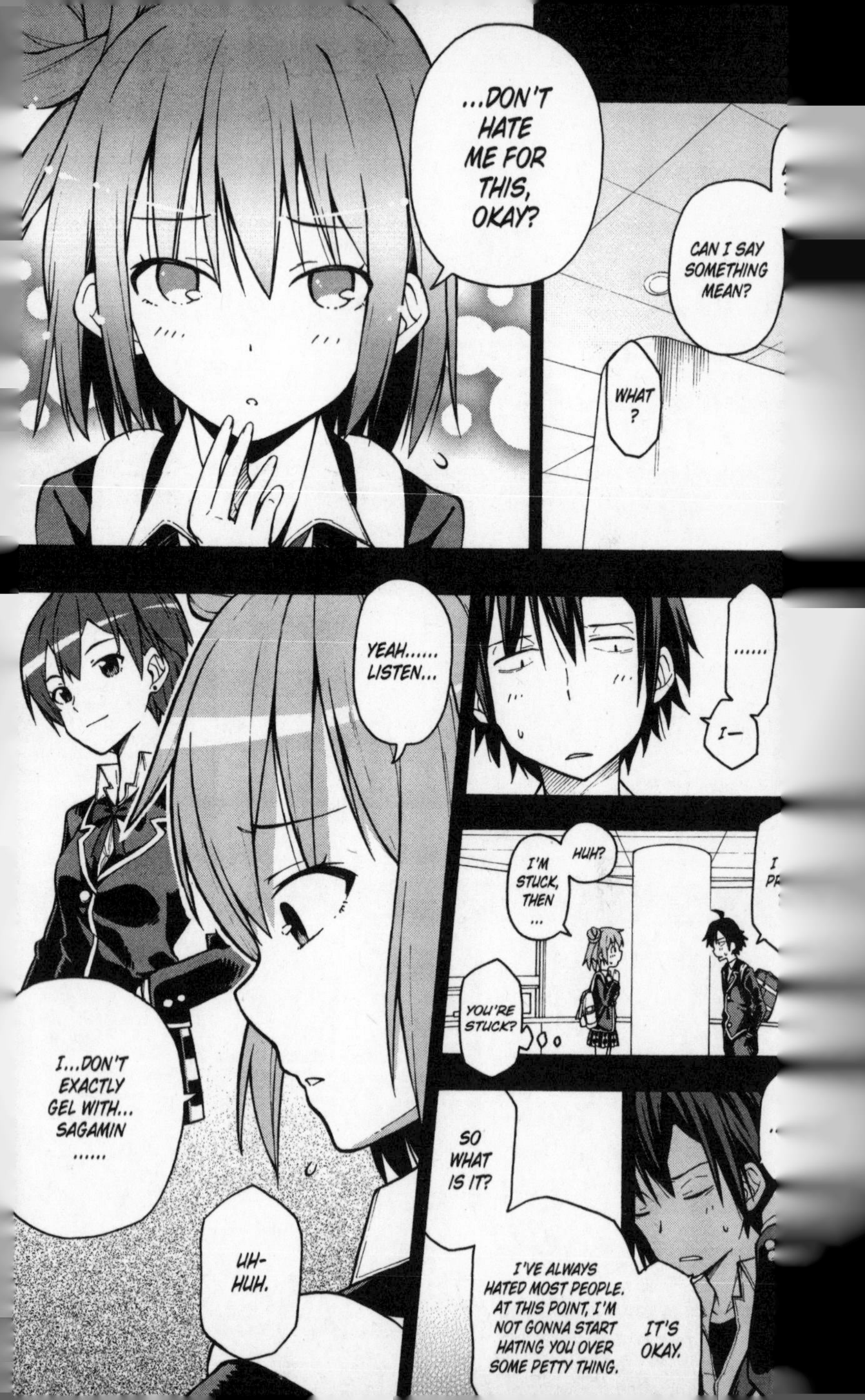
CAN I SAY SOMETHING MEAN?
WHAT ?
...DON'T HATE ME FOR THIS, OKAY?
......
I—
HUH?
I'M STUCK, THEN ...
YOU'RE STUCK?
SO WHAT IS IT?
IT'S OKAY.
I'VE ALWAYS HATED MOST PEOPLE. AT THIS POINT, I'M NOT GONNA START HATING YOU OVER SOME PETTY THING.
YEAH...... LISTEN...
I...DON'T EXACTLY GEL WITH... SAGAMIN ......
UH-HUH.

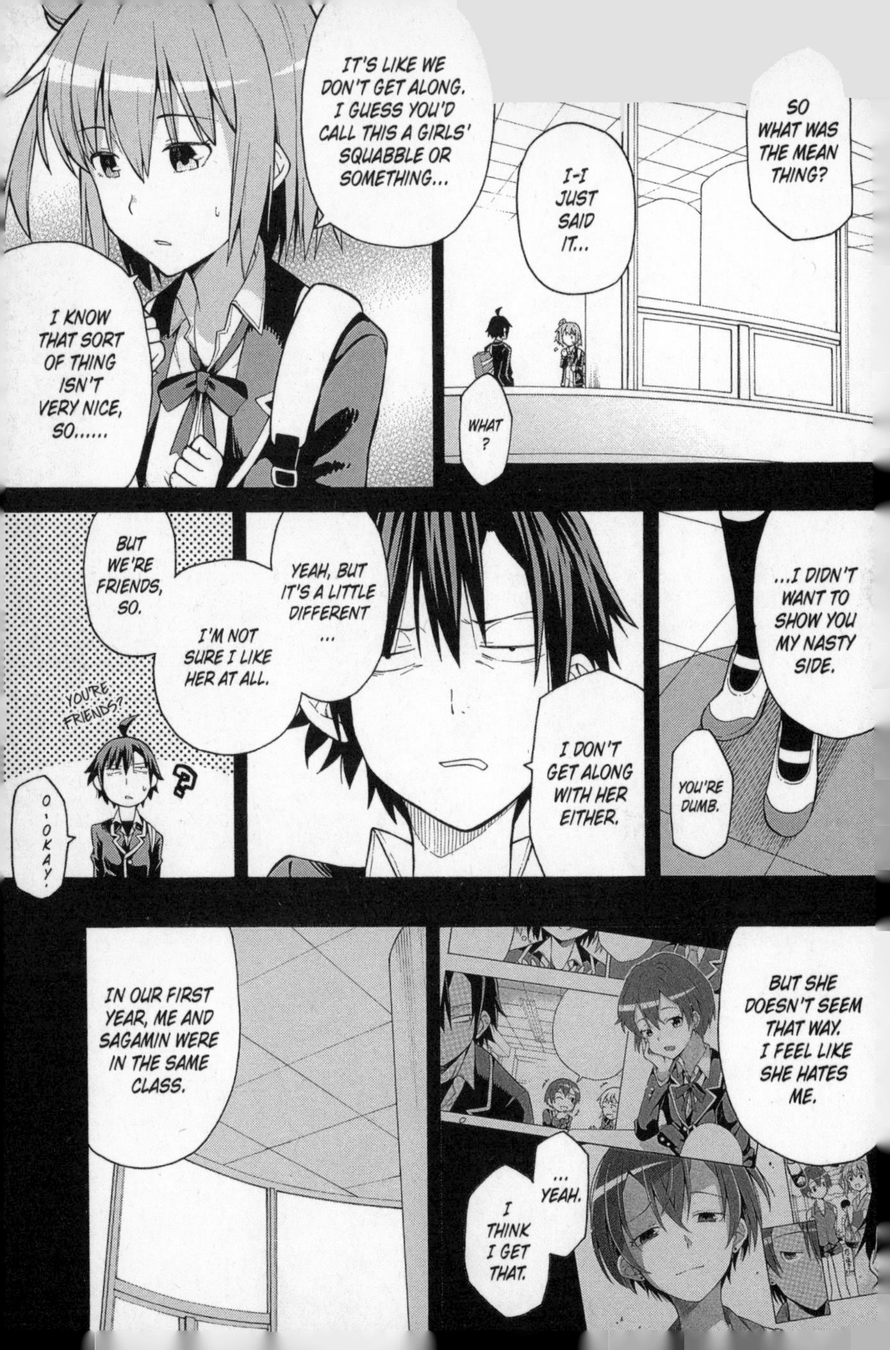
SO WHAT WAS THE MEAN THING?
I-I JUST SAID IT...
WHAT?
IT'S LIKE WE DON'T GET ALONG. I GUESS YOU'D CALL THIS A GIRLS' SQUABBLE OR SOMETHING...
I KNOW THAT SORT OF THING ISN'T VERY NICE, SO......
...I DIDN'T WANT TO SHOW YOU MY NASTY SIDE.
YOU'RE DUMB.
I DON'T GET ALONG WITH HER EITHER.
YEAH, BUT IT'S A LITTLE DIFFERENT ...
I'M NOT SURE I LIKE HER AT ALL.
BUT WE'RE FRIENDS, SO.
YOU'RE FRIENDS?
O-OKAY.
BUT SHE DOESN'T SEEM THAT WAY. I FEEL LIKE SHE HATES ME.
...YEAH.
I THINK I GET THAT.
IN OUR FIRST YEAR, ME AND SAGAMIN WERE IN THE SAME CLASS.

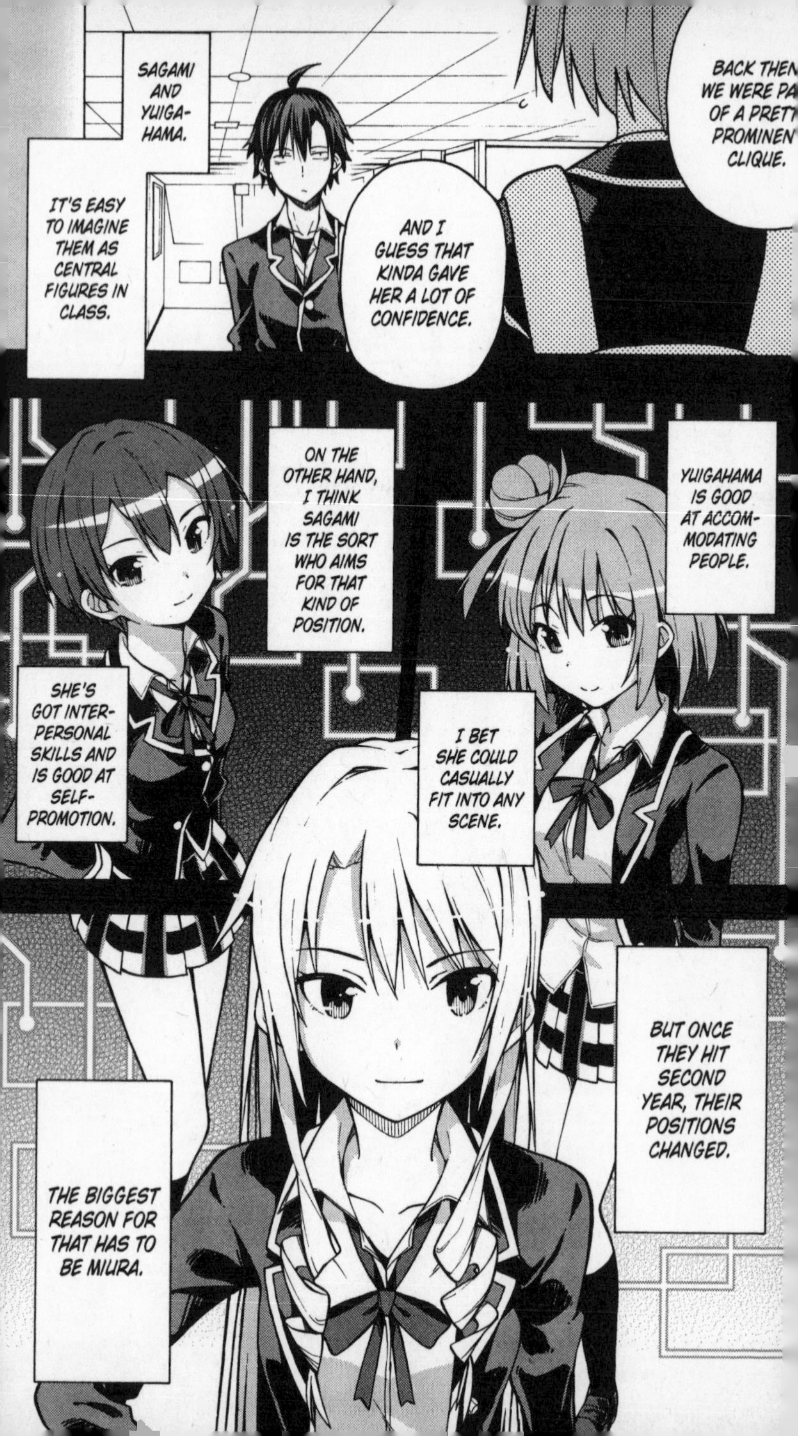
BACK THEN WE WERE PA OF A PRETT PROMINEN CLIQUE.
AND I GUESS THAT KINDA GAVE HER A LOT OF CONFIDENCE.
SAGAMI AND YUIGA-HAMA.
IT'S EASY TO IMAGINE THEM AS CENTRAL FIGURES IN CLASS.
YUIGAHAMA IS GOOD AT ACCOM-MODATING PEOPLE.
I BET SHE COULD CASUALLY FIT INTO ANY SCENE.
ON THE OTHER HAND, I THINK SAGAMI IS THE SORT WHO AIMS FOR THAT KIND OF POSITION.
SHE'S GOT INTER-PERSONAL SKILLS AND IS GOOD AT SELF-PROMOTION.
BUT ONCE THEY HIT SECOND YEAR, THEIR POSITIONS CHANGED.
THE BIGGEST REASON FOR THAT HAS TO BE MIURA.

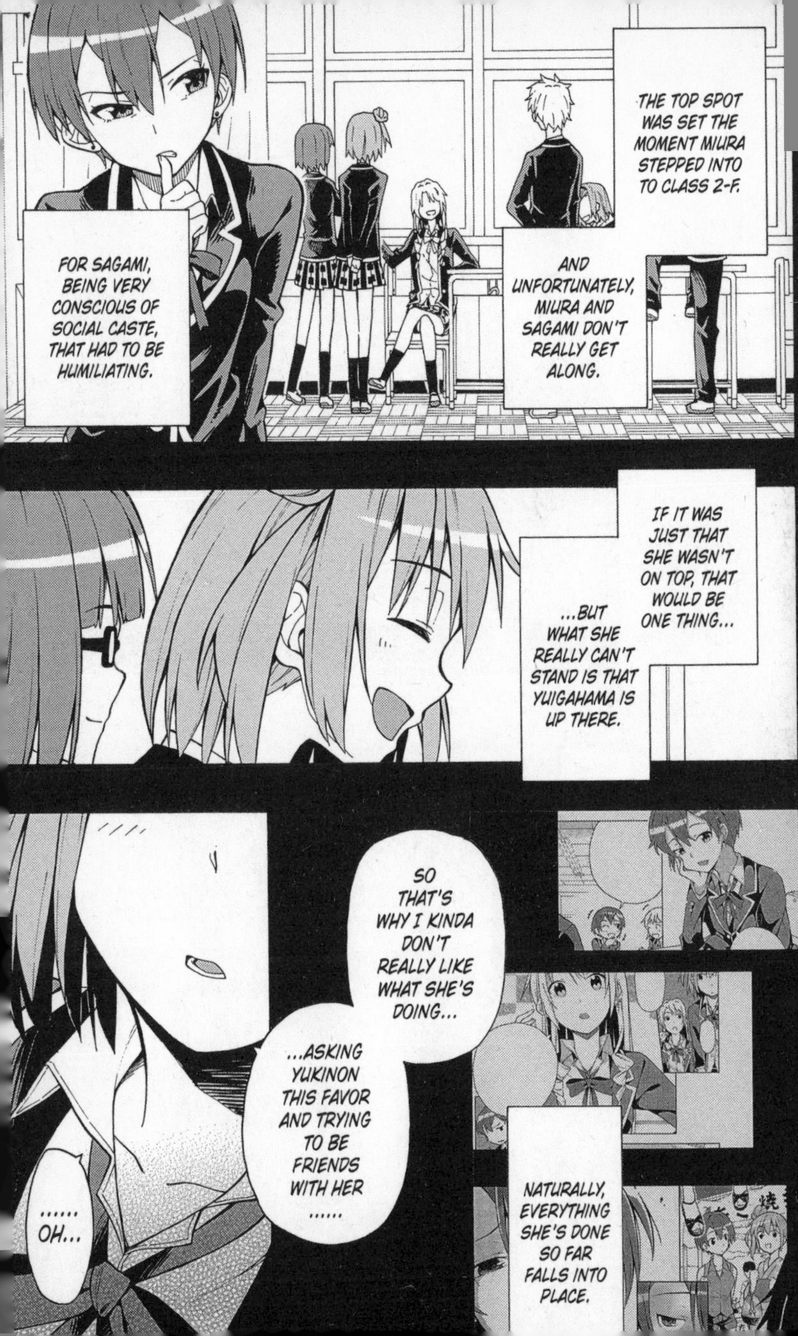
THE TOP SPOT WAS SET THE MOMENT MIURA STEPPED INTO TO CLASS 2-F.
AND UNFORTUNATELY, MIURA AND SAGAMI DON'T REALLY GET ALONG.
FOR SAGAMI, BEING VERY CONSCIOUS OF SOCIAL CASTE, THAT HAD TO BE HUMILIATING.
IF IT WAS JUST THAT SHE WASN'T ON TOP, THAT WOULD BE ONE THING...
...BUT WHAT SHE REALLY CAN'T STAND IS THAT YUIGAHAMA IS UP THERE.
SO THAT'S WHY I KINDA DON'T REALLY LIKE WHAT SHE'S DOING...
...ASKING YUKINON THIS FAVOR AND TRYING TO BE FRIENDS WITH HER ......
...... OH...
NATURALLY, EVERYTHING SHE'S DONE SO FAR FALLS INTO PLACE.

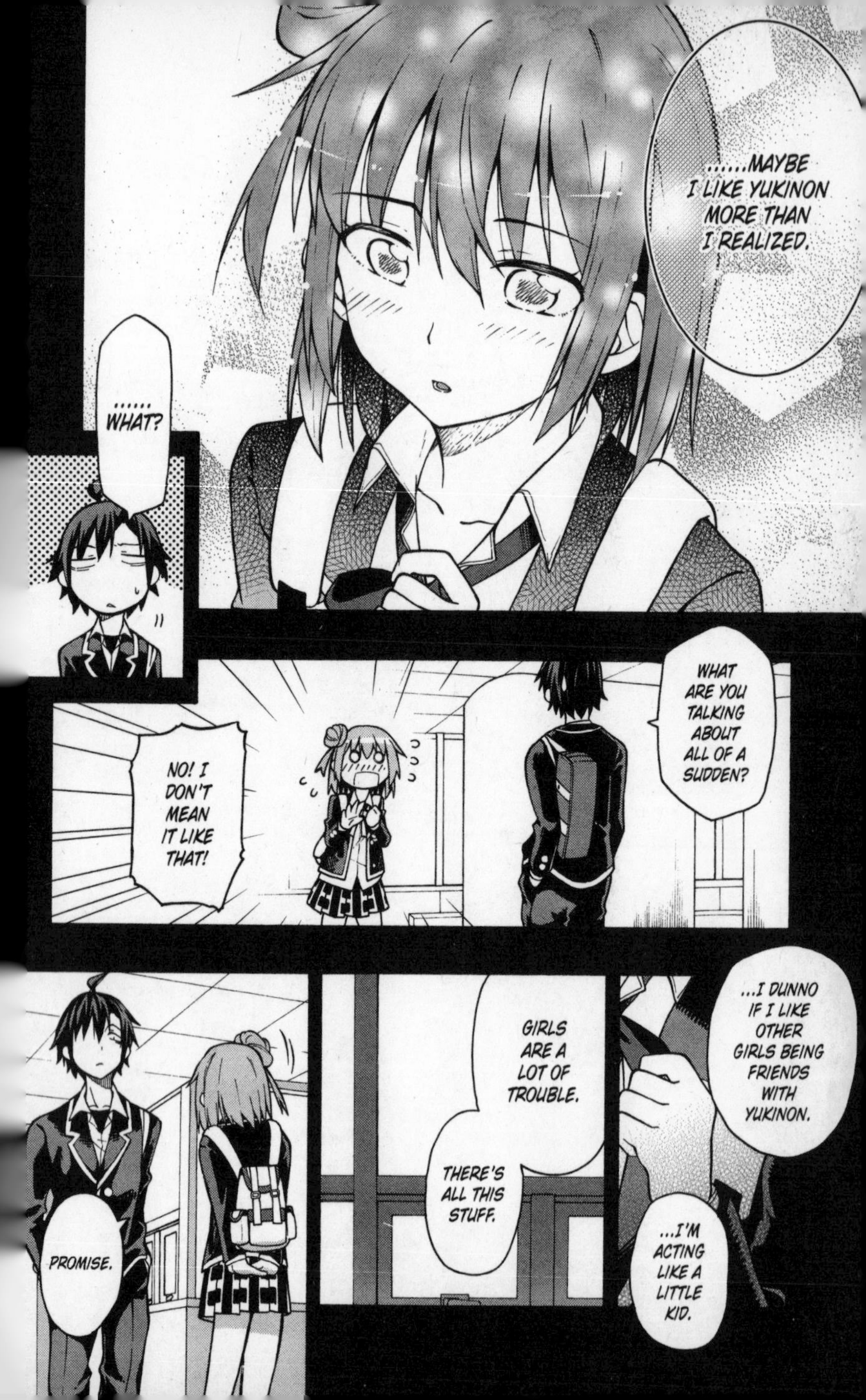
......MAYBE I LIKE YUKINON MORE THAN I REALIZED.
...... WHAT?
WHAT ARE YOU TALKING ABOUT ALL OF A SUDDEN?
NO! I DON'T MEAN IT LIKE THAT!
...I DUNNO IF I LIKE OTHER GIRLS BEING FRIENDS WITH YUKINON.
...I'M ACTING LIKE A LITTLE KID.
GIRLS ARE A LOT OF TROUBLE.
THERE'S ALL THIS STUFF.
PROMISE.

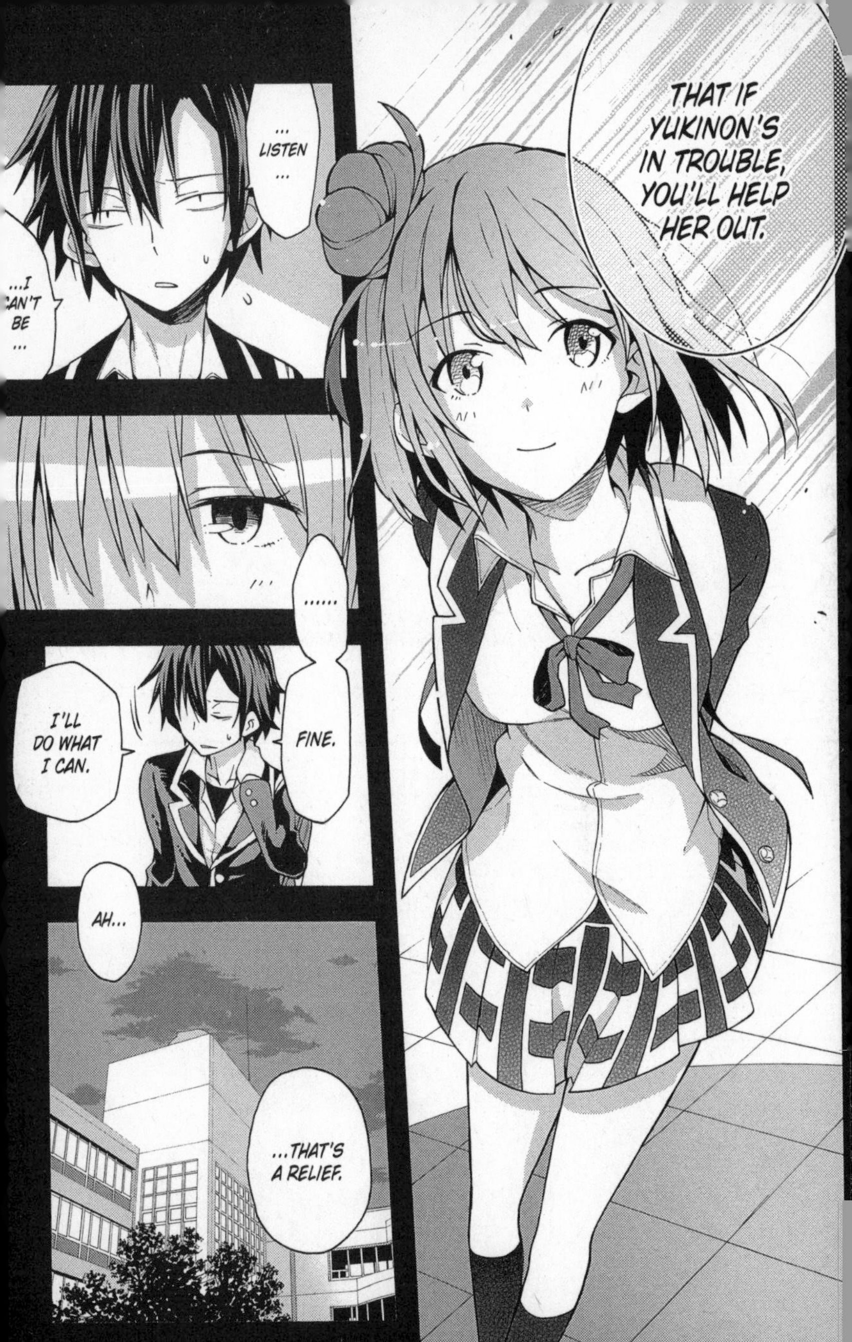
THAT IF YUKINON'S IN TROUBLE, YOU'LL HELP HER OUT.
... LISTEN ...
...I CAN'T BE ...
......
FINE.
I'LL DO WHAT I CAN.
AH...
...THAT'S A RELIEF.

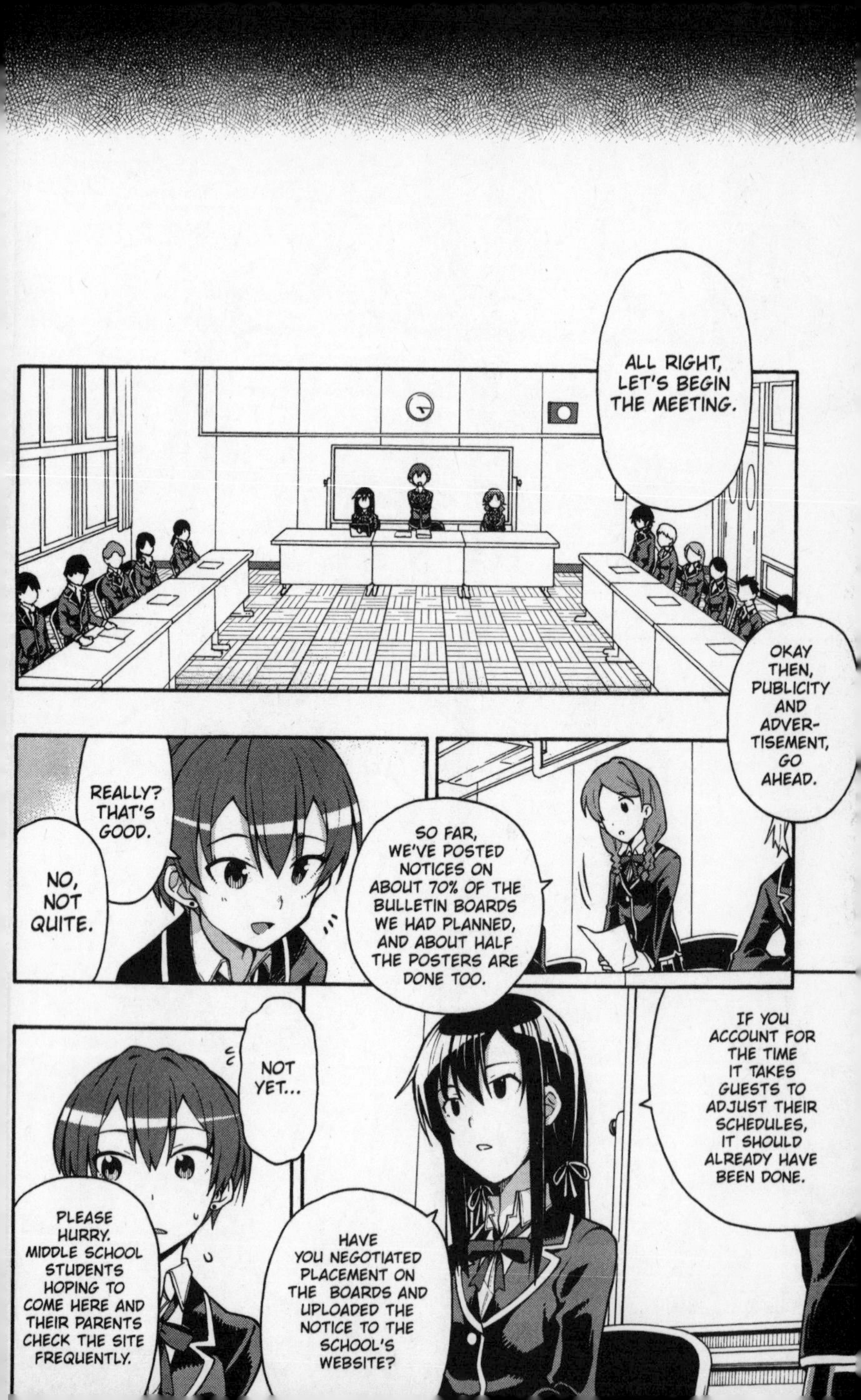

ALL RIGHT, LET'S BEGIN THE MEETING.
OKAY THEN, PUBLICITY AND ADVERTISEMENT, GO AHEAD.
SO FAR, WE'VE POSTED NOTICES ON ABOUT 70% OF THE BULLETIN BOARDS WE HAD PLANNED, AND ABOUT HALF THE POSTERS ARE DONE TOO.
REALLY? THAT'S GOOD.
NO, NOT QUITE.
HAVE YOU NEGOTIATED PLACEMENT ON THE BOARDS AND UPLOADED THE NOTICE TO THE SCHOOL'S WEBSITE?
NOT YET...
IF YOU ACCOUNT FOR THE TIME IT TAKES GUESTS TO ADJUST THEIR SCHEDULES, IT SHOULD ALREADY HAVE BEEN DONE.
PLEASE HURRY. MIDDLE SCHOOL STUDENTS HOPING TO COME HERE AND THEIR PARENTS CHECK THE SITE FREQUENTLY.

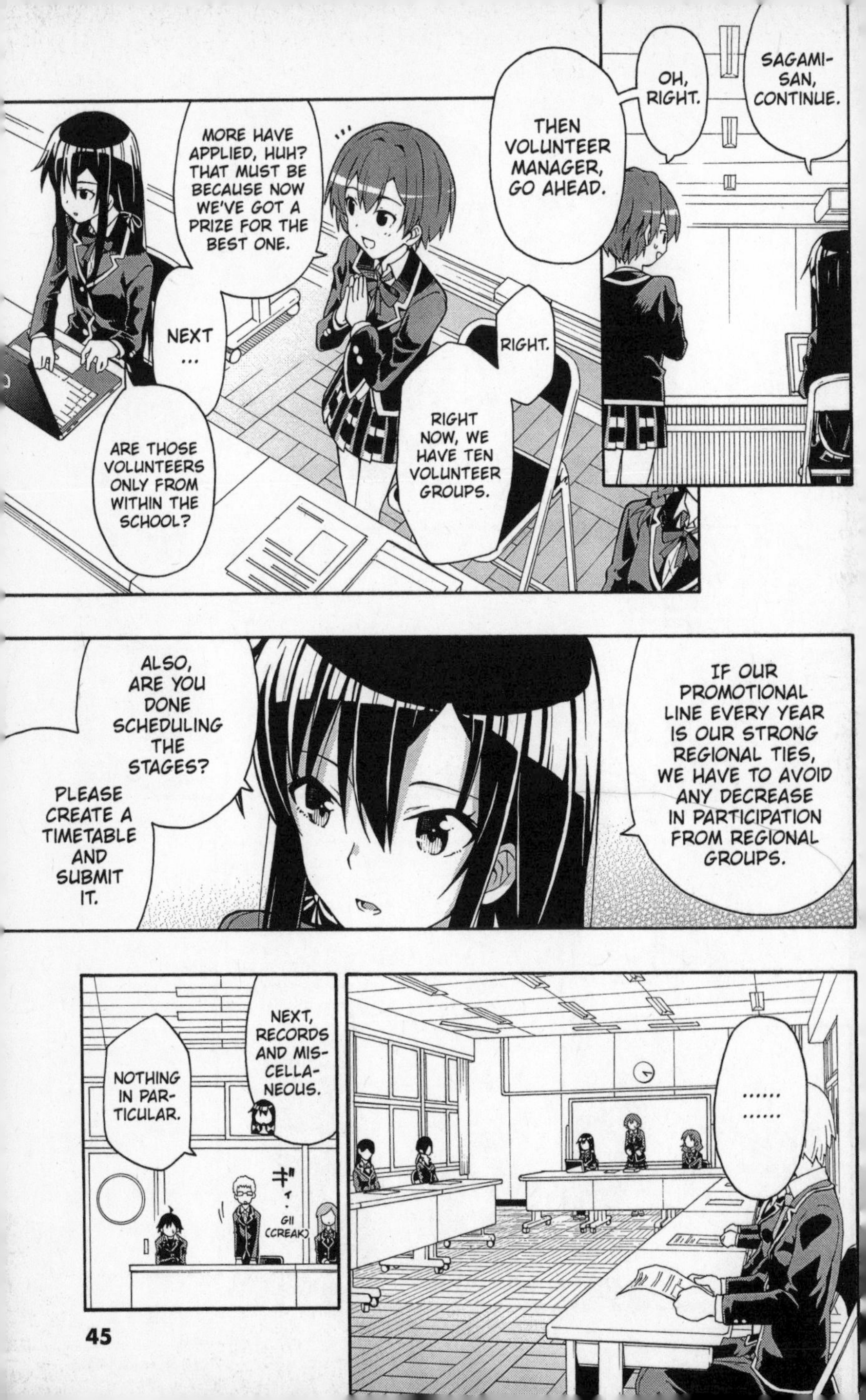
SAGAMI-SAN, CONTINUE.
OH, RIGHT.
THEN VOLUNTEER MANAGER, GO AHEAD.
RIGHT.
RIGHT NOW, WE HAVE TEN VOLUNTEER GROUPS.
MORE HAVE APPLIED, HUH? THAT MUST BE BECAUSE NOW WE'VE GOT A PRIZE FOR THE BEST ONE.
NEXT ...
ARE THOSE VOLUNTEERS ONLY FROM WITHIN THE SCHOOL?
IF OUR PROMOTIONAL LINE EVERY YEAR IS OUR STRONG REGIONAL TIES, WE HAVE TO AVOID ANY DECREASE IN PARTICIPATION FROM REGIONAL GROUPS.
ALSO, ARE YOU DONE SCHEDULING THE STAGES?
PLEASE CREATE A TIMETABLE AND SUBMIT IT.
......
......
NEXT, RECORDS AND MIS-CELLA-NEOUS.
ギィ
GII (CREAK)
NOTHING IN PAR-TICULAR.

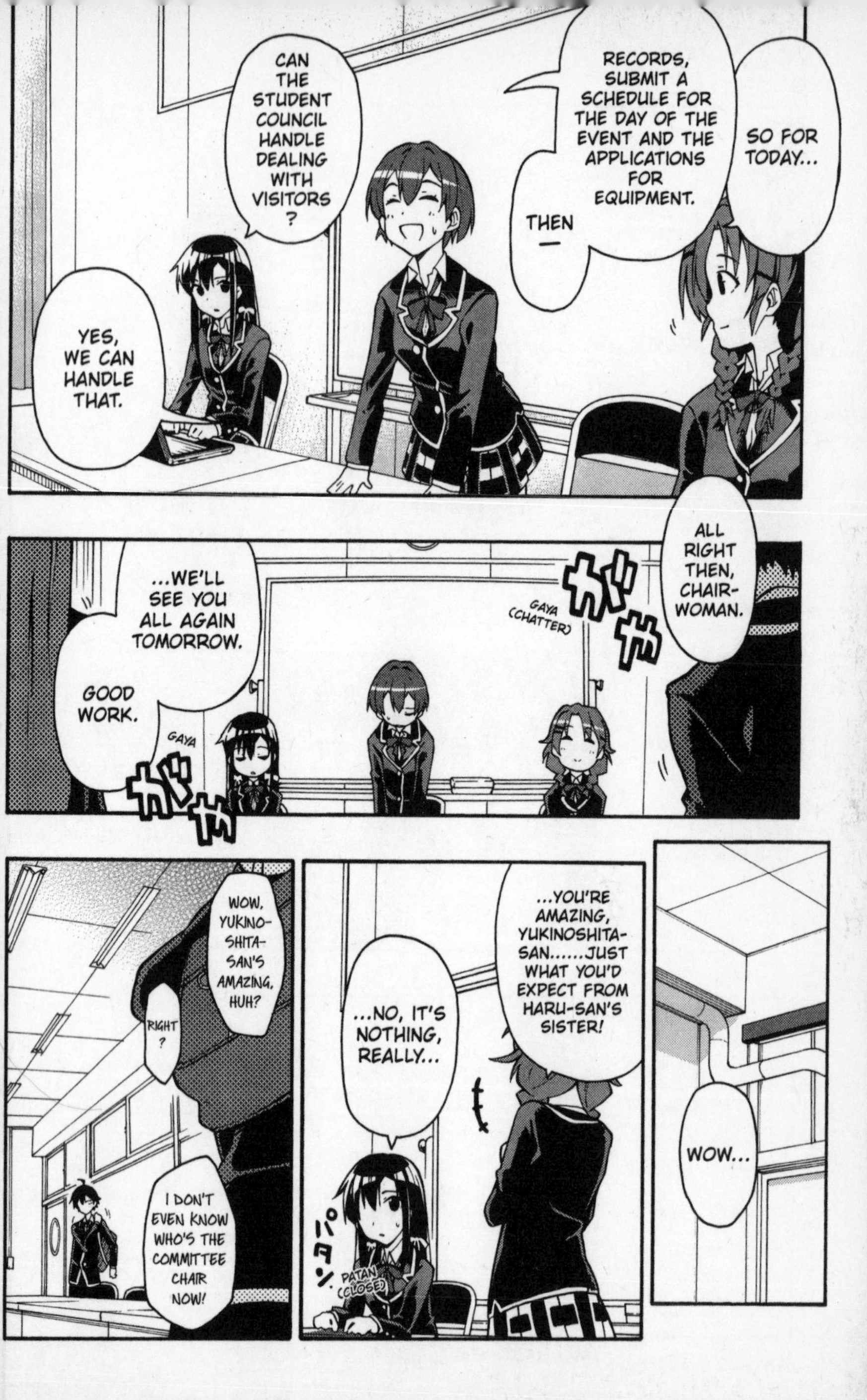
SO FOR TODAY...
RECORDS, SUBMIT A SCHEDULE FOR THE DAY OF THE EVENT AND THE APPLICATIONS FOR EQUIPMENT.
THEN—
CAN THE STUDENT COUNCIL HANDLE DEALING WITH VISITORS?
YES, WE CAN HANDLE THAT.
ALL RIGHT THEN, CHAIR-WOMAN.
GAYA (CHATTER)
...WE'LL SEE YOU ALL AGAIN TOMORROW.
GOOD WORK.
GAYA
WOW...
...YOU'RE AMAZING, YUKINOSHITA-SAN......JUST WHAT YOU'D EXPECT FROM HARU-SAN'S SISTER!
...NO, IT'S NOTHING, REALLY...
PATAN (CLOSE)
WOW, YUKINOSHITA-SAN'S AMAZING, HUH?
RIGHT?
I DON'T EVEN KNOW WHO'S THE COMMITTEE CHAIR NOW!

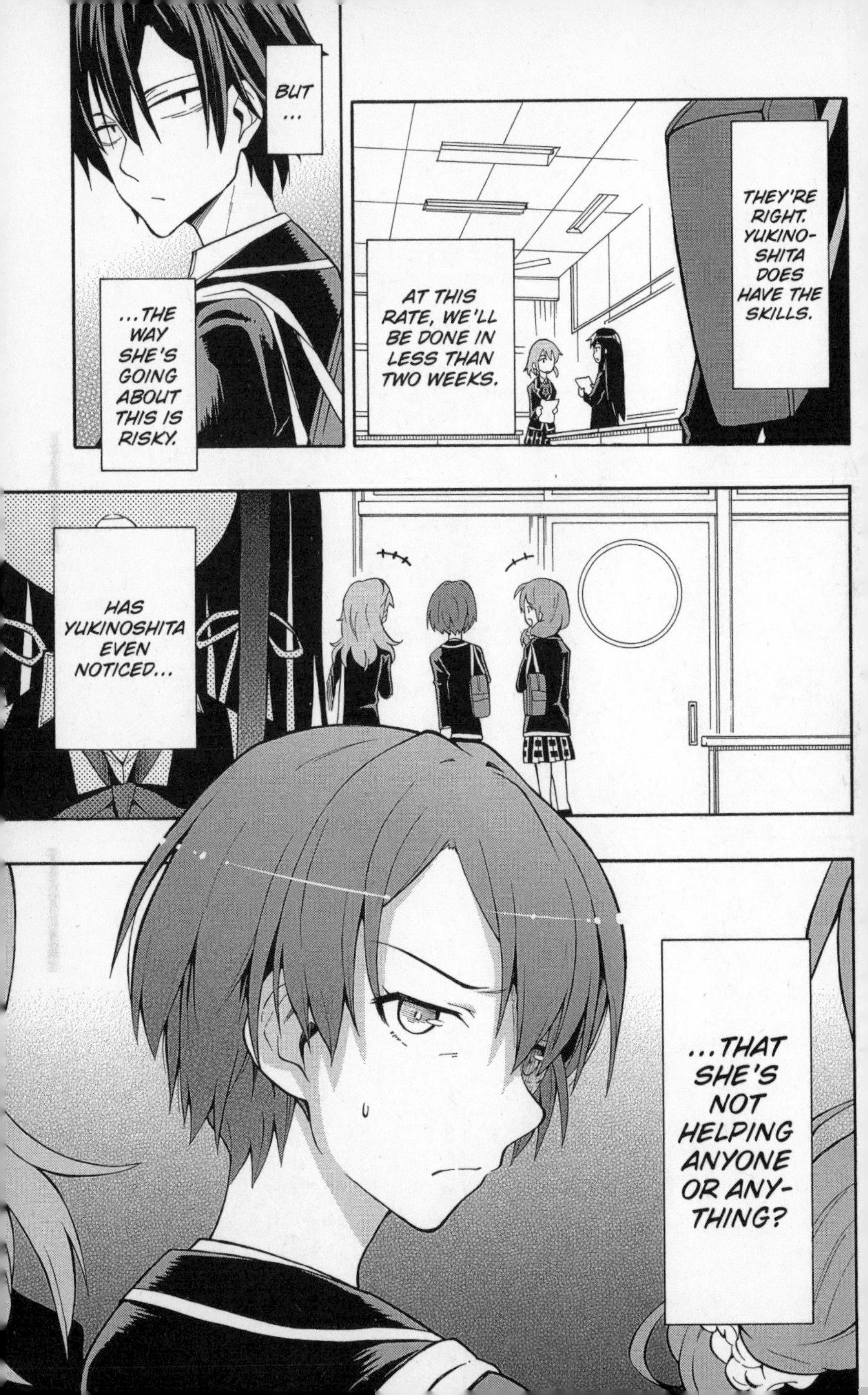

THEY'RE RIGHT. YUKINOSHITA DOES HAVE THE SKILLS.
AT THIS RATE, WE'LL BE DONE IN LESS THAN TWO WEEKS.
BUT...
...THE WAY SHE'S GOING ABOUT THIS IS RISKY.
HAS YUKINOSHITA EVEN NOTICED...
...THAT SHE'S NOT HELPING ANYONE OR ANYTHING?

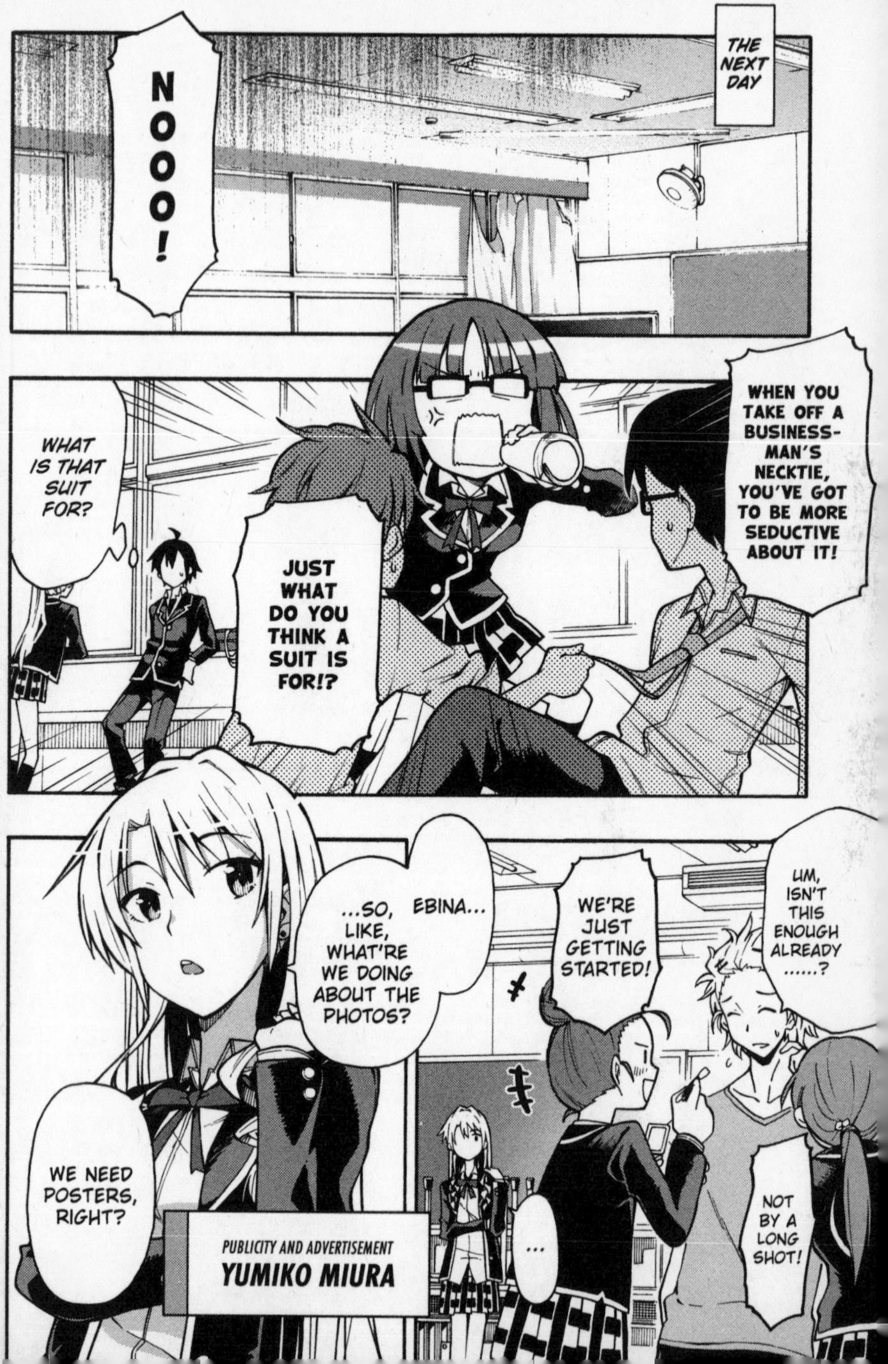
THE NEXT DAY
NOOO!
WHEN YOU TAKE OFF A BUSINESS-MAN'S NECKTIE, YOU'VE GOT TO BE MORE SEDUCTIVE ABOUT IT!
JUST WHAT DO YOU THINK A SUIT IS FOR!?
WHAT IS THAT SUIT FOR?
UM, ISN'T THIS ENOUGH ALREADY ......?
WE'RE JUST GETTING STARTED!
...SO, EBINA... LIKE, WHAT'RE WE DOING ABOUT THE PHOTOS?
NOT BY A LONG SHOT!
...
WE NEED POSTERS, RIGHT?
PUBLICITY AND ADVERTISEMENT
YUMIKO MIURA

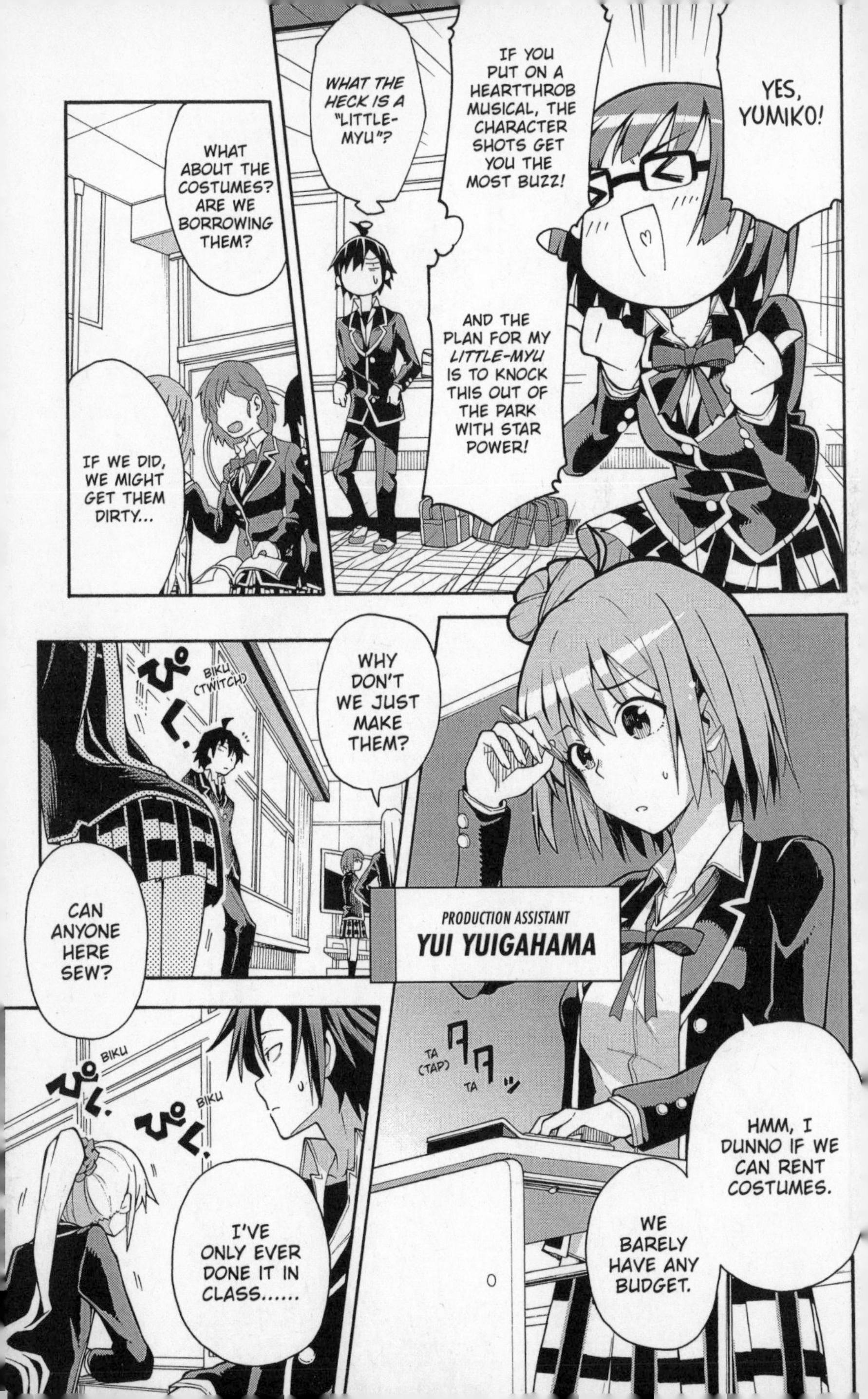
YES, YUMIKO!
IF YOU PUT ON A HEARTTHROB MUSICAL, THE CHARACTER SHOTS GET YOU THE MOST BUZZ!
AND THE PLAN FOR MY *LITTLE-MYU* IS TO KNOCK THIS OUT OF THE PARK WITH STAR POWER!
WHAT THE HECK IS A "LITTLE-MYU"?
WHAT ABOUT THE COSTUMES? ARE WE BORROWING THEM?
IF WE DID, WE MIGHT GET THEM DIRTY...
PRODUCTION ASSISTANT
YUI YUIGAHAMA
TA (TAP) TA
HMM, I DUNNO IF WE CAN RENT COSTUMES.
WE BARELY HAVE ANY BUDGET.
WHY DON'T WE JUST MAKE THEM?
BIKU (TWITCH)
CAN ANYONE HERE SEW?
BIKU
BIKU
I'VE ONLY EVER DONE IT IN CLASS......

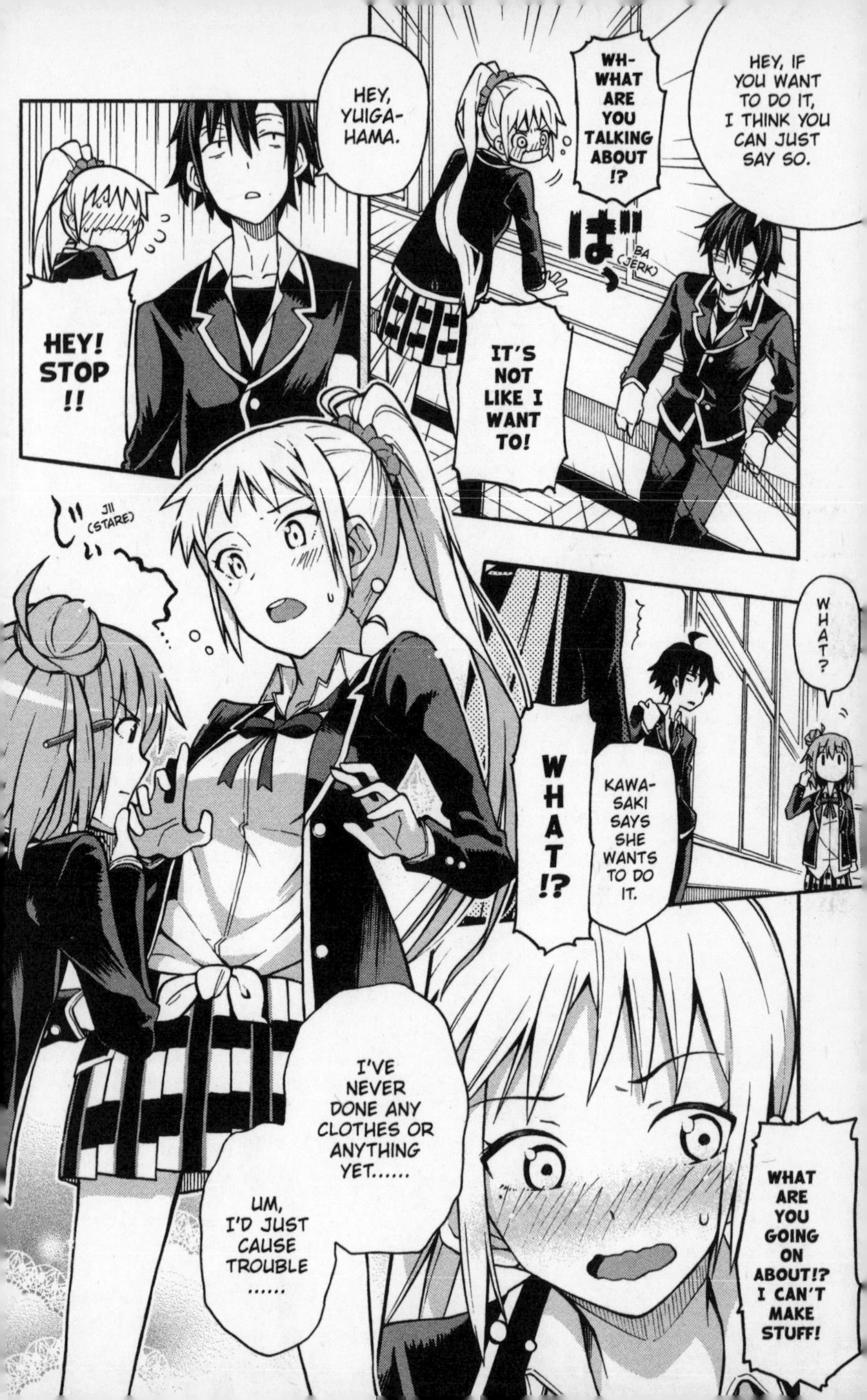
HEY, IF YOU WANT TO DO IT, I THINK YOU CAN JUST SAY SO.
WH- WHAT ARE YOU TALKING ABOUT !?
BA (JERK)
IT'S NOT LIKE I WANT TO!
HEY, YUIGA-HAMA.
HEY! STOP !!
WHAT?
KAWA-SAKI SAYS SHE WANTS TO DO IT.
WHAT !?
JII (STARE)
WHAT ARE YOU GOING ON ABOUT!? I CAN'T MAKE STUFF!
I'VE NEVER DONE ANY CLOTHES OR ANYTHING YET......
UM, I'D JUST CAUSE TROUBLE ......

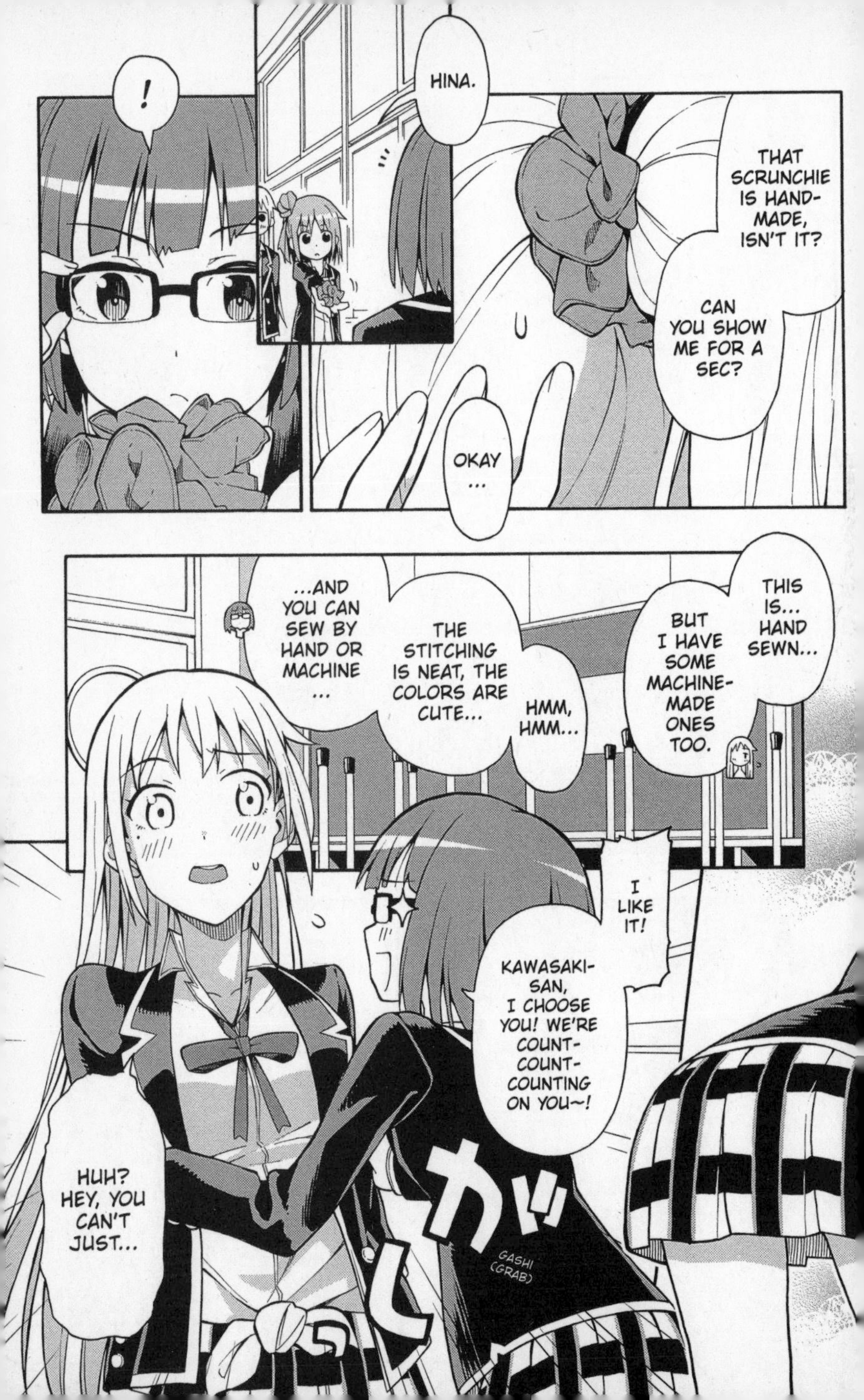
THAT SCRUNCHIE IS HAND-MADE, ISN'T IT?
CAN YOU SHOW ME FOR A SEC?
OKAY...
HINA.
!
THIS IS... HAND SEWN...
BUT I HAVE SOME MACHINE-MADE ONES TOO.
HMM, HMM...
THE STITCHING IS NEAT, THE COLORS ARE CUTE...
...AND YOU CAN SEW BY HAND OR MACHINE...
I LIKE IT!
KAWASAKI-SAN, I CHOOSE YOU! WE'RE COUNT-COUNT-COUNTING ON YOU~!
GASHI (GRAB)
HUH? HEY, YOU CAN'T JUST...

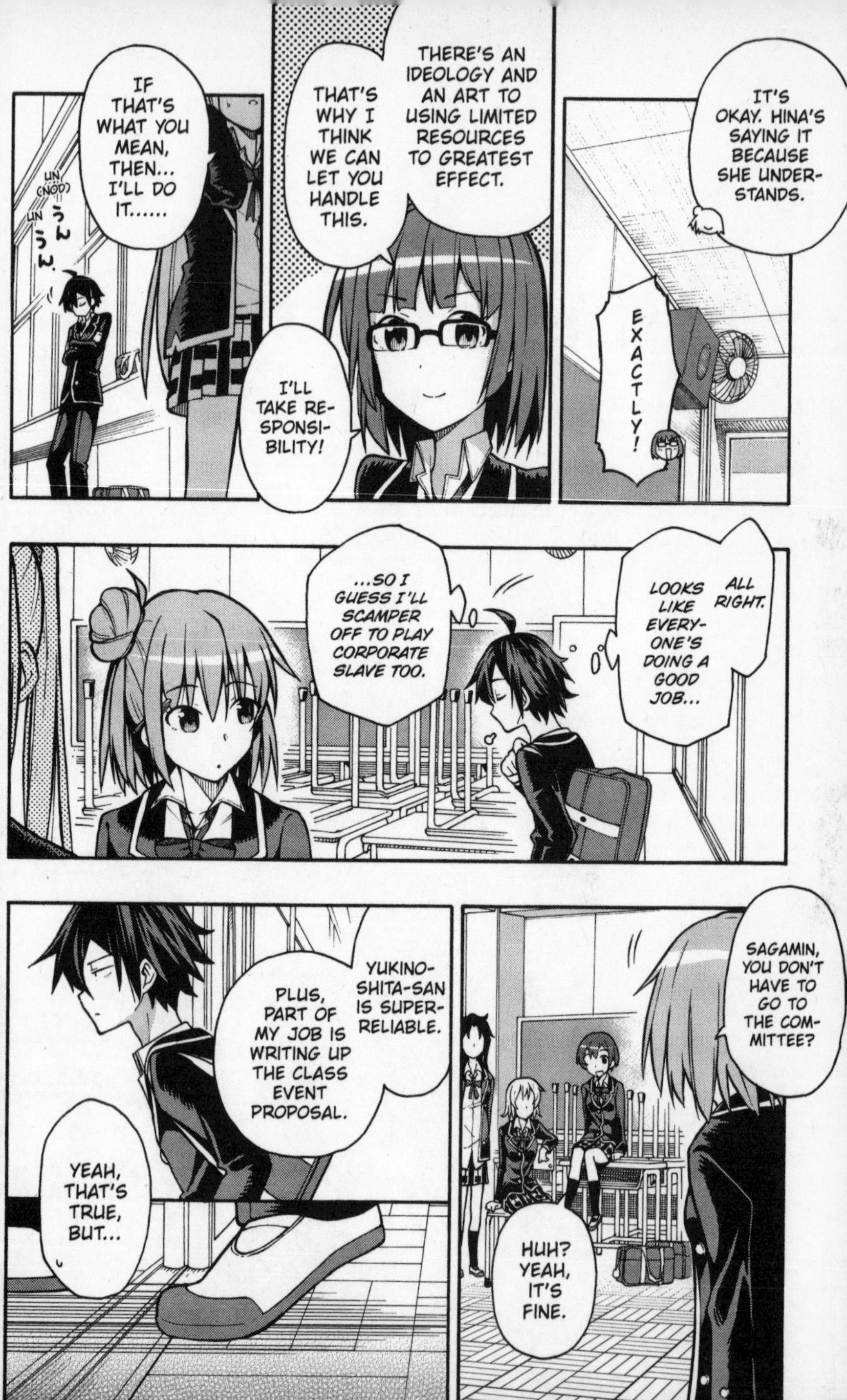
IT'S OKAY. HINA'S SAYING IT BECAUSE SHE UNDER-STANDS.
EXACTLY!
THERE'S AN IDEOLOGY AND AN ART TO USING LIMITED RESOURCES TO GREATEST EFFECT.
THAT'S WHY I THINK WE CAN LET YOU HANDLE THIS.
I'LL TAKE RE-SPONSI-BILITY!
IF THAT'S WHAT YOU MEAN, THEN... I'LL DO IT......
UN (NOD) UN
うんうん
ALL RIGHT.
LOOKS LIKE EVERY-ONE'S DOING A GOOD JOB...
...SO I GUESS I'LL SCAMPER OFF TO PLAY CORPORATE SLAVE TOO.
SAGAMIN, YOU DON'T HAVE TO GO TO THE COM-MITTEE?
HUH? YEAH, IT'S FINE.
YUKINO-SHITA-SAN IS SUPER-RELIABLE.
PLUS, PART OF MY JOB IS WRITING UP THE CLASS EVENT PROPOSAL.
YEAH, THAT'S TRUE, BUT...

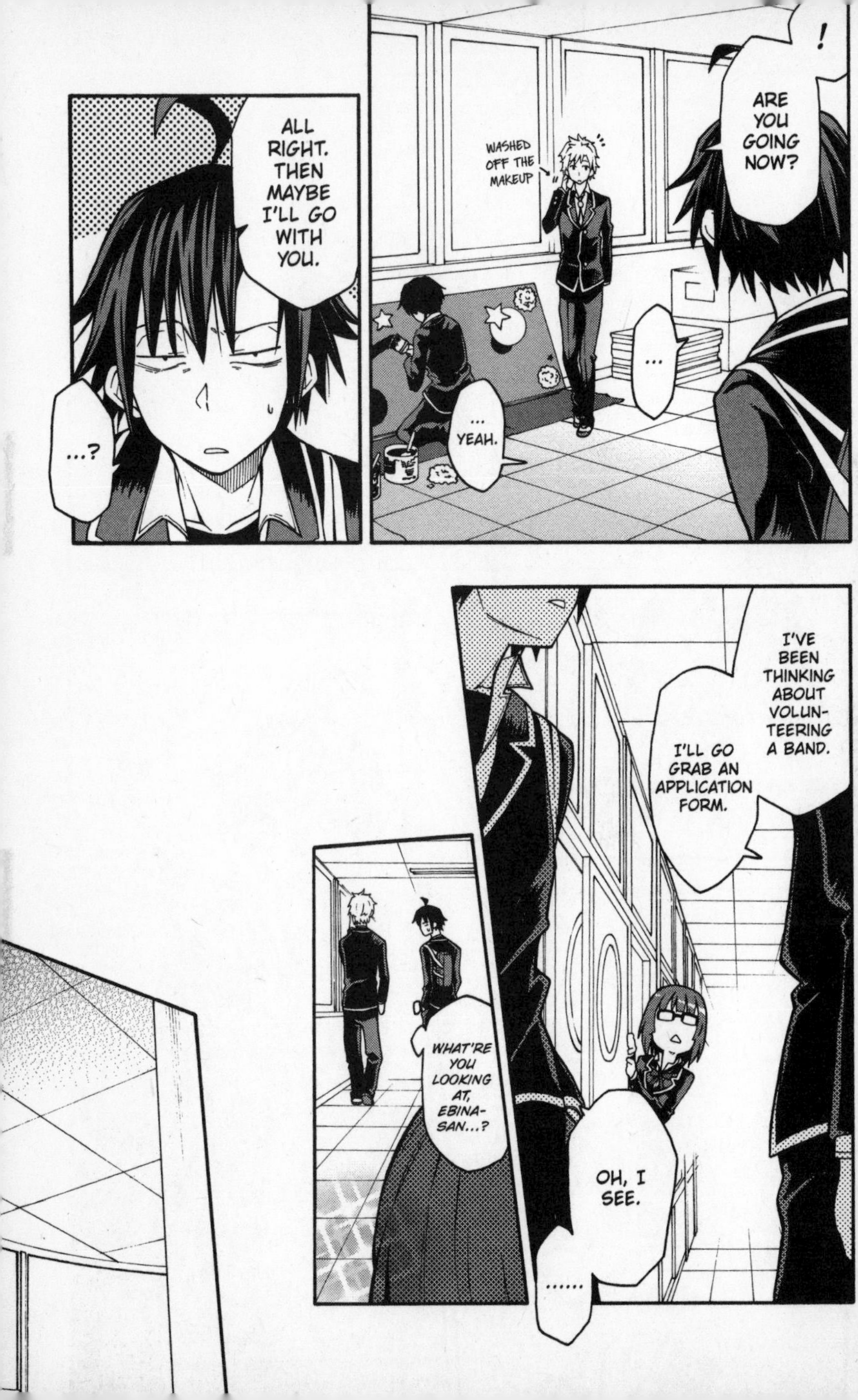
!
ARE YOU GOING NOW?
WASHED OFF THE MAKEUP
...
... YEAH.
ALL RIGHT. THEN MAYBE I'LL GO WITH YOU.
...?
I'VE BEEN THINKING ABOUT VOLUNTEERING A BAND.
I'LL GO GRAB AN APPLICATION FORM.
WHAT'RE YOU LOOKING AT, EBINA-SAN...?
OH, I SEE.
......

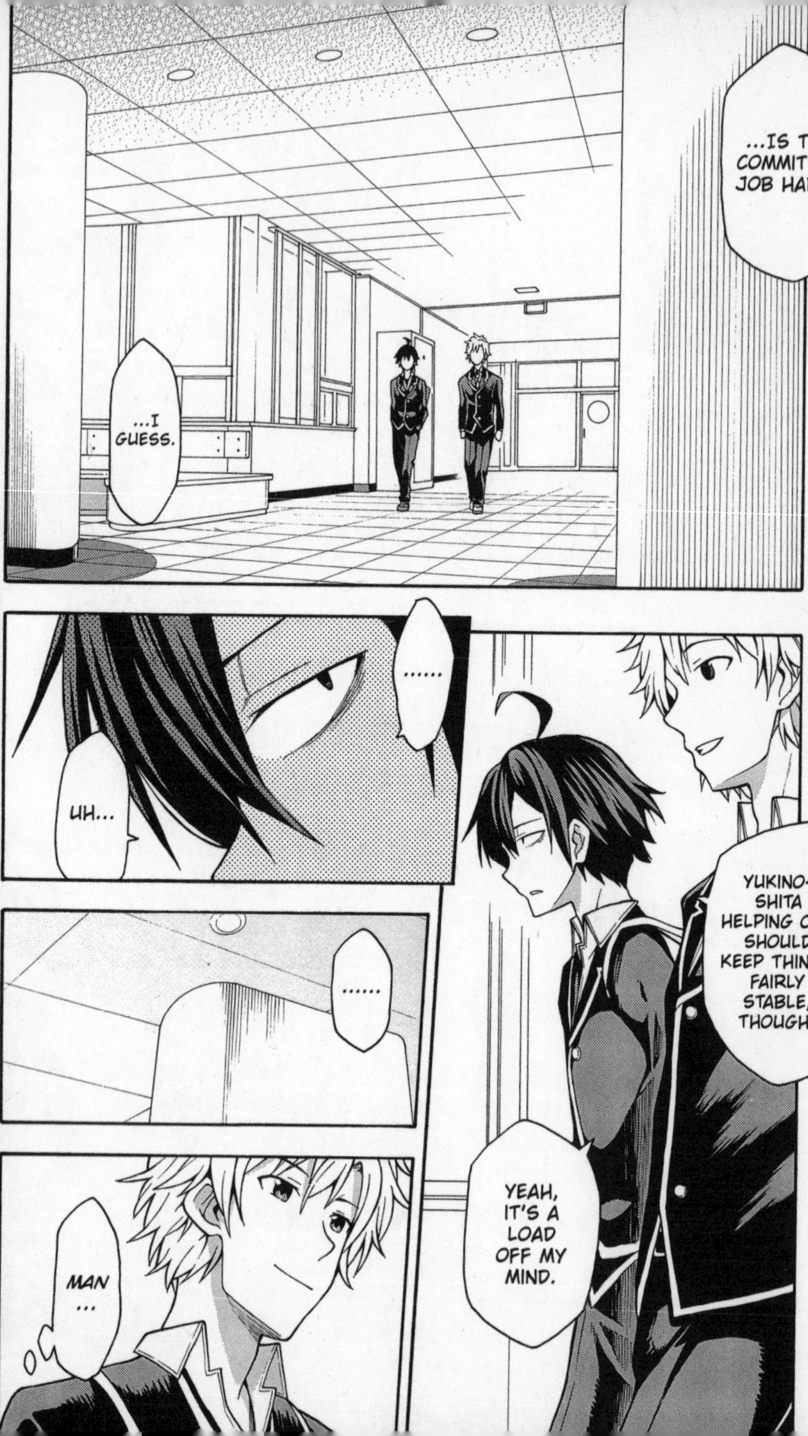
...IS THE COMMITTEE JOB HARD?
...I GUESS.
YUKINO-SHITA HELPING OUT SHOULD KEEP THINGS FAIRLY STABLE, THOUGH.
YEAH, IT'S A LOAD OFF MY MIND.
......
UH...
......
MAN ...

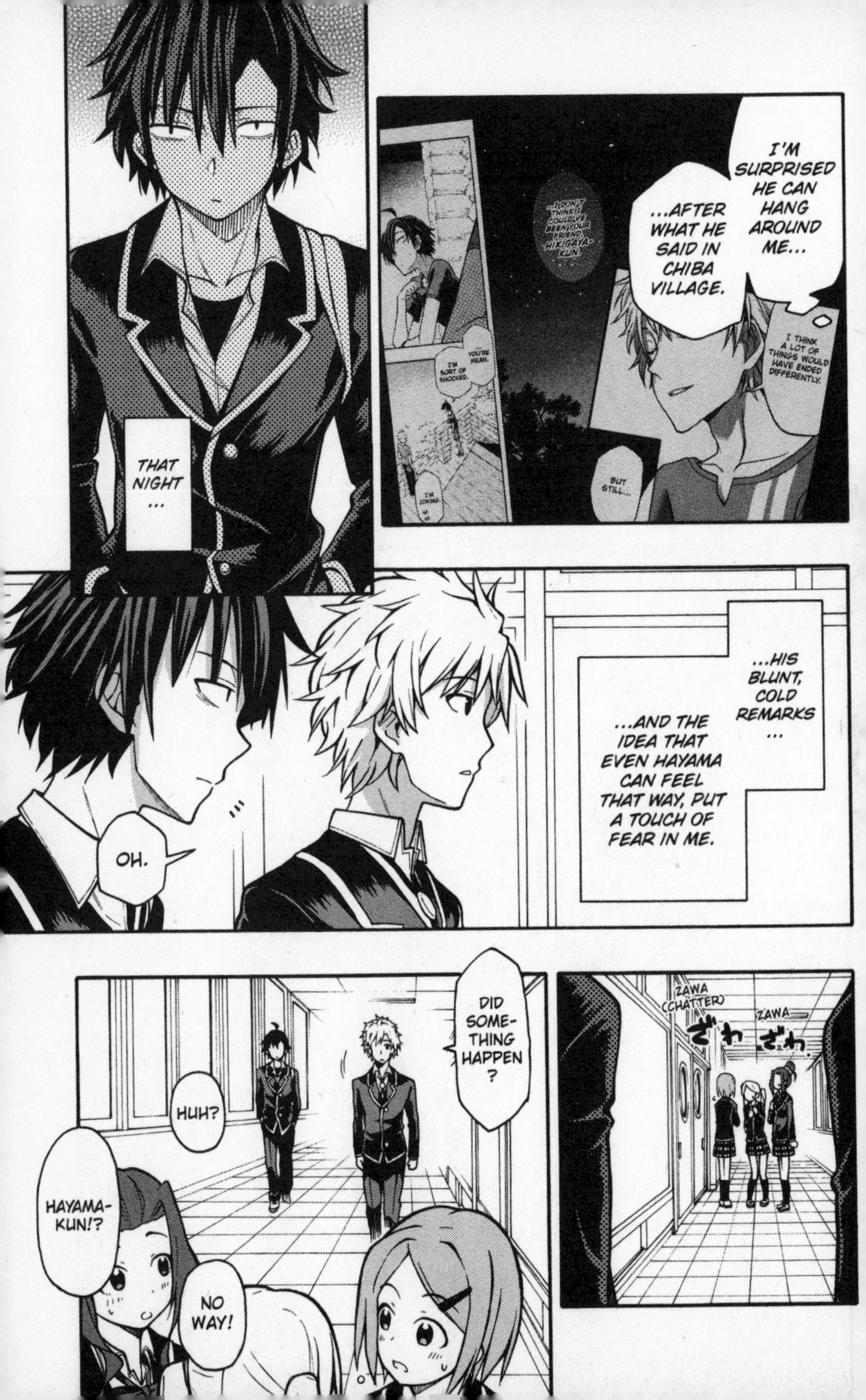
I'M SURPRISED HE CAN HANG AROUND ME...
...AFTER WHAT HE SAID IN CHIBA VILLAGE.
I THINK A LOT OF THINGS WOULD HAVE ENDED DIFFERENTLY.
...I DON'T THINK I COULD'VE BEEN YOUR FRIEND, HIKIGAYA-KUN.
BUT STILL...
YOU'RE MEAN.
I'M SORT OF SHOCKED.
I'M JOKING.
THAT NIGHT...
...HIS BLUNT, COLD REMARKS...
...AND THE IDEA THAT EVEN HAYAMA CAN FEEL THAT WAY, PUT A TOUCH OF FEAR IN ME.
OH.
ZAWA (CHATTER)
ざわ
ZAWA
ざわ
DID SOMETHING HAPPEN?
HUH?
HAYAMA-KUN!?
NO WAY!

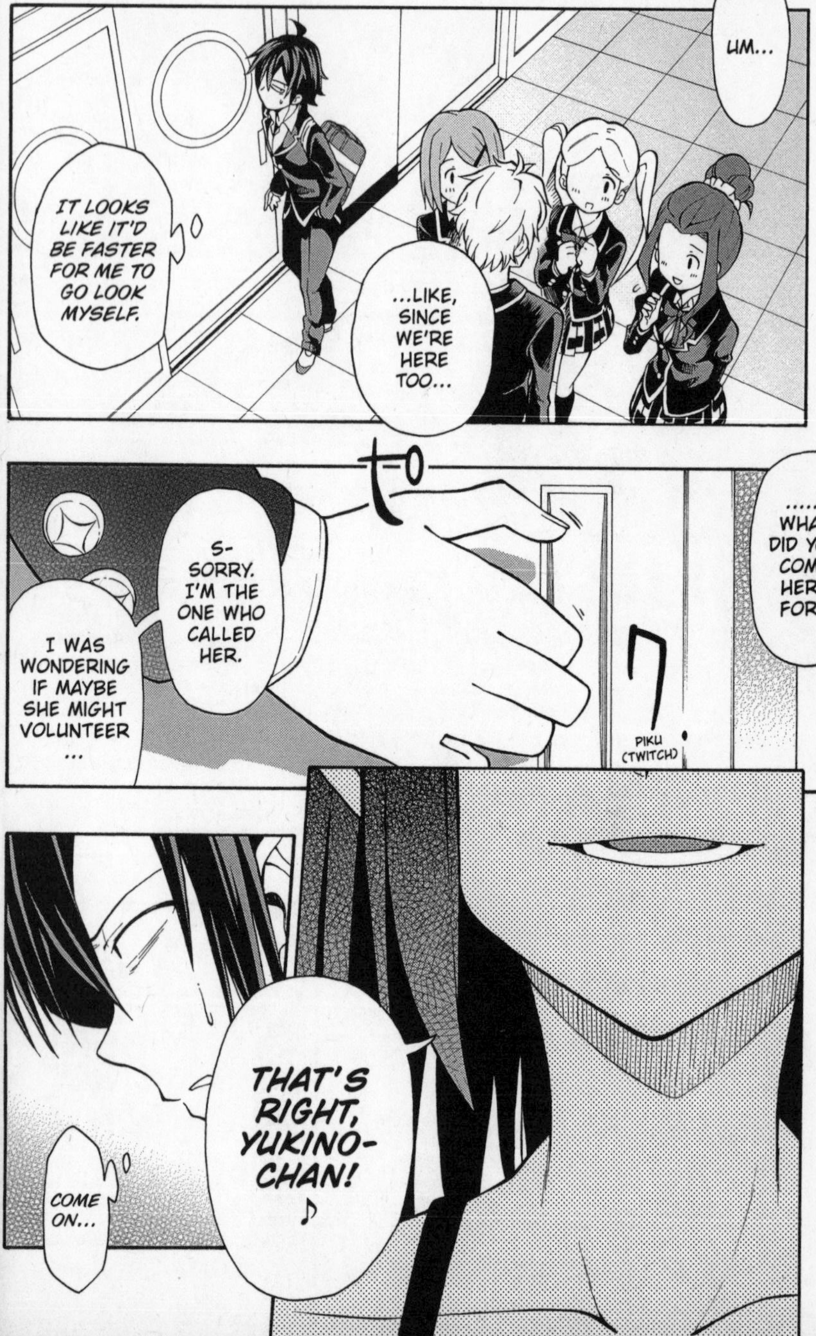
UM...
...LIKE, SINCE WE'RE HERE TOO...
IT LOOKS LIKE IT'D BE FASTER FOR ME TO GO LOOK MYSELF.
......WHAT DID YOU COME HERE FOR?
PIKU (TWITCH)
S-SORRY. I'M THE ONE WHO CALLED HER.
I WAS WONDERING IF MAYBE SHE MIGHT VOLUNTEER...
THAT'S RIGHT, YUKINO-CHAN! ♪
COME ON...

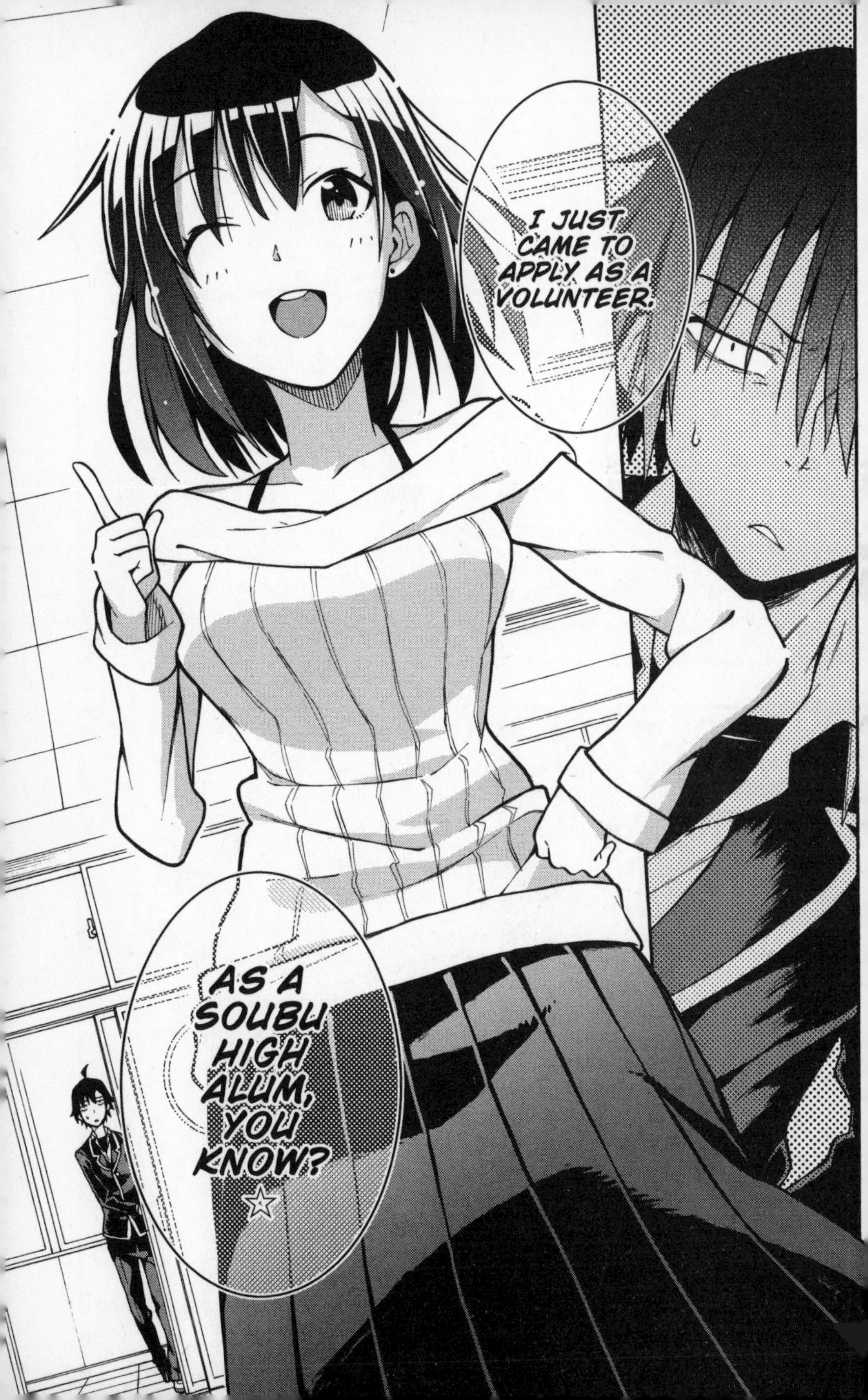
I JUST CAME TO APPLY AS A VOLUNTEER.
AS A SOUBU HIGH ALUM, YOU KNOW? ☆

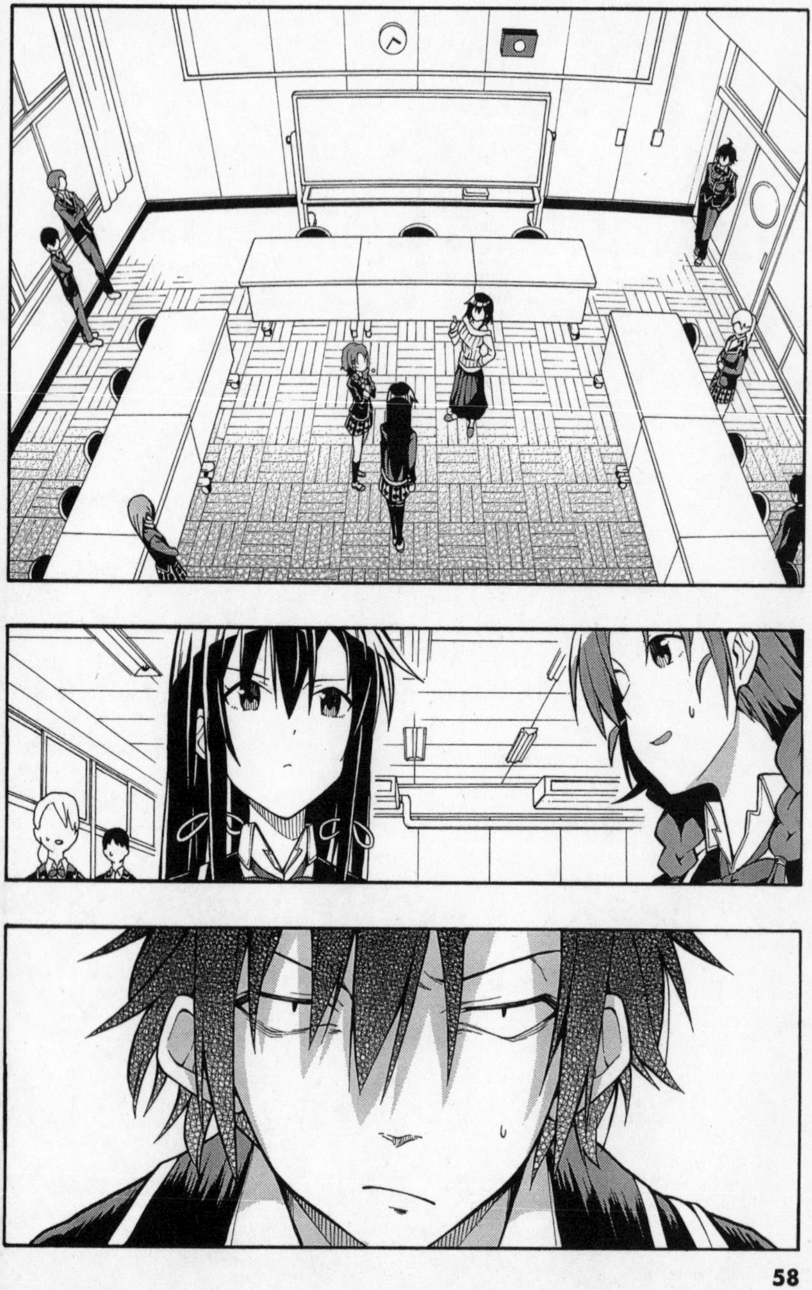

CHAPTER 38 ... SUDDENLY, HARUNO YUKINOSHITA ATTACKS.

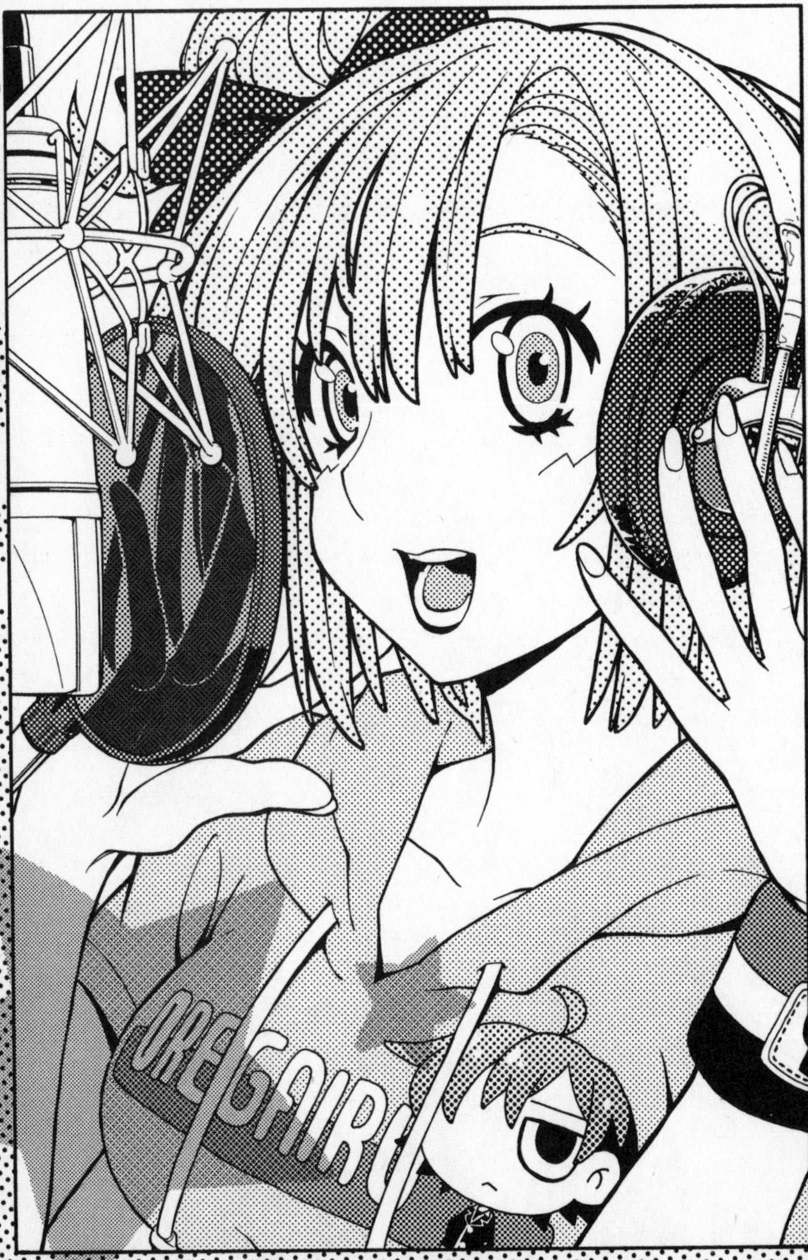
OREGAIRU

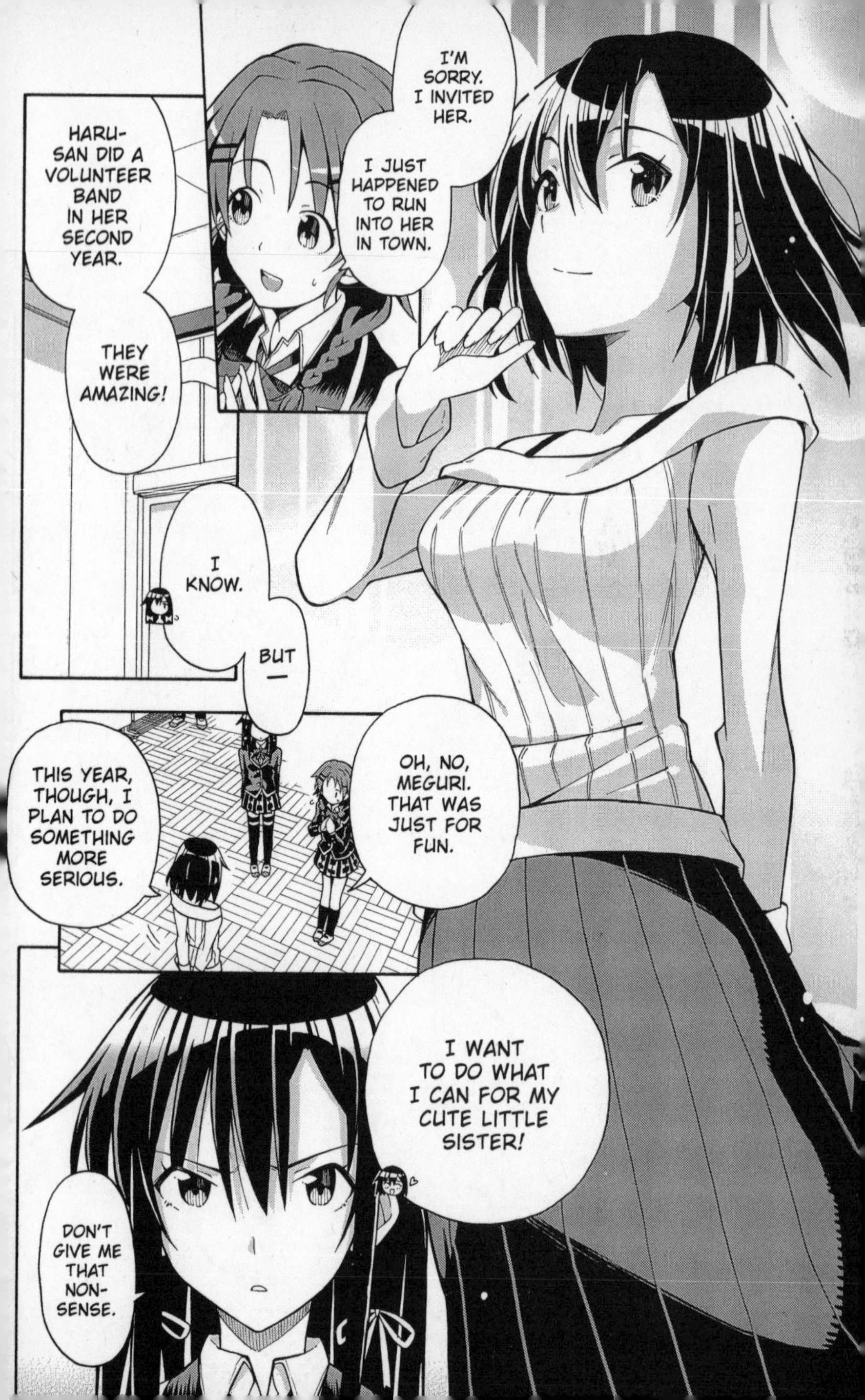
I'M SORRY. I INVITED HER.
I JUST HAPPENED TO RUN INTO HER IN TOWN.
HARU-SAN DID A VOLUNTEER BAND IN HER SECOND YEAR.
THEY WERE AMAZING!
I KNOW.
BUT —
OH, NO, MEGURI. THAT WAS JUST FOR FUN.
THIS YEAR, THOUGH, I PLAN TO DO SOMETHING MORE SERIOUS.
I WANT TO DO WHAT I CAN FOR MY CUTE LITTLE SISTER!
DON'T GIVE ME THAT NON-SENSE.

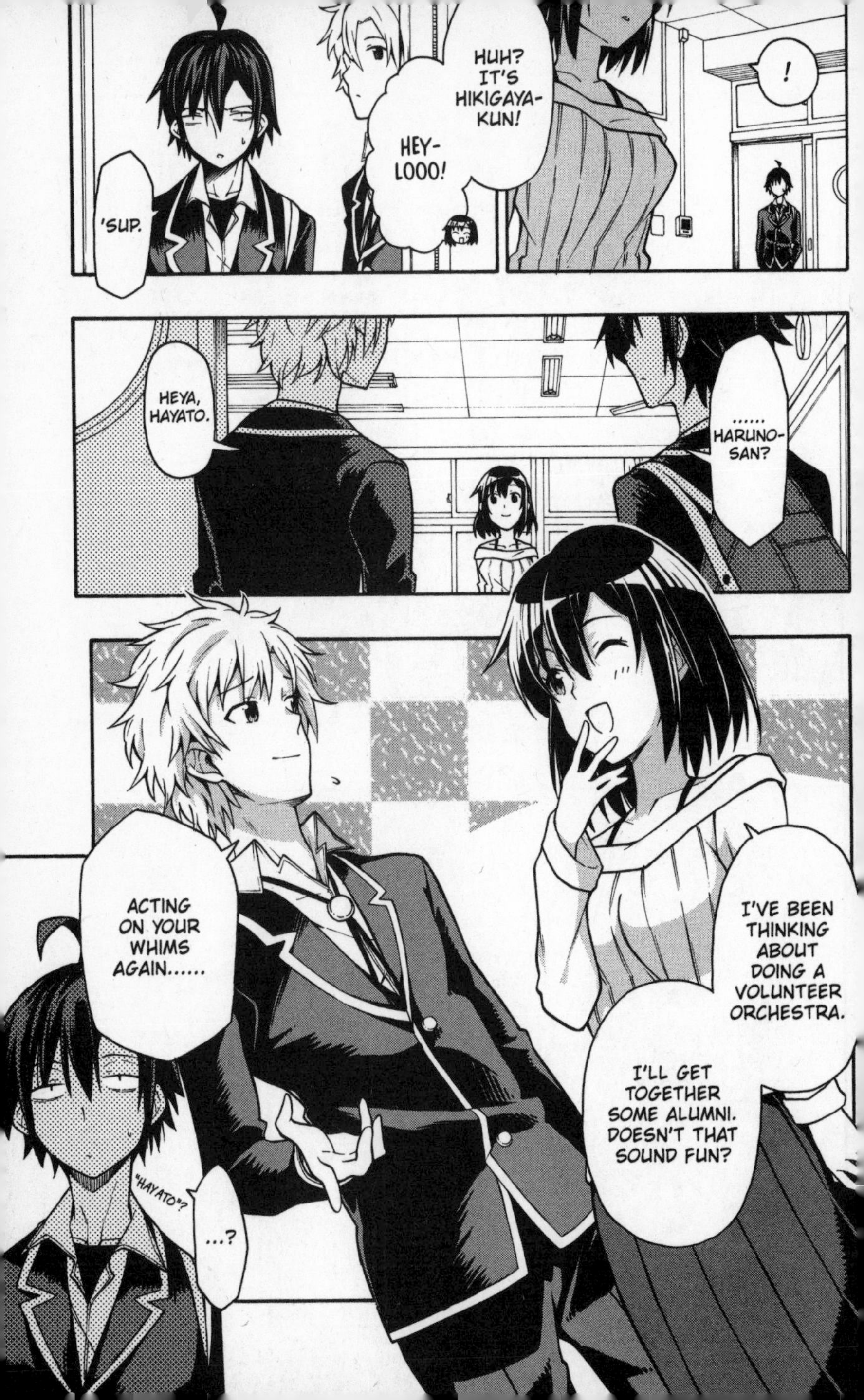
!
HUH? IT'S HIKIGAYA-KUN!
HEY-LOOO!
'SUP.
...... HARUNO-SAN?
HEYA, HAYATO.
I'VE BEEN THINKING ABOUT DOING A VOLUNTEER ORCHESTRA.
I'LL GET TOGETHER SOME ALUMNI. DOESN'T THAT SOUND FUN?
ACTING ON YOUR WHIMS AGAIN......
"HAYATO"?
...?

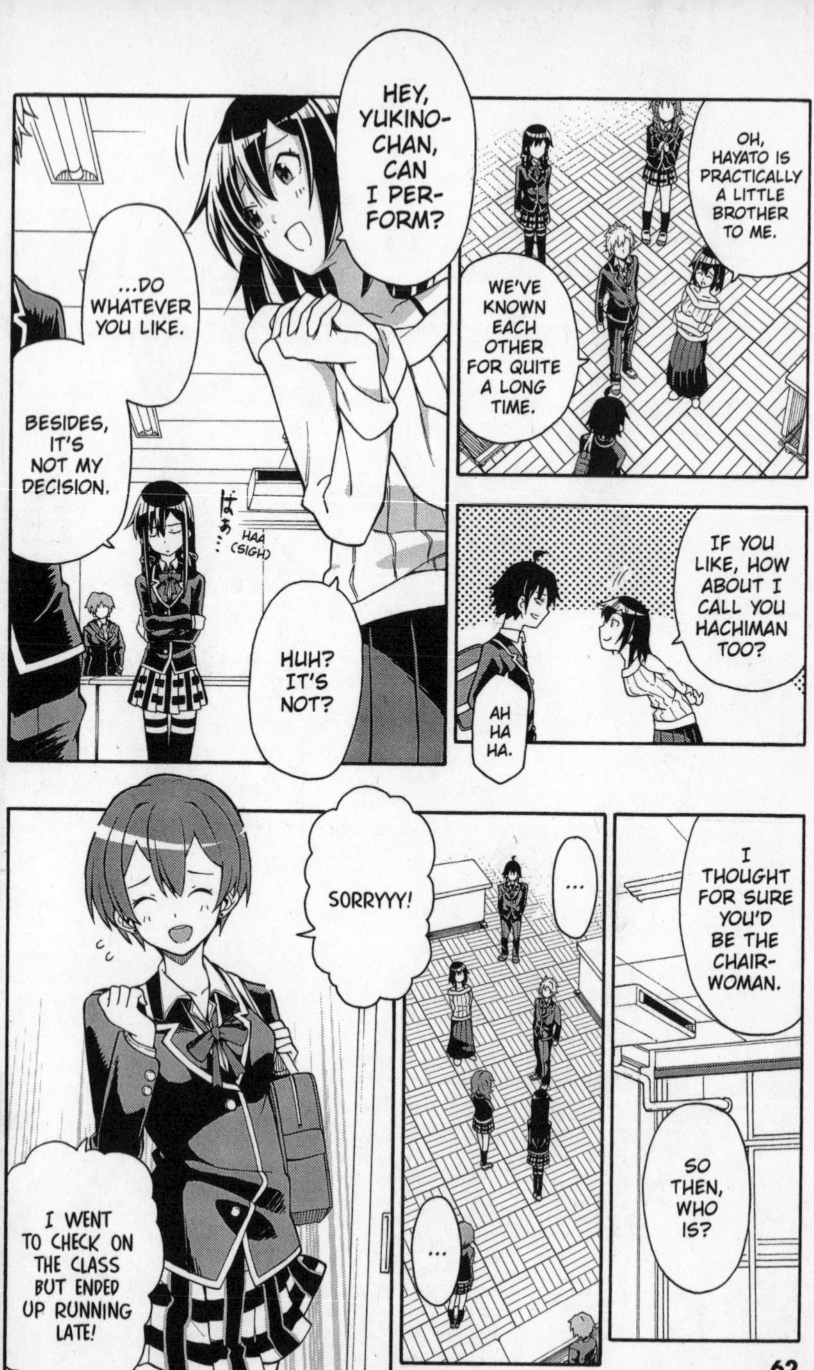
OH, HAYATO IS PRACTICALLY A LITTLE BROTHER TO ME.
WE'VE KNOWN EACH OTHER FOR QUITE A LONG TIME.
IF YOU LIKE, HOW ABOUT I CALL YOU HACHIMAN TOO?
AH HA HA.
HEY, YUKINO-CHAN, CAN I PER-FORM?
...DO WHATEVER YOU LIKE.
BESIDES, IT'S NOT MY DECISION.
はぁ…
HAA (SIGH)
HUH? IT'S NOT?
I THOUGHT FOR SURE YOU'D BE THE CHAIR-WOMAN.
SO THEN, WHO IS?
...
...
SORRYYY!
I WENT TO CHECK ON THE CLASS BUT ENDED UP RUNNING LATE!

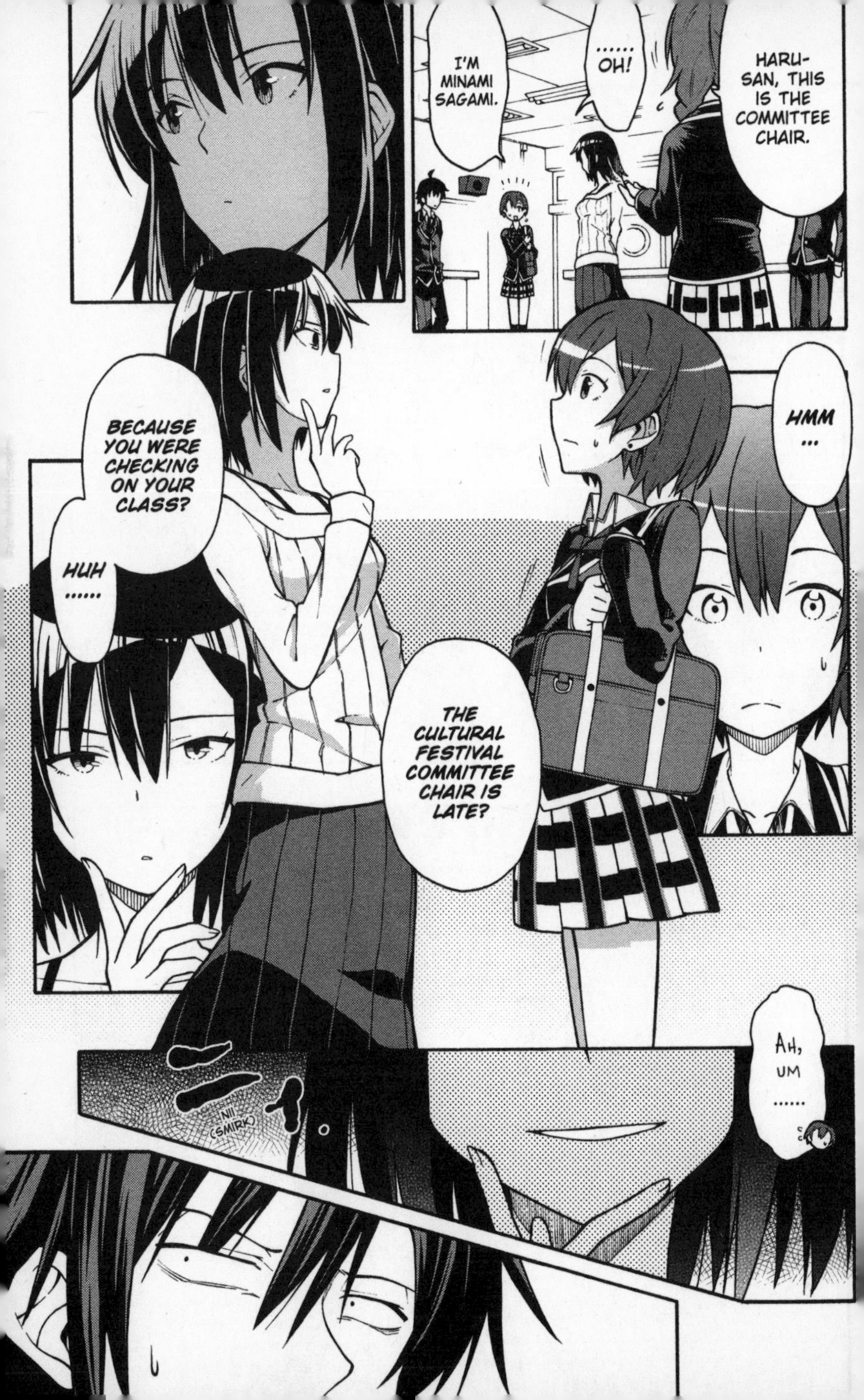
HARU-SAN, THIS IS THE COMMITTEE CHAIR.
......OH!
I'M MINAMI SAGAMI.
HMM...
THE CULTURAL FESTIVAL COMMITTEE CHAIR IS LATE?
BECAUSE YOU WERE CHECKING ON YOUR CLASS?
HUH......
AH, UM......
NII (SMIRK)

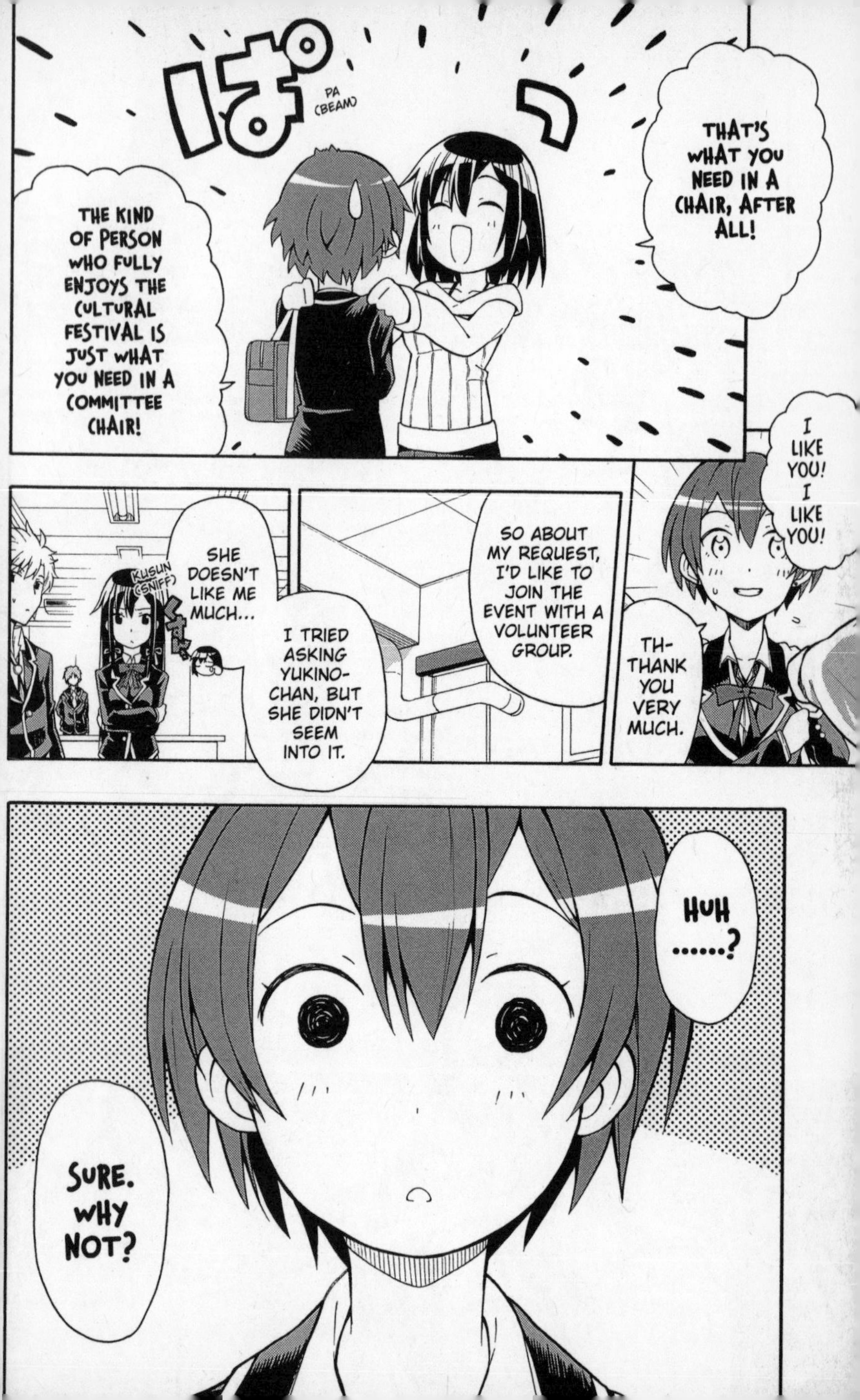
ぱっ
PA (BEAM)
THAT'S WHAT YOU NEED IN A CHAIR, AFTER ALL!
THE KIND OF PERSON WHO FULLY ENJOYS THE CULTURAL FESTIVAL IS JUST WHAT YOU NEED IN A COMMITTEE CHAIR!
I LIKE YOU! I LIKE YOU!
TH-THANK YOU VERY MUCH.
SO ABOUT MY REQUEST, I'D LIKE TO JOIN THE EVENT WITH A VOLUNTEER GROUP.
I TRIED ASKING YUKINO-CHAN, BUT SHE DIDN'T SEEM INTO IT.
SHE DOESN'T LIKE ME MUCH...
KUSUN (SNIFF)
HUH ......?
SURE. WHY NOT?

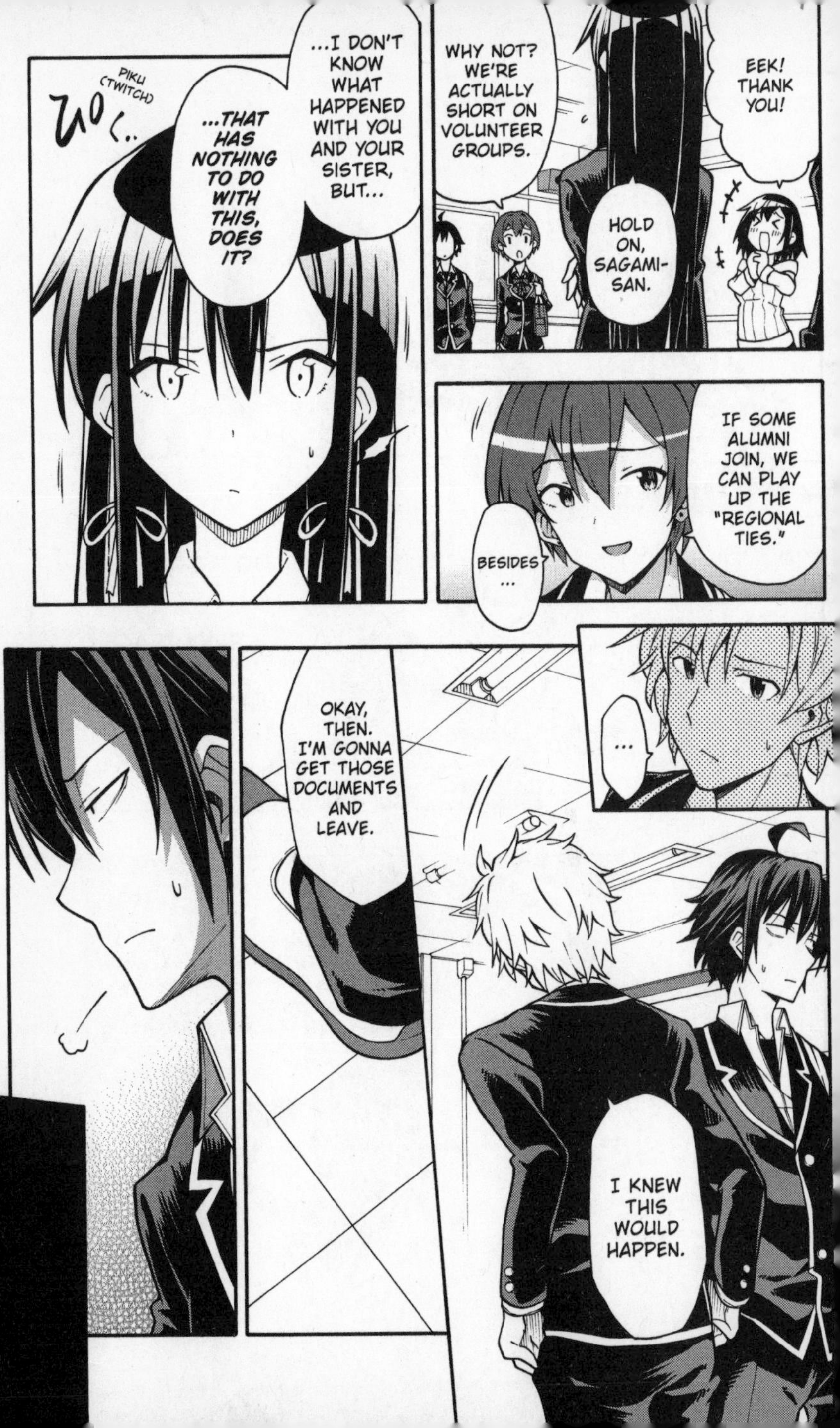
EEK! THANK YOU!
WHY NOT? WE'RE ACTUALLY SHORT ON VOLUNTEER GROUPS.
HOLD ON, SAGAMI-SAN.
IF SOME ALUMNI JOIN, WE CAN PLAY UP THE "REGIONAL TIES."
BESIDES...
...I DON'T KNOW WHAT HAPPENED WITH YOU AND YOUR SISTER, BUT...
...THAT HAS NOTHING TO DO WITH THIS, DOES IT?
PIKU (TWITCH)
...
OKAY, THEN. I'M GONNA GET THOSE DOCUMENTS AND LEAVE.
I KNEW THIS WOULD HAPPEN.

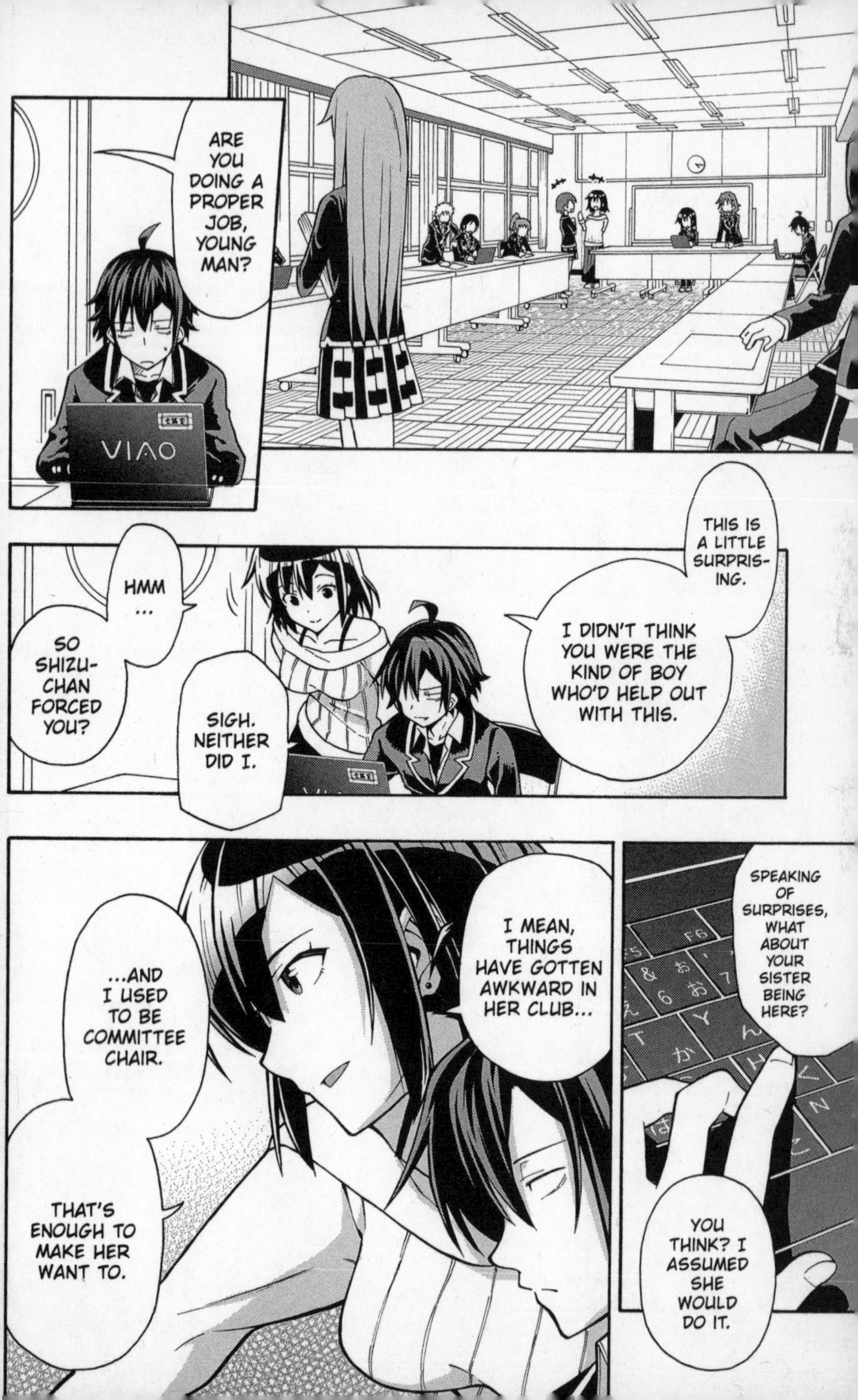
ARE YOU DOING A PROPER JOB, YOUNG MAN?
THIS IS A LITTLE SURPRIS-ING.
I DIDN'T THINK YOU WERE THE KIND OF BOY WHO'D HELP OUT WITH THIS.
SIGH. NEITHER DID I.
HMM ...
SO SHIZU-CHAN FORCED YOU?
SPEAKING OF SURPRISES, WHAT ABOUT YOUR SISTER BEING HERE?
YOU THINK? I ASSUMED SHE WOULD DO IT.
I MEAN, THINGS HAVE GOTTEN AWKWARD IN HER CLUB...
...AND I USED TO BE COMMITTEE CHAIR.
THAT'S ENOUGH TO MAKE HER WANT TO.

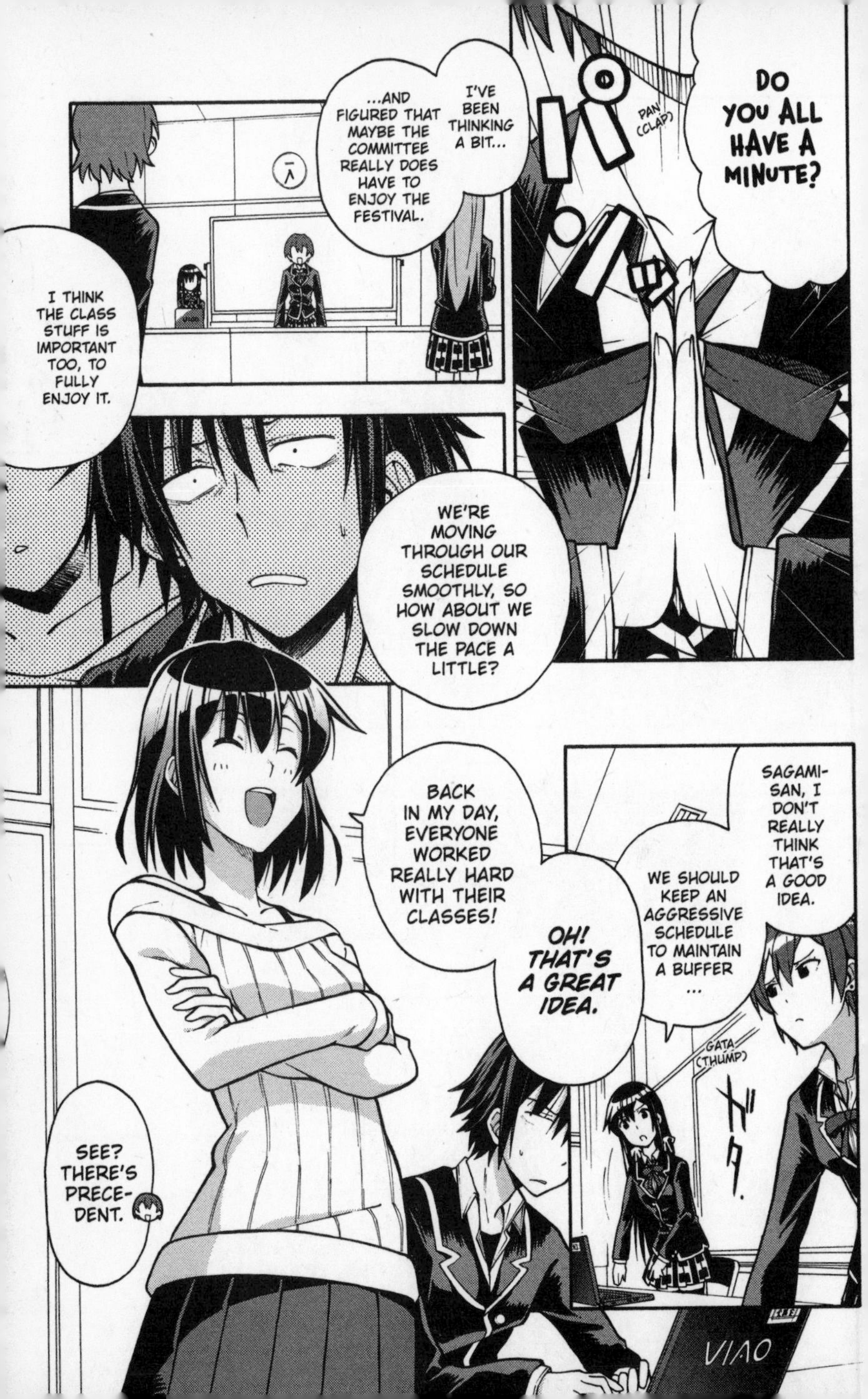
DO YOU ALL HAVE A MINUTE?
PAN (CLAP)
I'VE BEEN THINKING A BIT...
...AND FIGURED THAT MAYBE THE COMMITTEE REALLY DOES HAVE TO ENJOY THE FESTIVAL.
I THINK THE CLASS STUFF IS IMPORTANT TOO, TO FULLY ENJOY IT.
WE'RE MOVING THROUGH OUR SCHEDULE SMOOTHLY, SO HOW ABOUT WE SLOW DOWN THE PACE A LITTLE?
SAGAMI-SAN, I DON'T REALLY THINK THAT'S A GOOD IDEA.
WE SHOULD KEEP AN AGGRESSIVE SCHEDULE TO MAINTAIN A BUFFER ...
GATA (THUMP)
OH! THAT'S A GREAT IDEA.
BACK IN MY DAY, EVERYONE WORKED REALLY HARD WITH THEIR CLASSES!
SEE? THERE'S PRECE-DENT.
VIAO

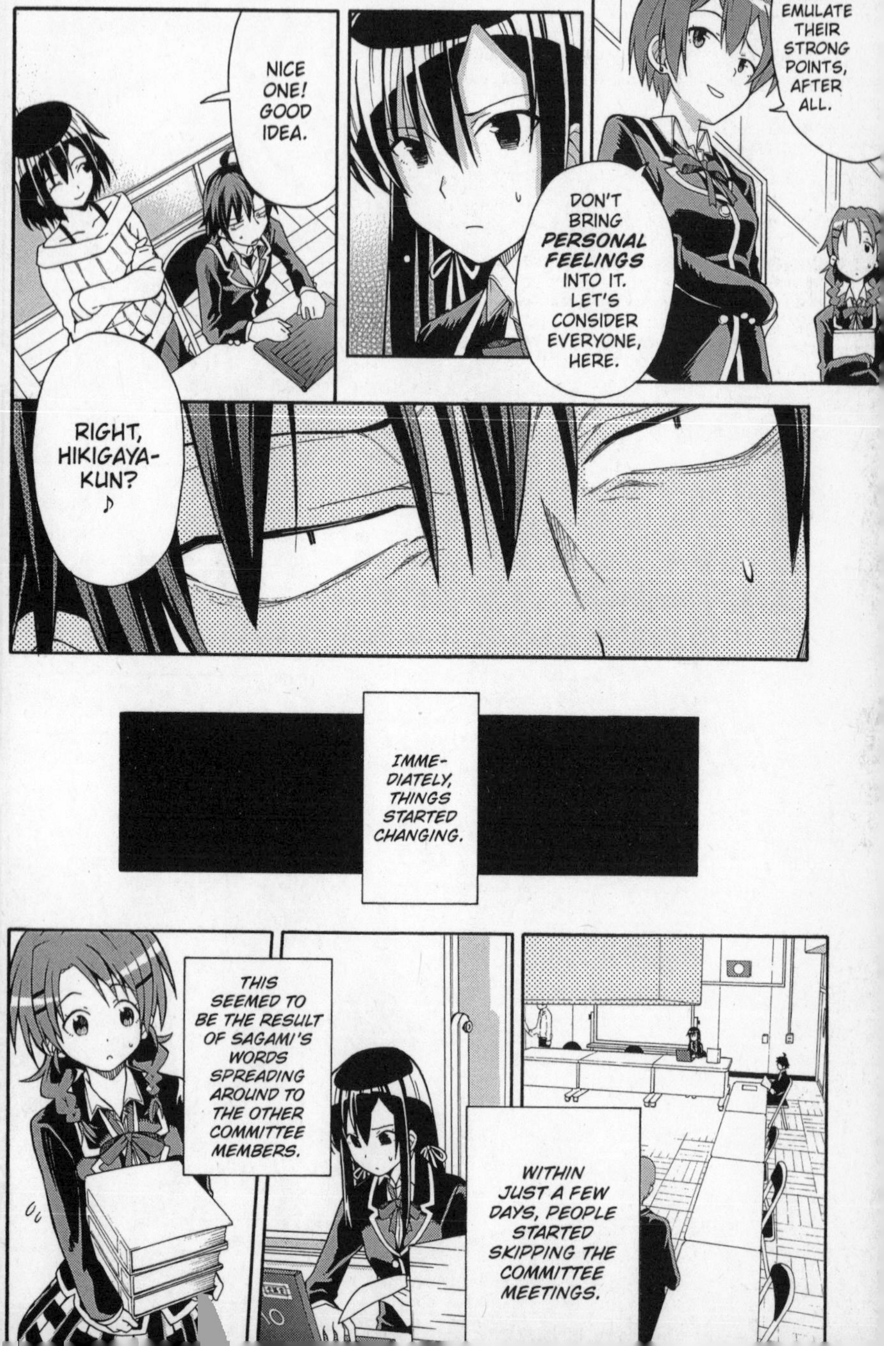
WE SHOULD EMULATE THEIR STRONG POINTS, AFTER ALL.
DON'T BRING PERSONAL FEELINGS INTO IT. LET'S CONSIDER EVERYONE, HERE.
NICE ONE! GOOD IDEA.
RIGHT, HIKIGAYA-KUN? ♪
IMME-DIATELY, THINGS STARTED CHANGING.
WITHIN JUST A FEW DAYS, PEOPLE STARTED SKIPPING THE COMMITTEE MEETINGS.
THIS SEEMED TO BE THE RESULT OF SAGAMI'S WORDS SPREADING AROUND TO THE OTHER COMMITTEE MEMBERS.

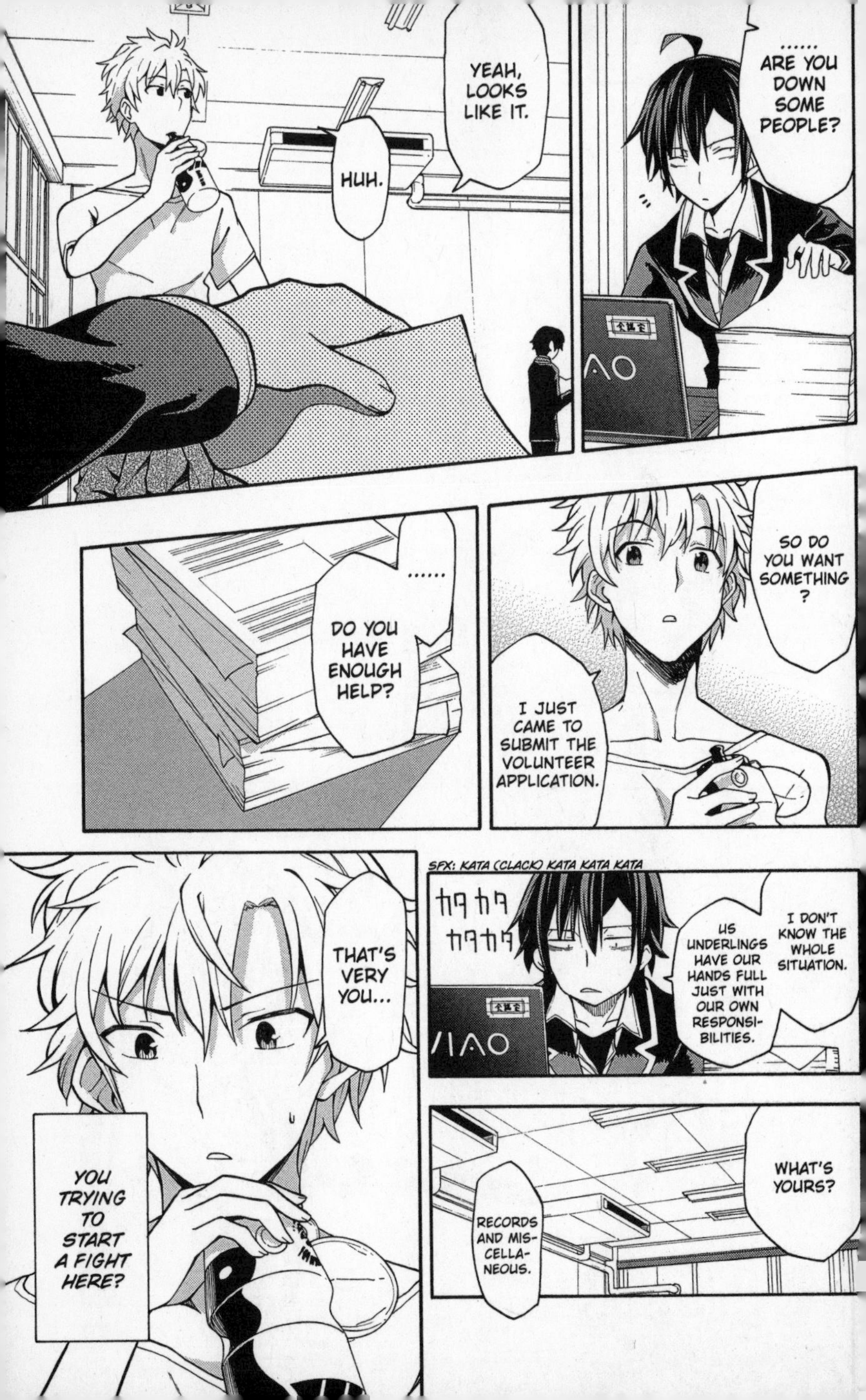

...... ARE YOU DOWN SOME PEOPLE?
YEAH, LOOKS LIKE IT.
HUH.
SO DO YOU WANT SOMETHING?
I JUST CAME TO SUBMIT THE VOLUNTEER APPLICATION.
...... DO YOU HAVE ENOUGH HELP?
SFX: KATA (CLACK) KATA KATA KATA
カタカタ
カタカタ
I DON'T KNOW THE WHOLE SITUATION.
US UNDERLINGS HAVE OUR HANDS FULL JUST WITH OUR OWN RESPONSI-BILITIES.
WHAT'S YOURS?
RECORDS AND MIS-CELLA-NEOUS.
THAT'S VERY YOU...
YOU TRYING TO START A FIGHT HERE?

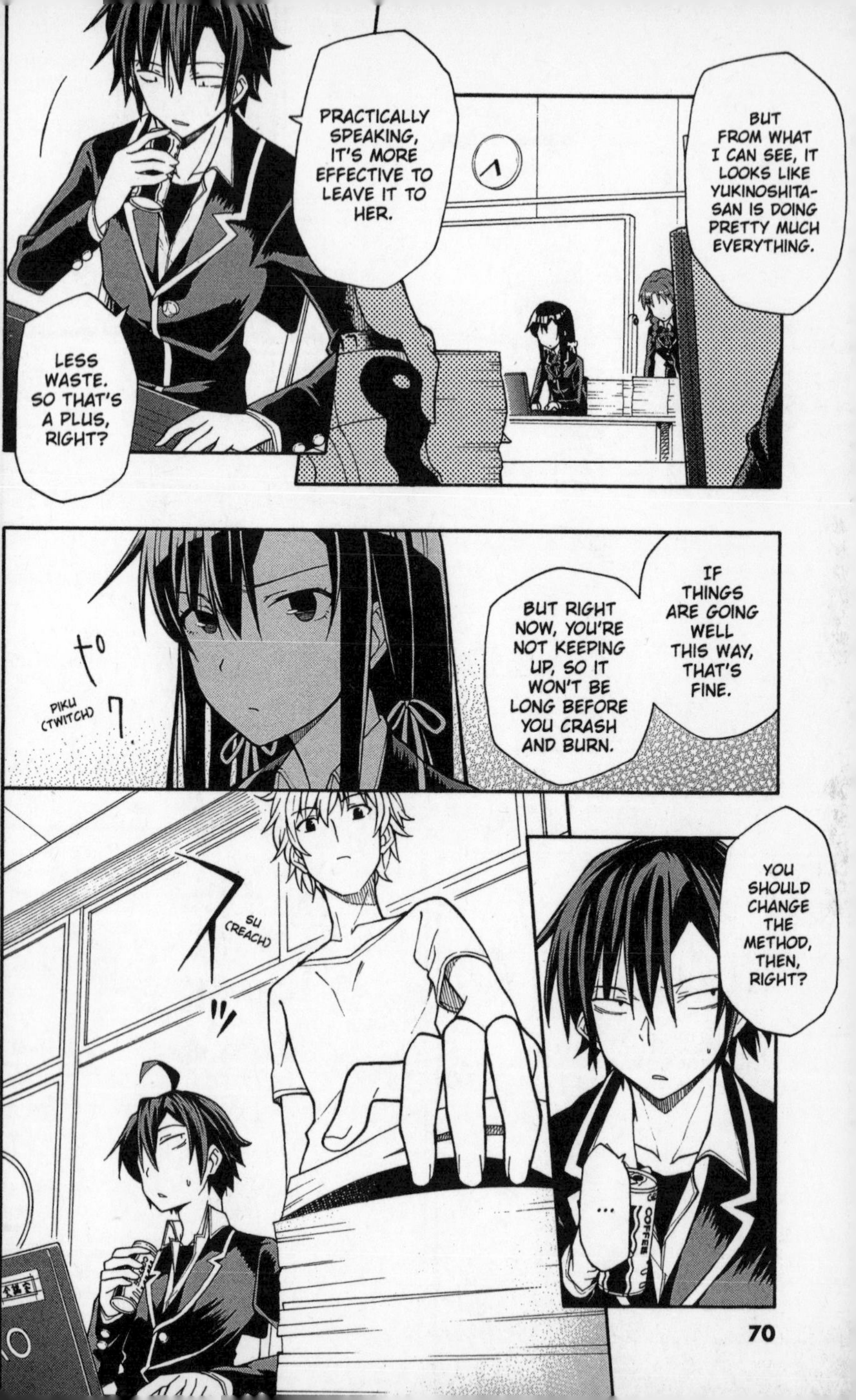
BUT FROM WHAT I CAN SEE, IT LOOKS LIKE YUKINOSHITA-SAN IS DOING PRETTY MUCH EVERYTHING.
PRACTICALLY SPEAKING, IT'S MORE EFFECTIVE TO LEAVE IT TO HER.
LESS WASTE. SO THAT'S A PLUS, RIGHT?
IF THINGS ARE GOING WELL THIS WAY, THAT'S FINE.
BUT RIGHT NOW, YOU'RE NOT KEEPING UP, SO IT WON'T BE LONG BEFORE YOU CRASH AND BURN.
PIKU (TWITCH)
YOU SHOULD CHANGE THE METHOD, THEN, RIGHT?
...
COFFEE
SU (REACH)

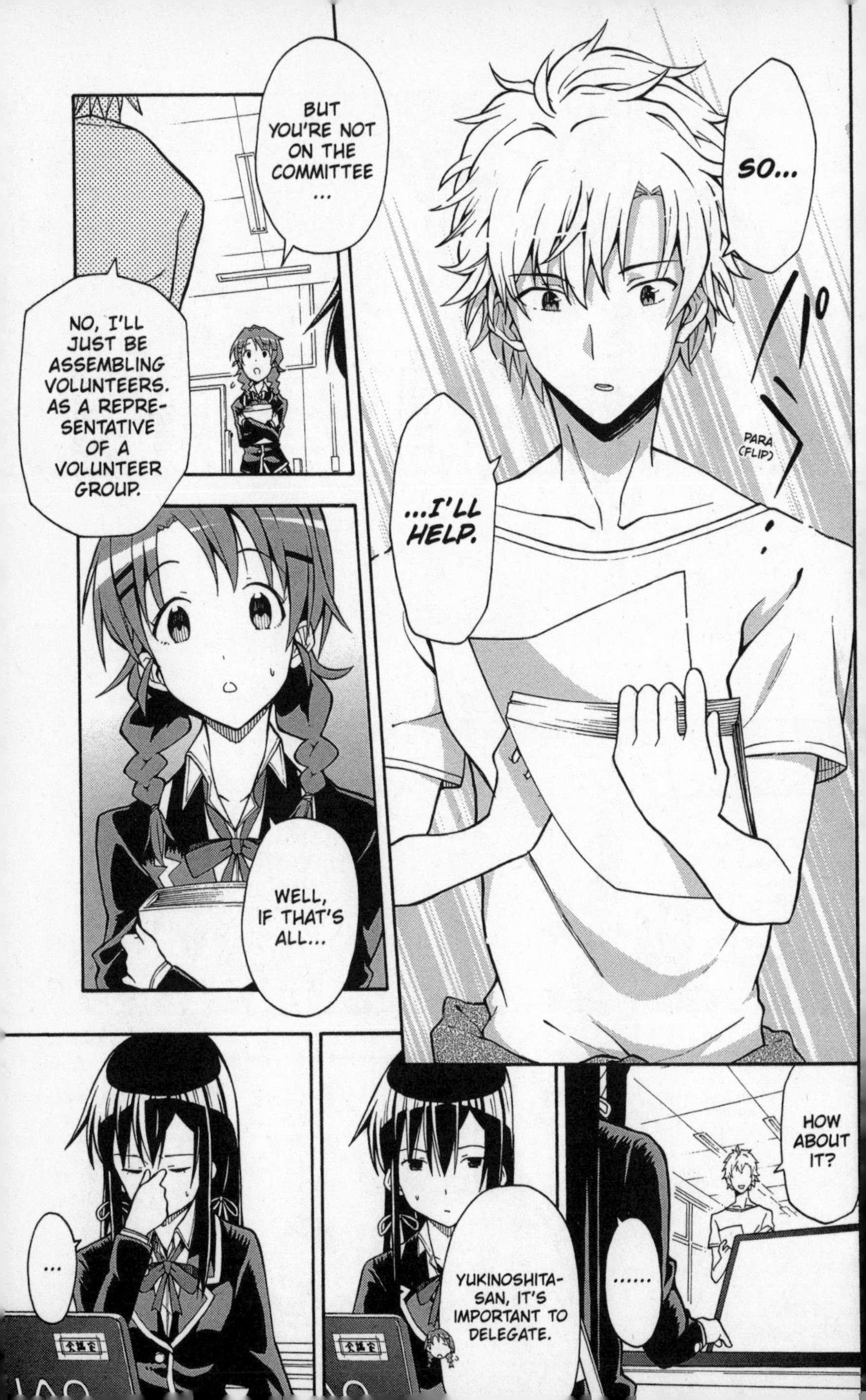
SO...
PARA (FLIP)
...I'LL HELP.
BUT YOU'RE NOT ON THE COMMITTEE ...
NO, I'LL JUST BE ASSEMBLING VOLUNTEERS. AS A REPRESENTATIVE OF A VOLUNTEER GROUP.
WELL, IF THAT'S ALL...
HOW ABOUT IT?
......
YUKINOSHITA-SAN, IT'S IMPORTANT TO DELEGATE.
...

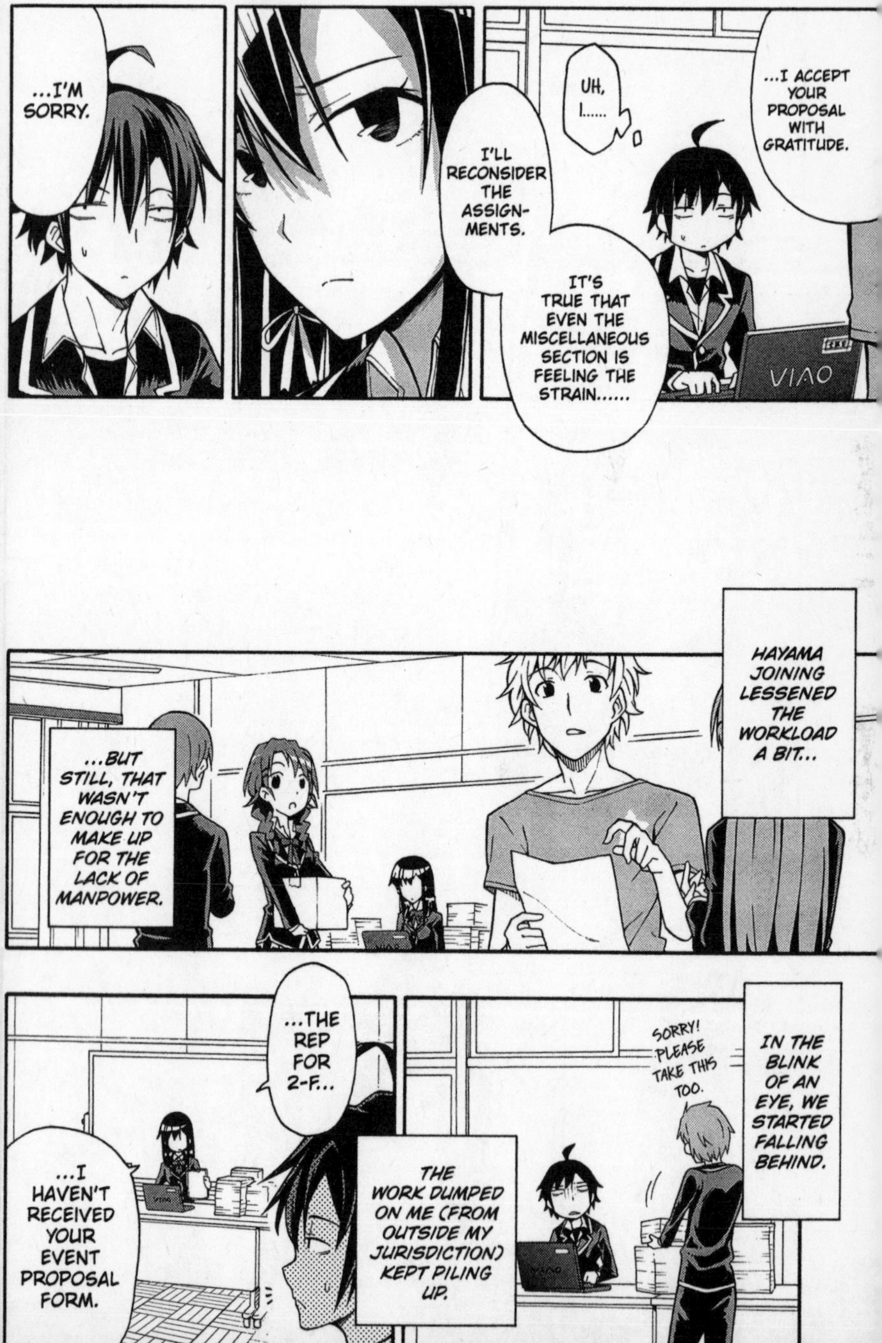
...I ACCEPT YOUR PROPOSAL WITH GRATITUDE.
UH, I......
VIAO
I'LL RECONSIDER THE ASSIGNMENTS.
IT'S TRUE THAT EVEN THE MISCELLANEOUS SECTION IS FEELING THE STRAIN......
...I'M SORRY.
HAYAMA JOINING LESSENED THE WORKLOAD A BIT...
...BUT STILL, THAT WASN'T ENOUGH TO MAKE UP FOR THE LACK OF MANPOWER.
IN THE BLINK OF AN EYE, WE STARTED FALLING BEHIND.
SORRY! PLEASE TAKE THIS TOO.
THE WORK DUMPED ON ME (FROM OUTSIDE MY JURISDICTION) KEPT PILING UP.
...THE REP FOR 2-F...
...I HAVEN'T RECEIVED YOUR EVENT PROPOSAL FORM.

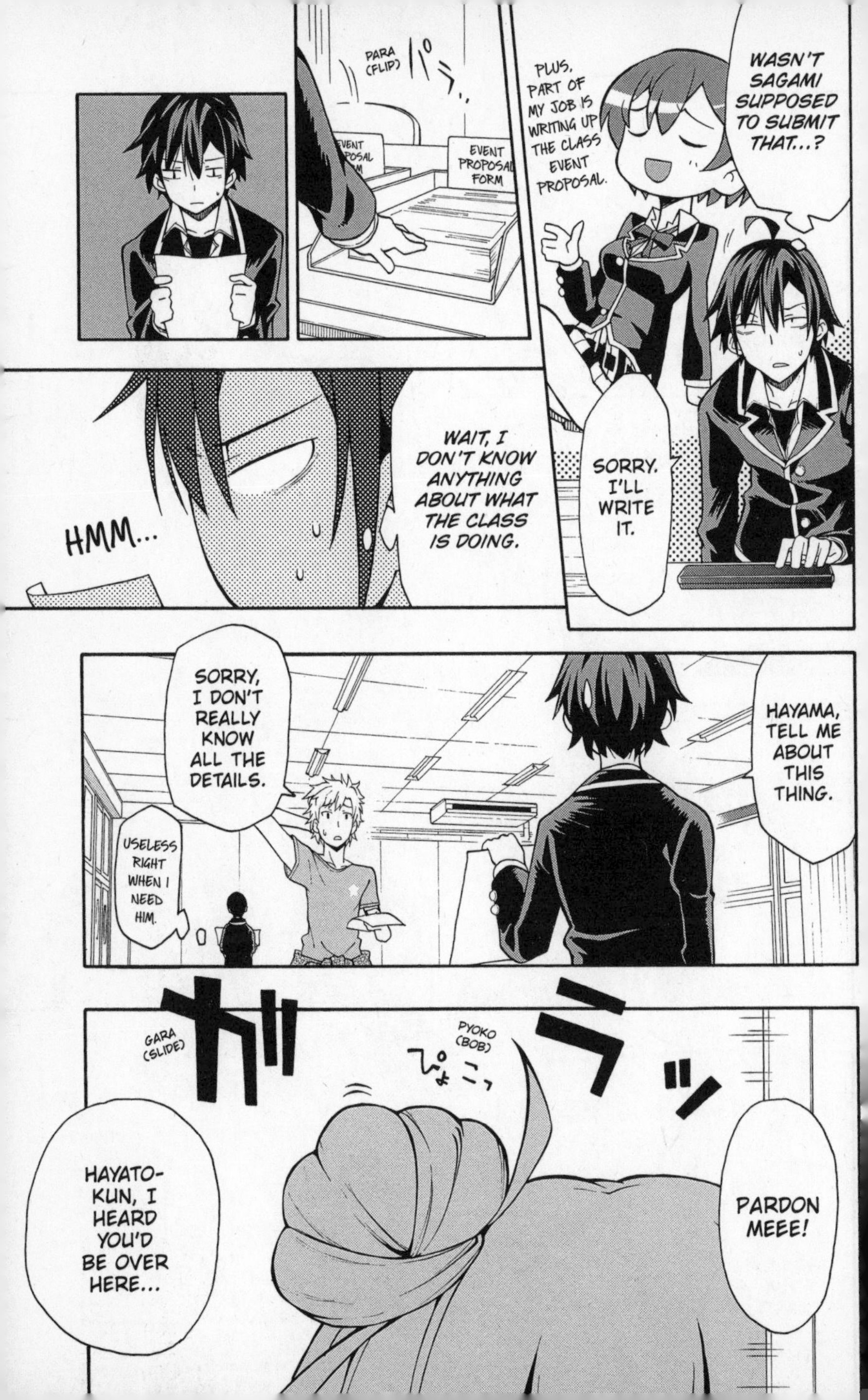

WASN'T SAGAMI SUPPOSED TO SUBMIT THAT...?
PLUS, PART OF MY JOB IS WRITING UP THE CLASS EVENT PROPOSAL.
SORRY. I'LL WRITE IT.
PARA (FLIP)
EVENT PROPOSAL FORM
WAIT, I DON'T KNOW ANYTHING ABOUT WHAT THE CLASS IS DOING.
HMM...
HAYAMA, TELL ME ABOUT THIS THING.
SORRY, I DON'T REALLY KNOW ALL THE DETAILS.
USELESS RIGHT WHEN I NEED HIM.
GARA (SLIDE)
PYOKO (BOB)
PARDON MEEE!
HAYATO-KUN, I HEARD YOU'D BE OVER HERE...

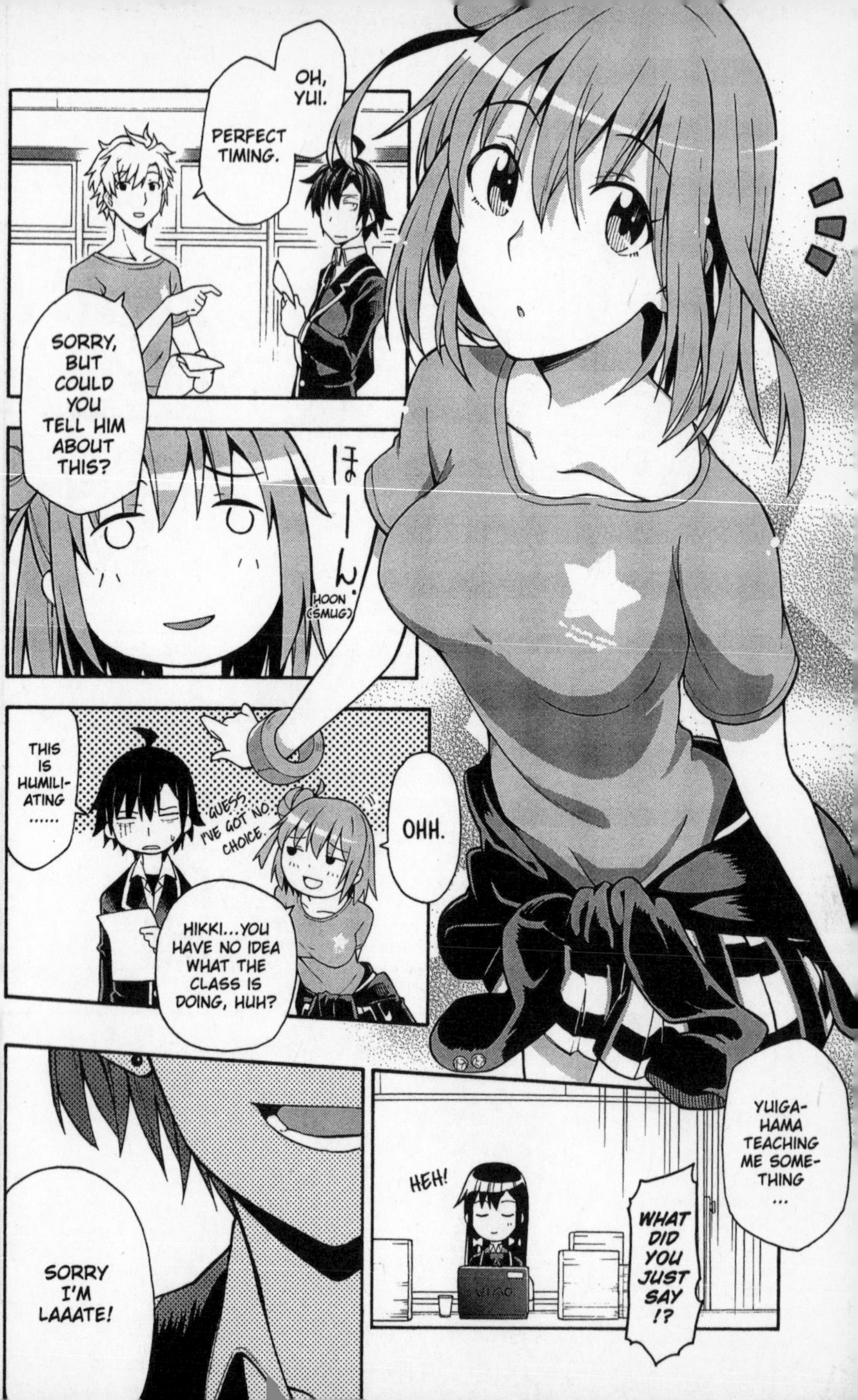
OH, YUI.
PERFECT TIMING.
SORRY, BUT COULD YOU TELL HIM ABOUT THIS?
ほーん
HOON (SMUG)
OHH.
GUESS I'VE GOT NO CHOICE.
HIKKI...YOU HAVE NO IDEA WHAT THE CLASS IS DOING, HUH?
THIS IS HUMILI-ATING ......
YUIGA-HAMA TEACHING ME SOME-THING ...
WHAT DID YOU JUST SAY !?
HEH!
SORRY I'M LAAATE!

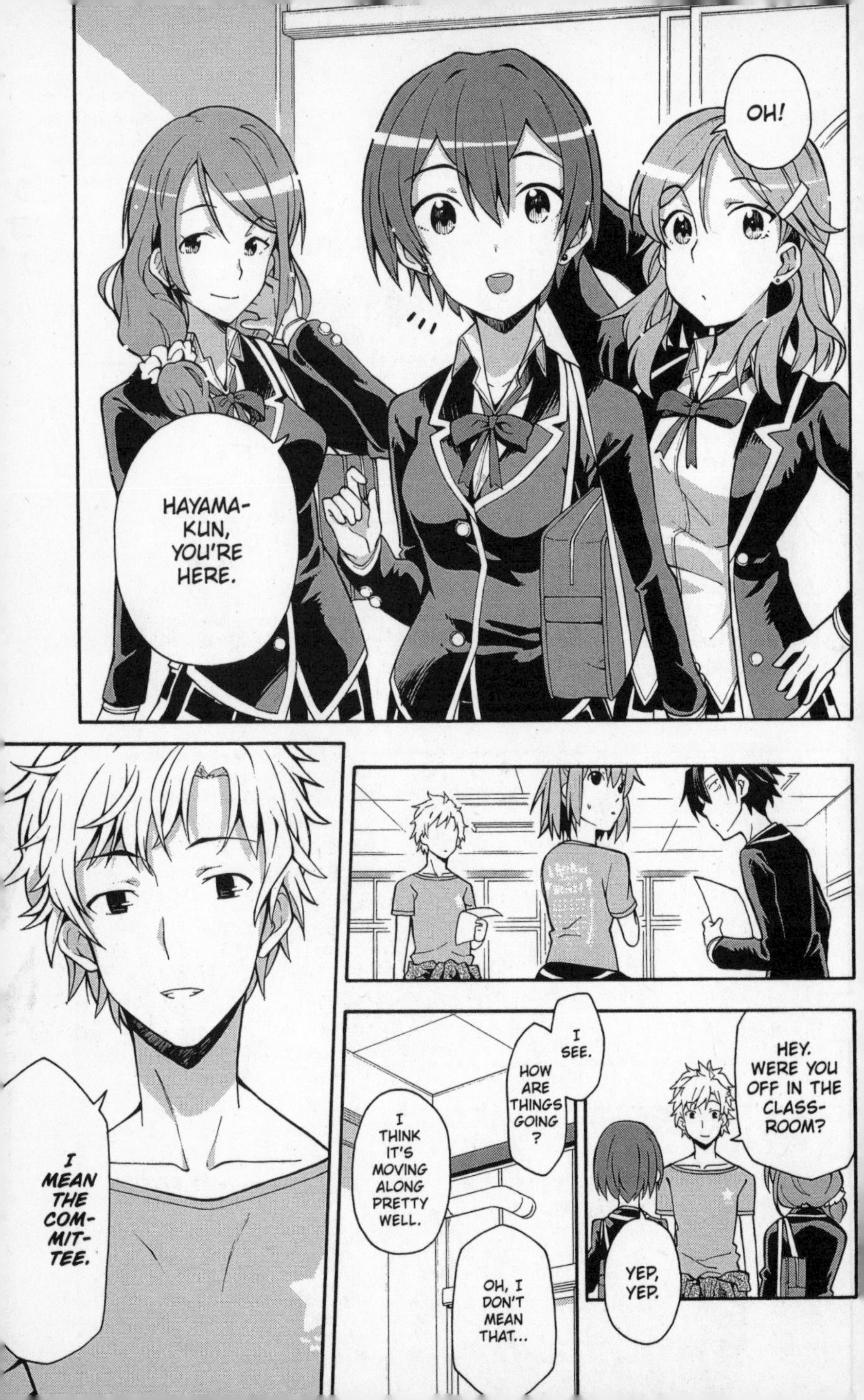
OH!
HAYAMA-KUN, YOU'RE HERE.
HEY. WERE YOU OFF IN THE CLASSROOM?
YEP, YEP.
I SEE.
HOW ARE THINGS GOING?
I THINK IT'S MOVING ALONG PRETTY WELL.
OH, I DON'T MEAN THAT...
I MEAN THE COMMITTEE.

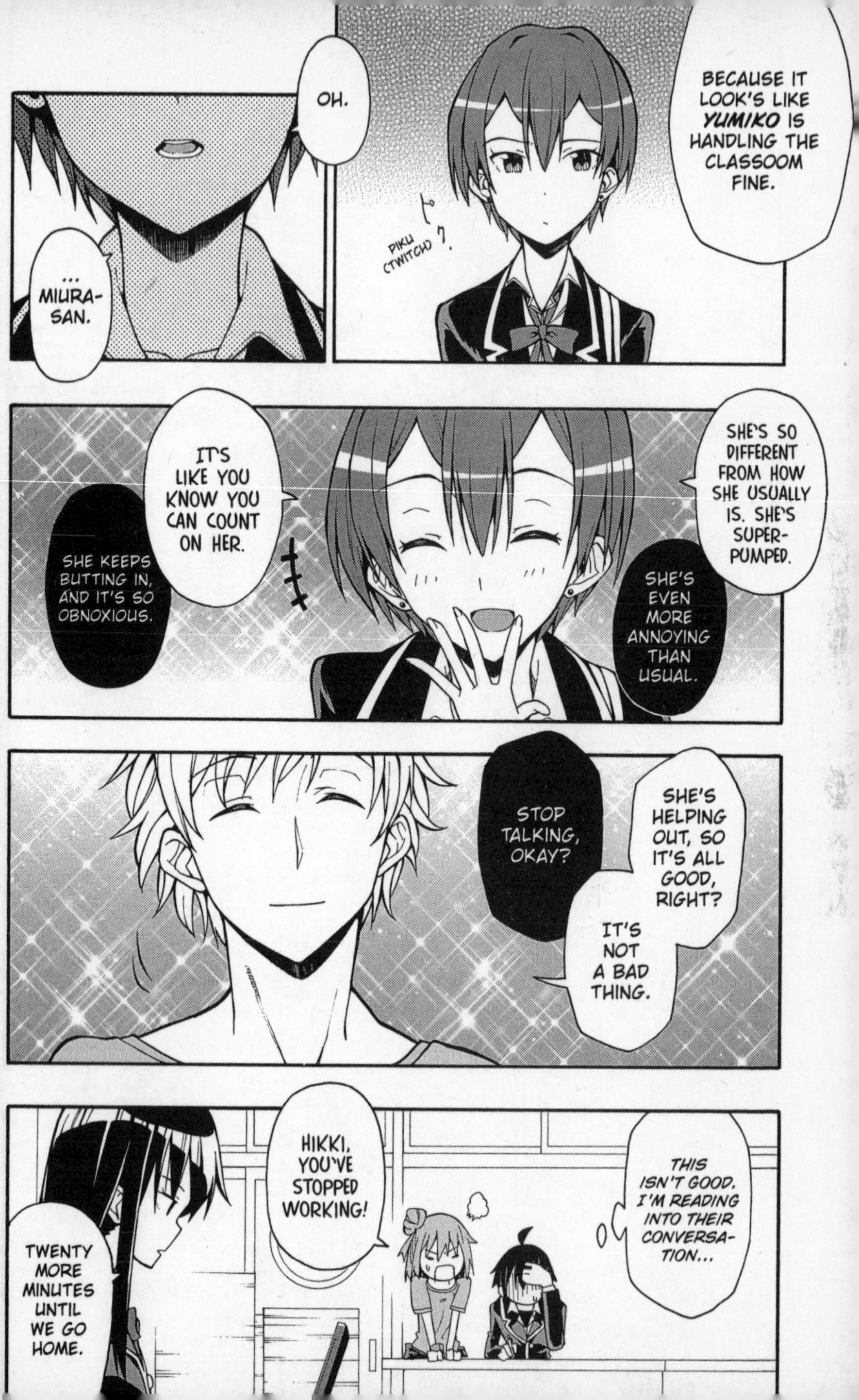
BECAUSE IT LOOK'S LIKE *YUMIKO* IS HANDLING THE CLASSOOM FINE.
PIKU (TWITCH)
OH.
... MIURA-SAN.
SHE'S SO DIFFERENT FROM HOW SHE USUALLY IS. SHE'S SUPER-PUMPED.
SHE'S EVEN MORE ANNOYING THAN USUAL.
IT'S LIKE YOU KNOW YOU CAN COUNT ON HER.
SHE KEEPS BUTTING IN, AND IT'S SO OBNOXIOUS.
SHE'S HELPING OUT, SO IT'S ALL GOOD, RIGHT?
STOP TALKING, OKAY?
IT'S NOT A BAD THING.
THIS ISN'T GOOD. I'M READING INTO THEIR CONVERSA-TION...
HIKKI, YOU'VE STOPPED WORKING!
TWENTY MORE MINUTES UNTIL WE GO HOME.

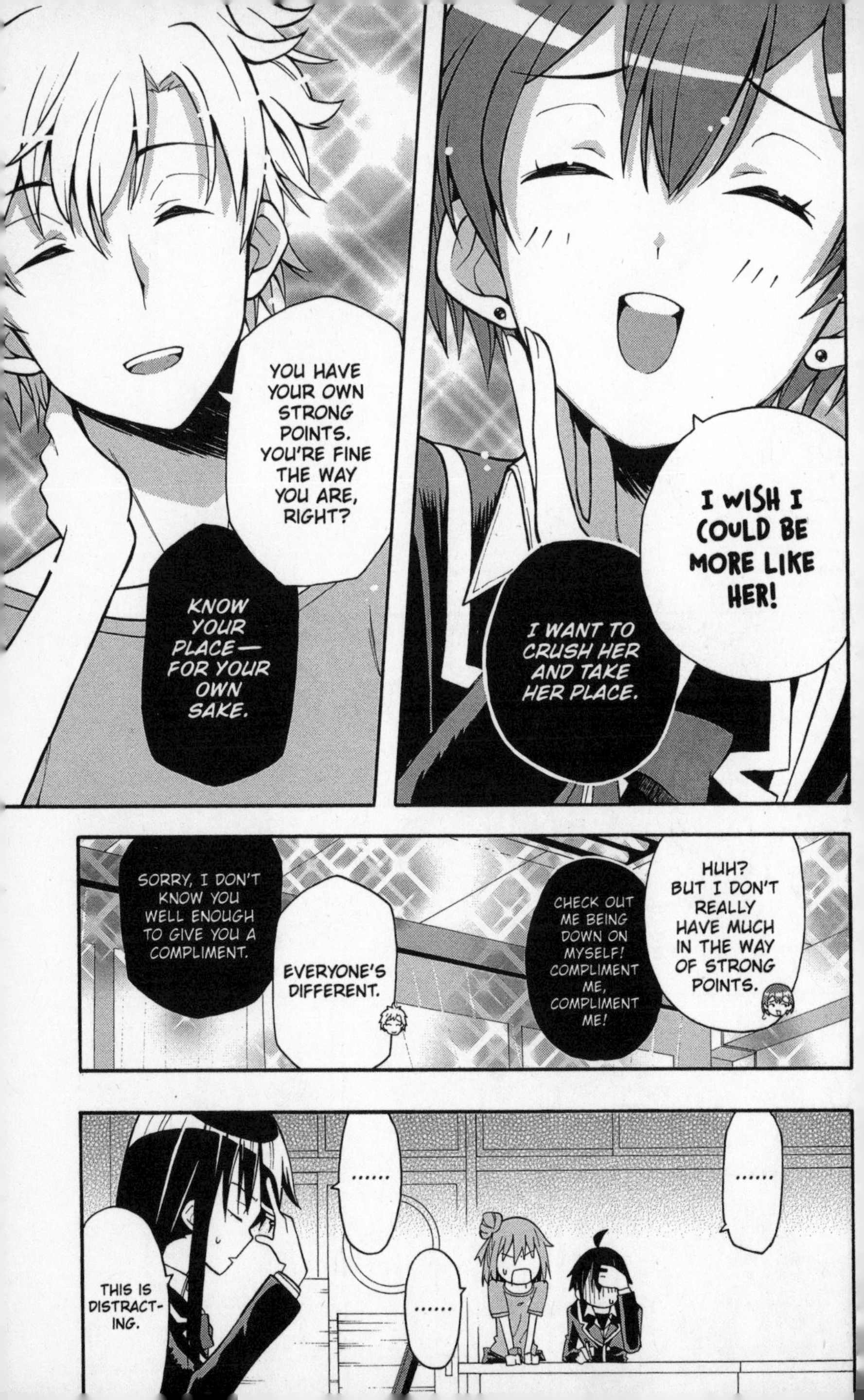
I WISH I COULD BE MORE LIKE HER!
I WANT TO CRUSH HER AND TAKE HER PLACE.
YOU HAVE YOUR OWN STRONG POINTS. YOU'RE FINE THE WAY YOU ARE, RIGHT?
KNOW YOUR PLACE—FOR YOUR OWN SAKE.
HUH? BUT I DON'T REALLY HAVE MUCH IN THE WAY OF STRONG POINTS.
CHECK OUT ME BEING DOWN ON MYSELF! COMPLIMENT ME, COMPLIMENT ME!
EVERYONE'S DIFFERENT.
SORRY, I DON'T KNOW YOU WELL ENOUGH TO GIVE YOU A COMPLIMENT.
......
......
......
THIS IS DISTRACT-ING.

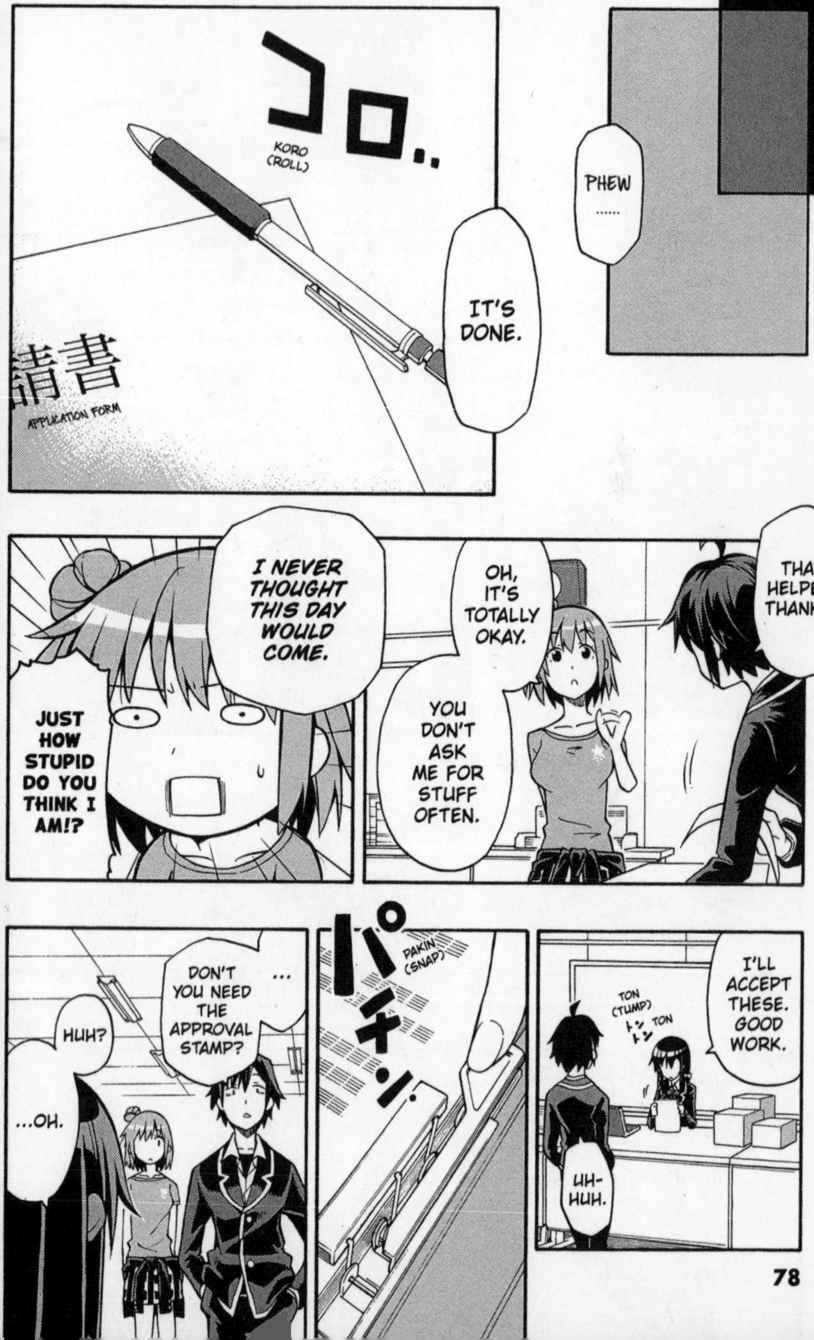
PHEW ......
コロ..
KORO (ROLL)
IT'S DONE.
請書
APPLICATION FORM
THAT HELPED. THANKS.
OH, IT'S TOTALLY OKAY.
YOU DON'T ASK ME FOR STUFF OFTEN.
I NEVER THOUGHT THIS DAY WOULD COME.
JUST HOW STUPID DO YOU THINK I AM!?
I'LL ACCEPT THESE. GOOD WORK.
TON (TUMP) TON
UH-HUH.
パキン
PAKIN (SNAP)
DON'T YOU NEED THE APPROVAL STAMP?
...
HUH?
...OH.

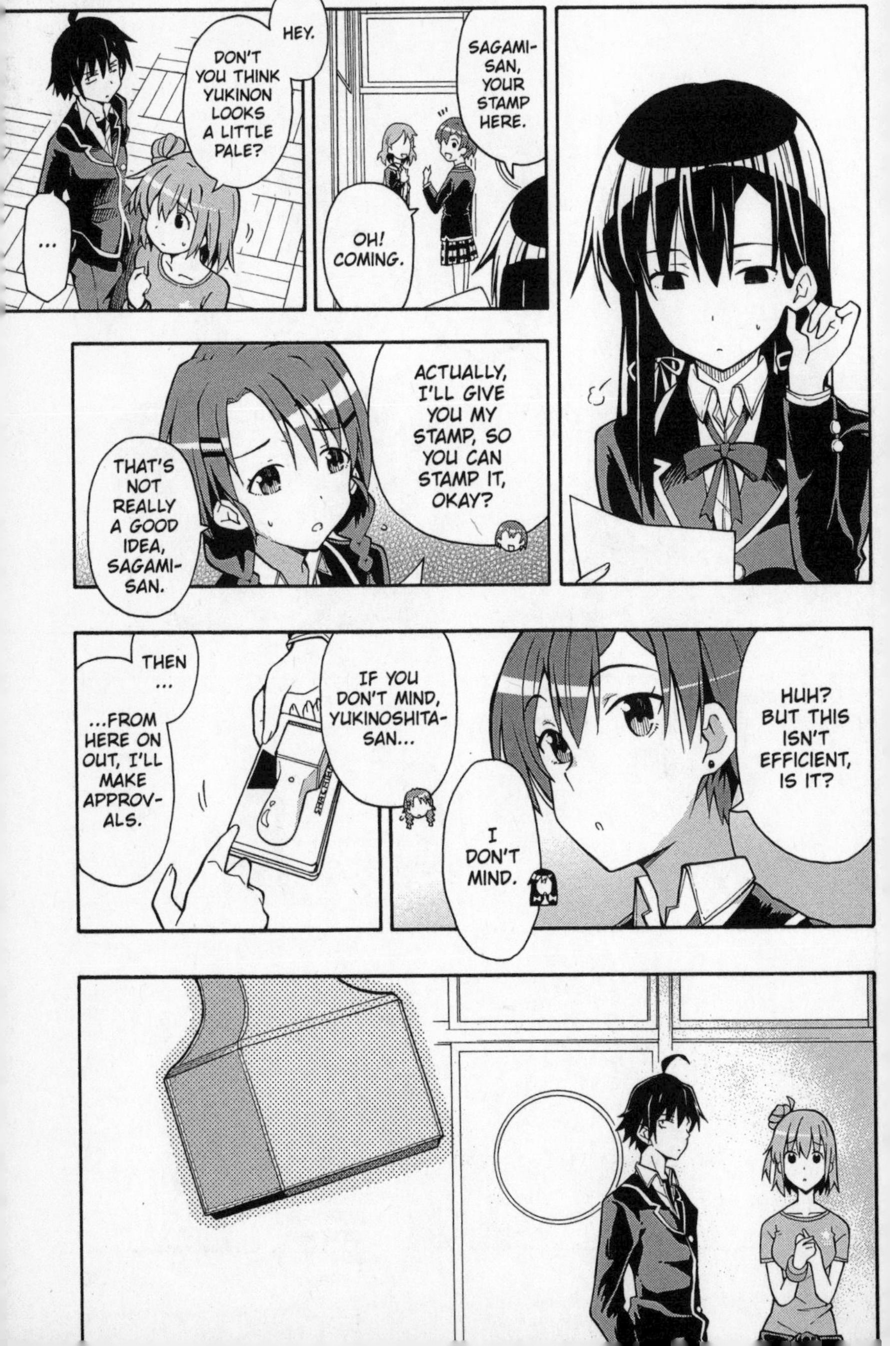
SAGAMI-SAN, YOUR STAMP HERE.
OH! COMING.
HEY.
DON'T YOU THINK YUKINON LOOKS A LITTLE PALE?
...
ACTUALLY, I'LL GIVE YOU MY STAMP, SO YOU CAN STAMP IT, OKAY?
THAT'S NOT REALLY A GOOD IDEA, SAGAMI-SAN.
HUH? BUT THIS ISN'T EFFICIENT, IS IT?
IF YOU DON'T MIND, YUKINOSHITA-SAN...
I DON'T MIND.
THEN...
...FROM HERE ON OUT, I'LL MAKE APPROVALS.

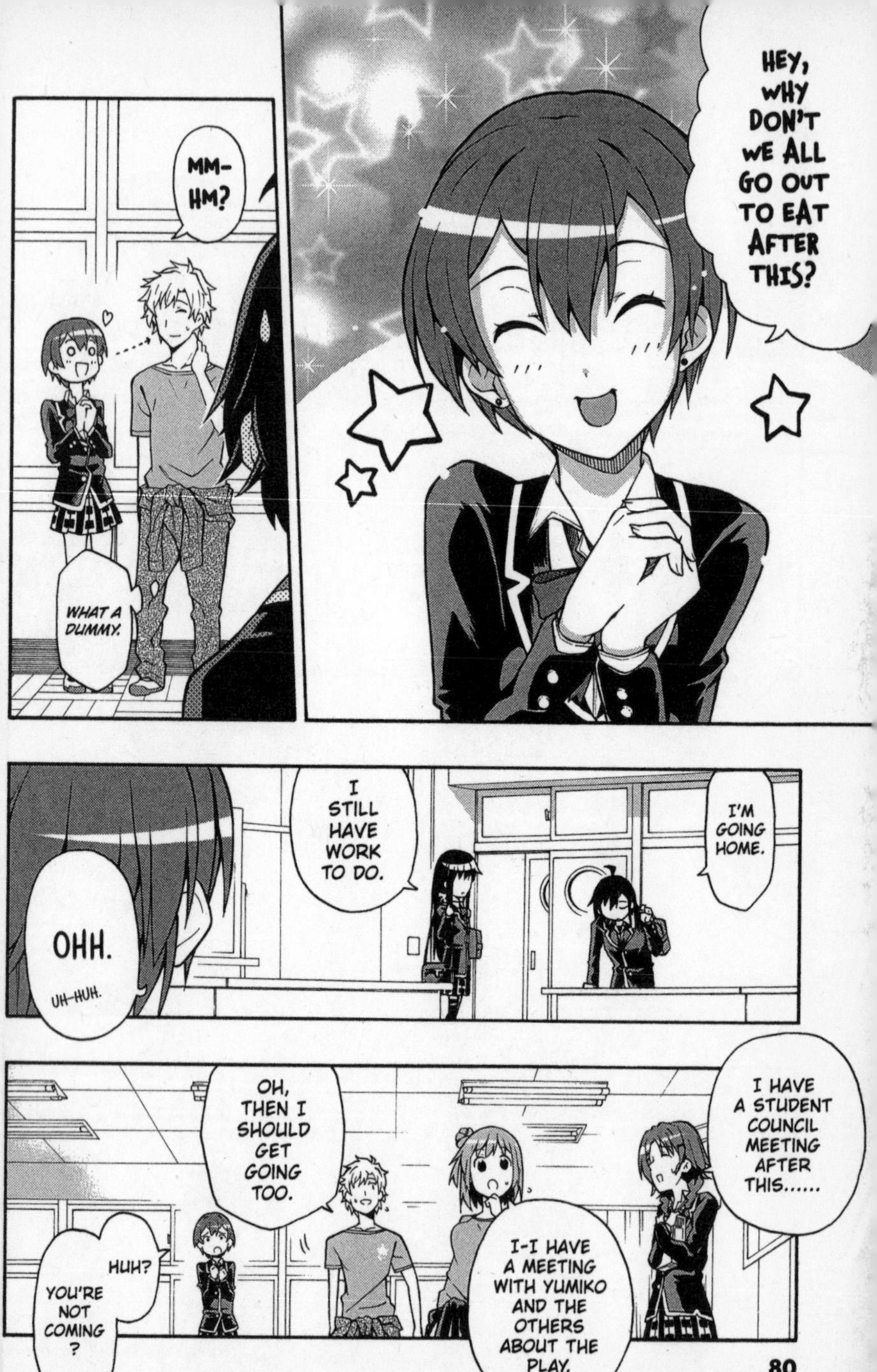
HEY, WHY DON'T WE ALL GO OUT TO EAT AFTER THIS?
MM-HM?
WHAT A DUMMY.
I'M GOING HOME.
I STILL HAVE WORK TO DO.
OHH.
UH-HUH.
I HAVE A STUDENT COUNCIL MEETING AFTER THIS......
I-I HAVE A MEETING WITH YUMIKO AND THE OTHERS ABOUT THE PLAY.
OH, THEN I SHOULD GET GOING TOO.
HUH?
YOU'RE NOT COMING?

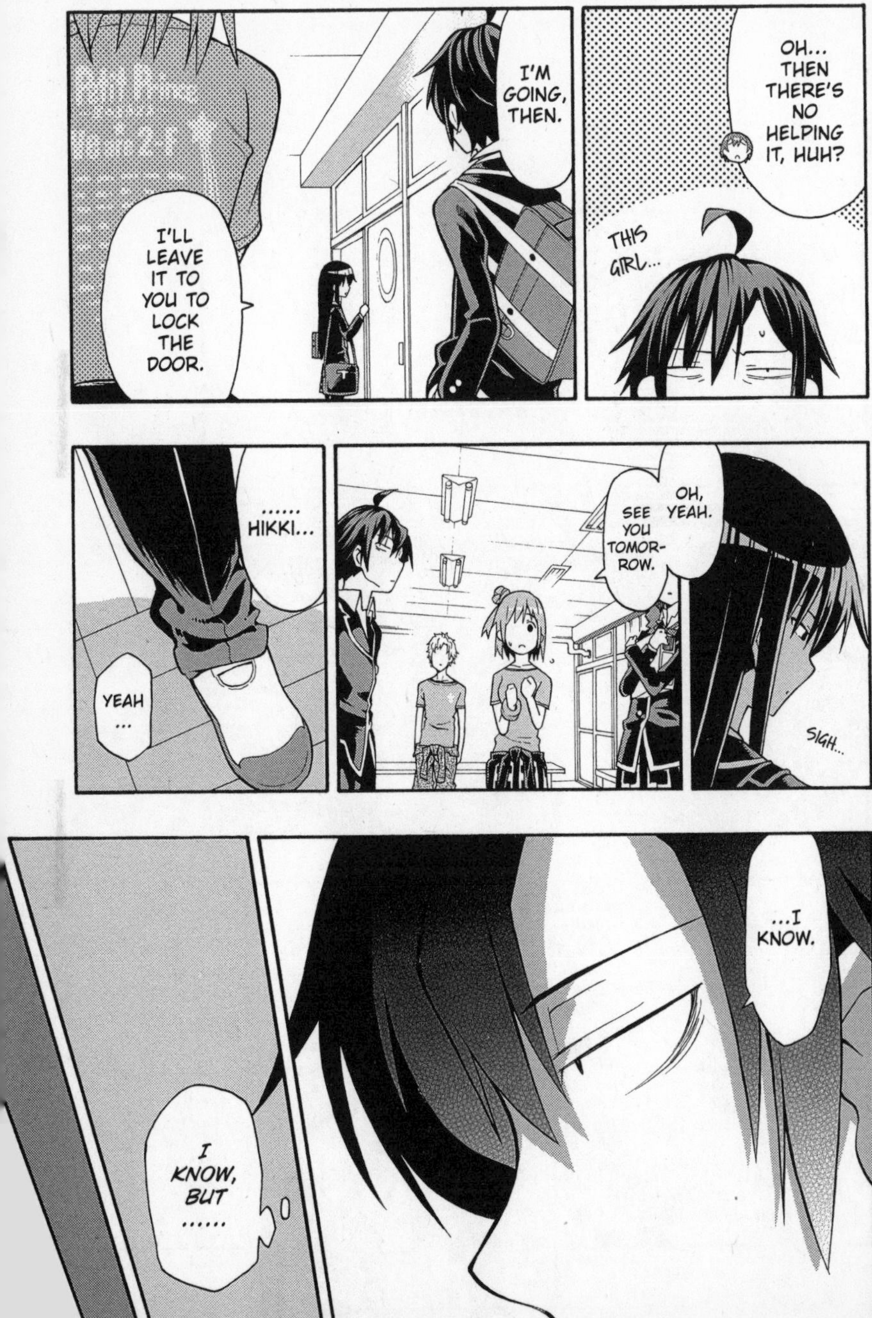
OH... THEN THERE'S NO HELPING IT, HUH?
THIS GIRL...
I'M GOING, THEN.
I'LL LEAVE IT TO YOU TO LOCK THE DOOR.
OH, YEAH. SEE YOU TOMORROW.
SIGH...
...... HIKKI...
YEAH ...
...I KNOW.
I KNOW, BUT ......

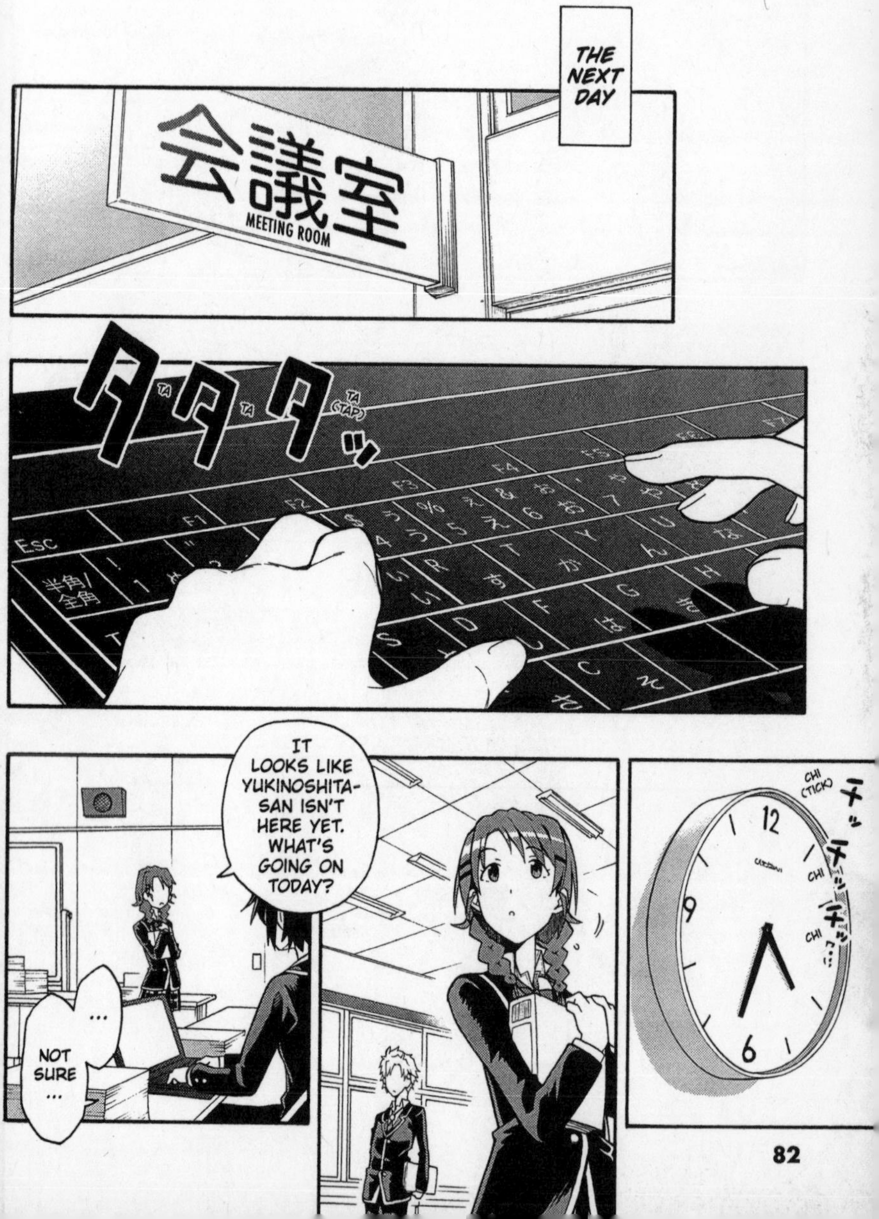
THE NEXT DAY
会議室
MEETING ROOM
TA TA TA (TAP)
CHI (TICK)
CHI
CHI
IT LOOKS LIKE YUKINOSHITA-SAN ISN'T HERE YET. WHAT'S GOING ON TODAY?
... NOT SURE ...

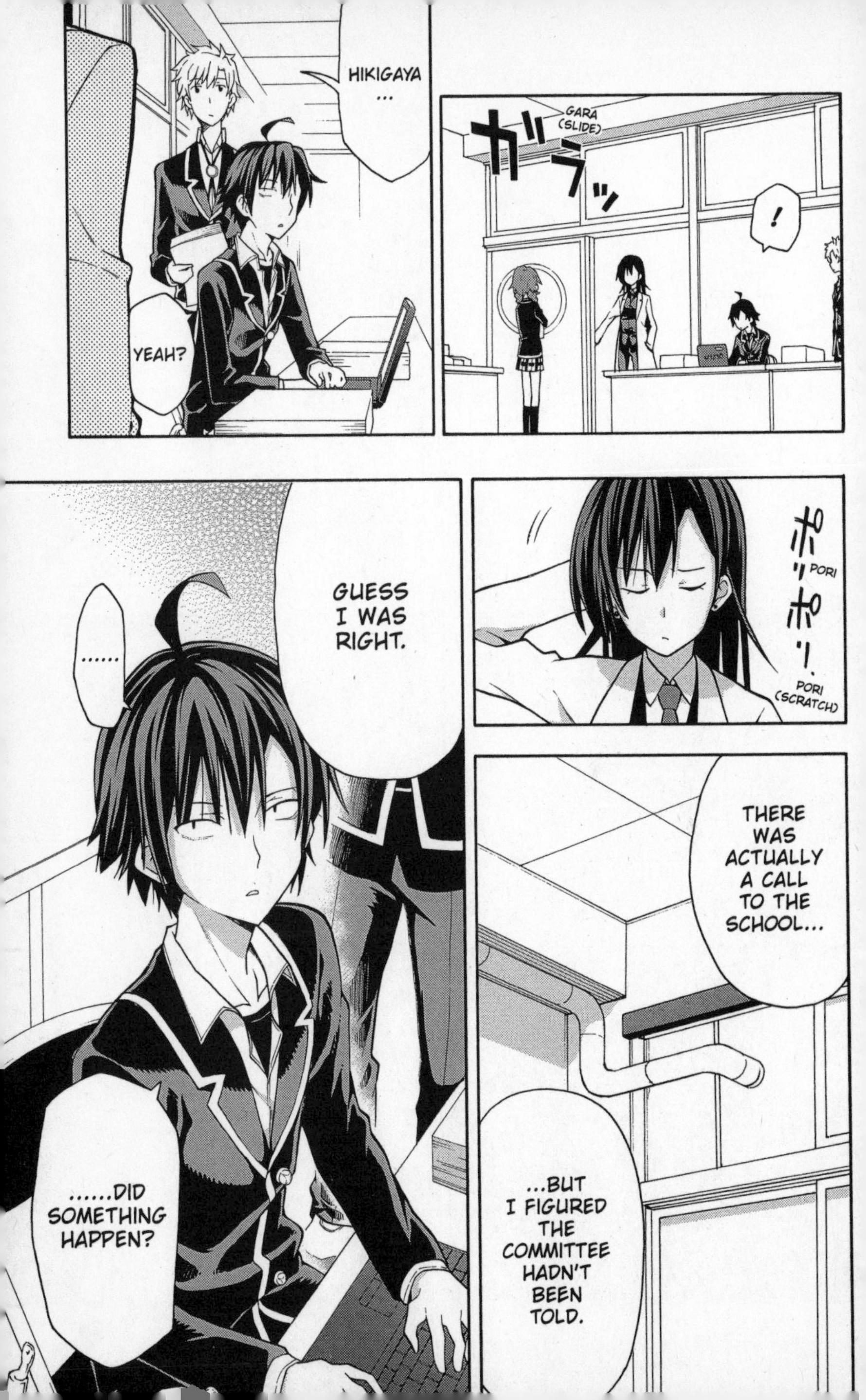
GARA (SLIDE)
!
HIKIGAYA ...
YEAH?
PORI
PORI (SCRATCH)
THERE WAS ACTUALLY A CALL TO THE SCHOOL...
...BUT I FIGURED THE COMMITTEE HADN'T BEEN TOLD.
......
GUESS I WAS RIGHT.
......DID SOMETHING HAPPEN?

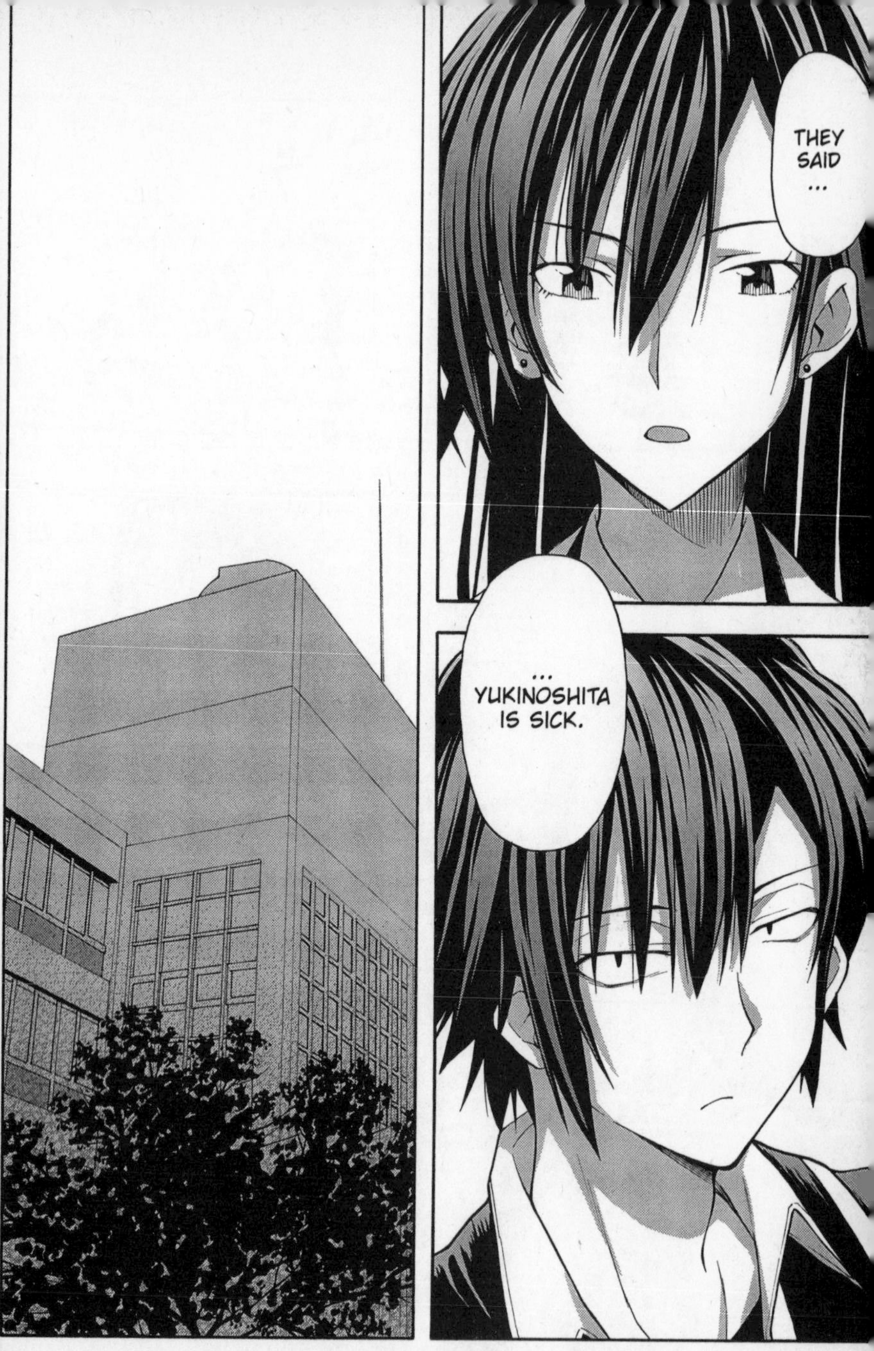
THEY SAID ...
... YUKINOSHITA IS SICK.

CHAPTER 39 ∞ UNUSUALLY, YUI YUIGAHAMA IS INDIGNANT.

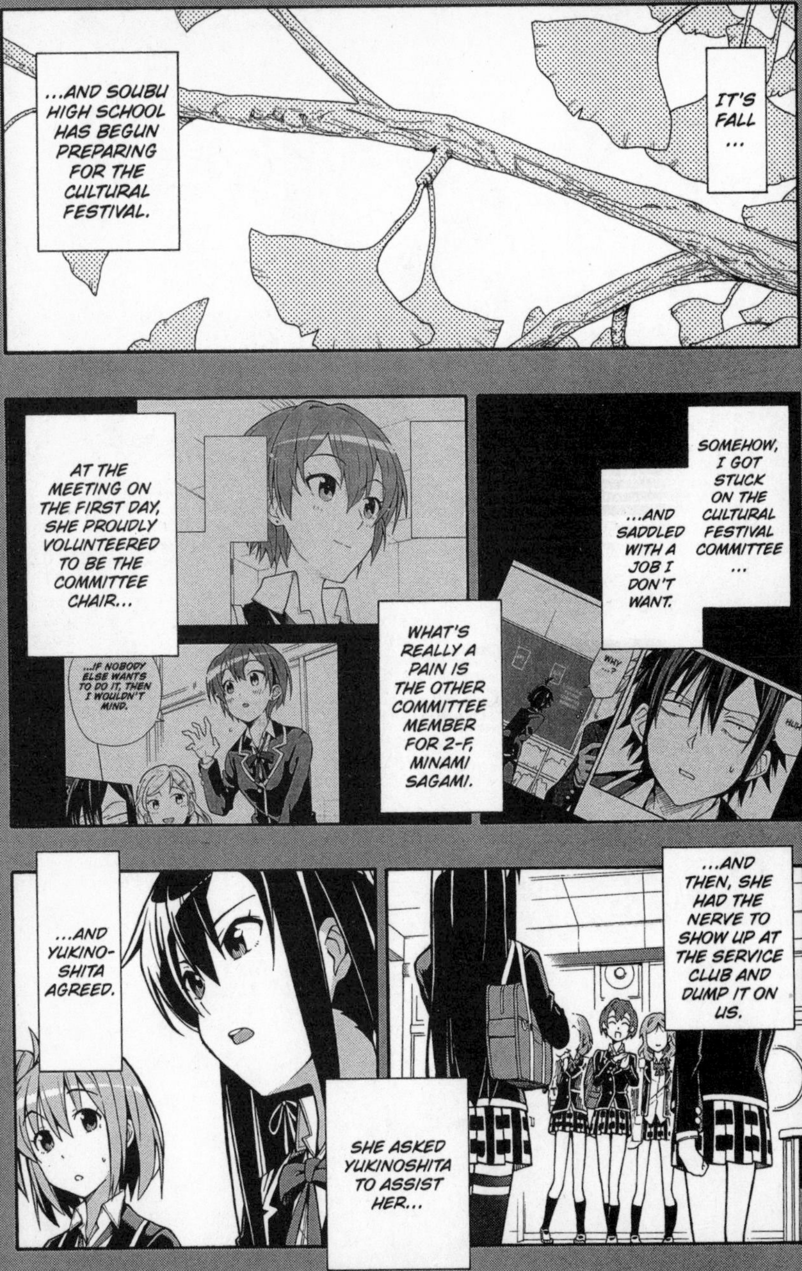
IT'S FALL...
...AND SOUBU HIGH SCHOOL HAS BEGUN PREPARING FOR THE CULTURAL FESTIVAL.
SOMEHOW, I GOT STUCK ON THE CULTURAL FESTIVAL COMMITTEE...
...AND SADDLED WITH A JOB I DON'T WANT.
WHY...?
WHAT'S REALLY A PAIN IS THE OTHER COMMITTEE MEMBER FOR 2-F, MINAMI SAGAMI.
AT THE MEETING ON THE FIRST DAY, SHE PROUDLY VOLUNTEERED TO BE THE COMMITTEE CHAIR...
...IF NOBODY ELSE WANTS TO DO IT, THEN I WOULDN'T MIND.
...AND THEN, SHE HAD THE NERVE TO SHOW UP AT THE SERVICE CLUB AND DUMP IT ON US.
SHE ASKED YUKINOSHITA TO ASSIST HER...
...AND YUKINO-SHITA AGREED.

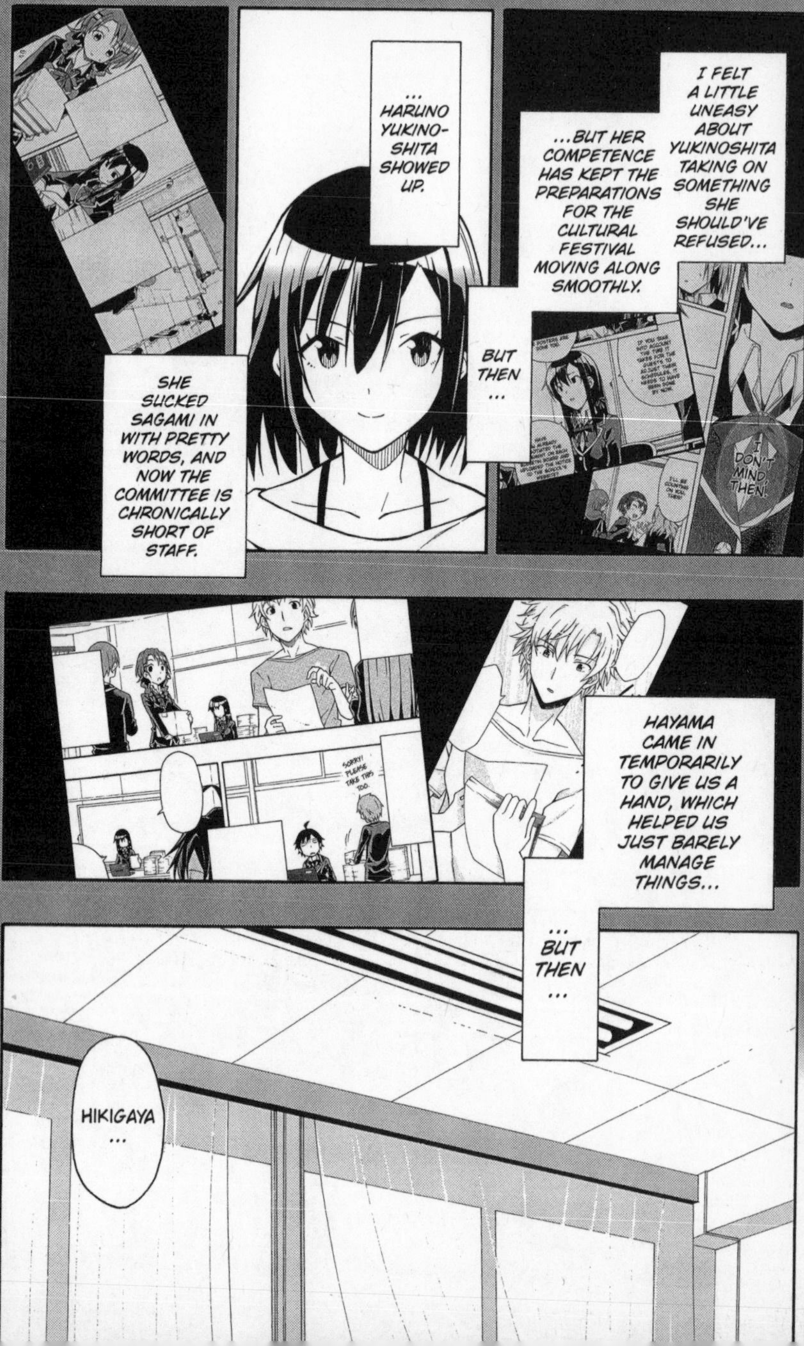
I FELT A LITTLE UNEASY ABOUT YUKINOSHITA TAKING ON SOMETHING SHE SHOULD'VE REFUSED...
...BUT HER COMPETENCE HAS KEPT THE PREPARATIONS FOR THE CULTURAL FESTIVAL MOVING ALONG SMOOTHLY.
IF YOU TAKE INTO ACCOUNT THE TIME IT TAKES FOR THE GUESTS TO ADJUST THEIR SCHEDULES, IT NEEDS TO HAVE BEEN DONE BY NOW.
I DON'T MIND THEN!
I'LL BE COUNTING ON YOU THEN!
BUT THEN ...
... HARUNO YUKINO-SHITA SHOWED UP.
SHE SUCKED SAGAMI IN WITH PRETTY WORDS, AND NOW THE COMMITTEE IS CHRONICALLY SHORT OF STAFF.
HAYAMA CAME IN TEMPORARILY TO GIVE US A HAND, WHICH HELPED US JUST BARELY MANAGE THINGS...
SORRY! PLEASE TAKE THIS TOO.
... BUT THEN ...
HIKIGAYA ...

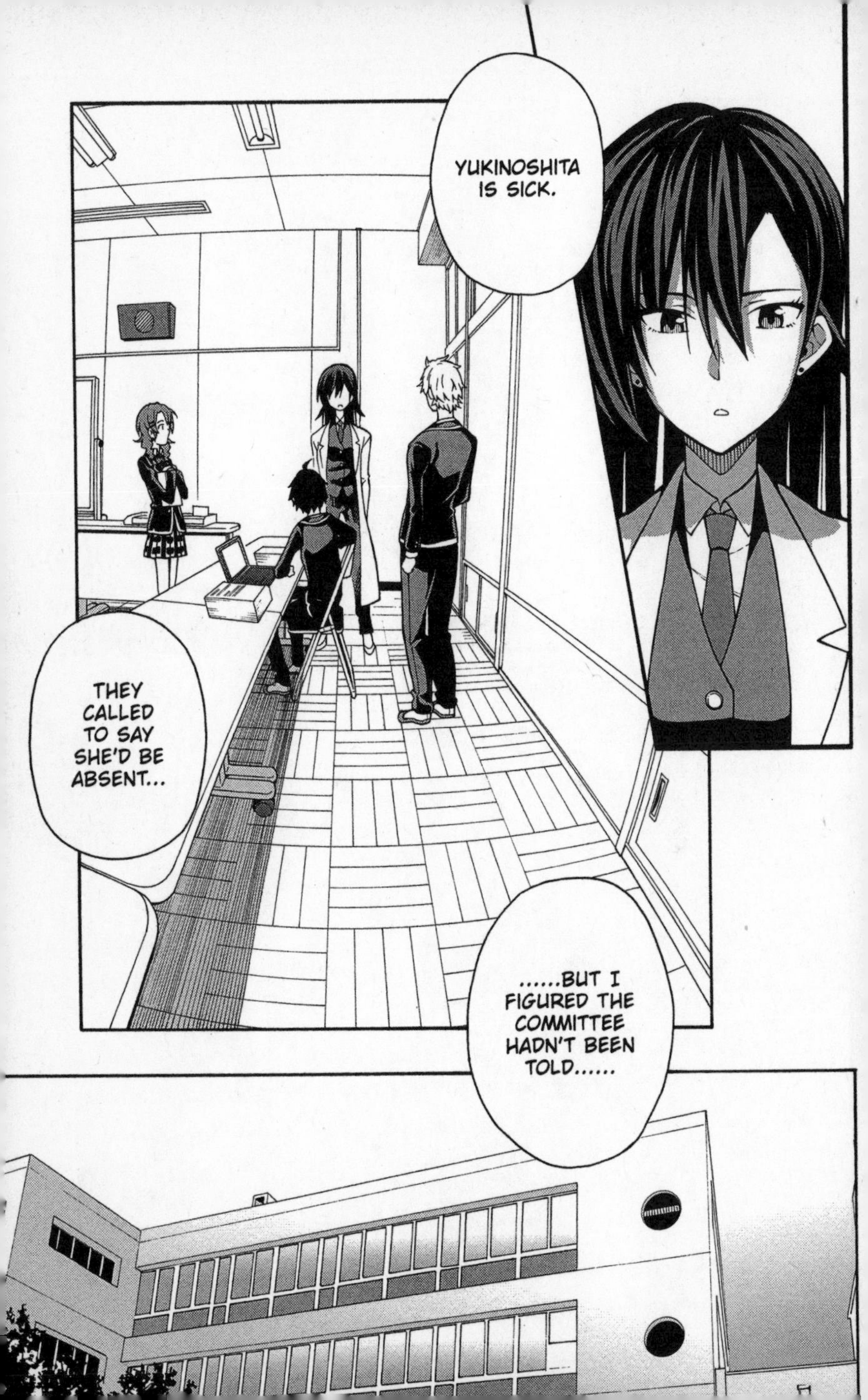
YUKINOSHITA IS SICK.
THEY CALLED TO SAY SHE'D BE ABSENT...
......BUT I FIGURED THE COMMITTEE HADN'T BEEN TOLD......

CHAPTER 39 ··· UNUSUALLY, YUI YUIGAHAMA IS INDIGNANT.

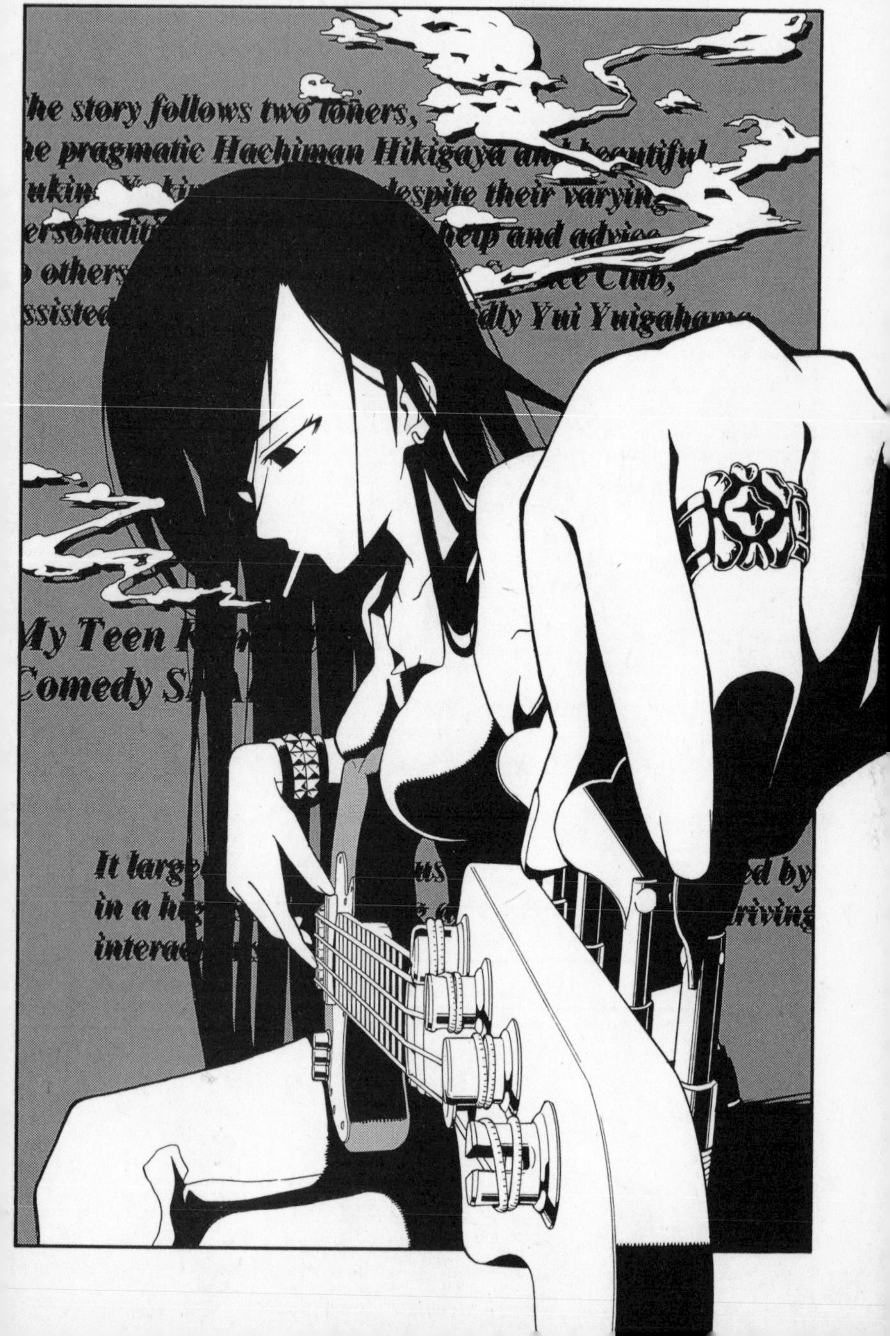
story follows two loners,
pragmatic Hachiman Hikigaya
despite their varying
help and advice
others
Yui
My Teen
Comedy

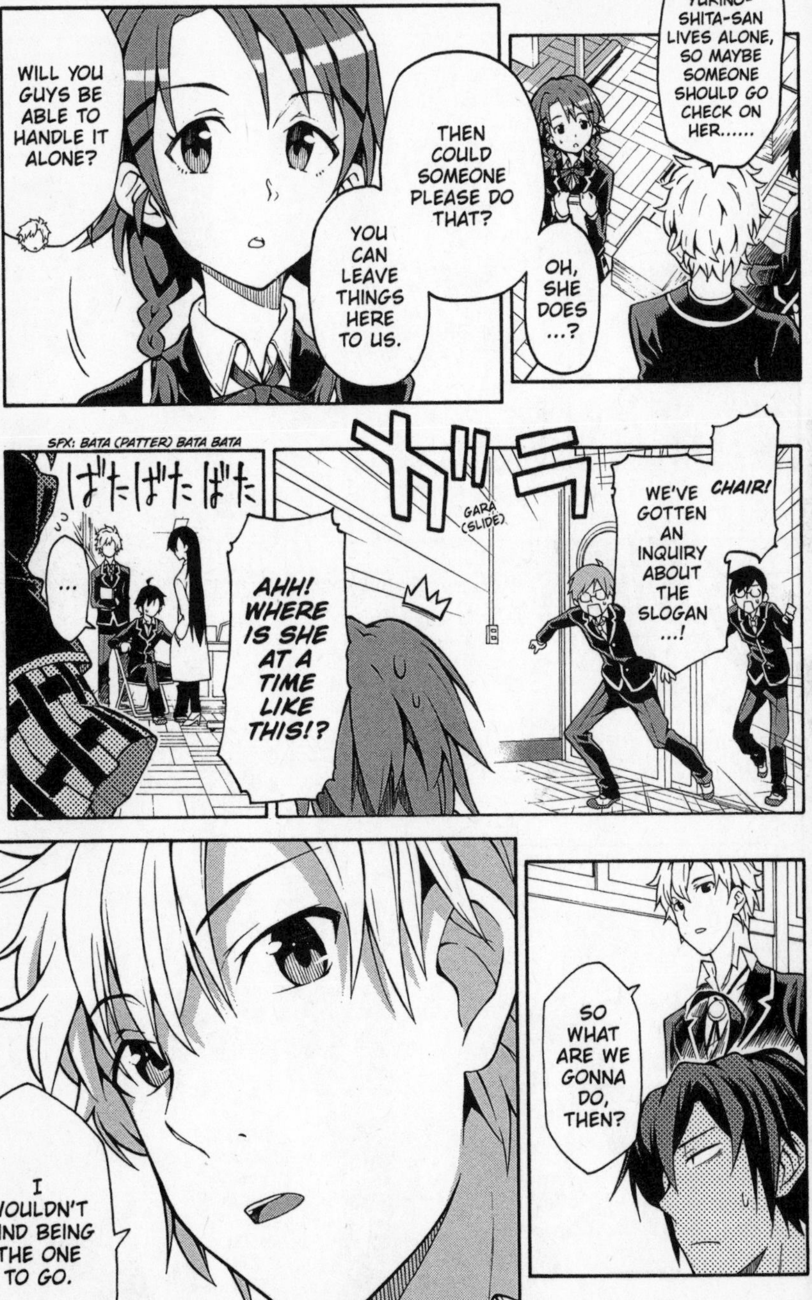
YUKINO-SHITA-SAN LIVES ALONE, SO MAYBE SOMEONE SHOULD GO CHECK ON HER......
OH, SHE DOES ...?
THEN COULD SOMEONE PLEASE DO THAT?
YOU CAN LEAVE THINGS HERE TO US.
WILL YOU GUYS BE ABLE TO HANDLE IT ALONE?
CHAIR!
WE'VE GOTTEN AN INQUIRY ABOUT THE SLOGAN ...!
ガラ
GARA (SLIDE)
AHH! WHERE IS SHE AT A TIME LIKE THIS!?
SFX: BATA (PATTER) BATA BATA
ばたばたばた
...
SO WHAT ARE WE GONNA DO, THEN?
I WOULDN'T MIND BEING THE ONE TO GO.

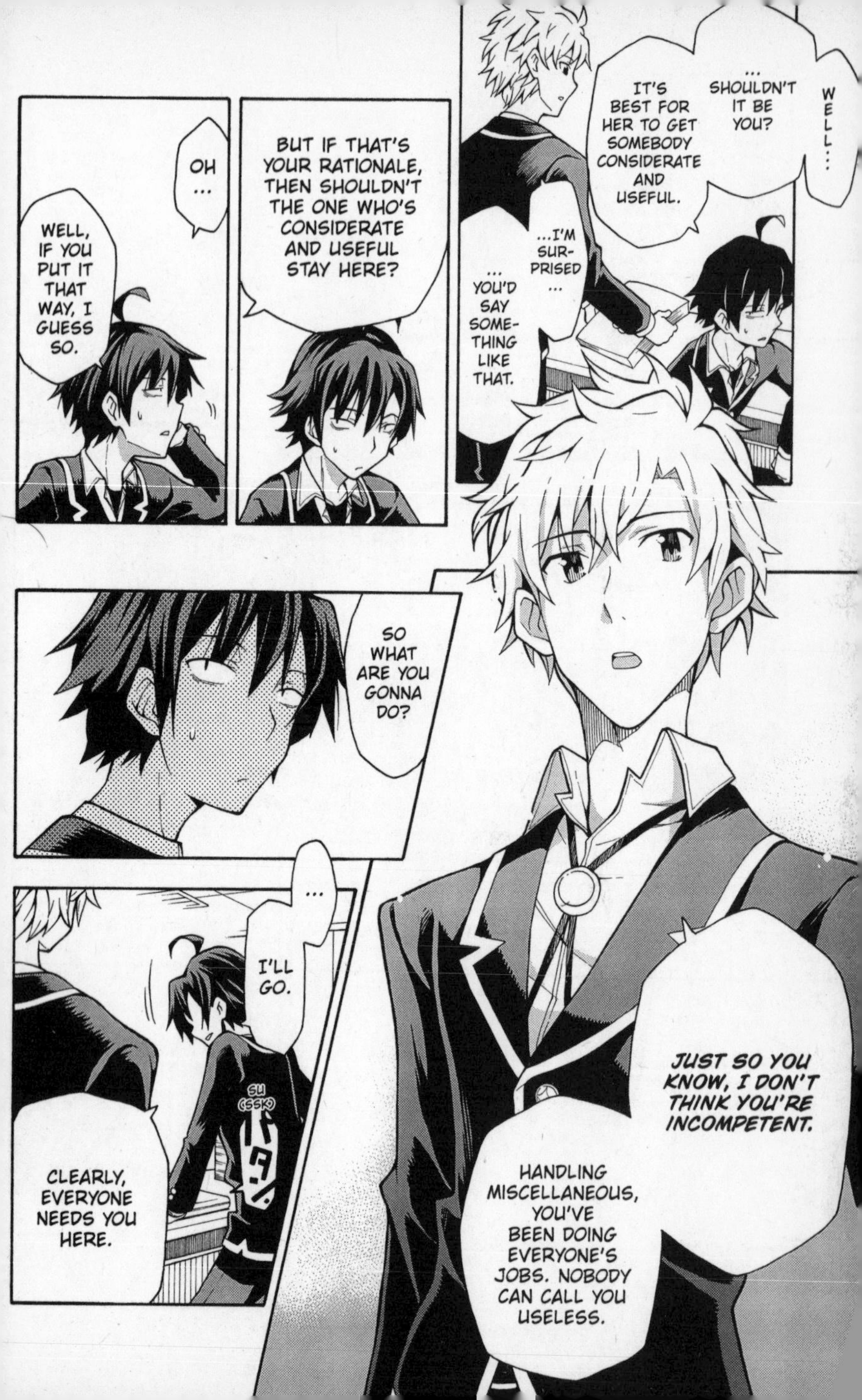
WELL...
...SHOULDN'T IT BE YOU?
IT'S BEST FOR HER TO GET SOMEBODY CONSIDERATE AND USEFUL.
...I'M SURPRISED...
...YOU'D SAY SOMETHING LIKE THAT.
BUT IF THAT'S YOUR RATIONALE, THEN SHOULDN'T THE ONE WHO'S CONSIDERATE AND USEFUL STAY HERE?
OH...
WELL, IF YOU PUT IT THAT WAY, I GUESS SO.
JUST SO YOU KNOW, I DON'T THINK YOU'RE INCOMPETENT.
HANDLING MISCELLANEOUS, YOU'VE BEEN DOING EVERYONE'S JOBS. NOBODY CAN CALL YOU USELESS.
SO WHAT ARE YOU GONNA DO?
...
I'LL GO.
SU (SSK)
CLEARLY, EVERYONE NEEDS YOU HERE.

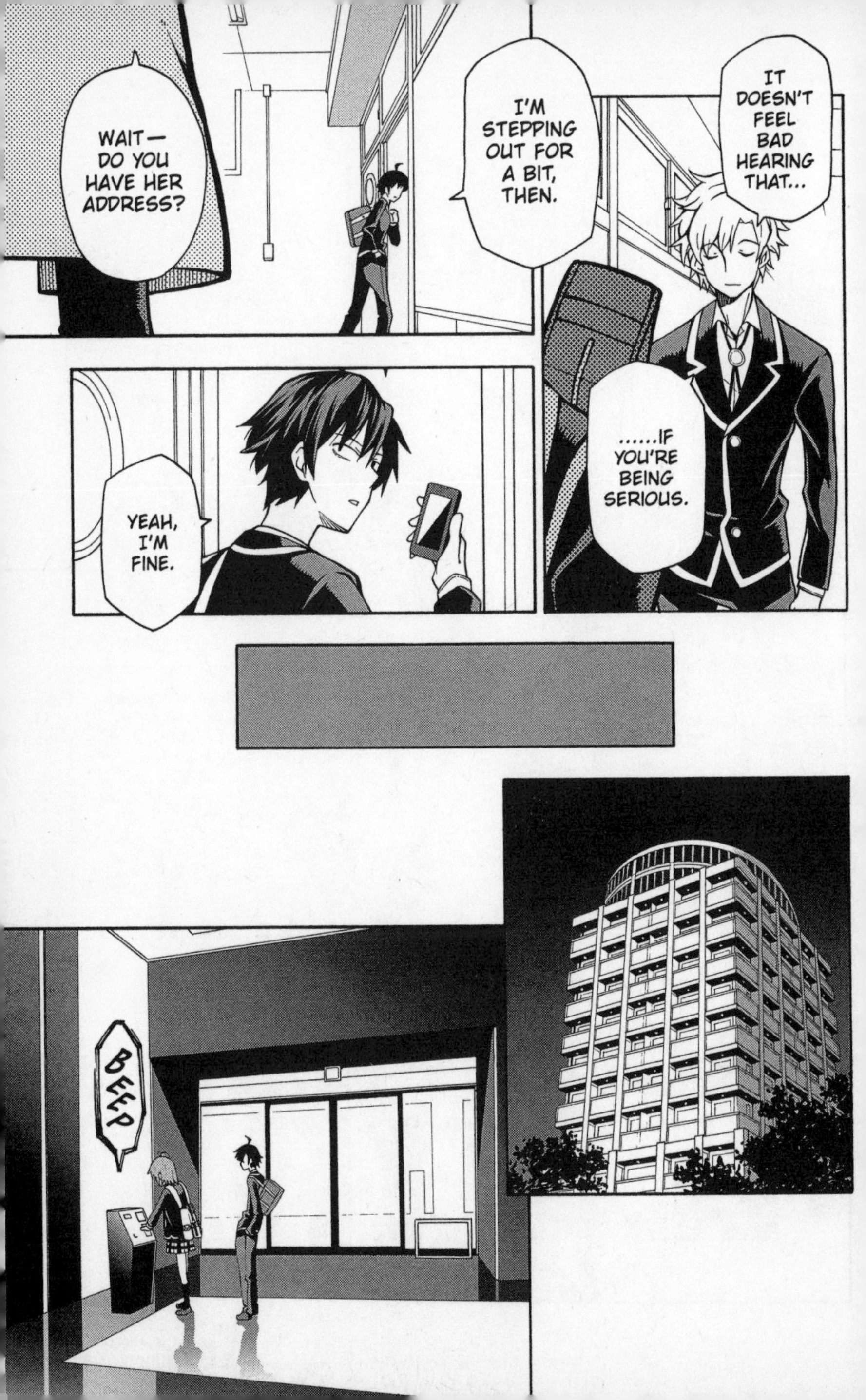
IT DOESN'T FEEL BAD HEARING THAT...
......IF YOU'RE BEING SERIOUS.
I'M STEPPING OUT FOR A BIT, THEN.
WAIT—DO YOU HAVE HER ADDRESS?
YEAH, I'M FINE.
BEEP

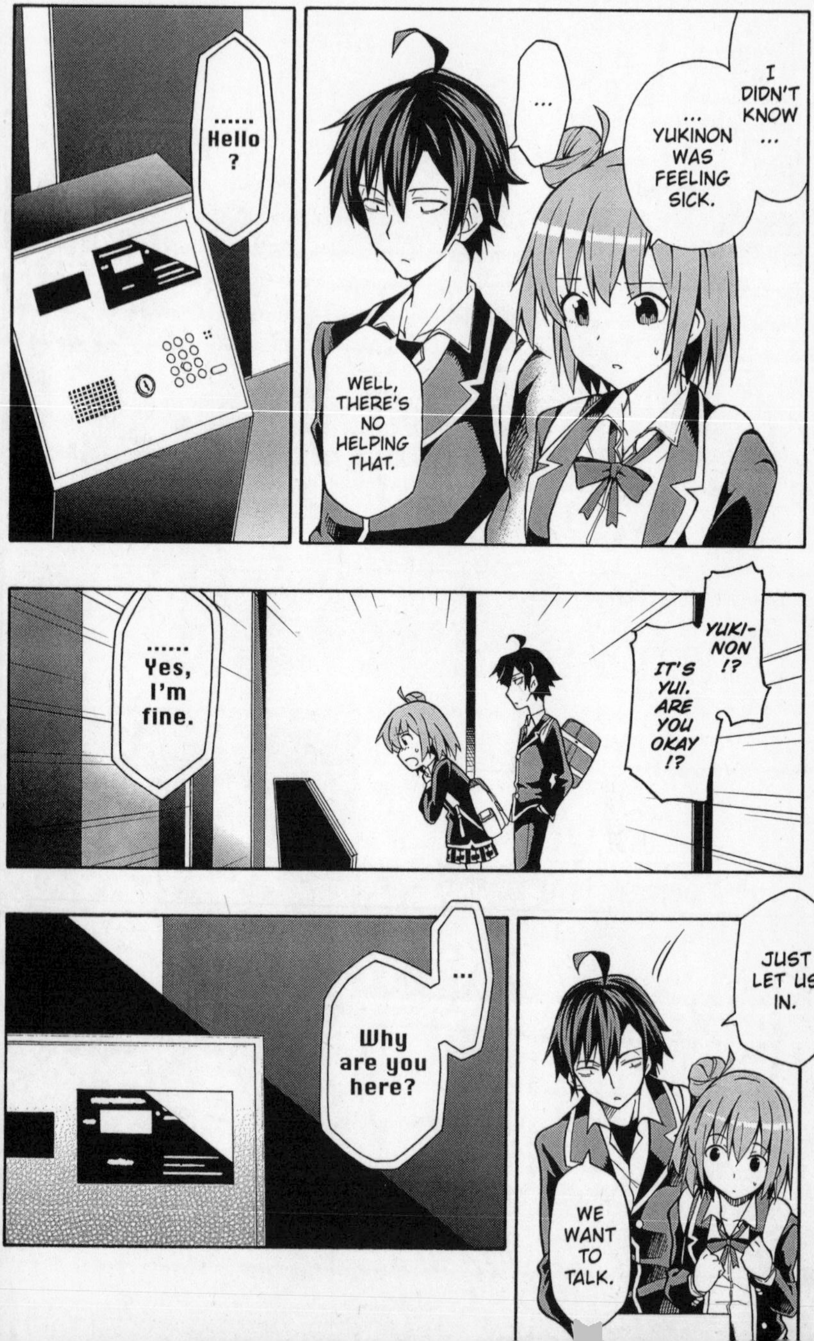
I DIDN'T KNOW...
...YUKINON WAS FEELING SICK.
...
WELL, THERE'S NO HELPING THAT.
......Hello?
YUKI-NON!?
IT'S YUI. ARE YOU OKAY!?
......Yes, I'm fine.
JUST LET US IN.
WE WANT TO TALK.
...
Why are you here?

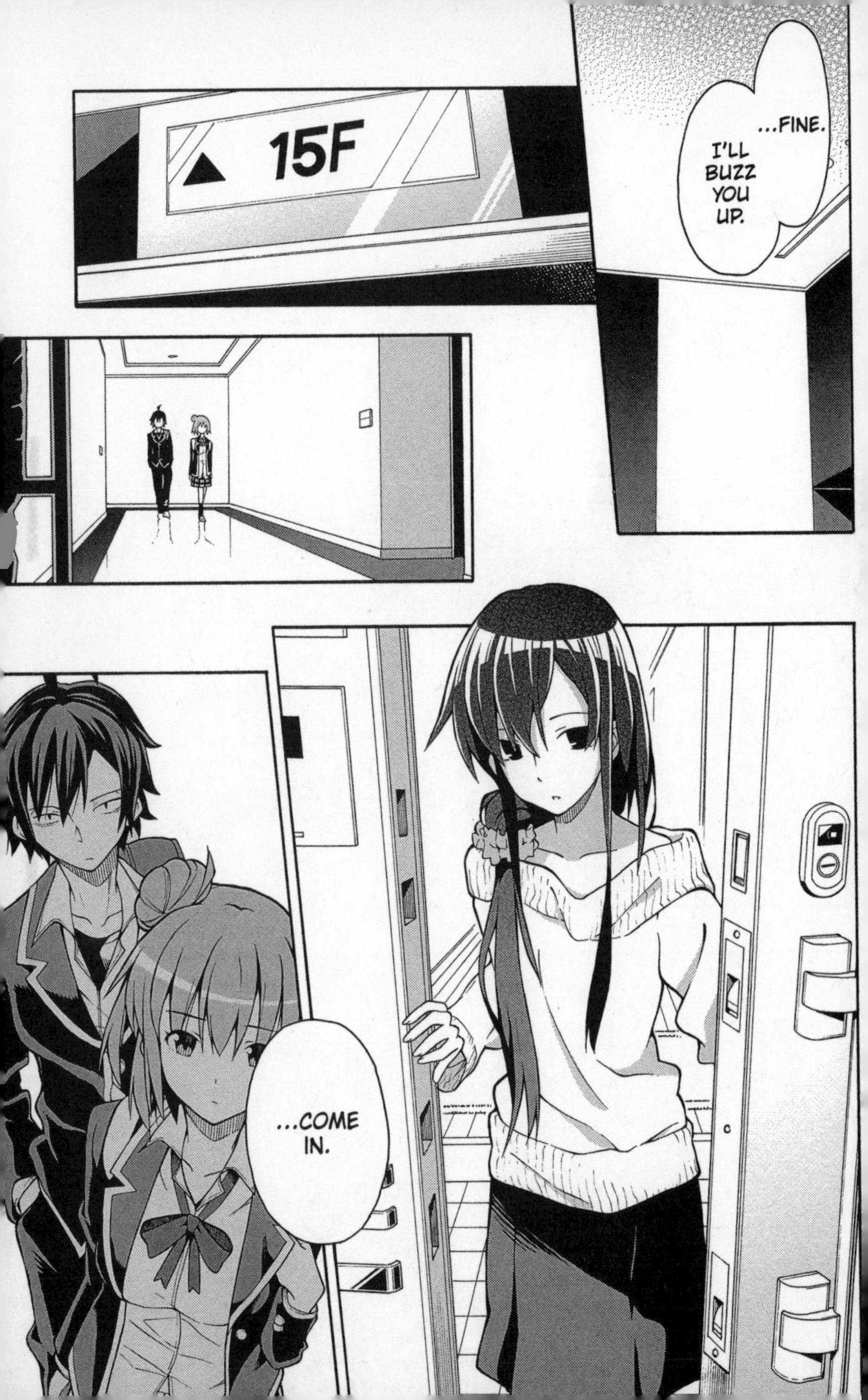
...FINE.
I'LL BUZZ YOU UP.
15F
...COME IN.

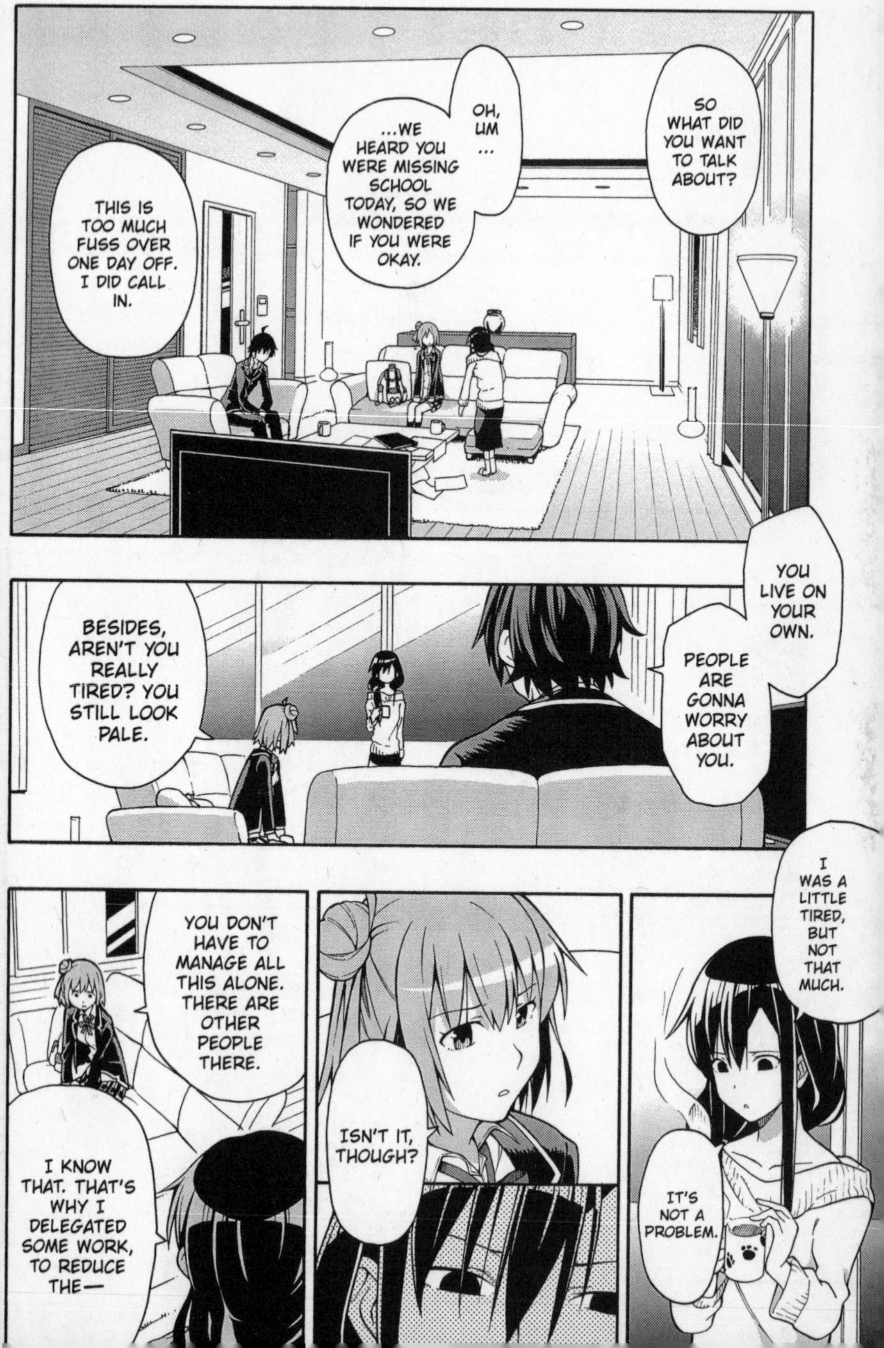
SO WHAT DID YOU WANT TO TALK ABOUT?
OH, UM ...
...WE HEARD YOU WERE MISSING SCHOOL TODAY, SO WE WONDERED IF YOU WERE OKAY.
THIS IS TOO MUCH FUSS OVER ONE DAY OFF. I DID CALL IN.
YOU LIVE ON YOUR OWN.
PEOPLE ARE GONNA WORRY ABOUT YOU.
BESIDES, AREN'T YOU REALLY TIRED? YOU STILL LOOK PALE.
I WAS A LITTLE TIRED, BUT NOT THAT MUCH.
IT'S NOT A PROBLEM.
ISN'T IT, THOUGH?
YOU DON'T HAVE TO MANAGE ALL THIS ALONE. THERE ARE OTHER PEOPLE THERE.
I KNOW THAT. THAT'S WHY I DELEGATED SOME WORK, TO REDUCE THE—

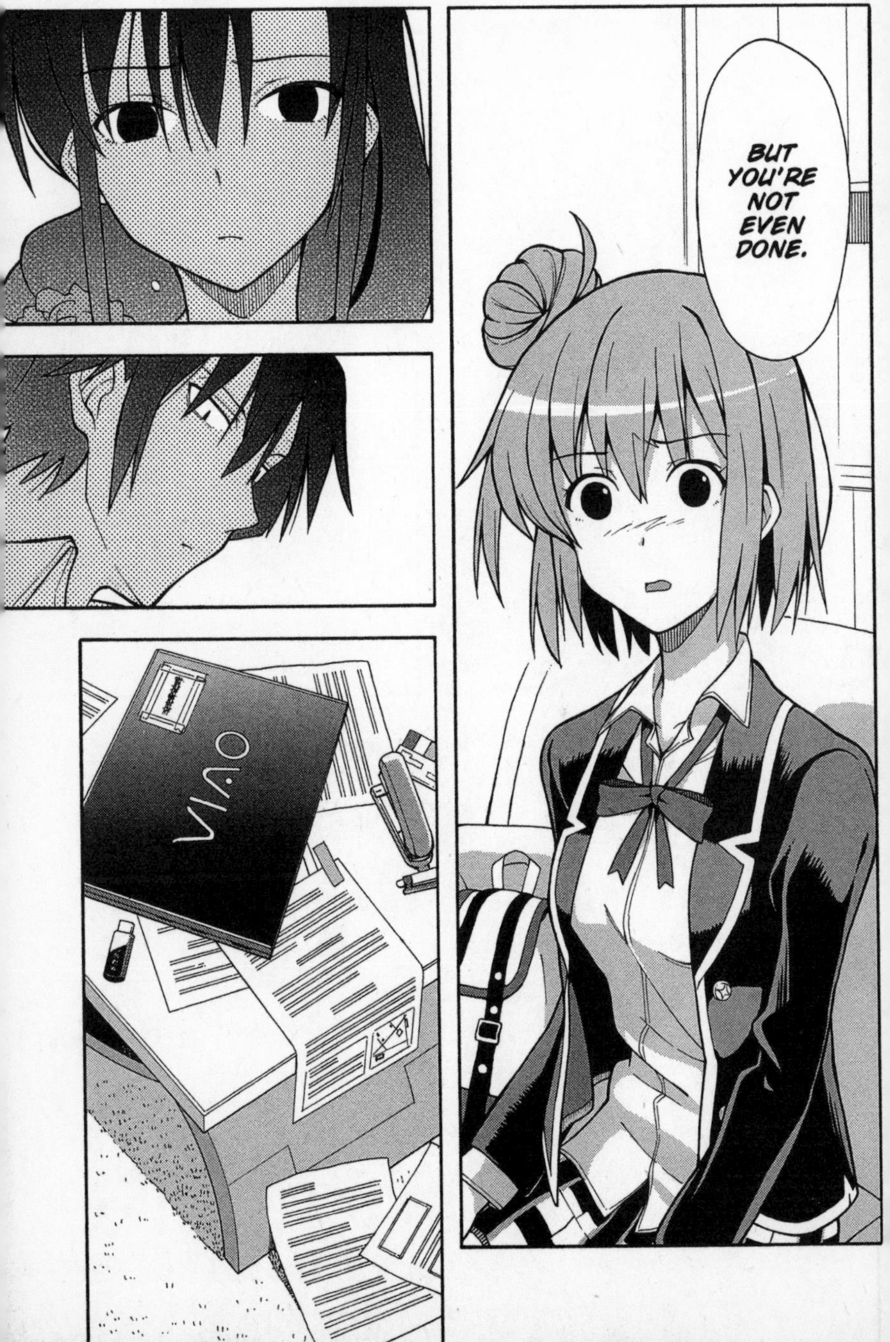
BUT YOU'RE NOT EVEN DONE.

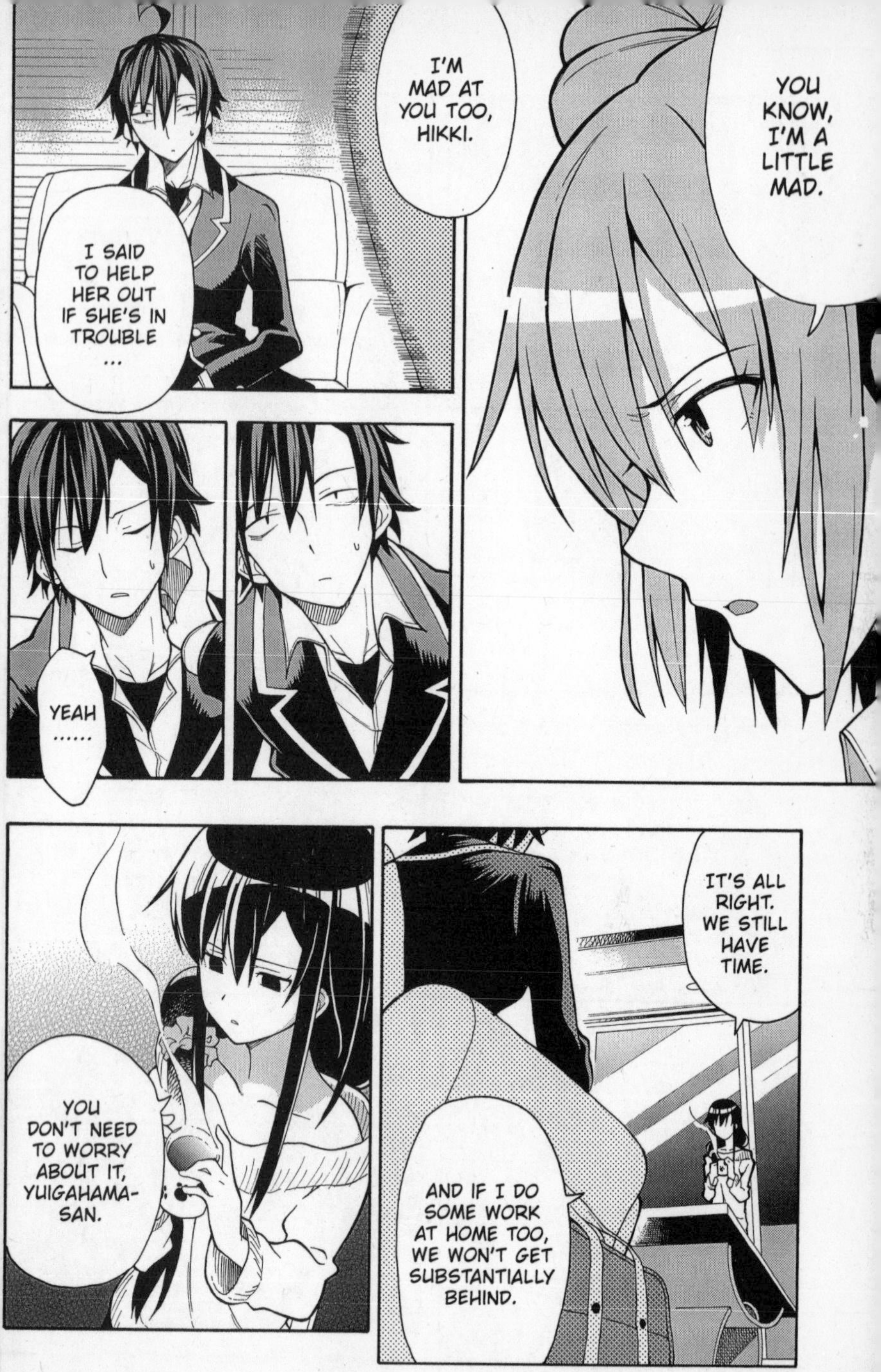
YOU KNOW, I'M A LITTLE MAD.
I'M MAD AT YOU TOO, HIKKI.
I SAID TO HELP HER OUT IF SHE'S IN TROUBLE...
YEAH......
IT'S ALL RIGHT. WE STILL HAVE TIME.
AND IF I DO SOME WORK AT HOME TOO, WE WON'T GET SUBSTANTIALLY BEHIND.
YOU DON'T NEED TO WORRY ABOUT IT, YUIGAHAMA-SAN.

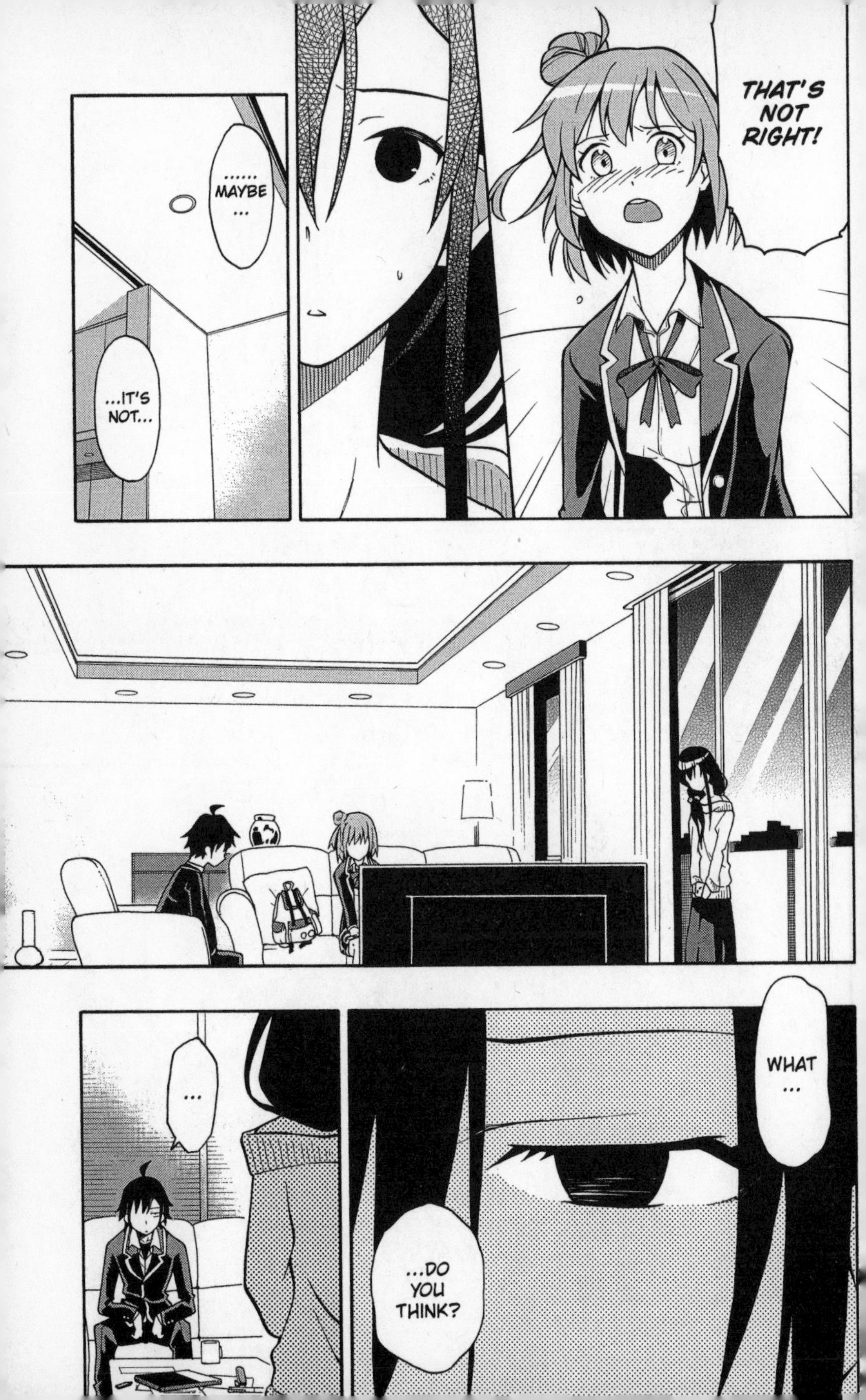
THAT'S NOT RIGHT!
...... MAYBE ...
...IT'S NOT...
WHAT ...
...DO YOU THINK?
...

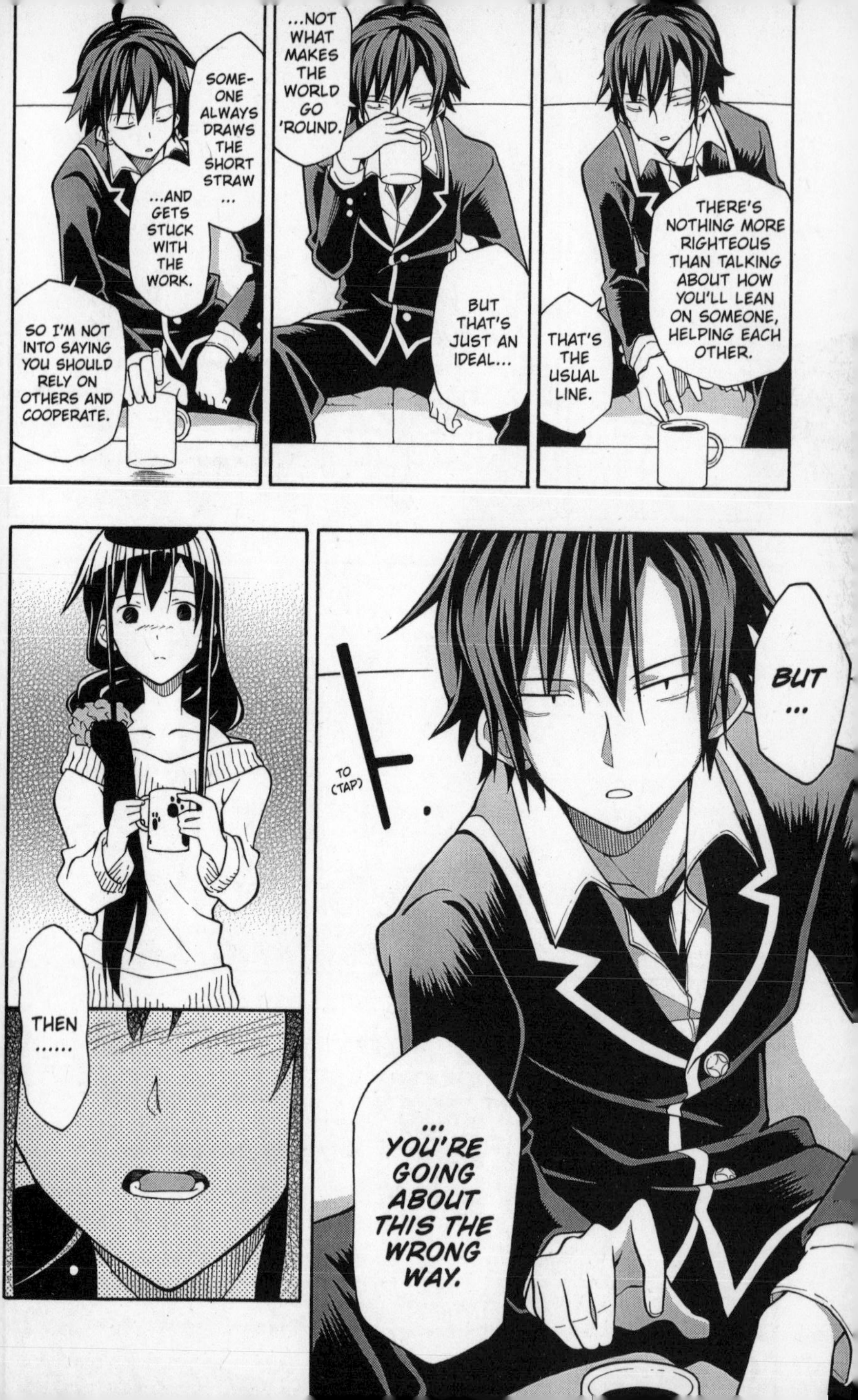
THERE'S NOTHING MORE RIGHTEOUS THAN TALKING ABOUT HOW YOU'LL LEAN ON SOMEONE, HELPING EACH OTHER.
THAT'S THE USUAL LINE.
BUT THAT'S JUST AN IDEAL...
...NOT WHAT MAKES THE WORLD GO 'ROUND.
SOME-ONE ALWAYS DRAWS THE SHORT STRAW ...
...AND GETS STUCK WITH THE WORK.
SO I'M NOT INTO SAYING YOU SHOULD RELY ON OTHERS AND COOPERATE.
BUT ...
TO (TAP)
... YOU'RE GOING ABOUT THIS THE WRONG WAY.
THEN ......

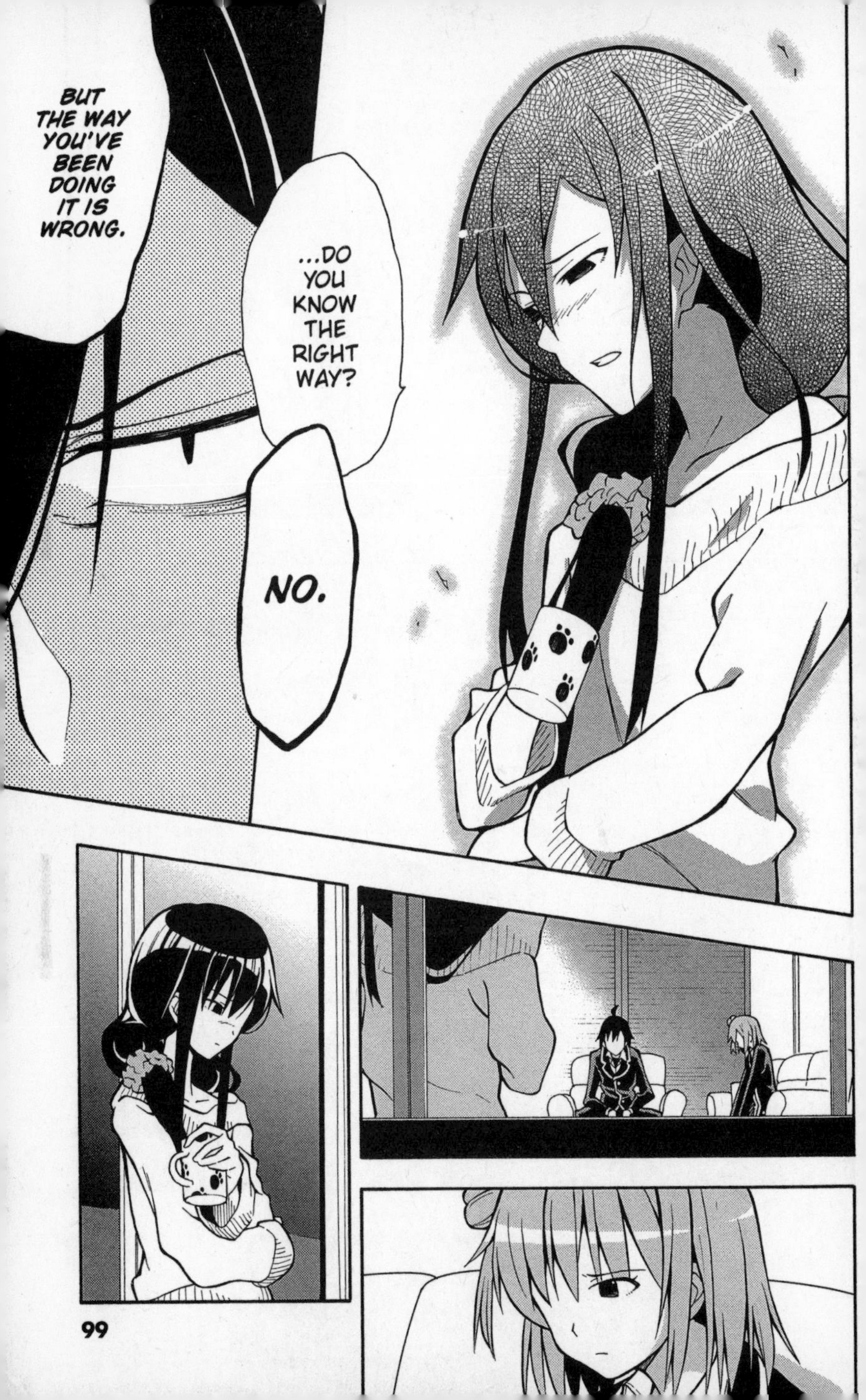
...DO YOU KNOW THE RIGHT WAY?
NO.
BUT THE WAY YOU'VE BEEN DOING IT IS WRONG.

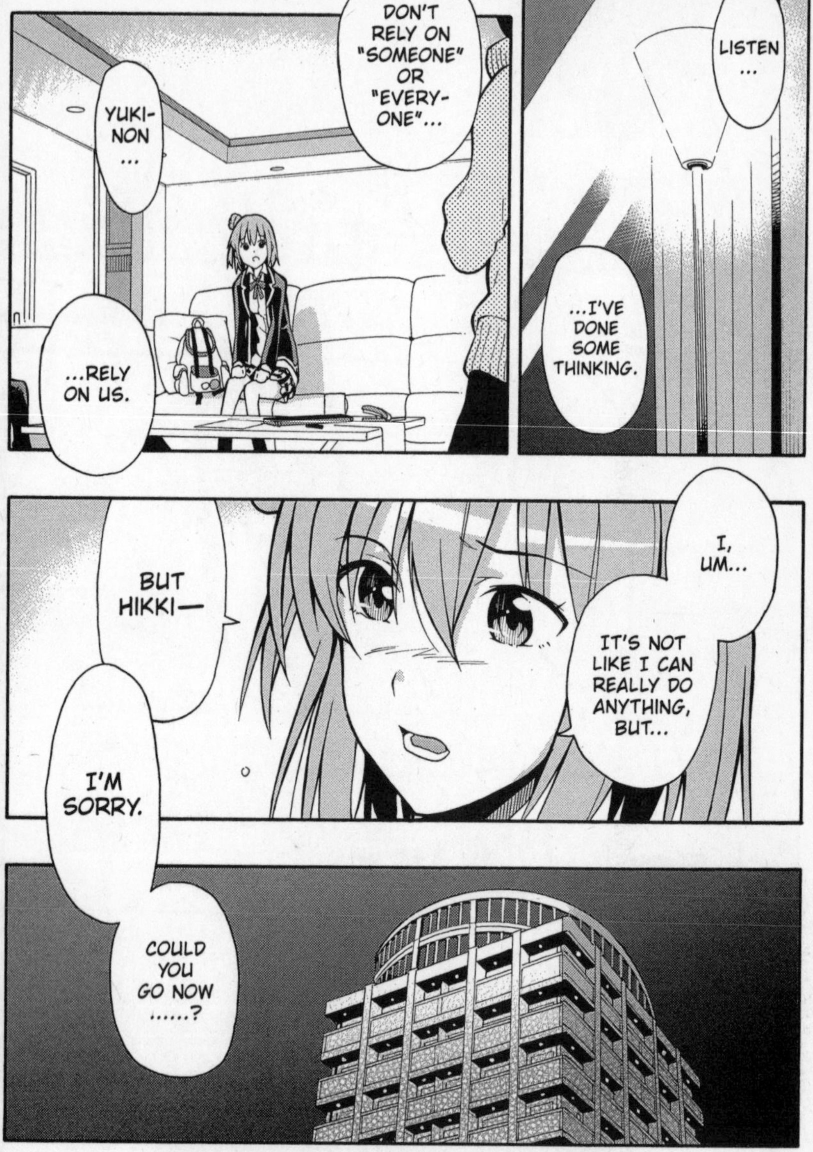
LISTEN...
...I'VE DONE SOME THINKING.
DON'T RELY ON "SOMEONE" OR "EVERY-ONE"...
YUKI-NON...
...RELY ON US.
I, UM...
IT'S NOT LIKE I CAN REALLY DO ANYTHING, BUT...
BUT HIKKI—
I'M SORRY.
COULD YOU GO NOW......?

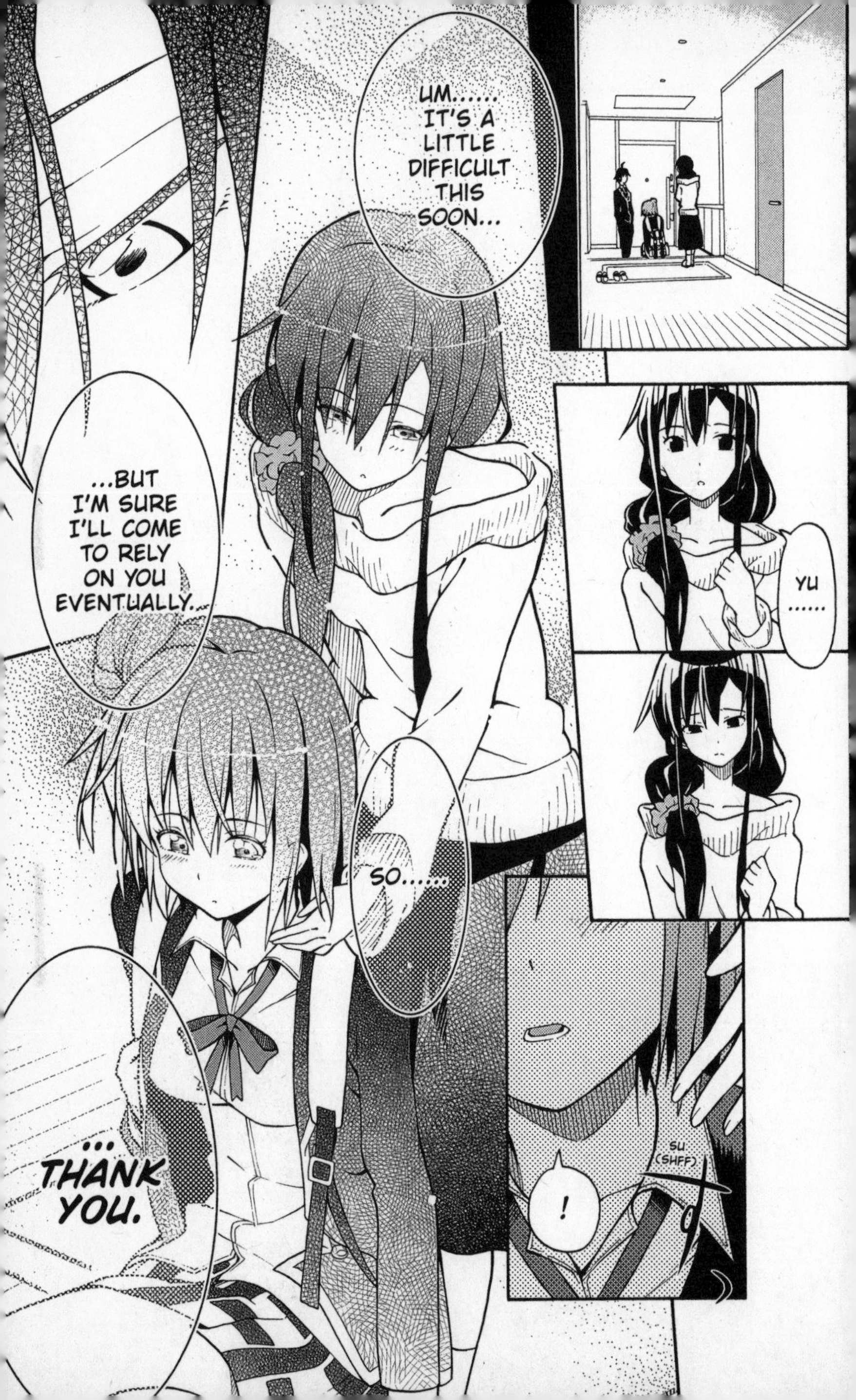
UM...... IT'S A LITTLE DIFFICULT THIS SOON...
...BUT I'M SURE I'LL COME TO RELY ON YOU EVENTUALLY.
YU ......
SO......
SU (SHFF)
!
... THANK YOU.

BUT I WANT TO THINK A LITTLE LONGER.

YUKI-NON...

GYU (SQUEEZE)

OKAY
......

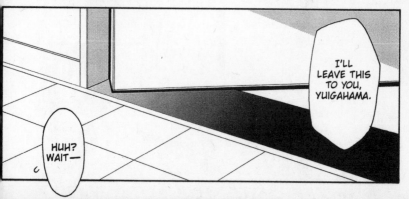

I'LL LEAVE THIS TO YOU, YUIGAHAMA.

HUH? WAIT—

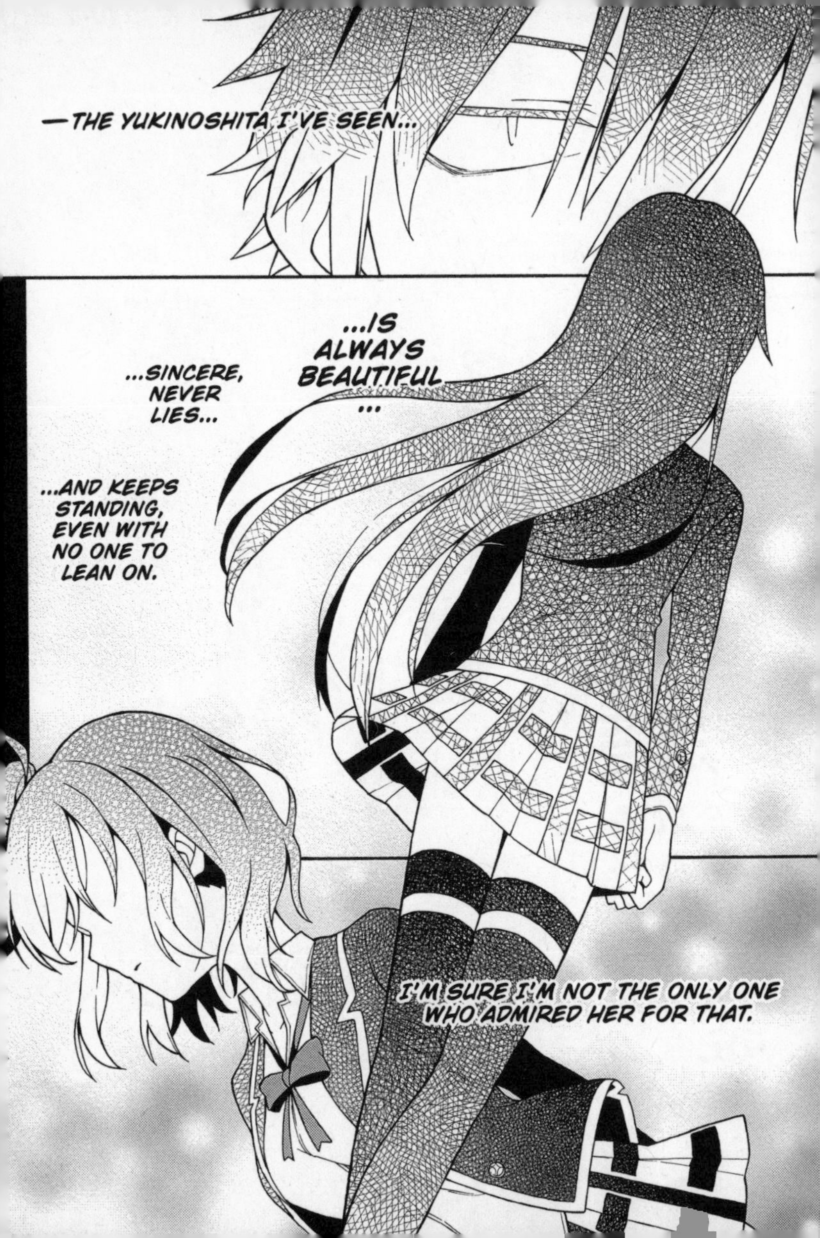
—THE YUKINOSHITA I'VE SEEN...
...IS ALWAYS BEAUTIFUL...
...SINCERE, NEVER LIES...
...AND KEEPS STANDING, EVEN WITH NO ONE TO LEAN ON.
I'M SURE I'M NOT THE ONLY ONE WHO ADMIRED HER FOR THAT.

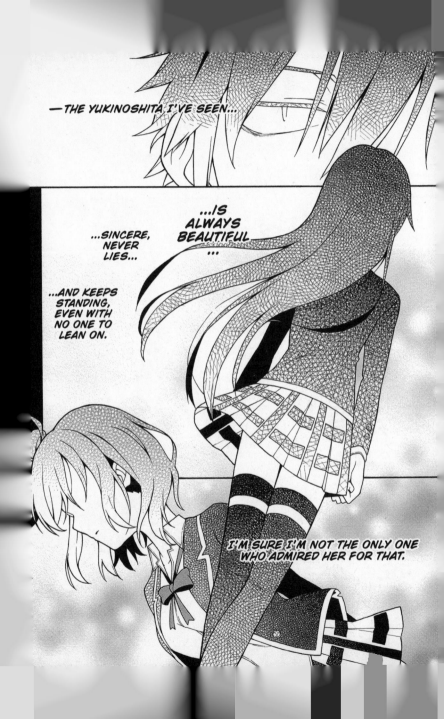

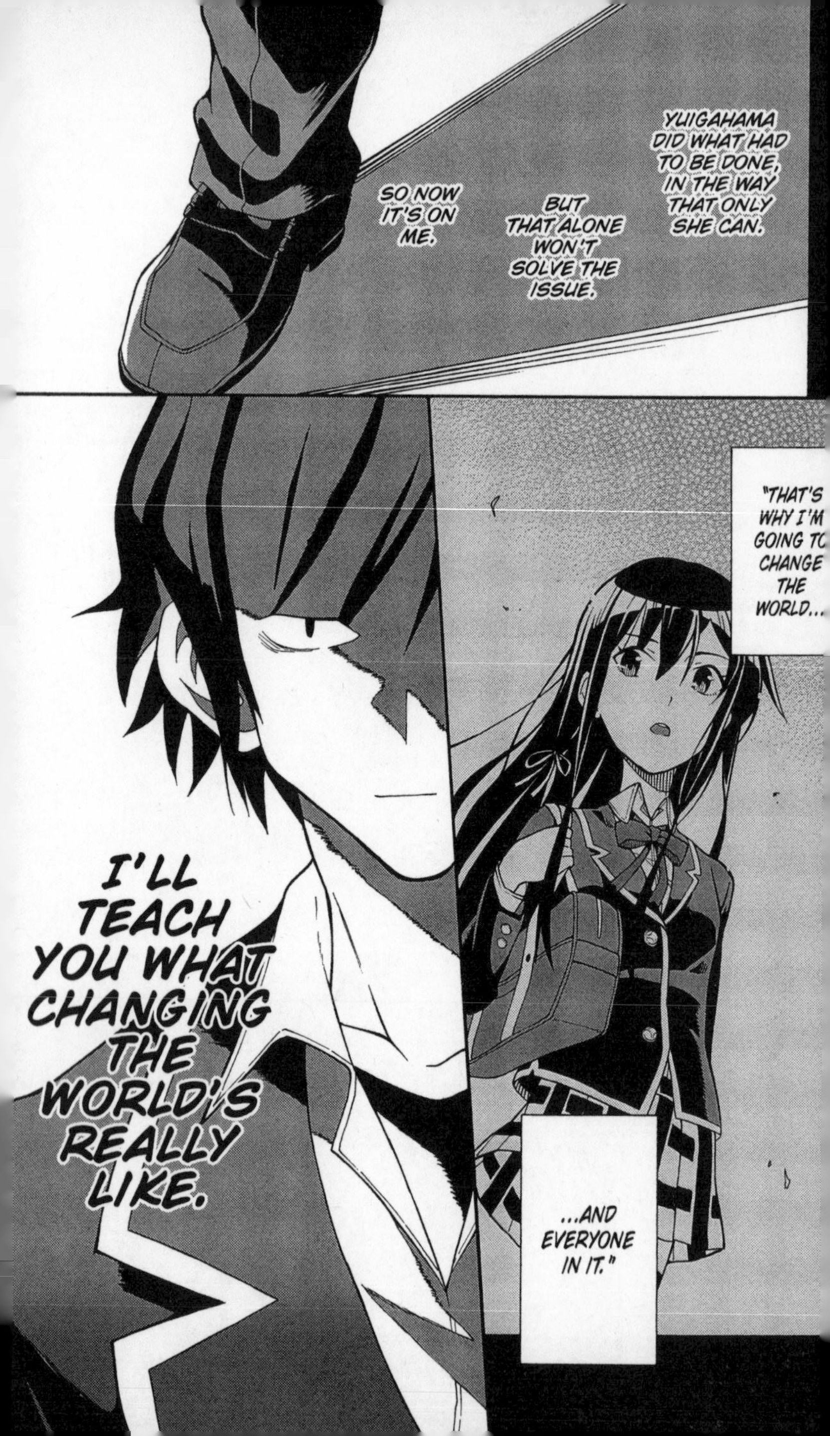
YUIGAHAMA DID WHAT HAD TO BE DONE, IN THE WAY THAT ONLY SHE CAN.
BUT THAT ALONE WON'T SOLVE THE ISSUE.
SO NOW IT'S ON ME.
"THAT'S WHY I'M GOING TO CHANGE THE WORLD...
...AND EVERYONE IN IT."
I'LL TEACH YOU WHAT CHANGING THE WORLD'S REALLY LIKE.

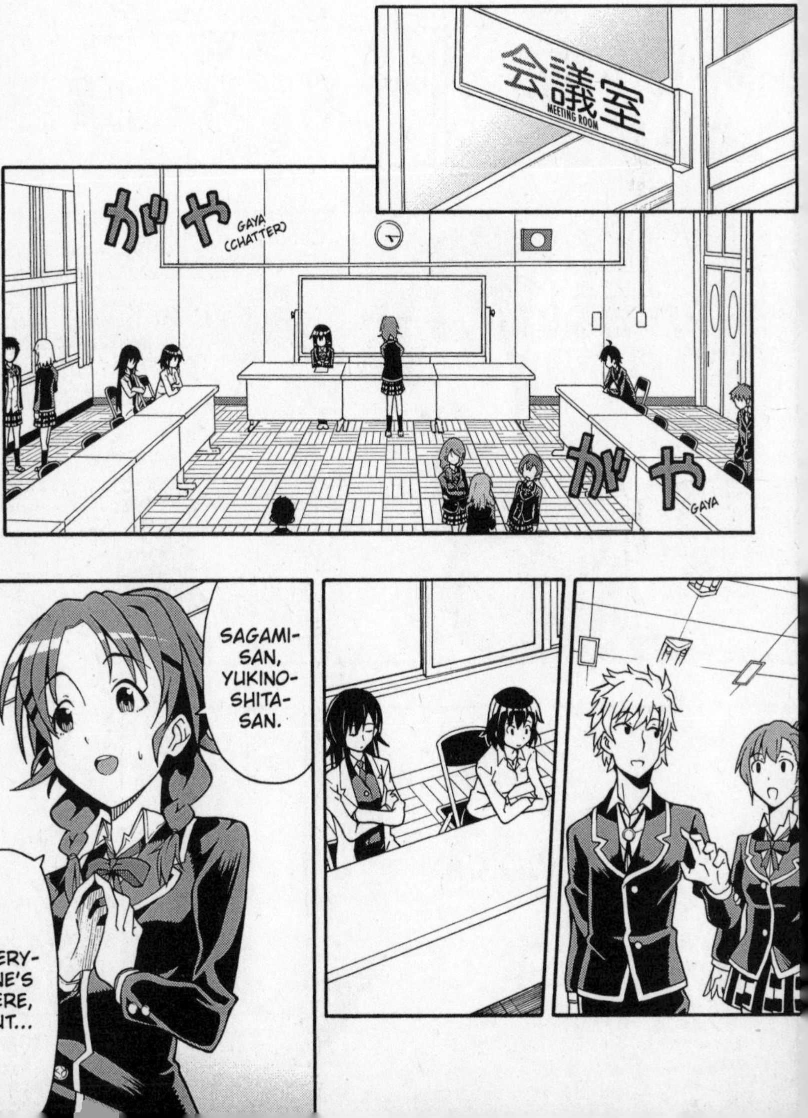
会議室
MEETING ROOM
がや
GAYA (CHATTER)
がや
GAYA
SAGAMI-SAN, YUKINO-SHITA-SAN.
EVERY-ONE'S HERE, BUT...

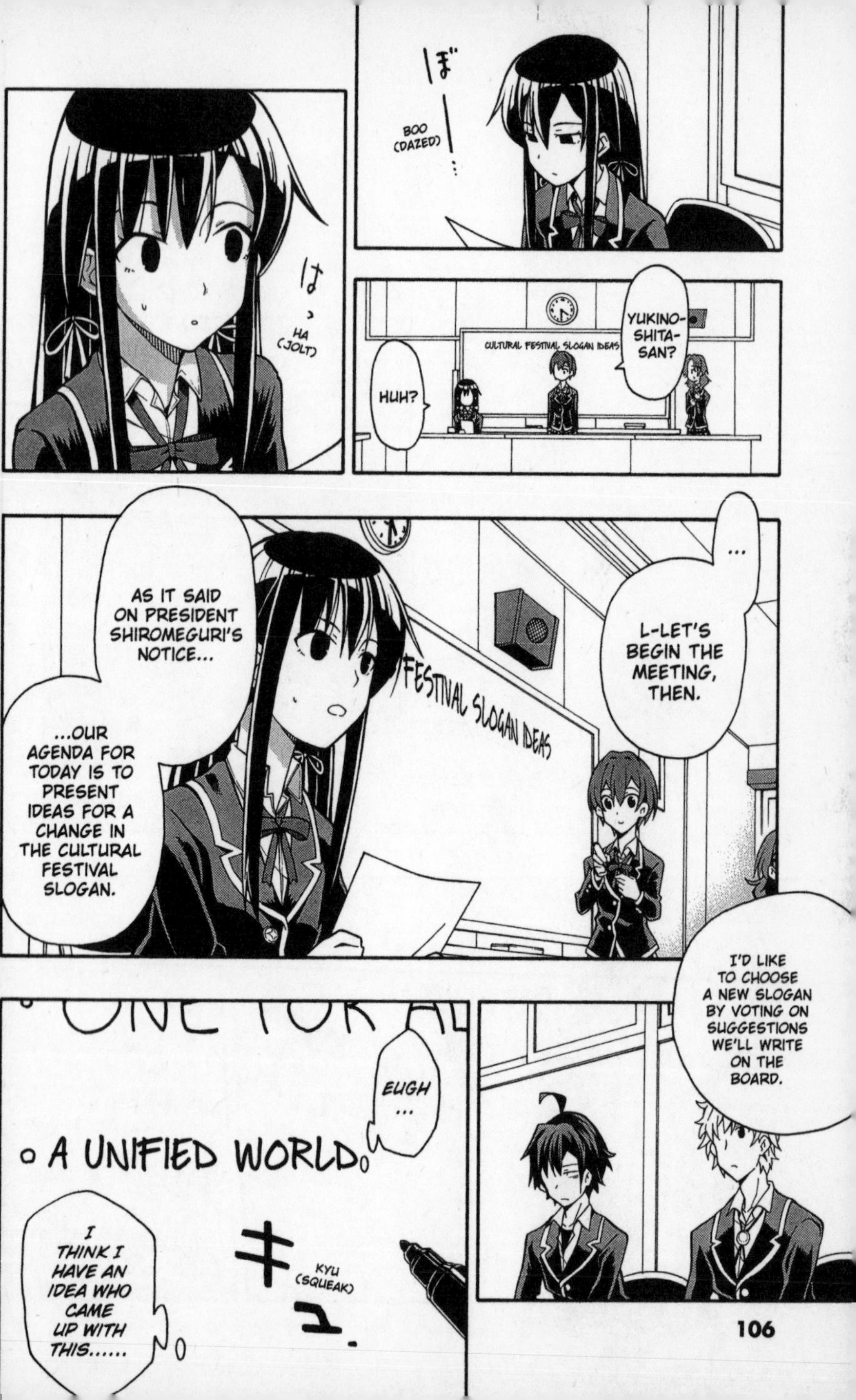
ぼ
BOO (DAZED)
CULTURAL FESTIVAL SLOGAN IDEAS
YUKINO-SHITA-SAN?
HUH?
は
HA (JOLT)
...
L-LET'S BEGIN THE MEETING, THEN.
FESTIVAL SLOGAN IDEAS
AS IT SAID ON PRESIDENT SHIROMEGURI'S NOTICE...
...OUR AGENDA FOR TODAY IS TO PRESENT IDEAS FOR A CHANGE IN THE CULTURAL FESTIVAL SLOGAN.
I'D LIKE TO CHOOSE A NEW SLOGAN BY VOTING ON SUGGESTIONS WE'LL WRITE ON THE BOARD.
ONE FOR AL
EUGH...
A UNIFIED WORLD
キュ
KYU (SQUEAK)
I THINK I HAVE AN IDEA WHO CAME UP WITH THIS......

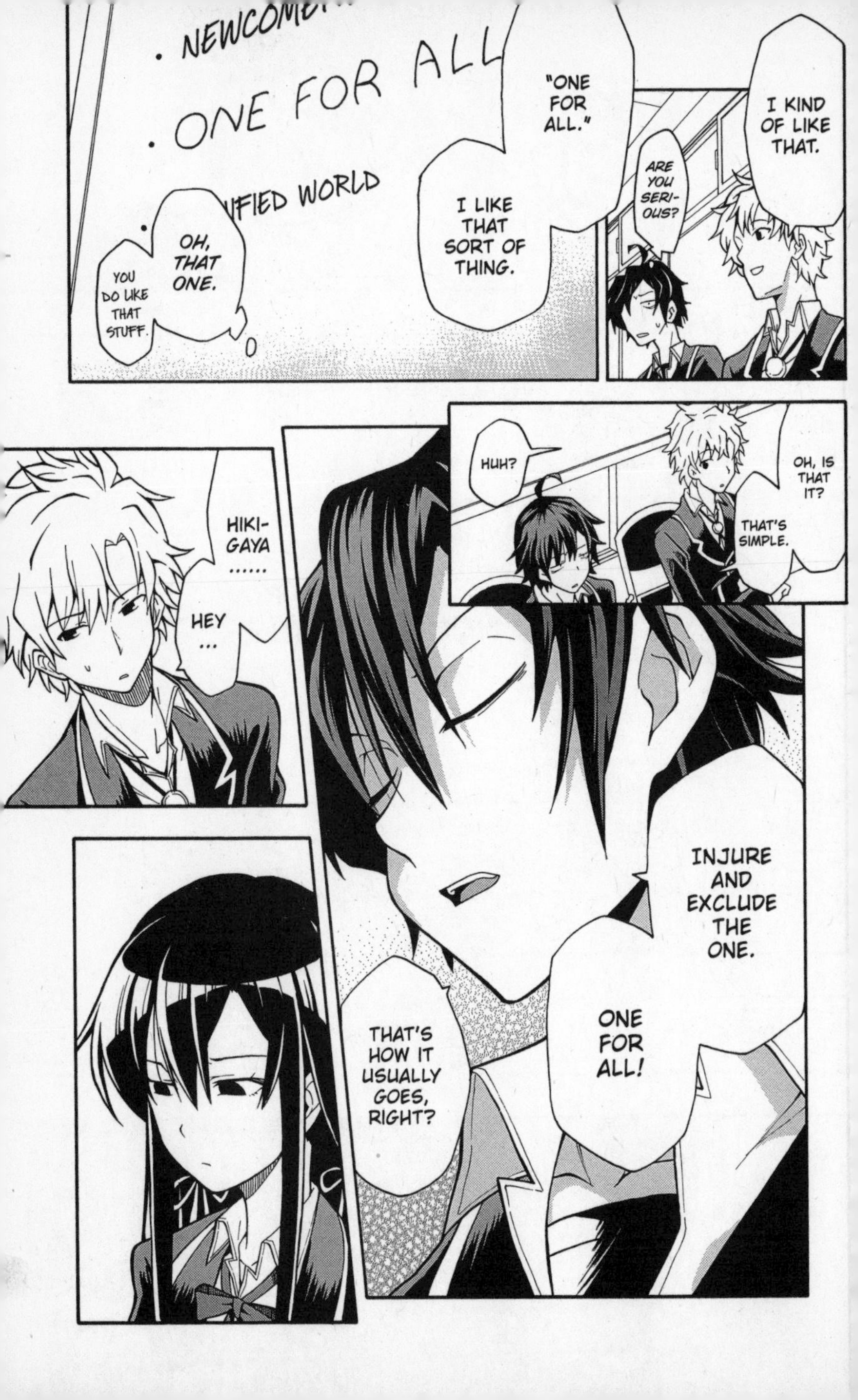
I KIND OF LIKE THAT.
ARE YOU SERIOUS?
• ONE FOR ALL
"ONE FOR ALL."
I LIKE THAT SORT OF THING.
OH, THAT ONE.
YOU DO LIKE THAT STUFF.
OH, IS THAT IT?
THAT'S SIMPLE.
HUH?
INJURE AND EXCLUDE THE ONE.
ONE FOR ALL!
THAT'S HOW IT USUALLY GOES, RIGHT?
HIKIGAYA ......
HEY ...

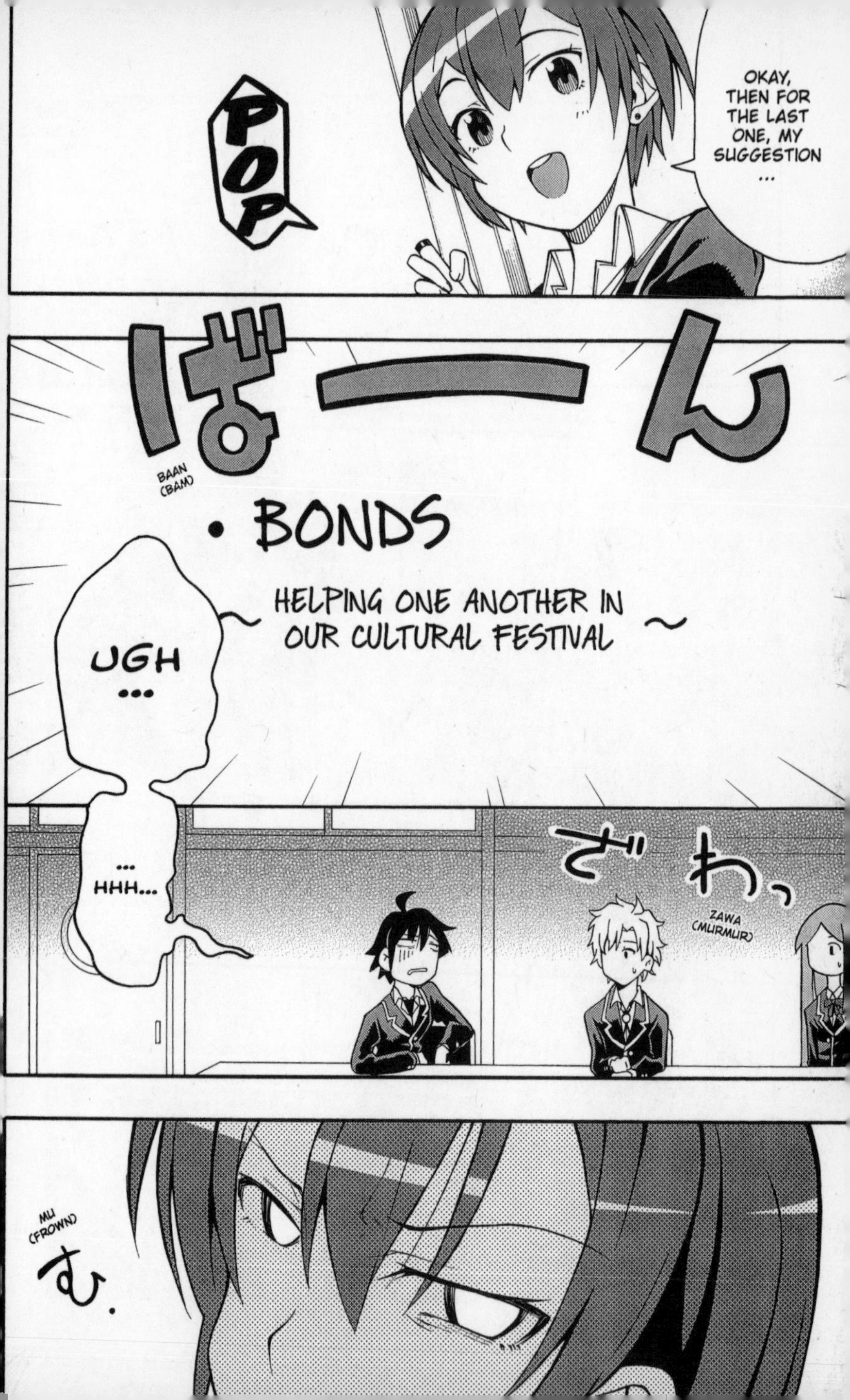
OKAY, THEN FOR THE LAST ONE, MY SUGGESTION ...
POP
ばーーん
BAAN (BAM)
• BONDS
~HELPING ONE ANOTHER IN OUR CULTURAL FESTIVAL~
UGH ...
... HHH...
ざわっ
ZAWA (MURMUR)
MU (FROWN)
む.

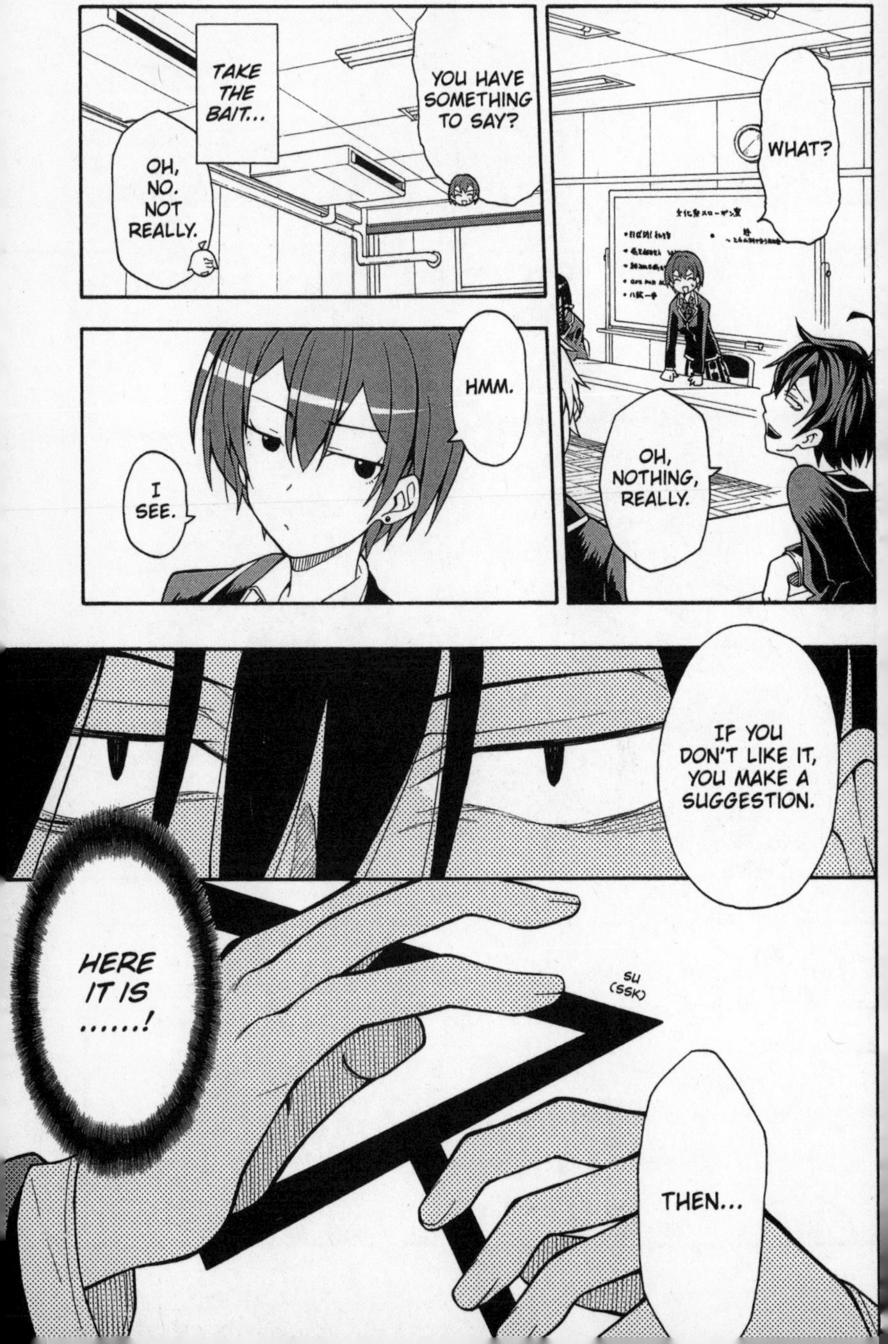
WHAT?
OH, NOTHING, REALLY.
YOU HAVE SOMETHING TO SAY?
TAKE THE BAIT...
OH, NO. NOT REALLY.
HMM.
I SEE.
IF YOU DON'T LIKE IT, YOU MAKE A SUGGESTION.
HERE IT IS ......!
SU (SSK)
THEN...

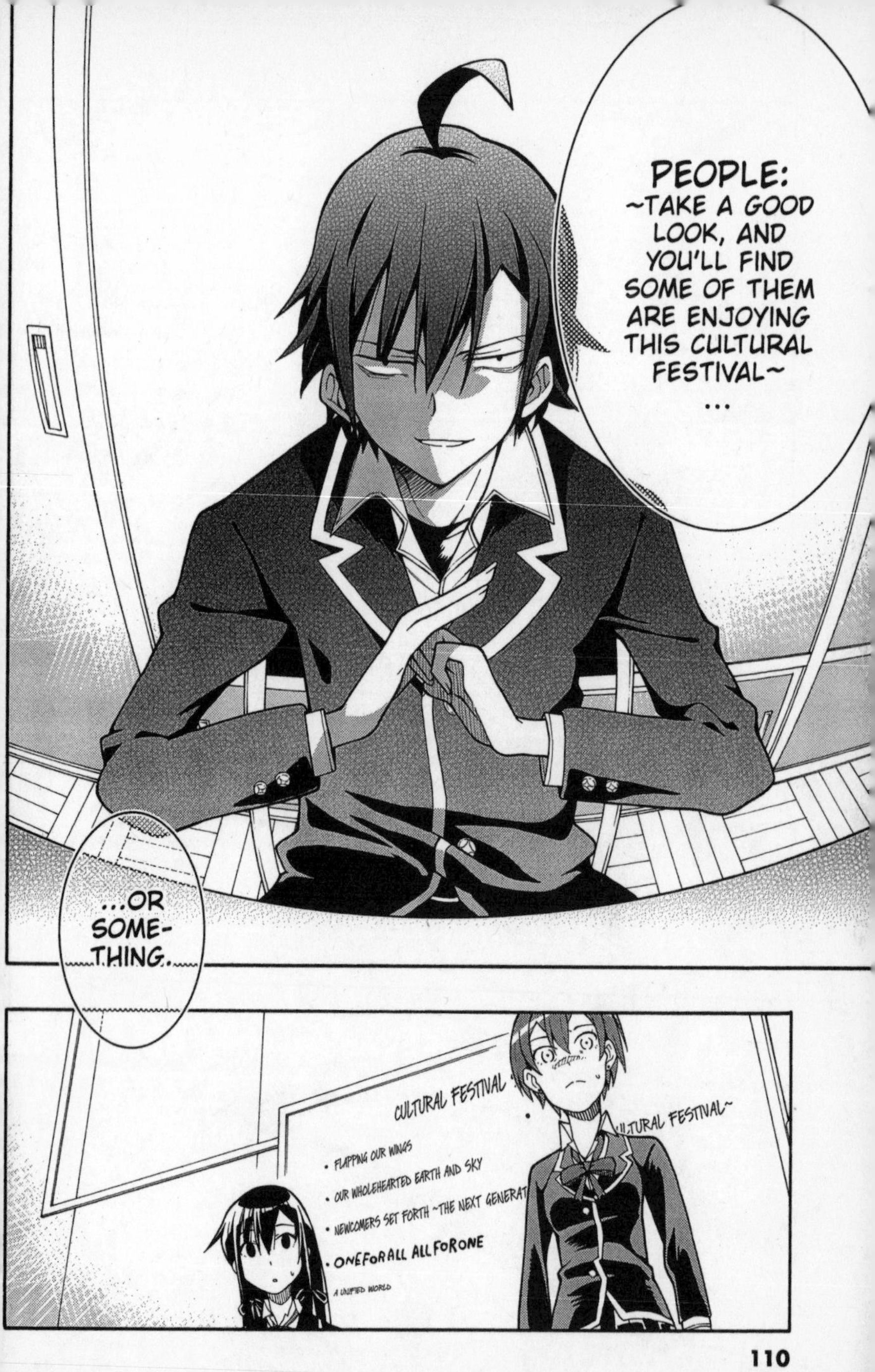
PEOPLE: ~TAKE A GOOD LOOK, AND YOU'LL FIND SOME OF THEM ARE ENJOYING THIS CULTURAL FESTIVAL~ ...
...OR SOME-THING.
CULTURAL FESTIVAL
ULTURAL FESTIVAL~
• FLAPPING OUR WINGS
• OUR WHOLEHEARTED EARTH AND SKY
• NEWCOMERS SET FORTH ~THE NEXT GENERAT
• ONEFORALL ALLFORONE
A UNIFIED WORLD

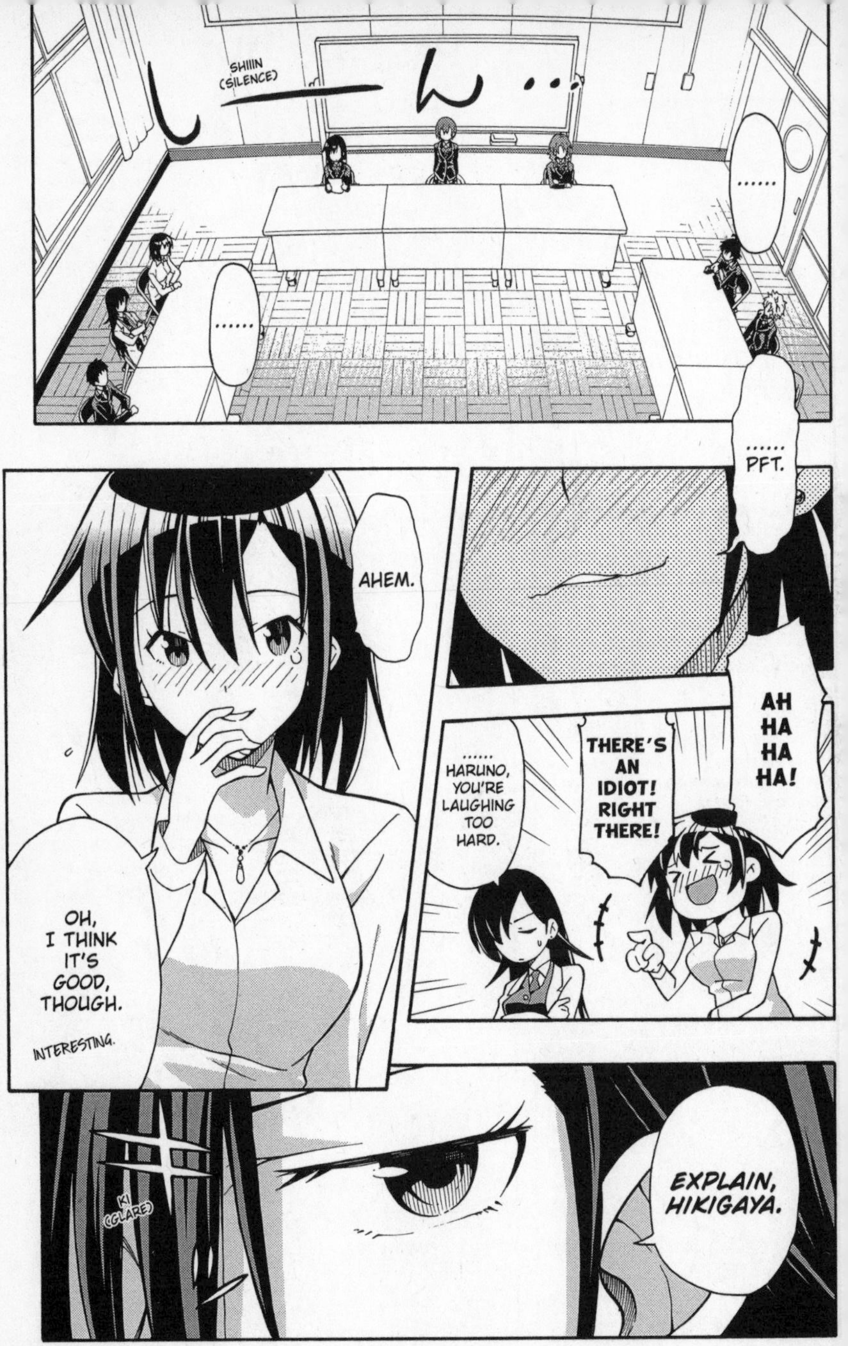

SHIIIN (SILENCE)
......
......
......PFT.
AH HA HA HA!
THERE'S AN IDIOT! RIGHT THERE!
...... HARUNO, YOU'RE LAUGHING TOO HARD.
AHEM.
OH, I THINK IT'S GOOD, THOUGH.
INTERESTING.
EXPLAIN, HIKIGAYA.
KI (GLARE)

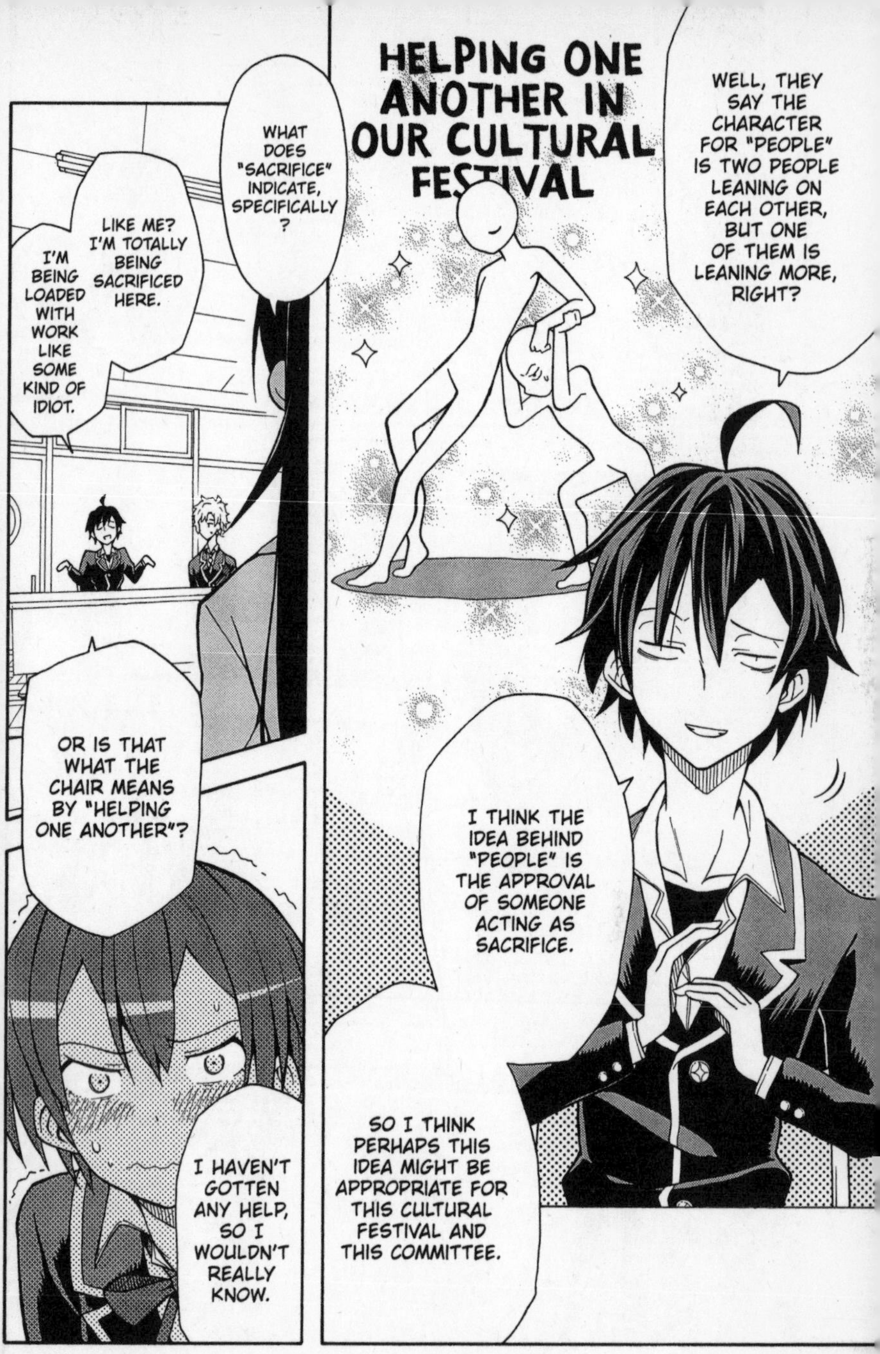
HELPING ONE ANOTHER IN OUR CULTURAL FESTIVAL
WELL, THEY SAY THE CHARACTER FOR "PEOPLE" IS TWO PEOPLE LEANING ON EACH OTHER, BUT ONE OF THEM IS LEANING MORE, RIGHT?
I THINK THE IDEA BEHIND "PEOPLE" IS THE APPROVAL OF SOMEONE ACTING AS SACRIFICE.
SO I THINK PERHAPS THIS IDEA MIGHT BE APPROPRIATE FOR THIS CULTURAL FESTIVAL AND THIS COMMITTEE.
WHAT DOES "SACRIFICE" INDICATE, SPECIFICALLY?
LIKE ME? I'M TOTALLY BEING SACRIFICED HERE.
I'M BEING LOADED WITH WORK LIKE SOME KIND OF IDIOT.
OR IS THAT WHAT THE CHAIR MEANS BY "HELPING ONE ANOTHER"?
I HAVEN'T GOTTEN ANY HELP, SO I WOULDN'T REALLY KNOW.

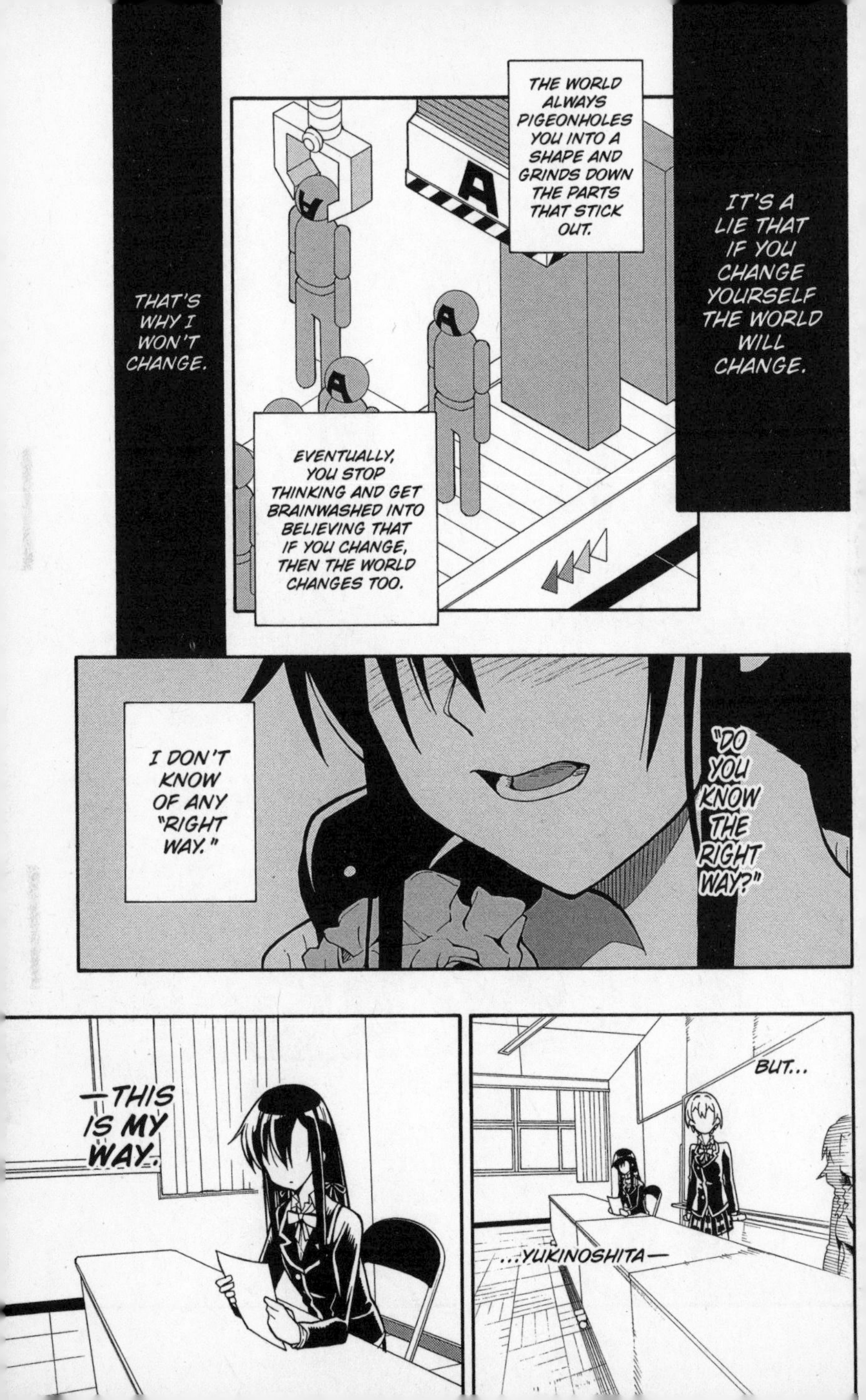
IT'S A LIE THAT IF YOU CHANGE YOURSELF THE WORLD WILL CHANGE.
THE WORLD ALWAYS PIGEONHOLES YOU INTO A SHAPE AND GRINDS DOWN THE PARTS THAT STICK OUT.
EVENTUALLY, YOU STOP THINKING AND GET BRAINWASHED INTO BELIEVING THAT IF YOU CHANGE, THEN THE WORLD CHANGES TOO.
THAT'S WHY I WON'T CHANGE.
"DO YOU KNOW THE RIGHT WAY?"
I DON'T KNOW OF ANY "RIGHT WAY."
BUT...
...YUKINOSHITA—
—THIS IS MY WAY.

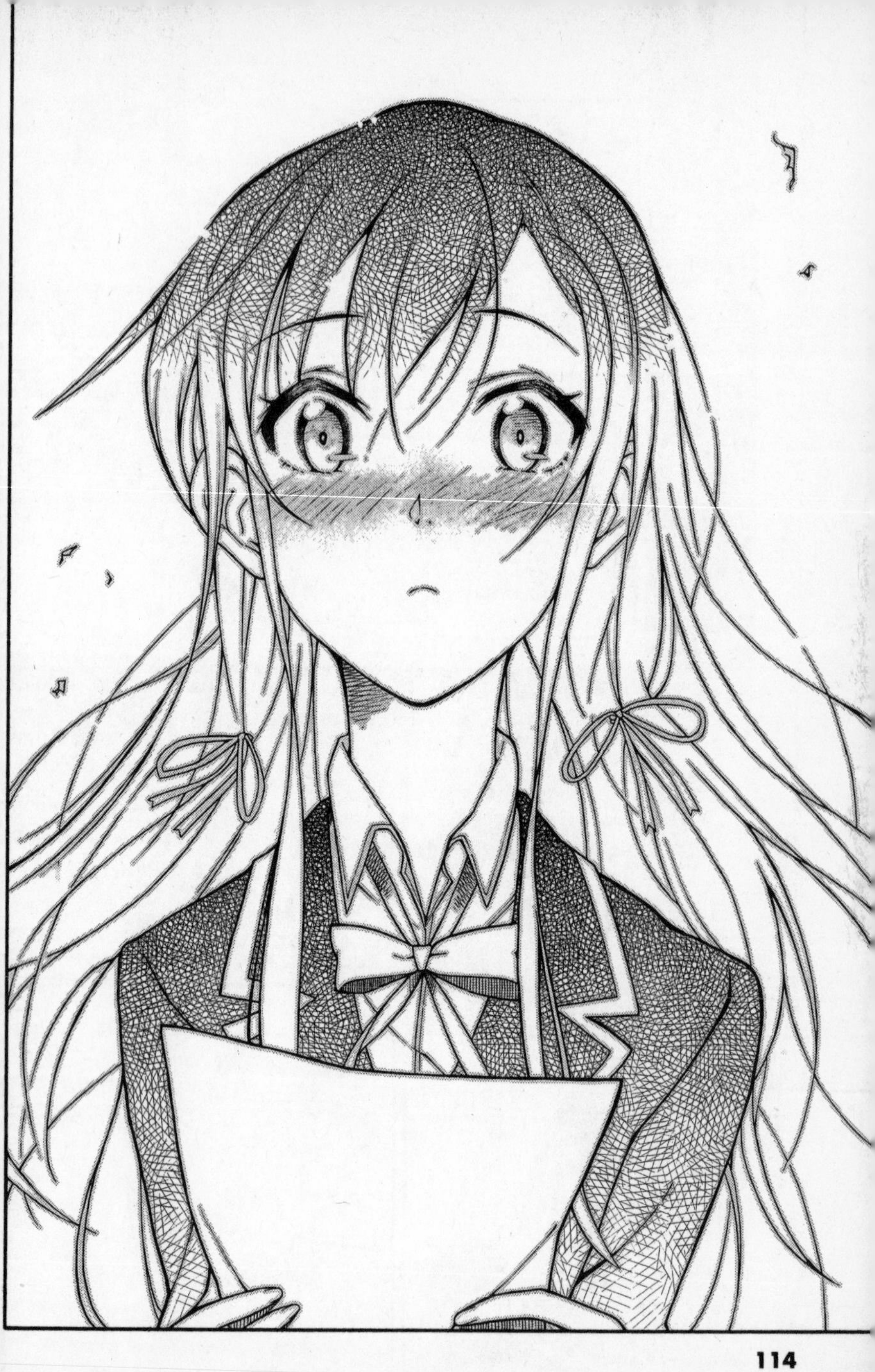

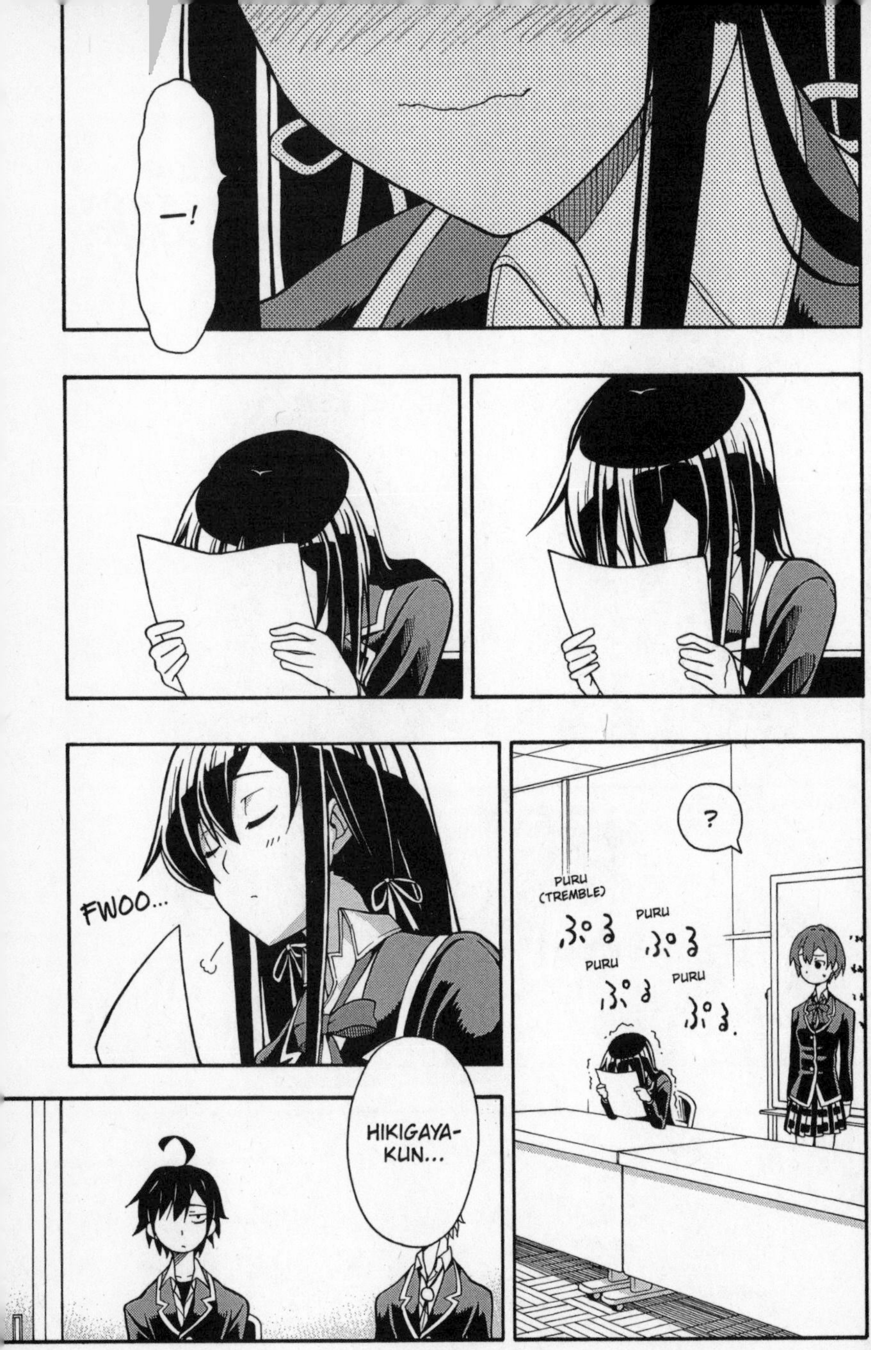
—!
?
PURU (TREMBLE)
ぷる
PURU
ぷる
PURU
ぷる
PURU
ぷる。
FWOO...
HIKIGAYA-KUN...

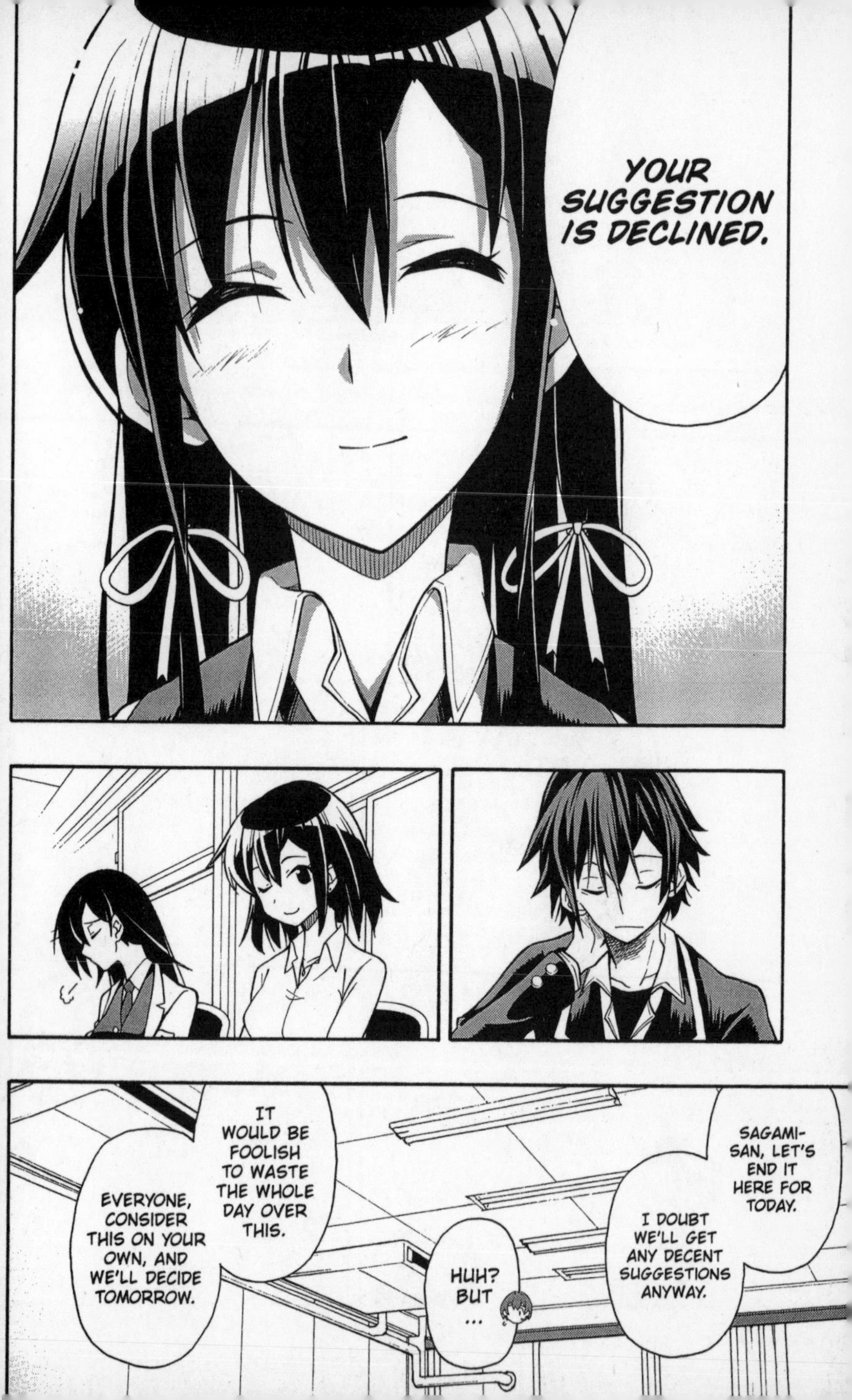
YOUR SUGGESTION IS DECLINED.
SAGAMI-SAN, LET'S END IT HERE FOR TODAY.
I DOUBT WE'LL GET ANY DECENT SUGGESTIONS ANYWAY.
HUH? BUT ...
IT WOULD BE FOOLISH TO WASTE THE WHOLE DAY OVER THIS.
EVERYONE, CONSIDER THIS ON YOUR OWN, AND WE'LL DECIDE TOMORROW.

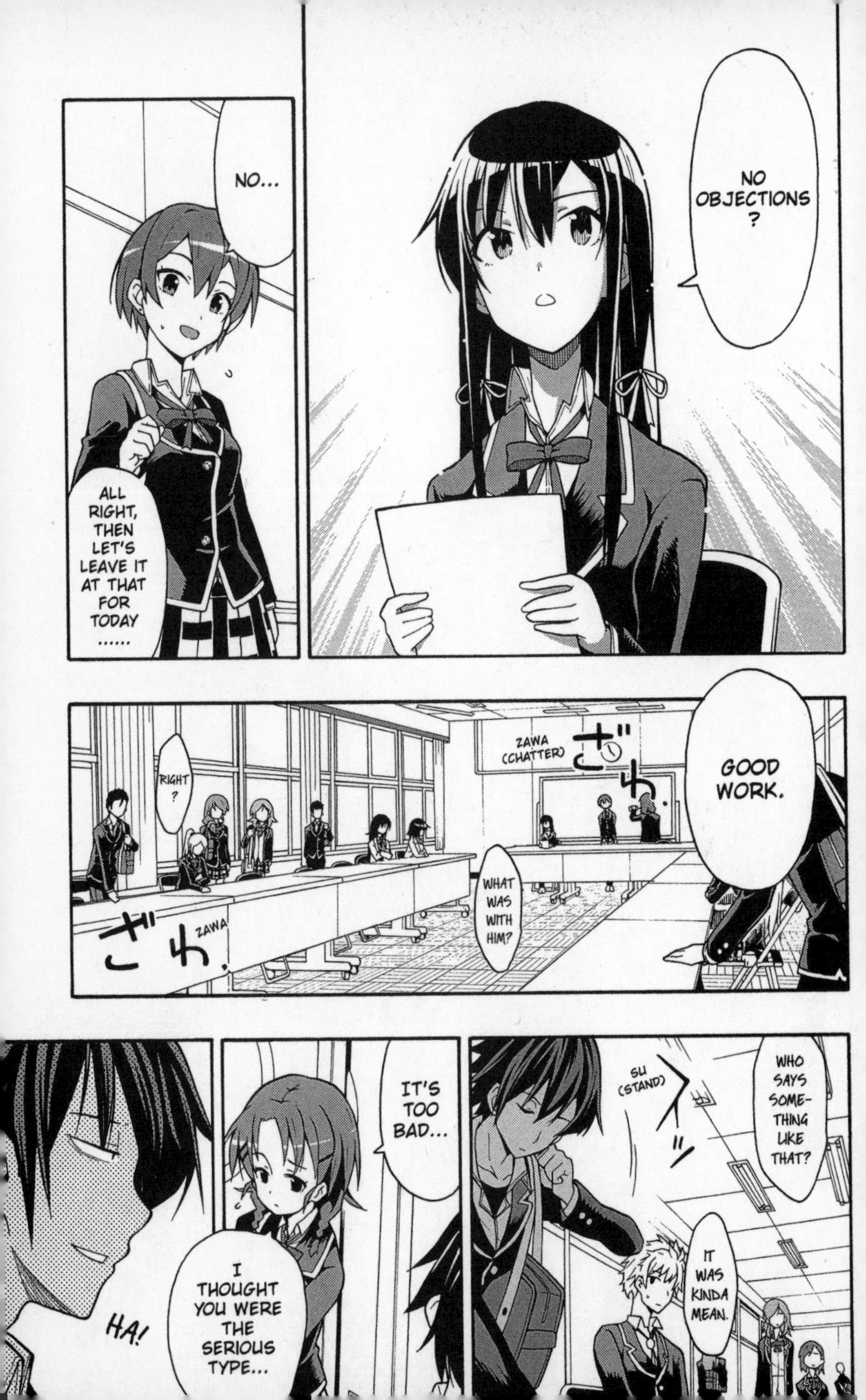
NO OBJECTIONS?
NO...
ALL RIGHT, THEN LET'S LEAVE IT AT THAT FOR TODAY ......
GOOD WORK.
ZAWA (CHATTER)
WHAT WAS WITH HIM?
RIGHT?
ZAWA
SU (STAND)
WHO SAYS SOME-THING LIKE THAT?
IT WAS KINDA MEAN.
IT'S TOO BAD...
I THOUGHT YOU WERE THE SERIOUS TYPE...
HA!

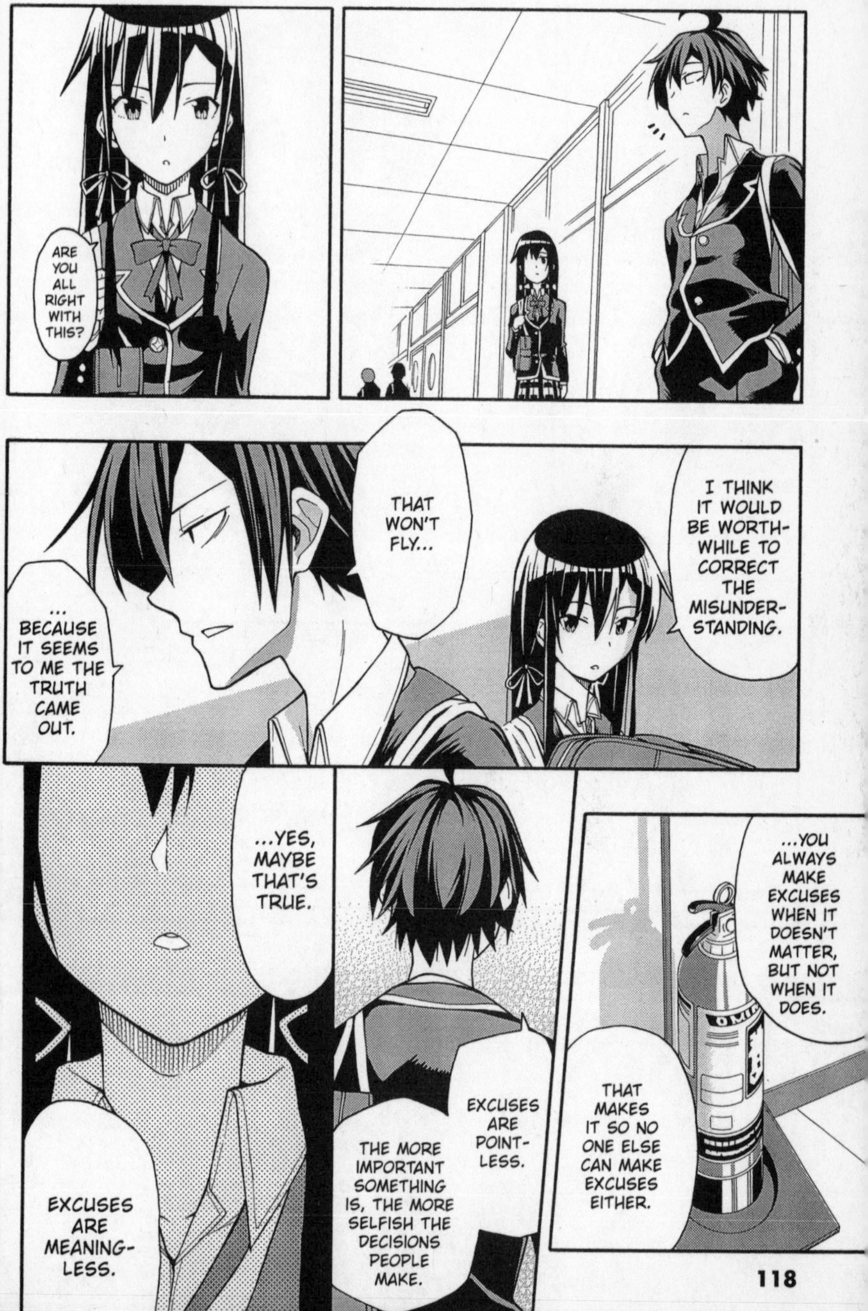
ARE YOU ALL RIGHT WITH THIS?
I THINK IT WOULD BE WORTH-WHILE TO CORRECT THE MISUNDER-STANDING.
THAT WON'T FLY...
...BECAUSE IT SEEMS TO ME THE TRUTH CAME OUT.
...YOU ALWAYS MAKE EXCUSES WHEN IT DOESN'T MATTER, BUT NOT WHEN IT DOES.
THAT MAKES IT SO NO ONE ELSE CAN MAKE EXCUSES EITHER.
EXCUSES ARE POINT-LESS.
THE MORE IMPORTANT SOMETHING IS, THE MORE SELFISH THE DECISIONS PEOPLE MAKE.
...YES, MAYBE THAT'S TRUE.
EXCUSES ARE MEANING-LESS.

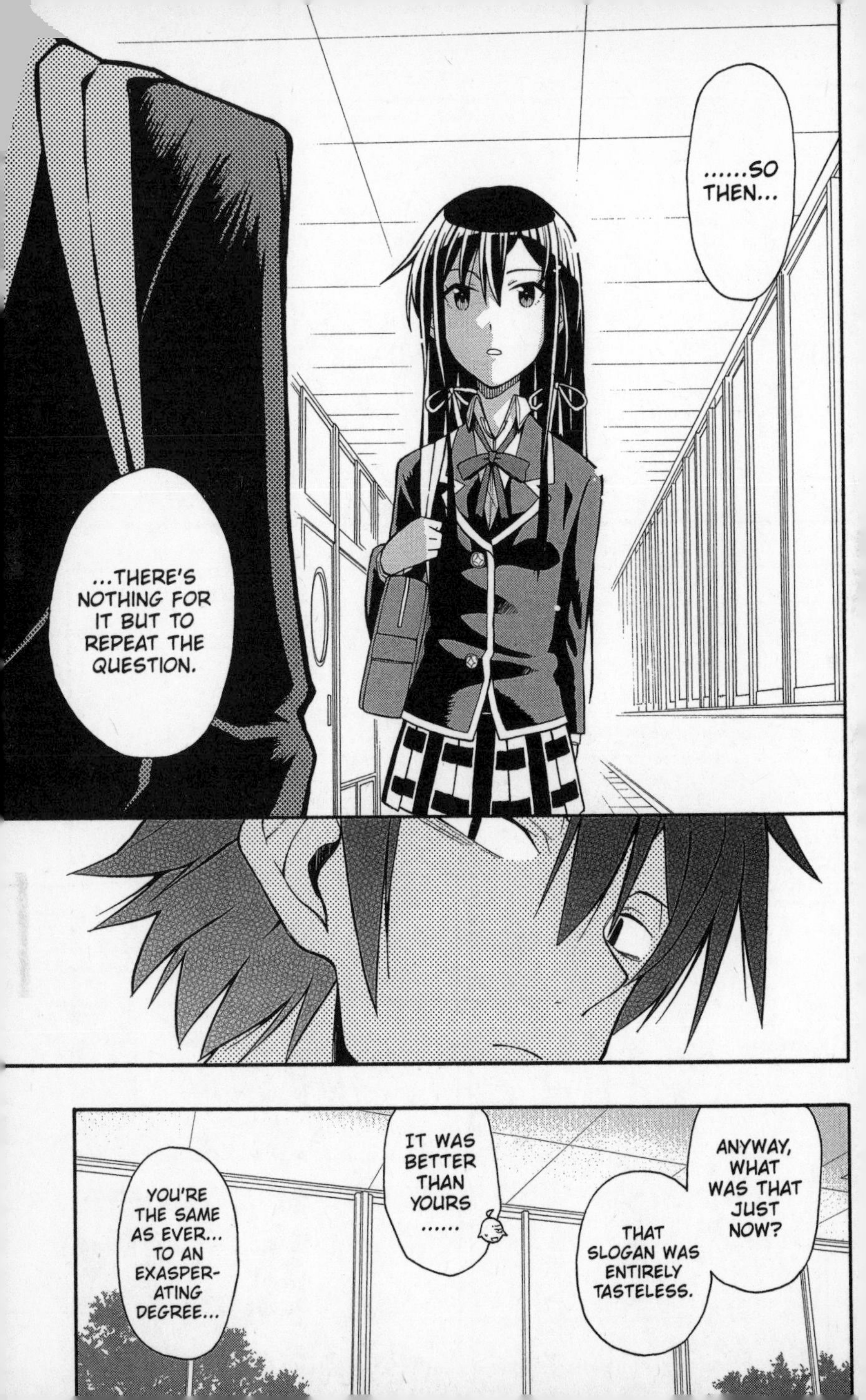
......SO THEN...
...THERE'S NOTHING FOR IT BUT TO REPEAT THE QUESTION.
ANYWAY, WHAT WAS THAT JUST NOW?
THAT SLOGAN WAS ENTIRELY TASTELESS.
IT WAS BETTER THAN YOURS ......
YOU'RE THE SAME AS EVER... TO AN EXASPER-ATING DEGREE...

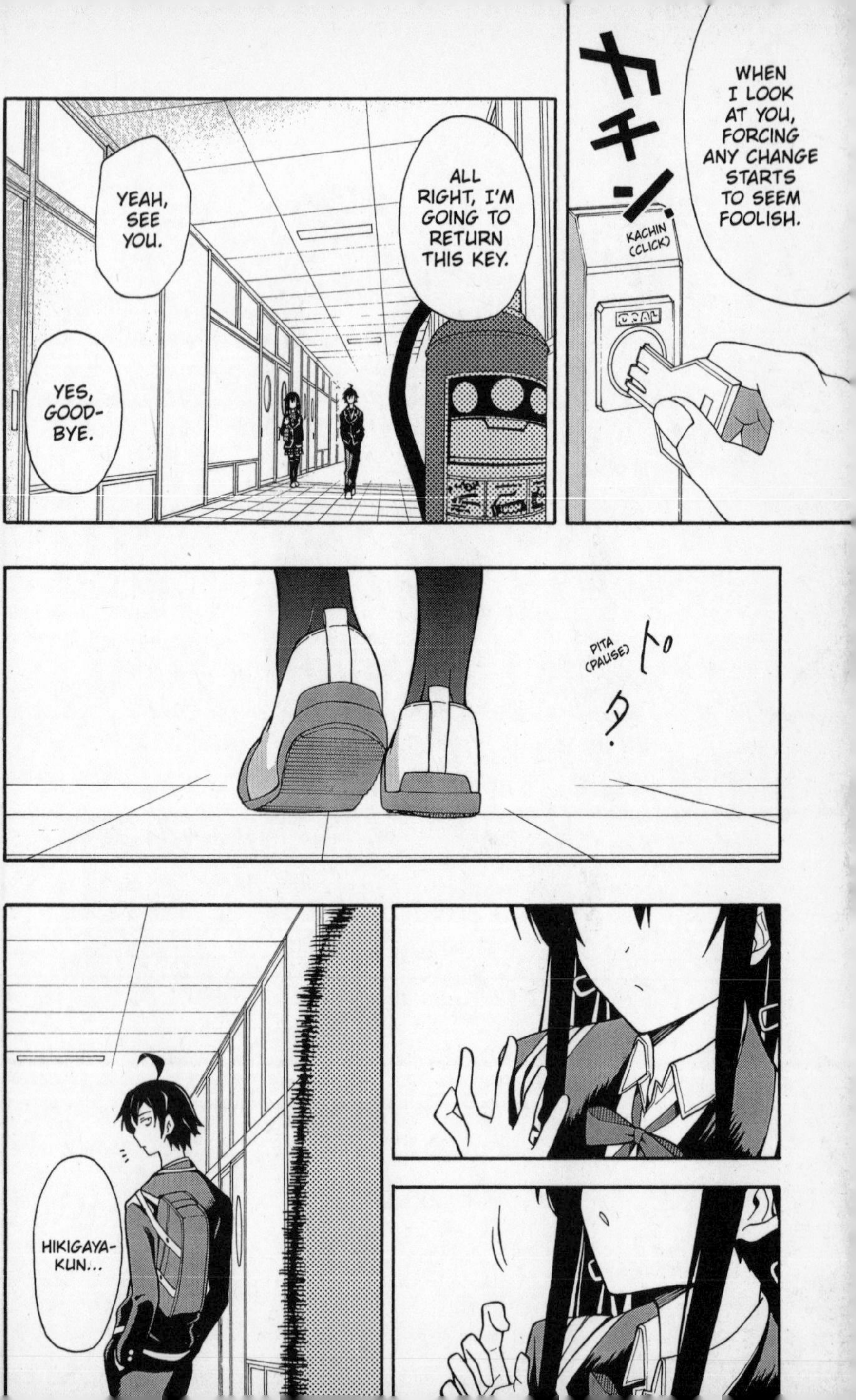
WHEN I LOOK AT YOU, FORCING ANY CHANGE STARTS TO SEEM FOOLISH.
KACHIN (CLICK)
ALL RIGHT, I'M GOING TO RETURN THIS KEY.
YEAH, SEE YOU.
YES, GOOD-BYE.
PITA (PAUSE)
HIKIGAYA-KUN...

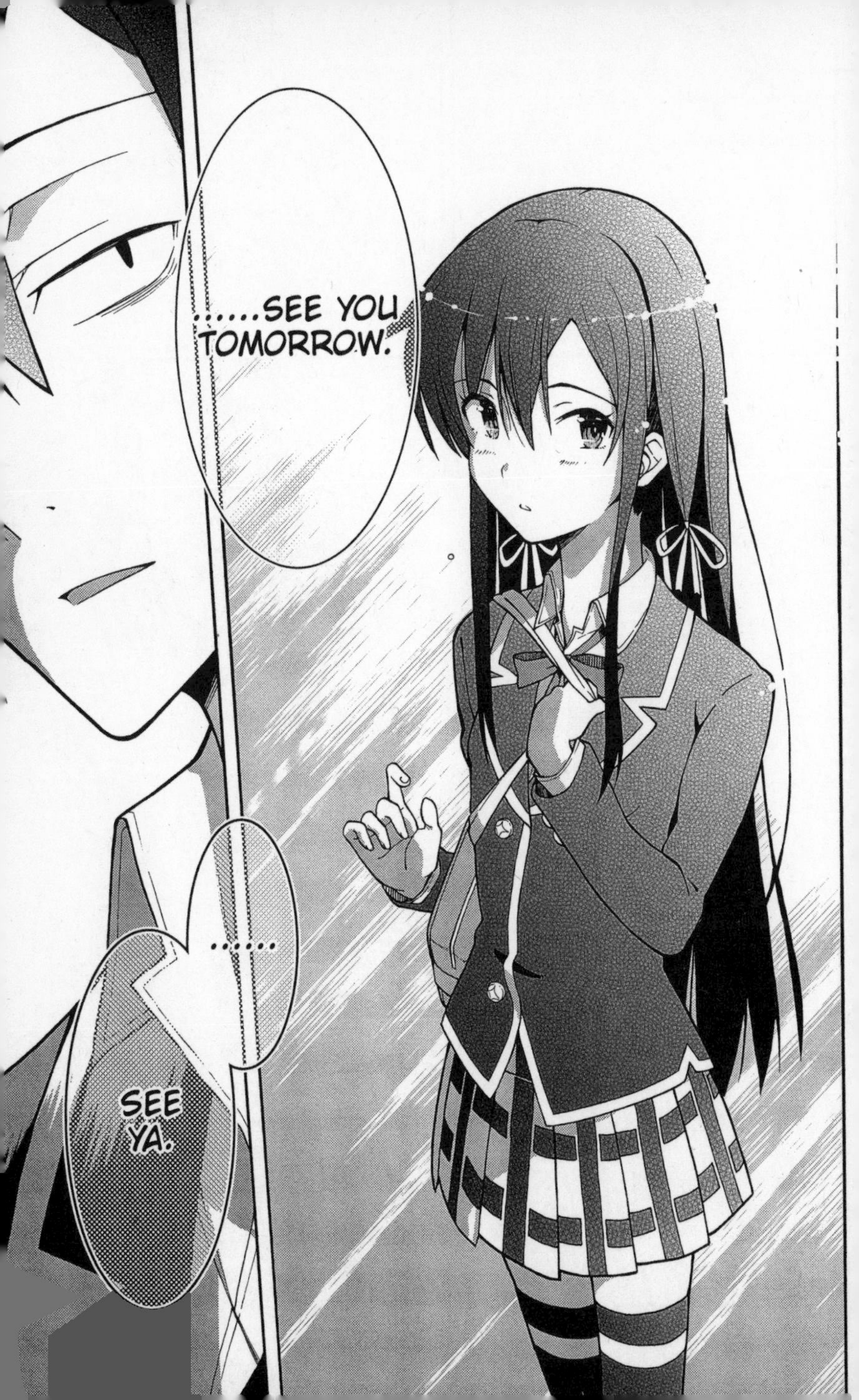
.....SEE YOU TOMORROW.
......
SEE YA.

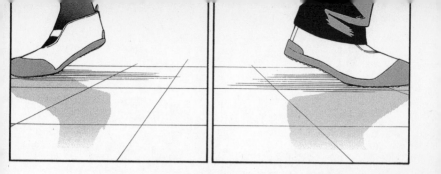

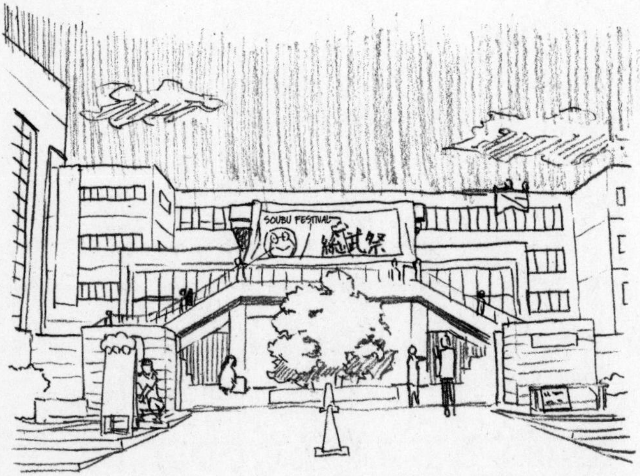
SOUBU FESTIVAL
総武祭

SOUBU FESTIVAL
総武祭

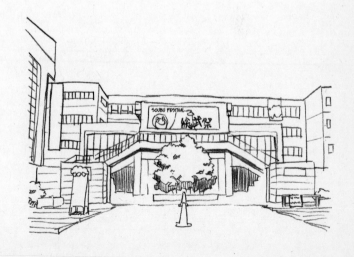

CHAPTER 40 … THIS IS THE MOMENT SOUBU HIGH SCHOOL IS FESTIVALING HARDEST.

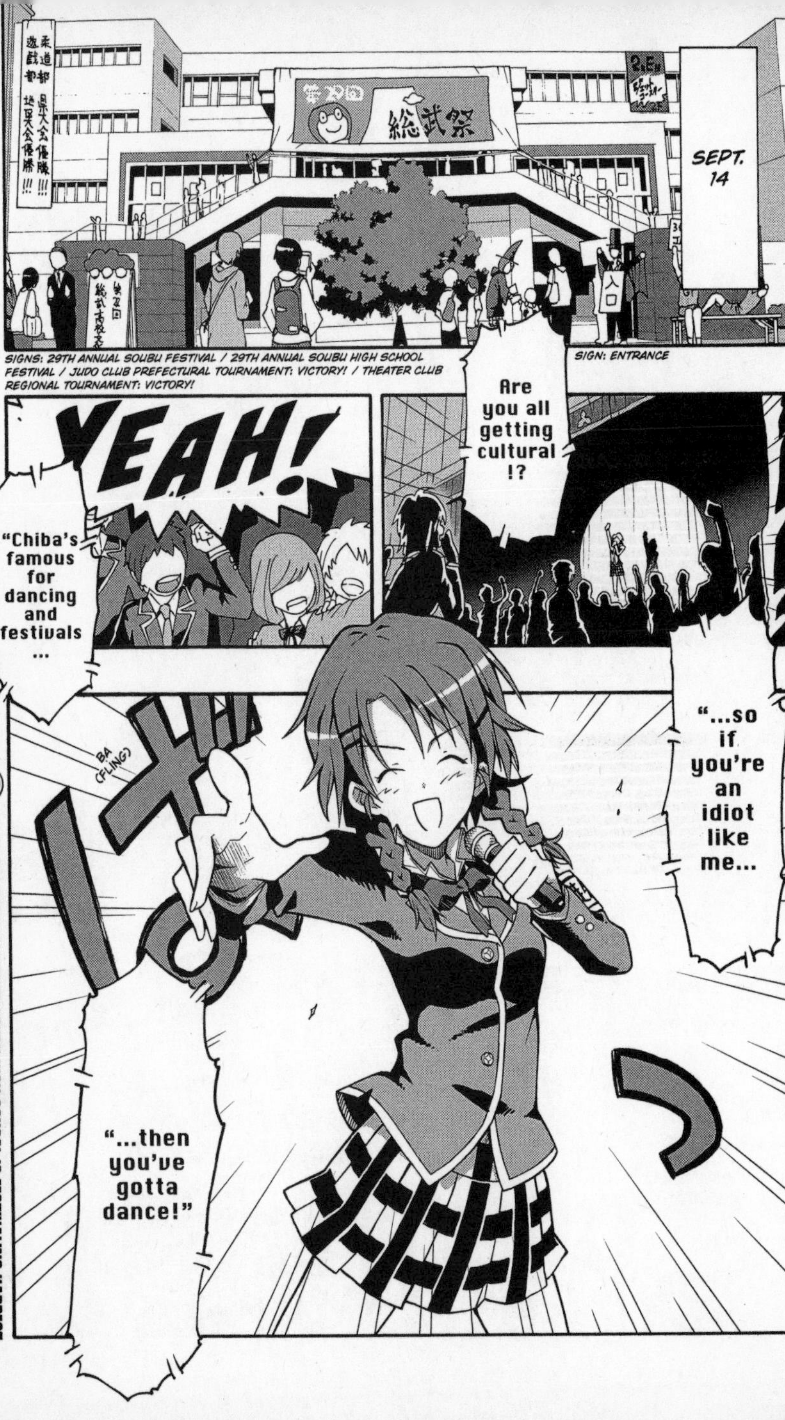

総武祭
SEPT. 14
SIGN: ENTRANCE
SIGNS: 29TH ANNUAL SOUBU FESTIVAL / 29TH ANNUAL SOUBU HIGH SCHOOL FESTIVAL / JUDO CLUB PREFECTURAL TOURNAMENT: VICTORY! / THEATER CLUB REGIONAL TOURNAMENT: VICTORY!
Are you all getting cultural !?
YEAH!
"Chiba's famous for dancing and festivals …
"…so if you're an idiot like me…
BA (FLING)
"…then you've gotta dance!"

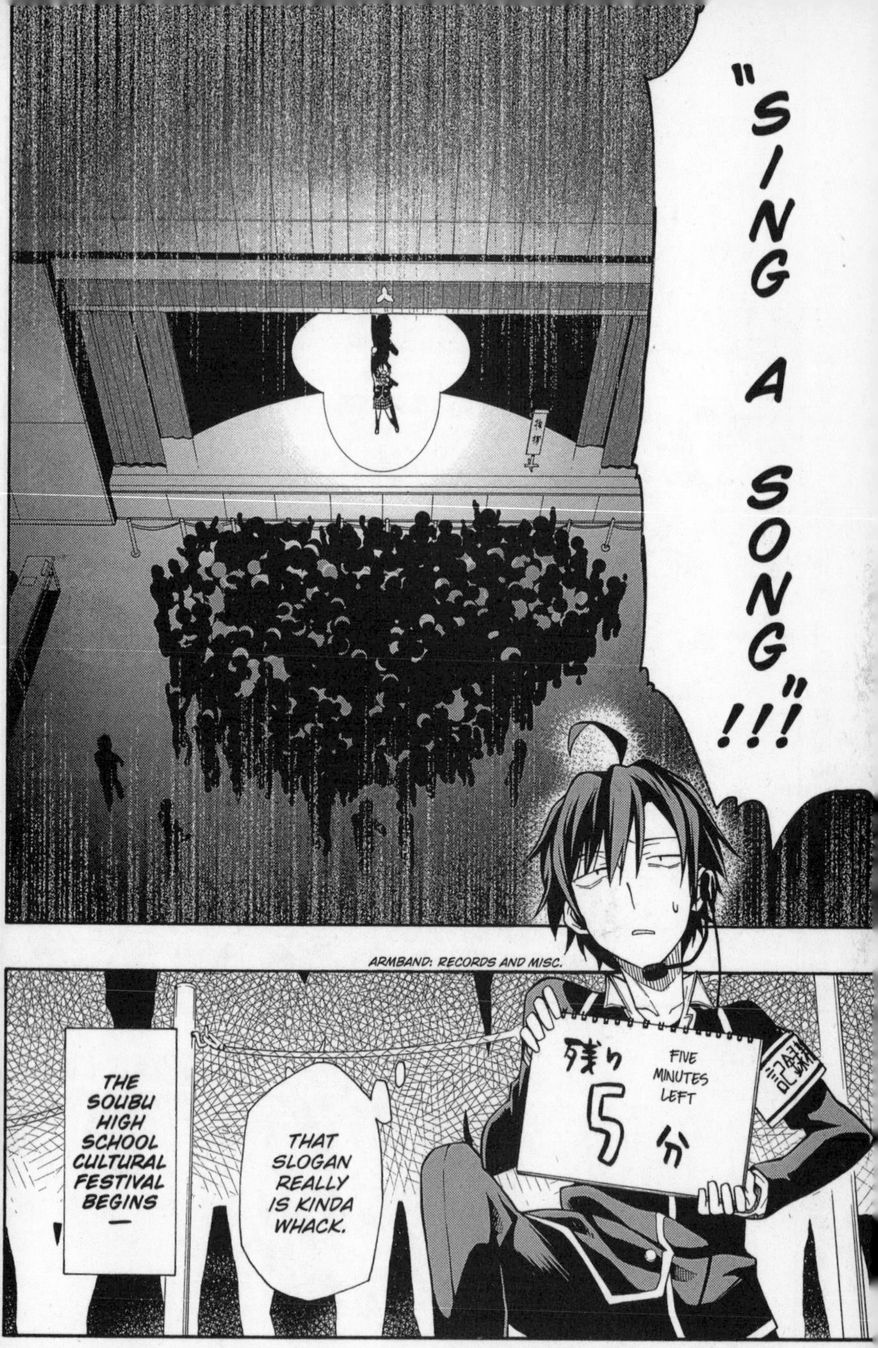
"SING A SONG"!!!
ARMBAND: RECORDS AND MISC.
残り 5 分
FIVE MINUTES LEFT
THAT SLOGAN REALLY IS KINDA WHACK.
THE SOUBU HIGH SCHOOL CULTURAL FESTIVAL BEGINS —

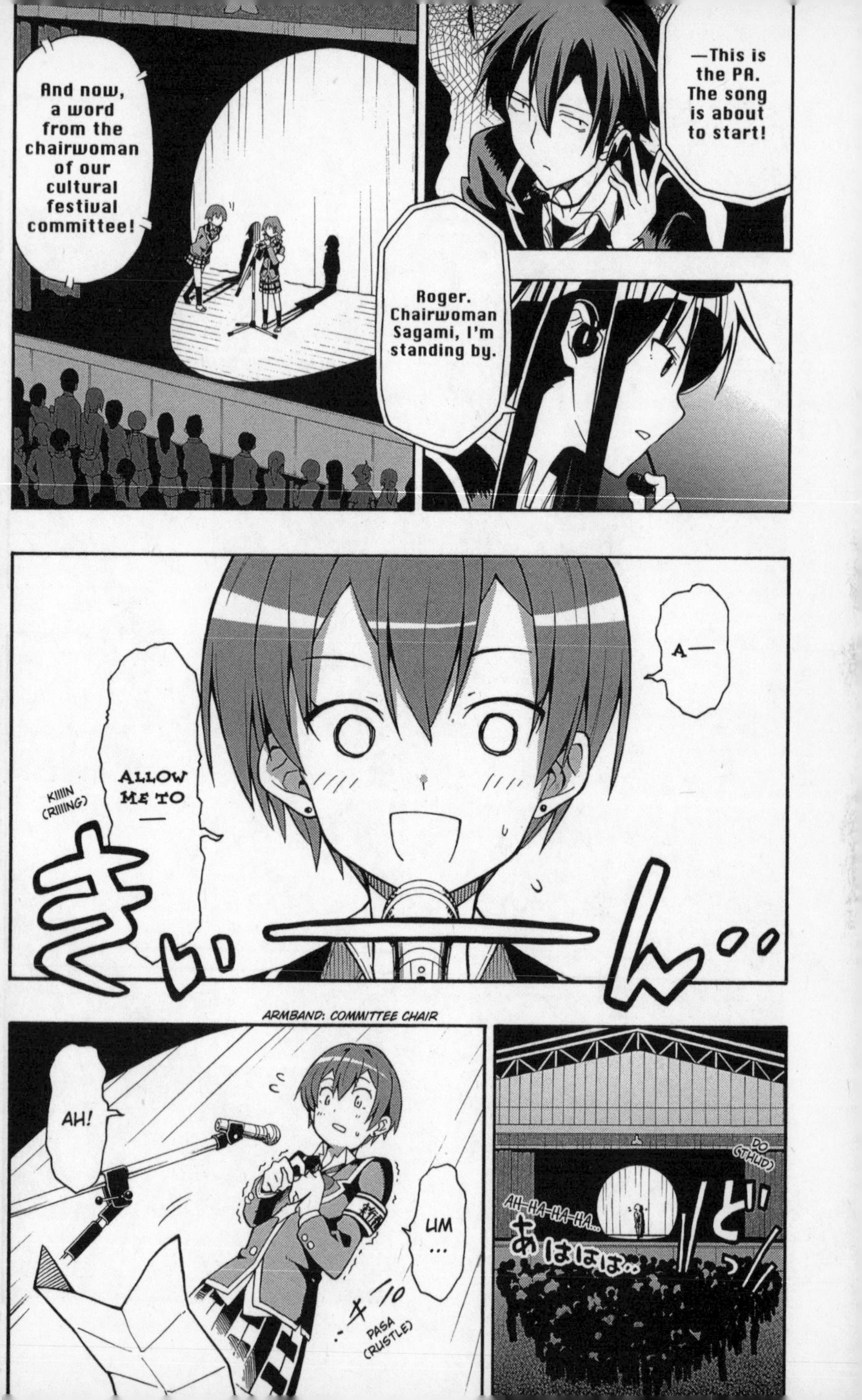
—This is the PA. The song is about to start!
Roger. Chairwoman Sagami, I'm standing by.
And now, a word from the chairwoman of our cultural festival committee!
A—
ALLOW ME TO —
KIIIIN (RIIIING)
きぃーーん
ARMBAND: COMMITTEE CHAIR
DO (THUD)
どっ
AH-HA-HA-HA...
あははは‥
AH!
UM ...
PASA (RUSTLE)

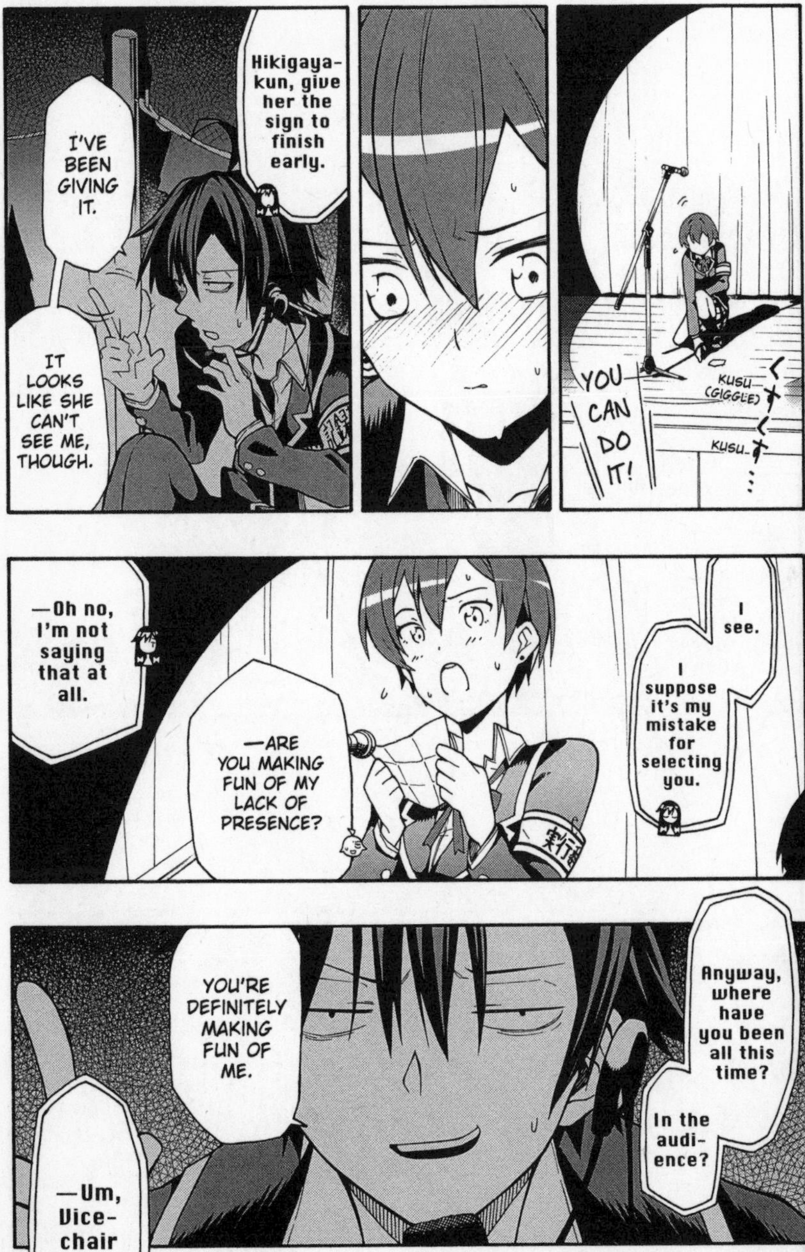

YOU CAN DO IT!
KUSU (GIGGLE)
KUSU...
Hikigaya-kun, give her the sign to finish early.
I'VE BEEN GIVING IT.
IT LOOKS LIKE SHE CAN'T SEE ME, THOUGH.
I see.
I suppose it's my mistake for selecting you.
—ARE YOU MAKING FUN OF MY LACK OF PRESENCE?
—Oh no, I'm not saying that at all.
Anyway, where have you been all this time?
In the audience?
YOU'RE DEFINITELY MAKING FUN OF ME.
—Um, Vice-chair ......

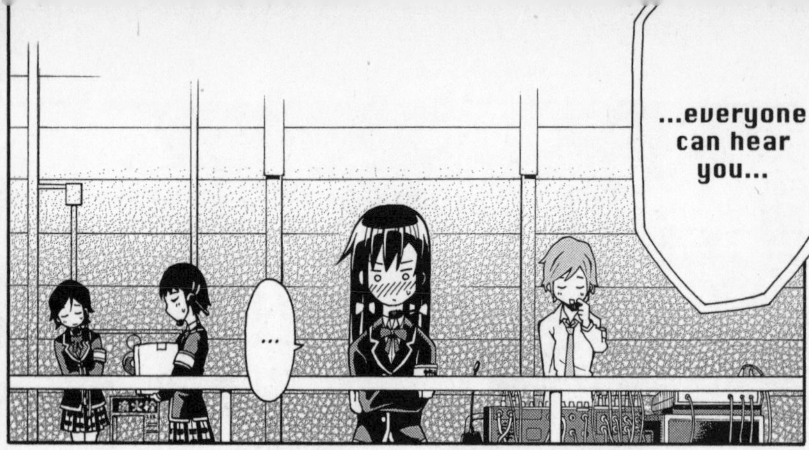
...everyone can hear you...
...

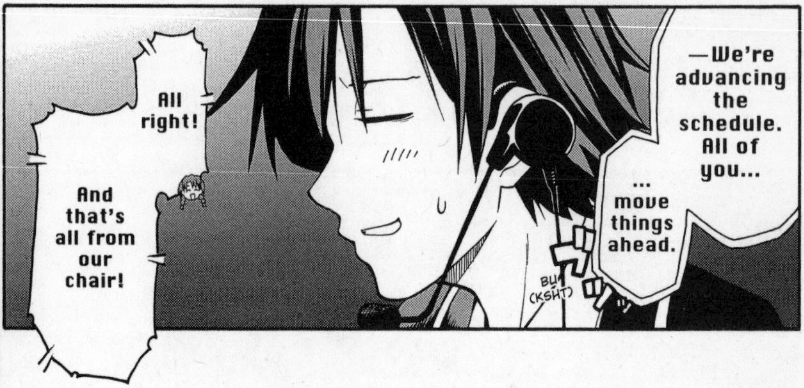
—We're advancing the schedule. All of you... ... move things ahead.
BU (KSHT)
All right! And that's all from our chair!

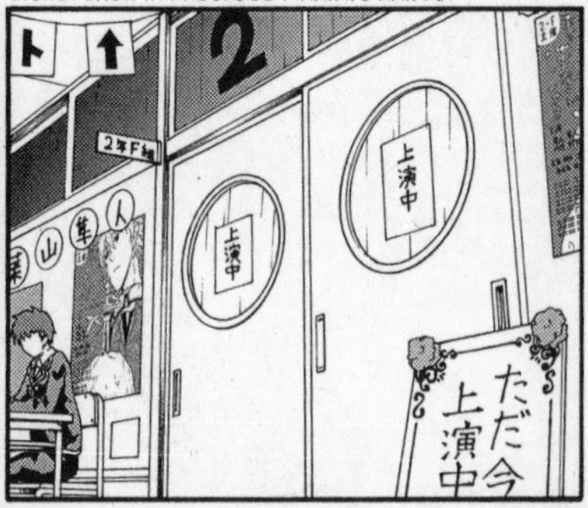
SIGNS: SHOW IN PROGRESS / HAYATO HAYAMA
2
上演中
上演中
ただ今上演中

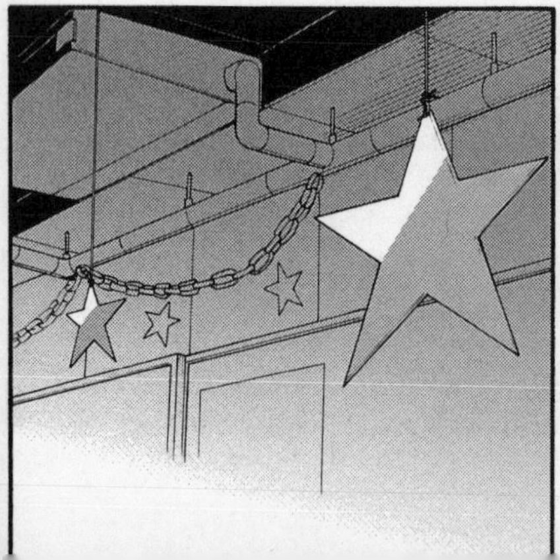

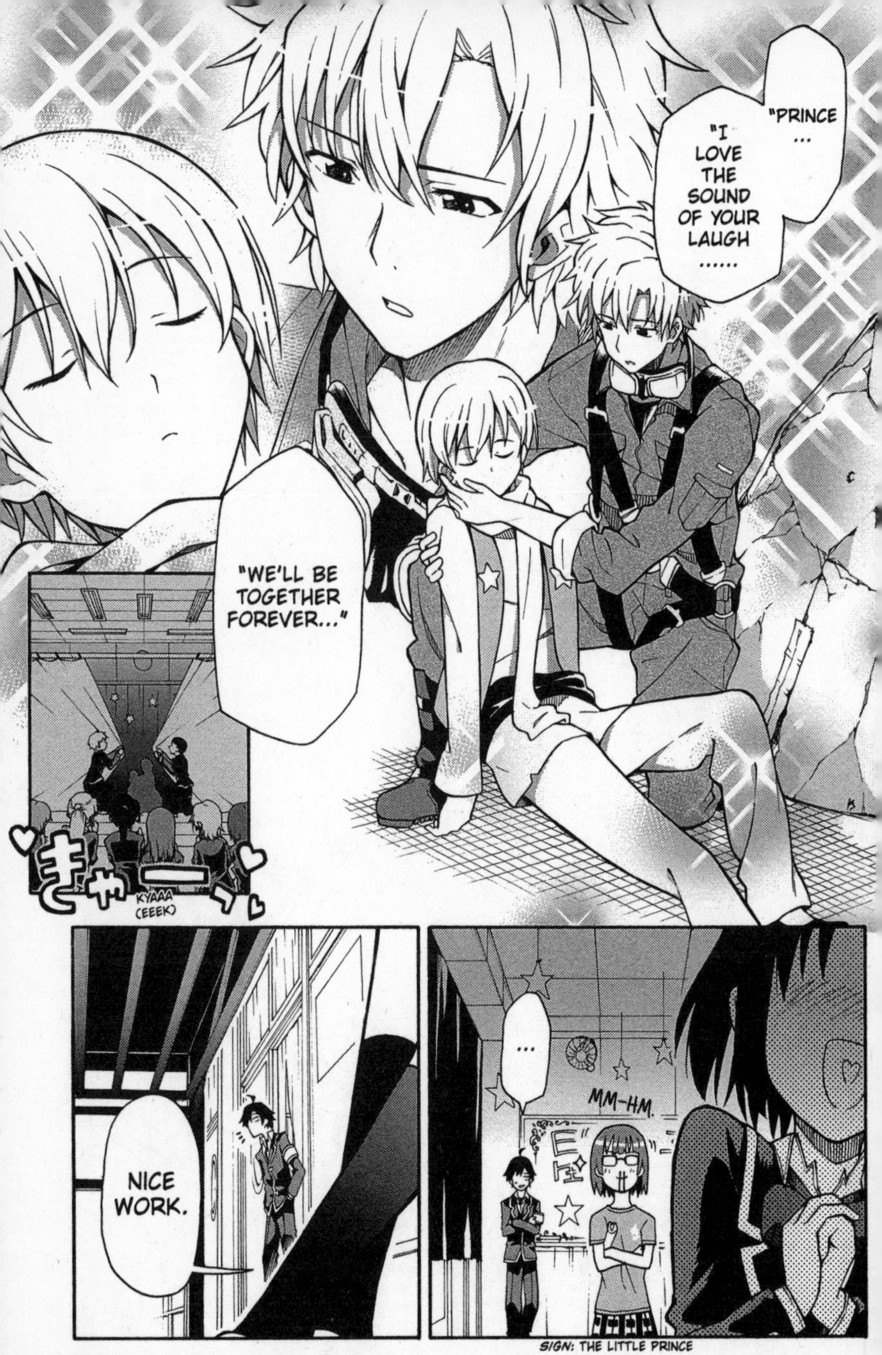

"PRINCE...
"I LOVE THE SOUND OF YOUR LAUGH......
"WE'LL BE TOGETHER FOREVER..."
きゃーっ
KYAAA (EEEK)
...
MM-HM.
NICE WORK.

SIGN: THE LITTLE PRINCE

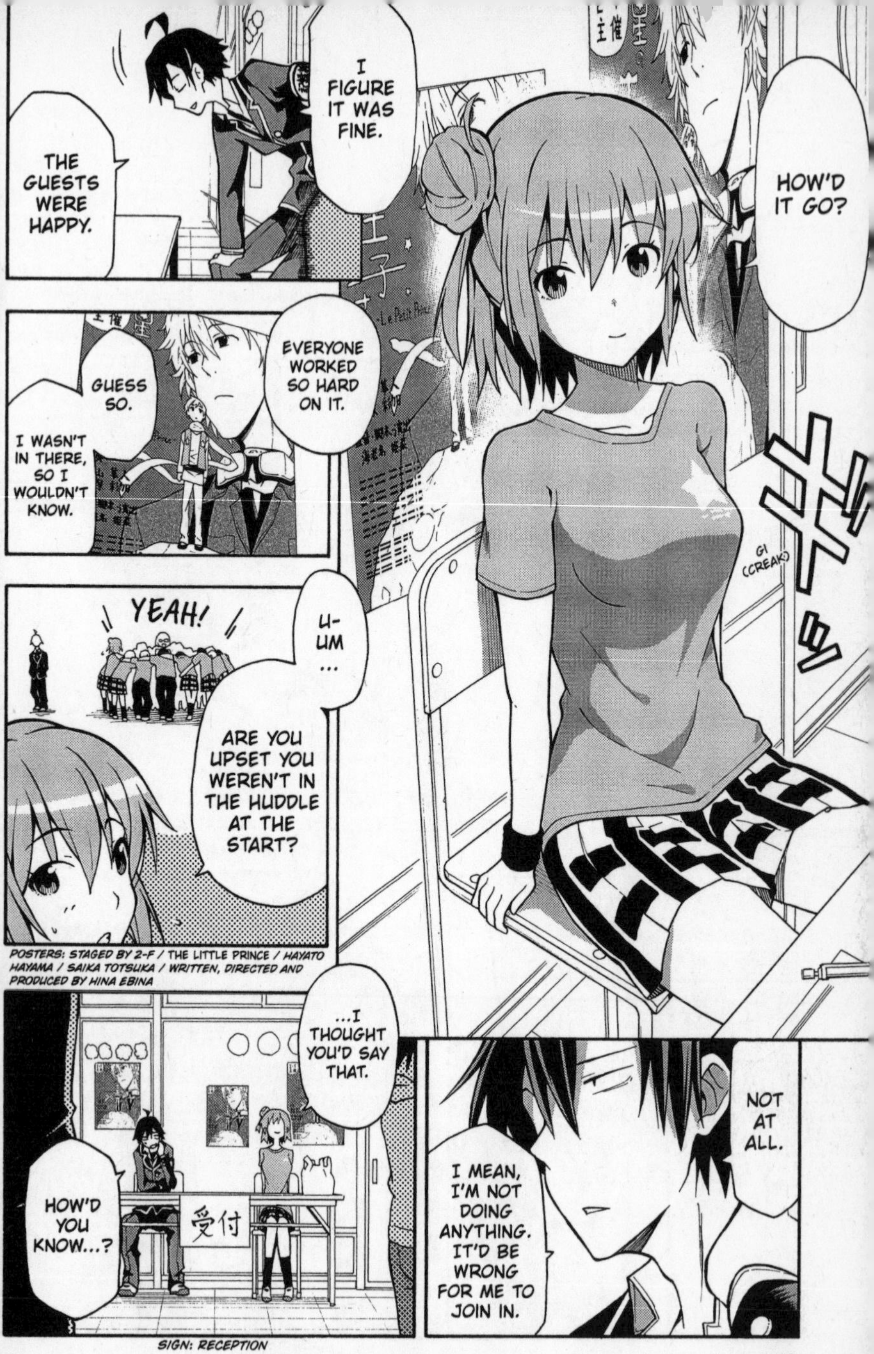
HOW'D IT GO?
GI (CREAK)
I FIGURE IT WAS FINE.
THE GUESTS WERE HAPPY.
EVERYONE WORKED SO HARD ON IT.
GUESS SO.
I WASN'T IN THERE, SO I WOULDN'T KNOW.
U-UM...
YEAH!
ARE YOU UPSET YOU WEREN'T IN THE HUDDLE AT THE START?
NOT AT ALL.
I MEAN, I'M NOT DOING ANYTHING. IT'D BE WRONG FOR ME TO JOIN IN.
...I THOUGHT YOU'D SAY THAT.
HOW'D YOU KNOW...?
受付
POSTERS: STAGED BY 2-F / THE LITTLE PRINCE / HAYATO HAYAMA / SAIKA TOTSUKA / WRITTEN, DIRECTED AND PRODUCED BY HINA EBINA

SIGN: RECEPTION

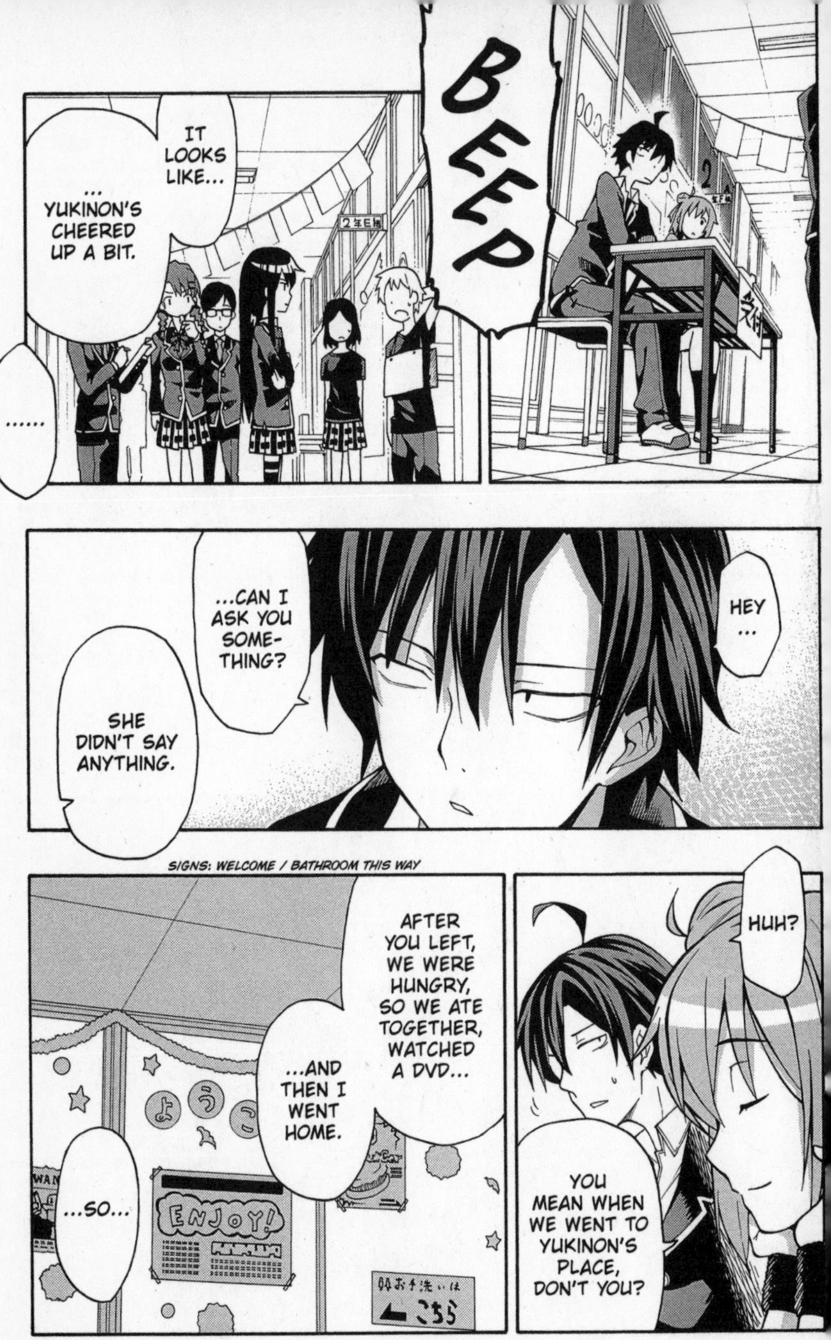
BEEP
IT LOOKS LIKE...
...YUKINON'S CHEERED UP A BIT.
......
HEY...
...CAN I ASK YOU SOMETHING?
SHE DIDN'T SAY ANYTHING.
SIGNS: WELCOME / BATHROOM THIS WAY
HUH?
YOU MEAN WHEN WE WENT TO YUKINON'S PLACE, DON'T YOU?
AFTER YOU LEFT, WE WERE HUNGRY, SO WE ATE TOGETHER, WATCHED A DVD...
...AND THEN I WENT HOME.
...SO...
ENJOY!
こちら

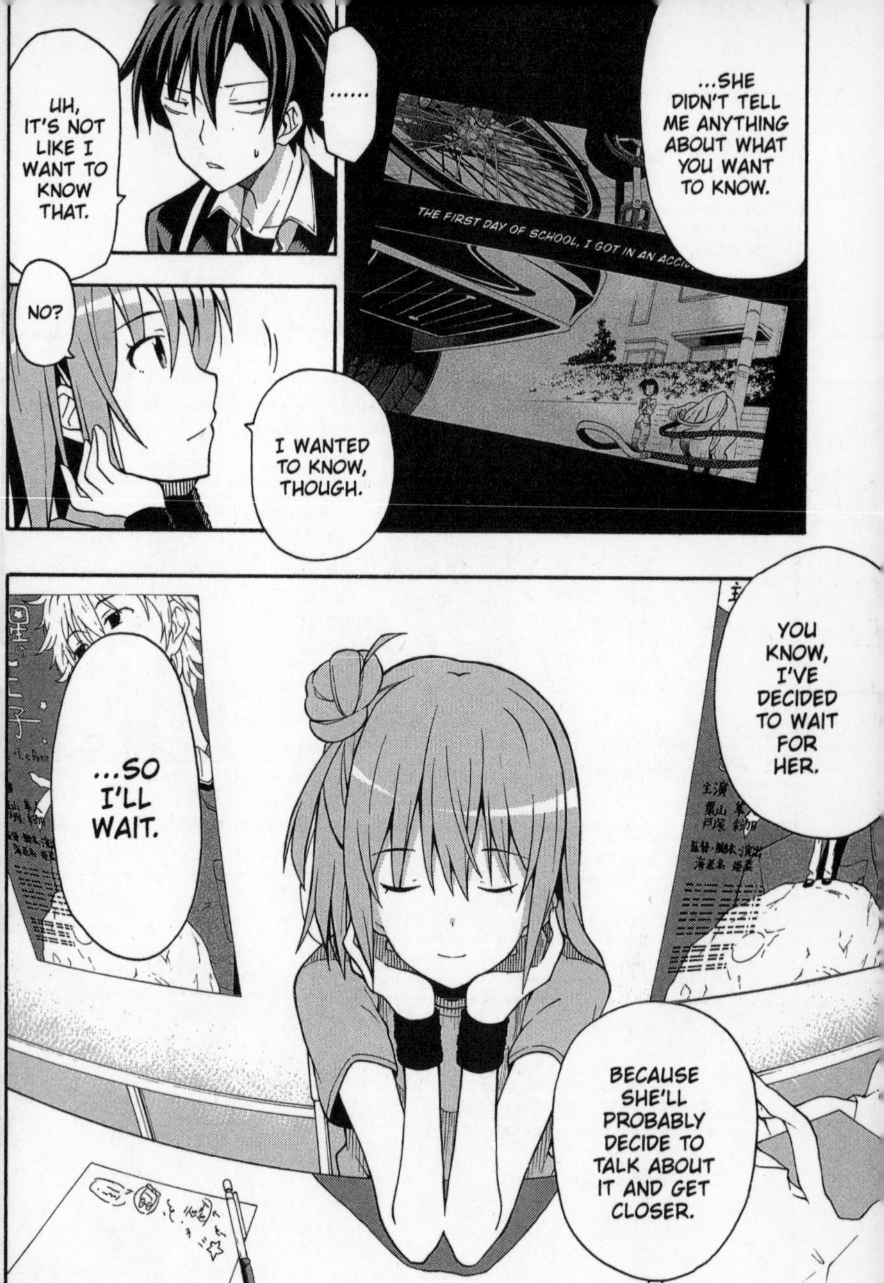
...SHE DIDN'T TELL ME ANYTHING ABOUT WHAT YOU WANT TO KNOW.
THE FIRST DAY OF SCHOOL, I GOT IN AN ACCI
......
UH, IT'S NOT LIKE I WANT TO KNOW THAT.
NO?
I WANTED TO KNOW, THOUGH.
YOU KNOW, I'VE DECIDED TO WAIT FOR HER.
BECAUSE SHE'LL PROBABLY DECIDE TO TALK ABOUT IT AND GET CLOSER.
...SO I'LL WAIT.

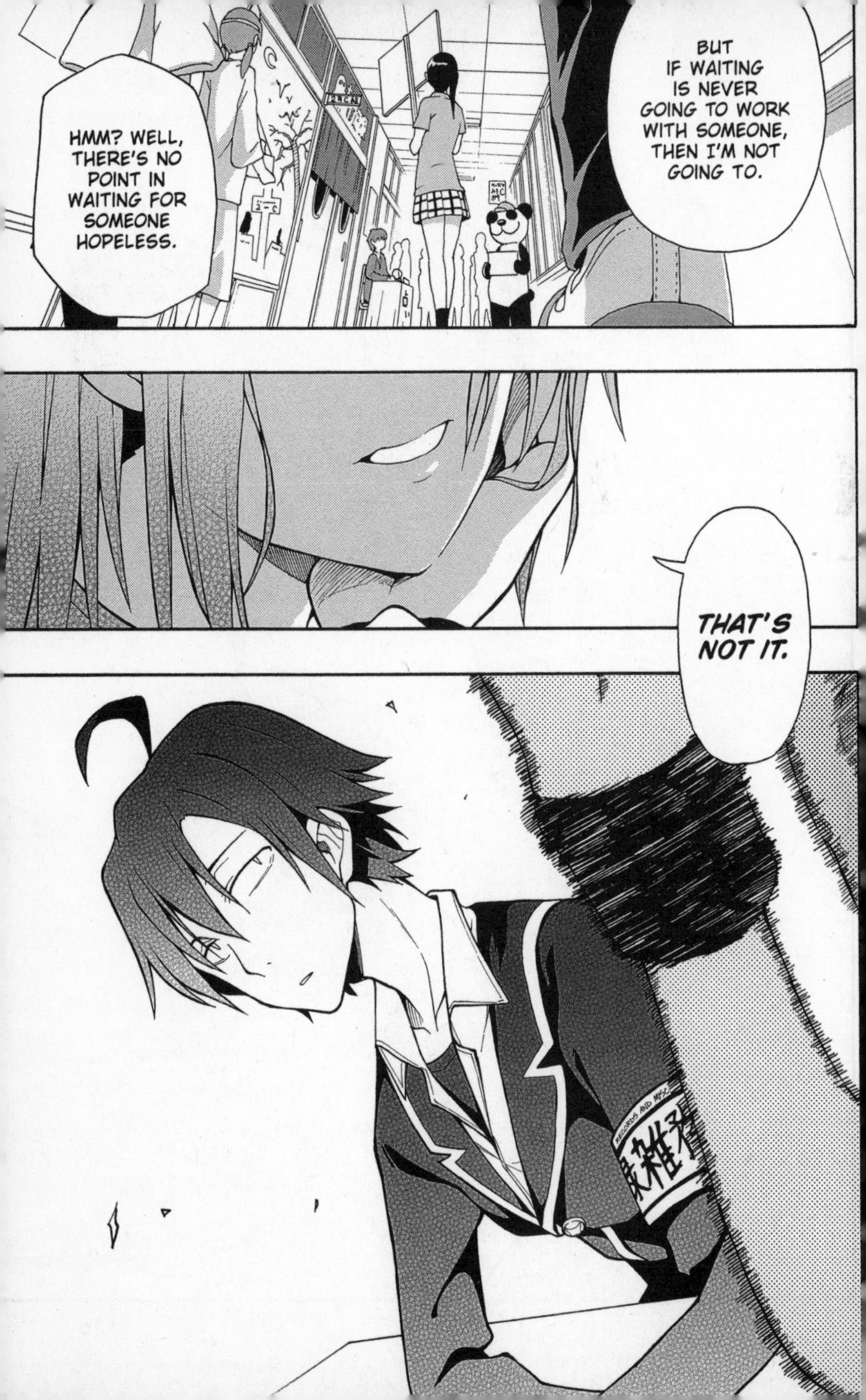
BUT IF WAITING IS NEVER GOING TO WORK WITH SOMEONE, THEN I'M NOT GOING TO.
HMM? WELL, THERE'S NO POINT IN WAITING FOR SOMEONE HOPELESS.
THAT'S NOT IT.
RECORDS AND MISC.

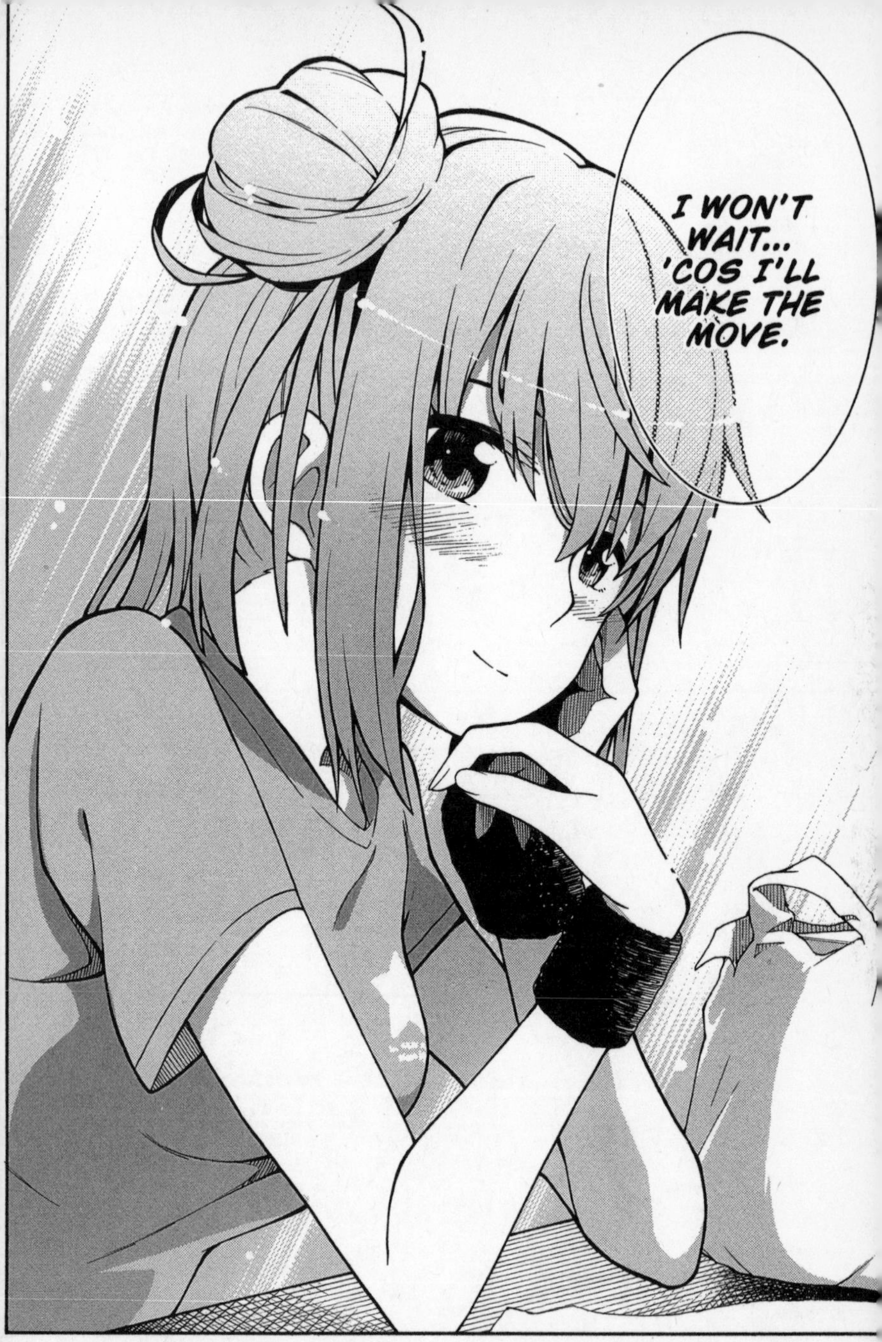
I WON'T WAIT... 'COS I'LL MAKE THE MOVE.

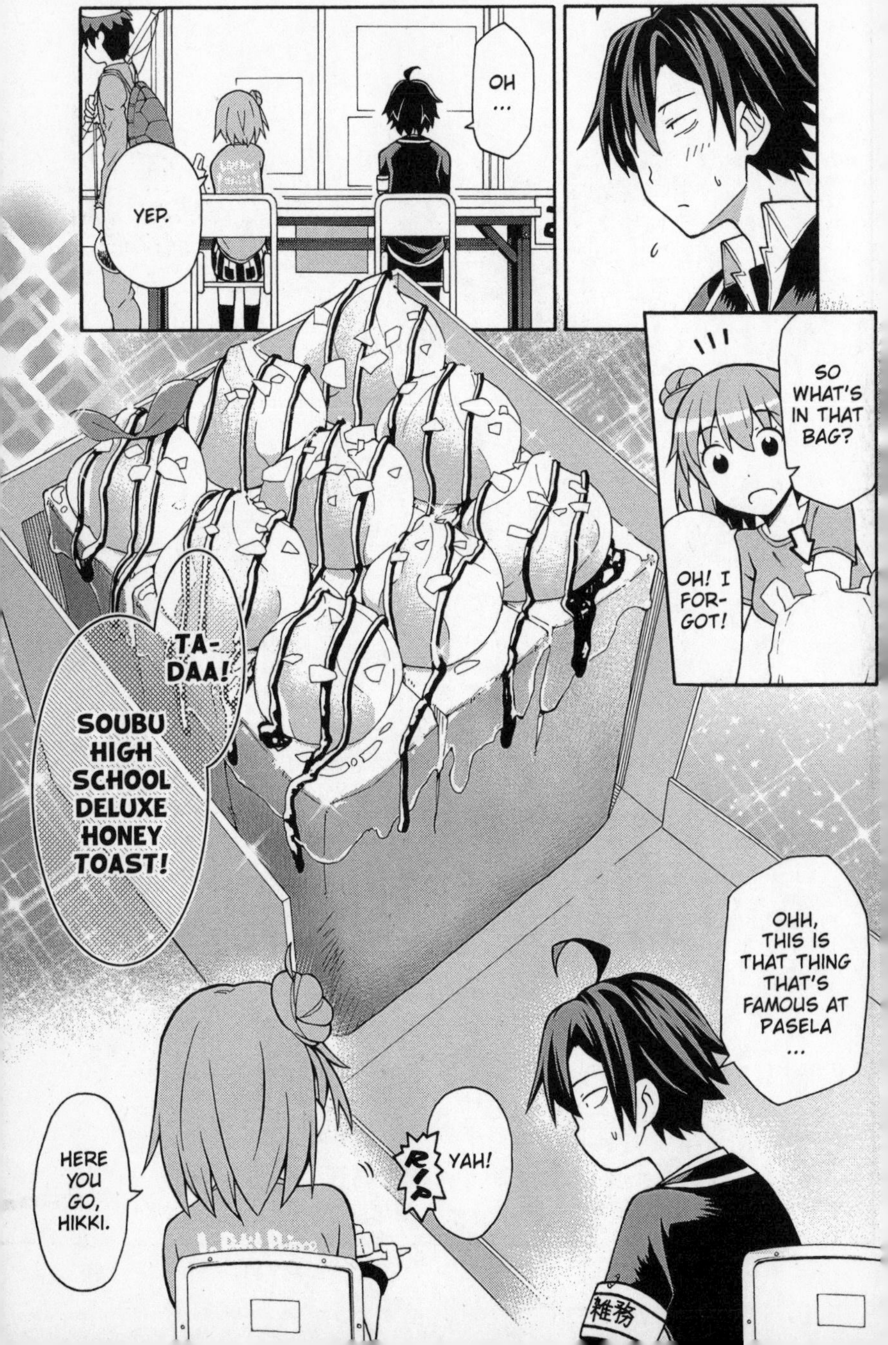
OH ...
YEP.
SO WHAT'S IN THAT BAG?
OH! I FOR-GOT!
YAH!
RIP
TA-DAA!
SOUBU HIGH SCHOOL DELUXE HONEY TOAST!
OHH, THIS IS THAT THING THAT'S FAMOUS AT PASELA ...
HERE YOU GO, HIKKI.
雑務

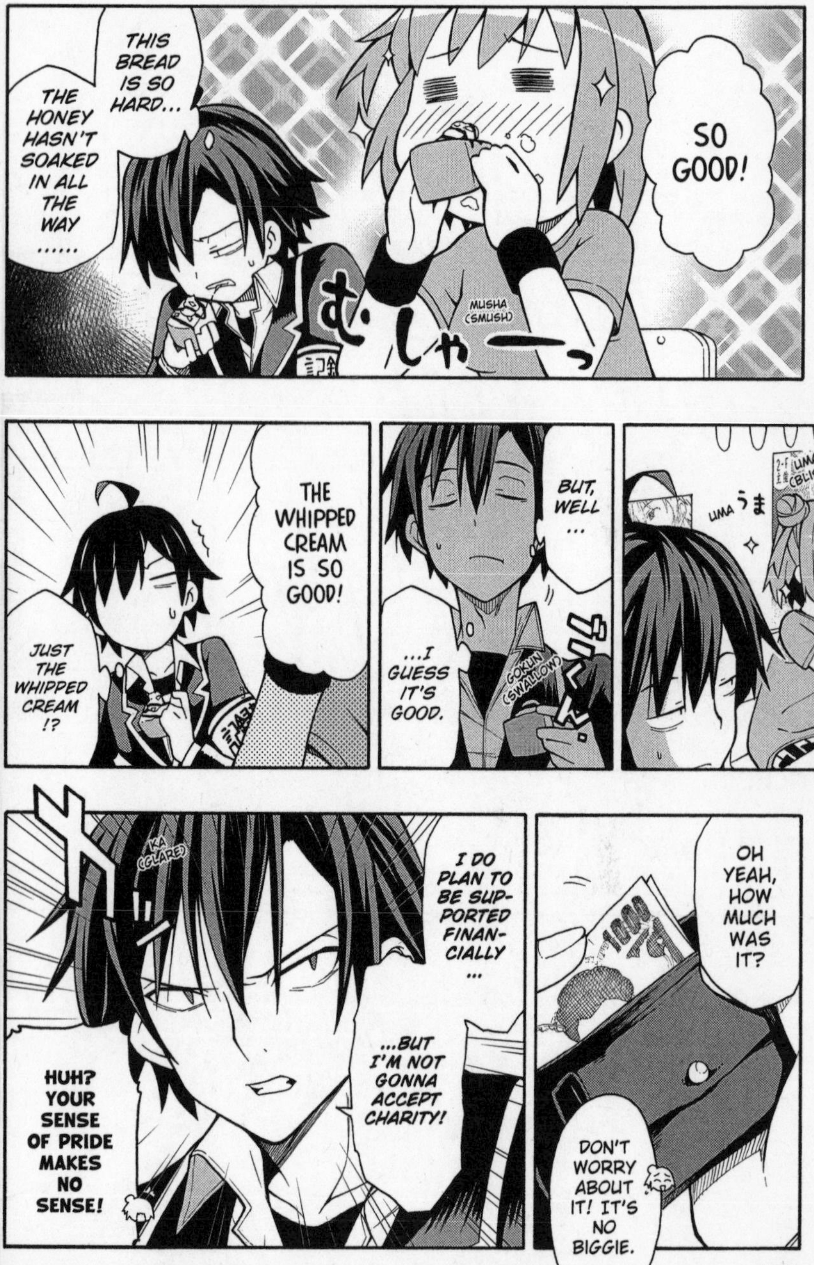
SO GOOD!
むしゃーーっ
MUSHA (SMUSH)
THIS BREAD IS SO HARD...
THE HONEY HASN'T SOAKED IN ALL THE WAY......
うま UMA (BLISS)
UMA うま
BUT, WELL...
ごくん。
GOKUN (SWALLOW)
...I GUESS IT'S GOOD.
THE WHIPPED CREAM IS SO GOOD!
JUST THE WHIPPED CREAM!?
OH YEAH, HOW MUCH WAS IT?
DON'T WORRY ABOUT IT! IT'S NO BIGGIE.
KA (GLARE)
I DO PLAN TO BE SUPPORTED FINANCIALLY...
...BUT I'M NOT GONNA ACCEPT CHARITY!
HUH? YOUR SENSE OF PRIDE MAKES NO SENSE!

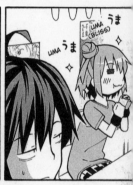

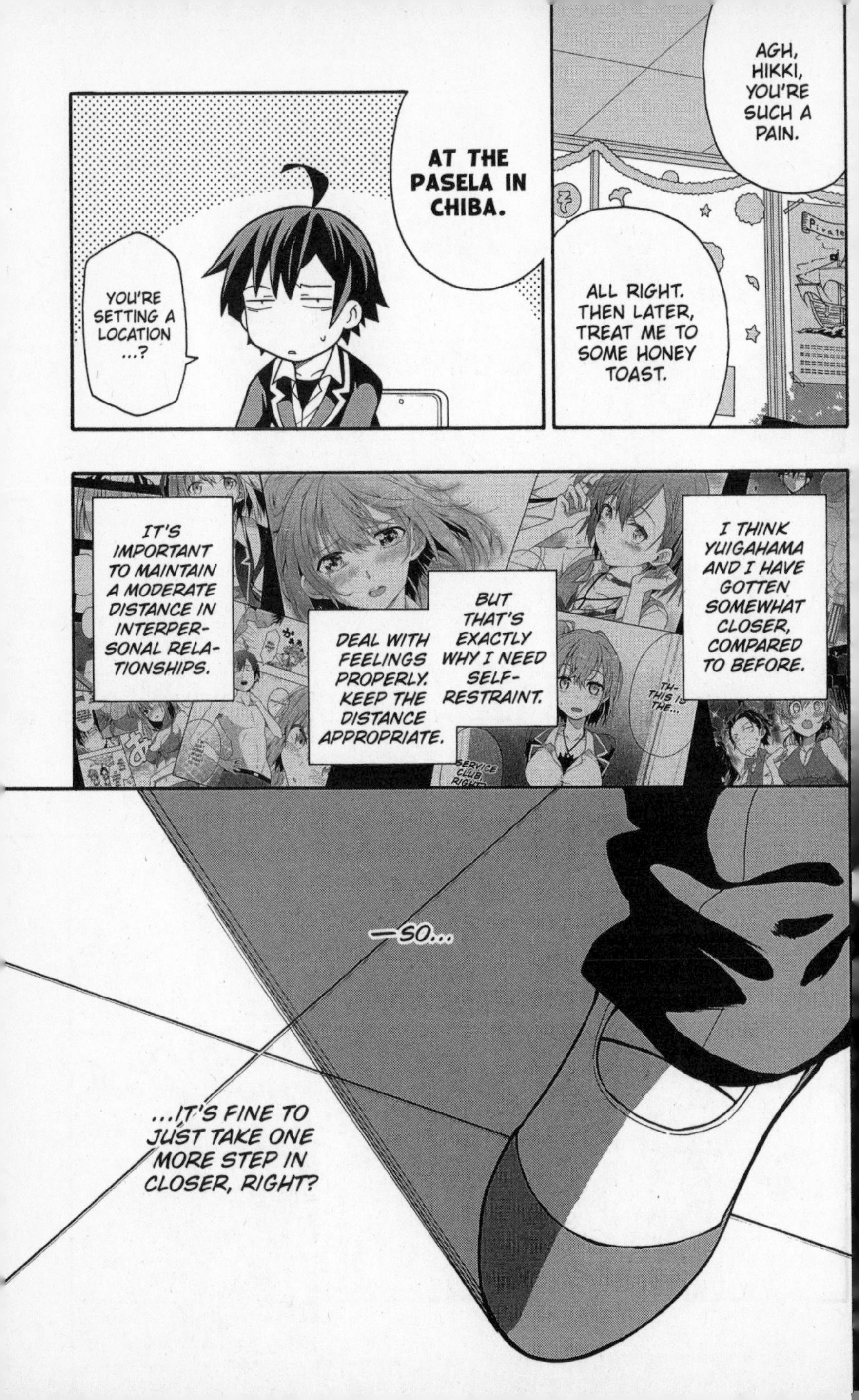
AGH, HIKKI, YOU'RE SUCH A PAIN.
ALL RIGHT. THEN LATER, TREAT ME TO SOME HONEY TOAST.
AT THE PASELA IN CHIBA.
YOU'RE SETTING A LOCATION ...?
I THINK YUIGAHAMA AND I HAVE GOTTEN SOMEWHAT CLOSER, COMPARED TO BEFORE.
TH- THIS IS THE...
BUT THAT'S EXACTLY WHY I NEED SELF-RESTRAINT.
DEAL WITH FEELINGS PROPERLY. KEEP THE DISTANCE APPROPRIATE.
IT'S IMPORTANT TO MAINTAIN A MODERATE DISTANCE IN INTERPERSONAL RELATIONSHIPS.
—SO...
...IT'S FINE TO JUST TAKE ONE MORE STEP IN CLOSER, RIGHT?

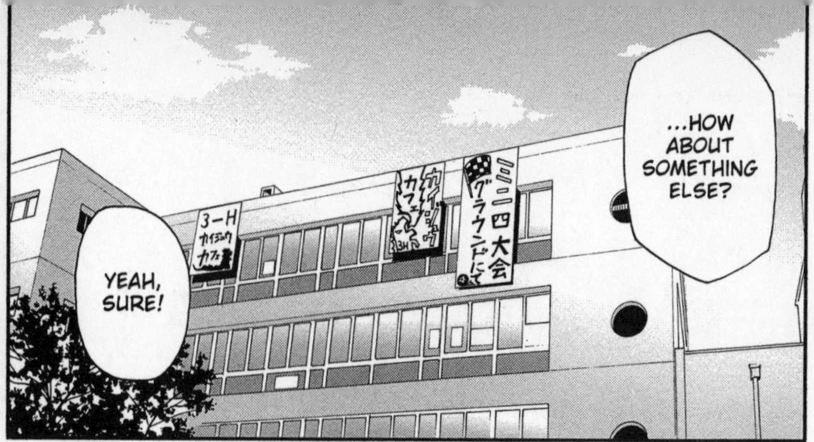
...HOW ABOUT SOMETHING ELSE?
YEAH, SURE!
SIGNS: MINI 4WD TOURNAMENT ON THE BASEBALL DIAMOND / KAIJUU CAFÉ / 3-H KAIJUU CAFÉ

SIGNS: SPECIALLY MADE BY THE TENNIS CLUB / FRANKFURTERS / TOTSUKA-YA / TWO HUNDRED YEN

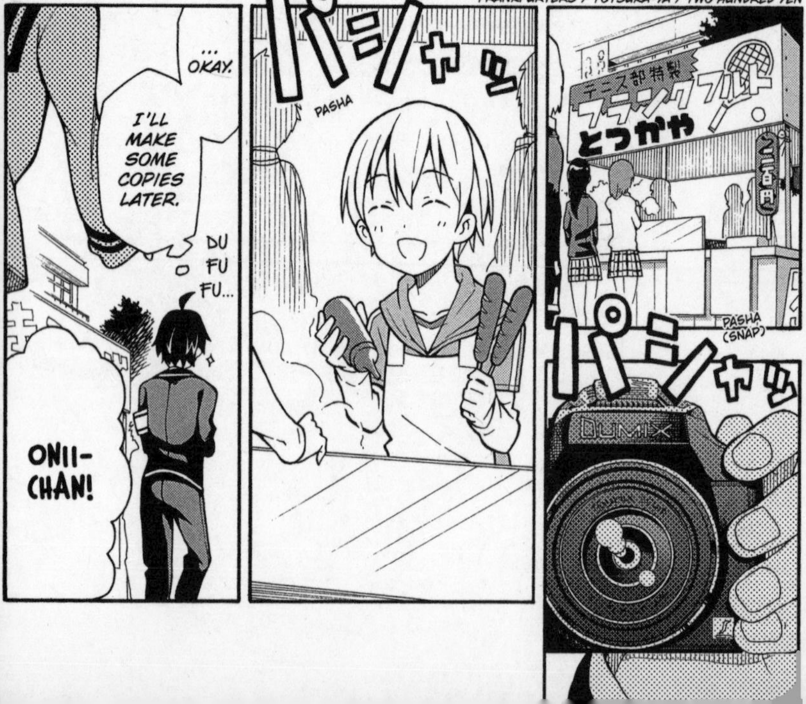
PASHA (SNAP)
パシャッ
パシャッ
PASHA
...OKAY.
I'LL MAKE SOME COPIES LATER.
DU FU FU...
ONII-CHAN!

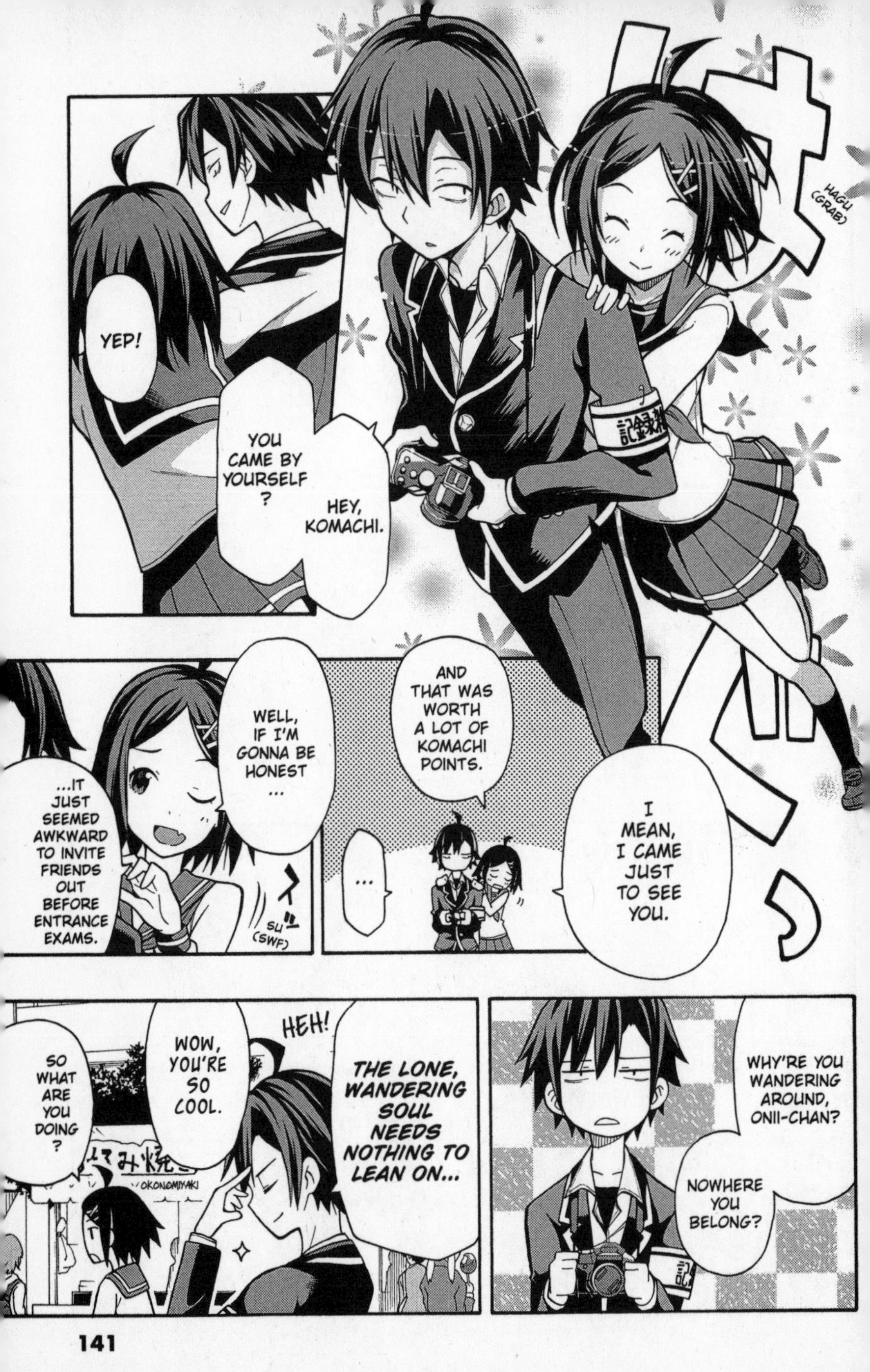
HAGU (GRAB)
HEY, KOMACHI.
YOU CAME BY YOURSELF?
YEP!
I MEAN, I CAME JUST TO SEE YOU.
AND THAT WAS WORTH A LOT OF KOMACHI POINTS.
...
WELL, IF I'M GONNA BE HONEST...
...IT JUST SEEMED AWKWARD TO INVITE FRIENDS OUT BEFORE ENTRANCE EXAMS.
SU (SWF)
WHY'RE YOU WANDERING AROUND, ONII-CHAN?
NOWHERE YOU BELONG?
THE LONE, WANDERING SOUL NEEDS NOTHING TO LEAN ON...
HEH!
WOW, YOU'RE SO COOL.
SO WHAT ARE YOU DOING?
OKONOMIYAKI

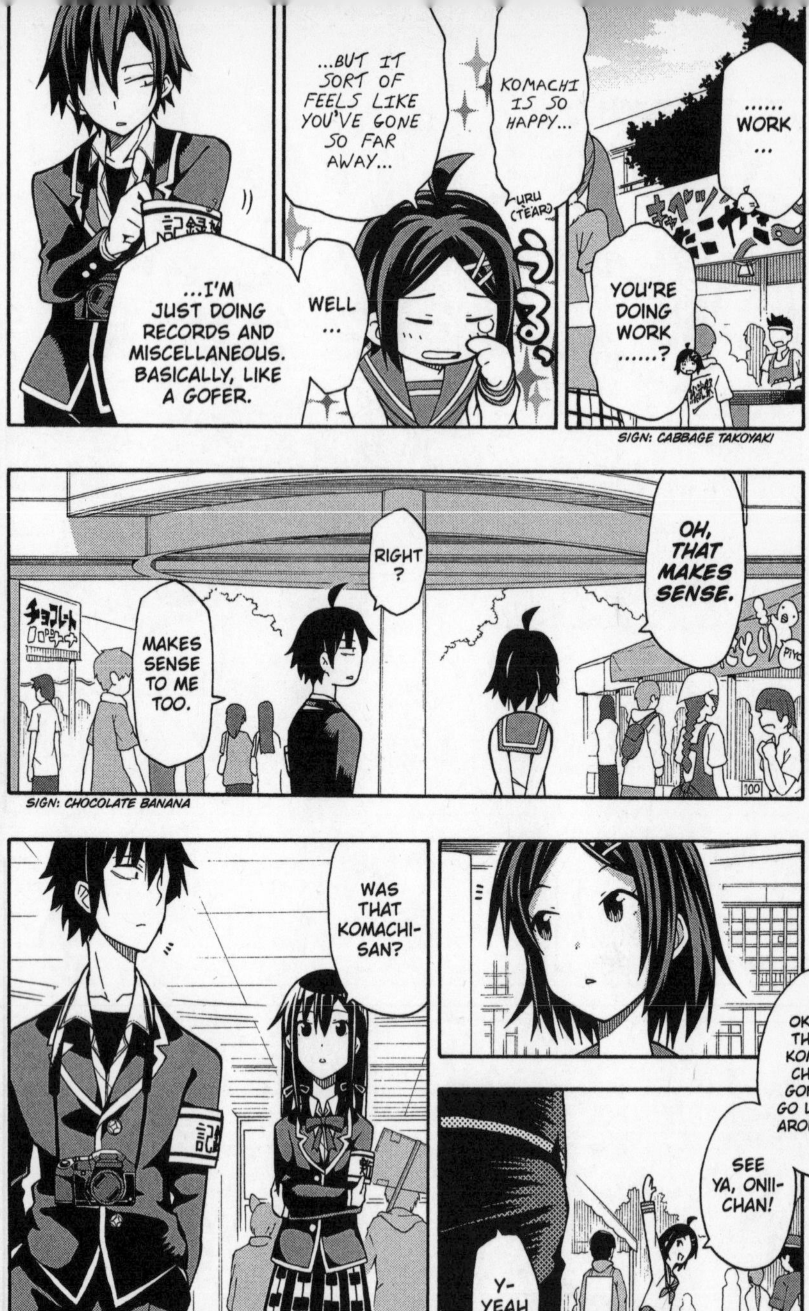
...... WORK ...
YOU'RE DOING WORK ......?
KOMACHI IS SO HAPPY...
URU (TEAR)
...BUT IT SORT OF FEELS LIKE YOU'VE GONE SO FAR AWAY...
WELL ...
...I'M JUST DOING RECORDS AND MISCELLANEOUS. BASICALLY, LIKE A GOFER.
OH, THAT MAKES SENSE.
PIYO
RIGHT?
MAKES SENSE TO ME TOO.
OKAY, THEN KOMACHI'S GONNA GO LOOK AROUND.
SEE YA, ONII-CHAN!
Y-YEAH ...
WAS THAT KOMACHI-SAN?

SIGN: CABBAGE TAKOYAKI

SIGN: CHOCOLATE BANANA

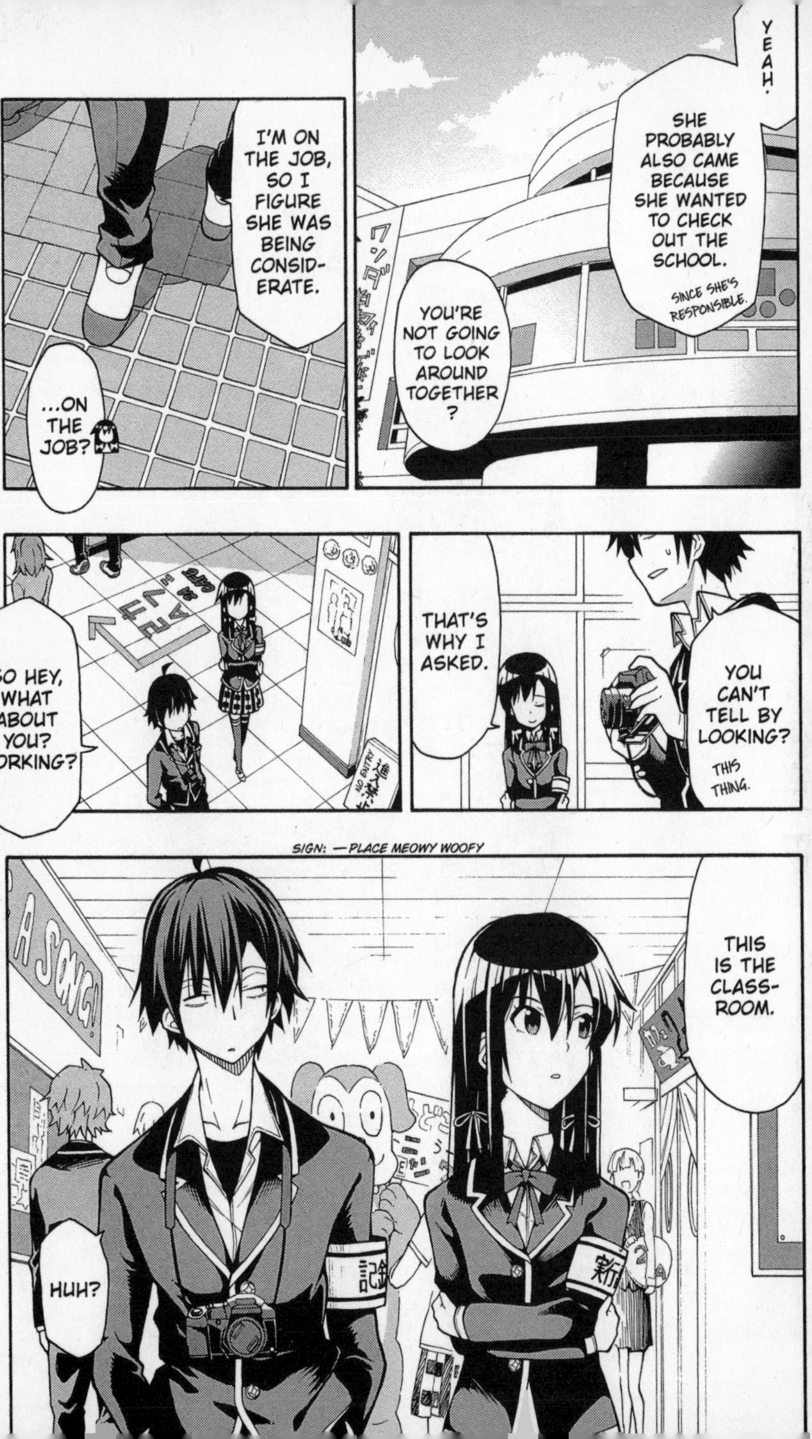
YEAH.
SHE PROBABLY ALSO CAME BECAUSE SHE WANTED TO CHECK OUT THE SCHOOL.
SINCE SHE'S RESPONSIBLE.
YOU'RE NOT GOING TO LOOK AROUND TOGETHER?
I'M ON THE JOB, SO I FIGURE SHE WAS BEING CONSIDERATE.
...ON THE JOB?
YOU CAN'T TELL BY LOOKING?
THIS THING.
THAT'S WHY I ASKED.
SO HEY, WHAT ABOUT YOU? WORKING?
SIGN: —PLACE MEOWY WOOFY
THIS IS THE CLASSROOM.
A SONG!
HUH?

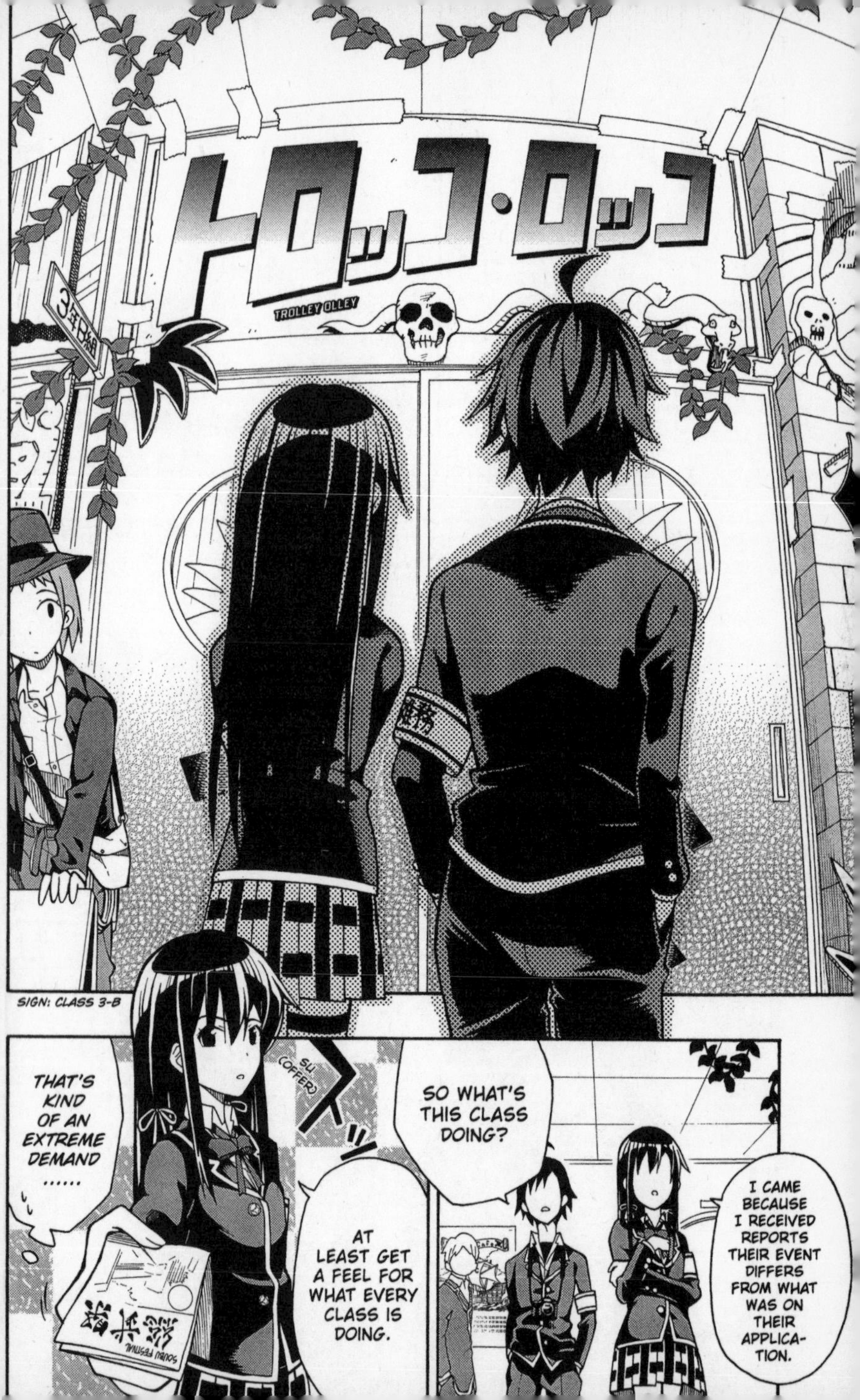
トロッコ・ロッコ
TROLLEY OLLEY
3年B組
SIGN: CLASS 3-B
SO WHAT'S THIS CLASS DOING?
I CAME BECAUSE I RECEIVED REPORTS THEIR EVENT DIFFERS FROM WHAT WAS ON THEIR APPLICATION.
SU (OFFER)
AT LEAST GET A FEEL FOR WHAT EVERY CLASS IS DOING.
THAT'S KIND OF AN EXTREME DEMAND......

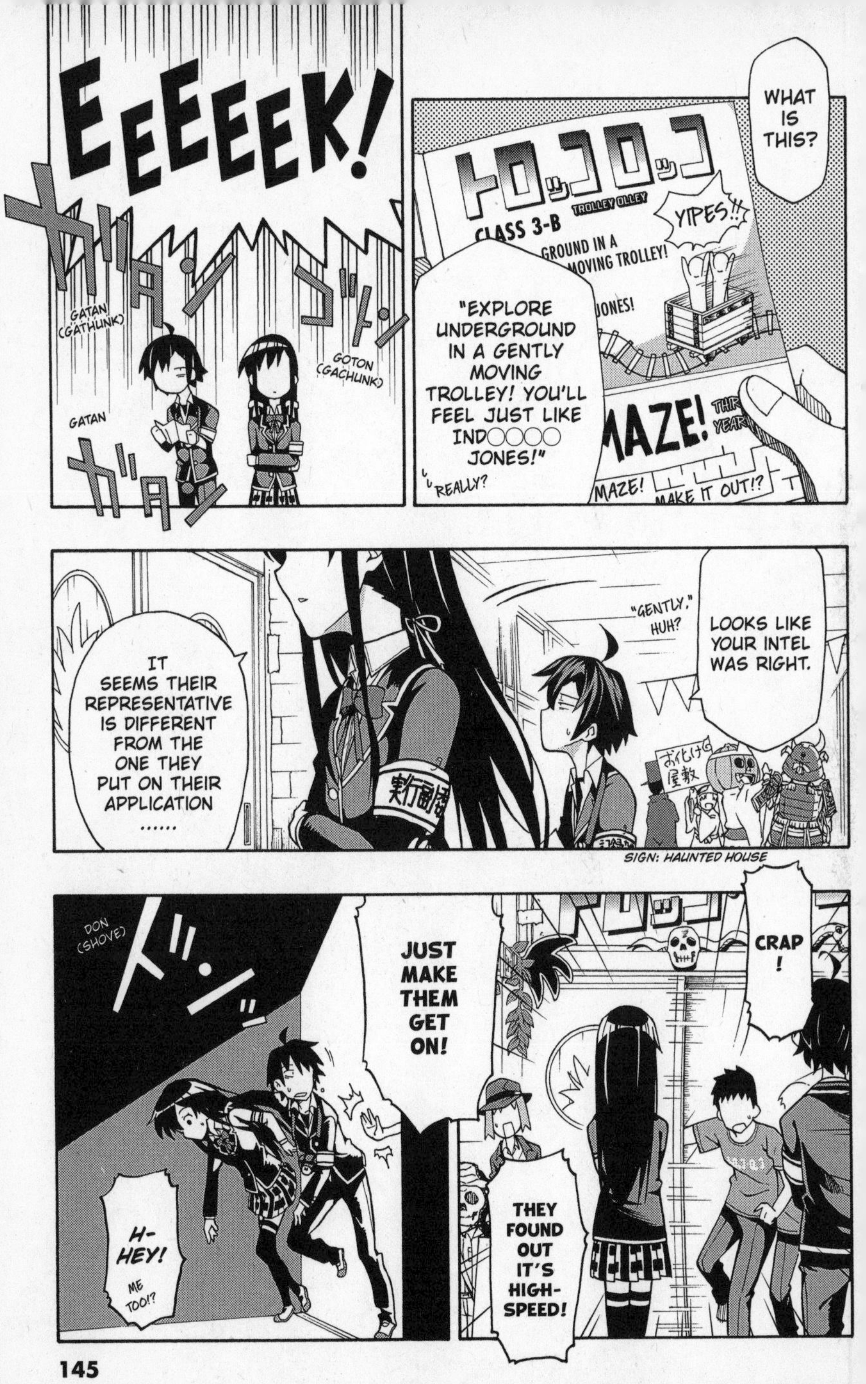
WHAT IS THIS?
トロッコロッコ
TROLLEY OLLEY
CLASS 3-B
GROUND IN A MOVING TROLLEY!
JONES!
YIPES!!
"EXPLORE UNDERGROUND IN A GENTLY MOVING TROLLEY! YOU'LL FEEL JUST LIKE IND○○○○○ JONES!"
REALLY?
MAZE!
MAZE! MAKE IT OUT!?
EEEEEK!
GATAN (GATHUNK)
GOTON (GACHUNK)
GATAN
"GENTLY," HUH?
LOOKS LIKE YOUR INTEL WAS RIGHT.
IT SEEMS THEIR REPRESENTATIVE IS DIFFERENT FROM THE ONE THEY PUT ON THEIR APPLICATION ......
SIGN: HAUNTED HOUSE
CRAP!
JUST MAKE THEM GET ON!
THEY FOUND OUT IT'S HIGH-SPEED!
DON (SHOVE)
H-HEY!
ME TOO!?

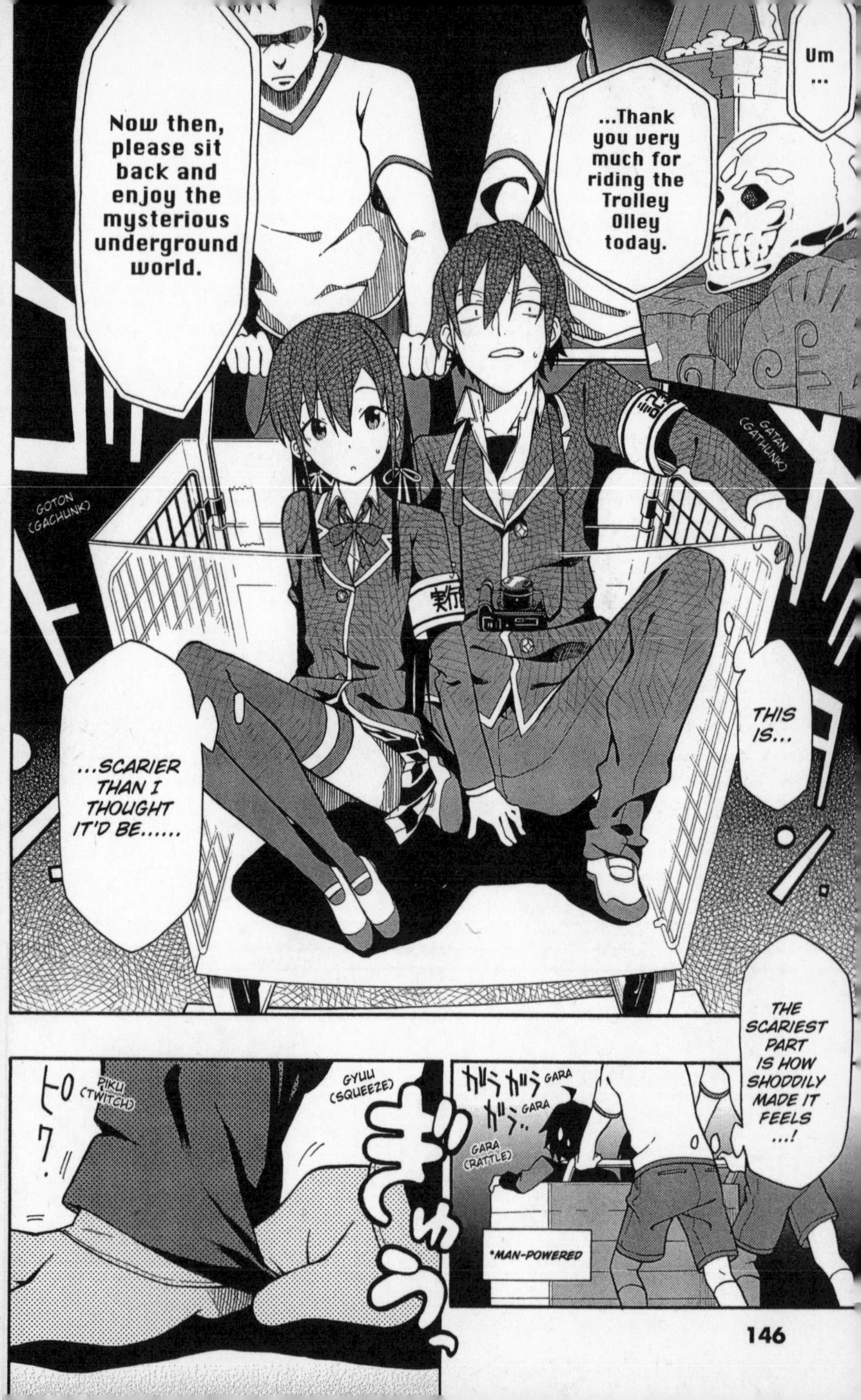
Um ...
...Thank you very much for riding the Trolley Olley today.
Now then, please sit back and enjoy the mysterious underground world.
GATAN (GATHUNK)
GOTON (GACHUNK)
THIS IS...
...SCARIER THAN I THOUGHT IT'D BE......
THE SCARIEST PART IS HOW SHODDILY MADE IT FEELS ...!
GARA GARA
GARA
GARA (RATTLE)
*MAN-POWERED
GYUU (SQUEEZE)
PIKU (TWITCH)

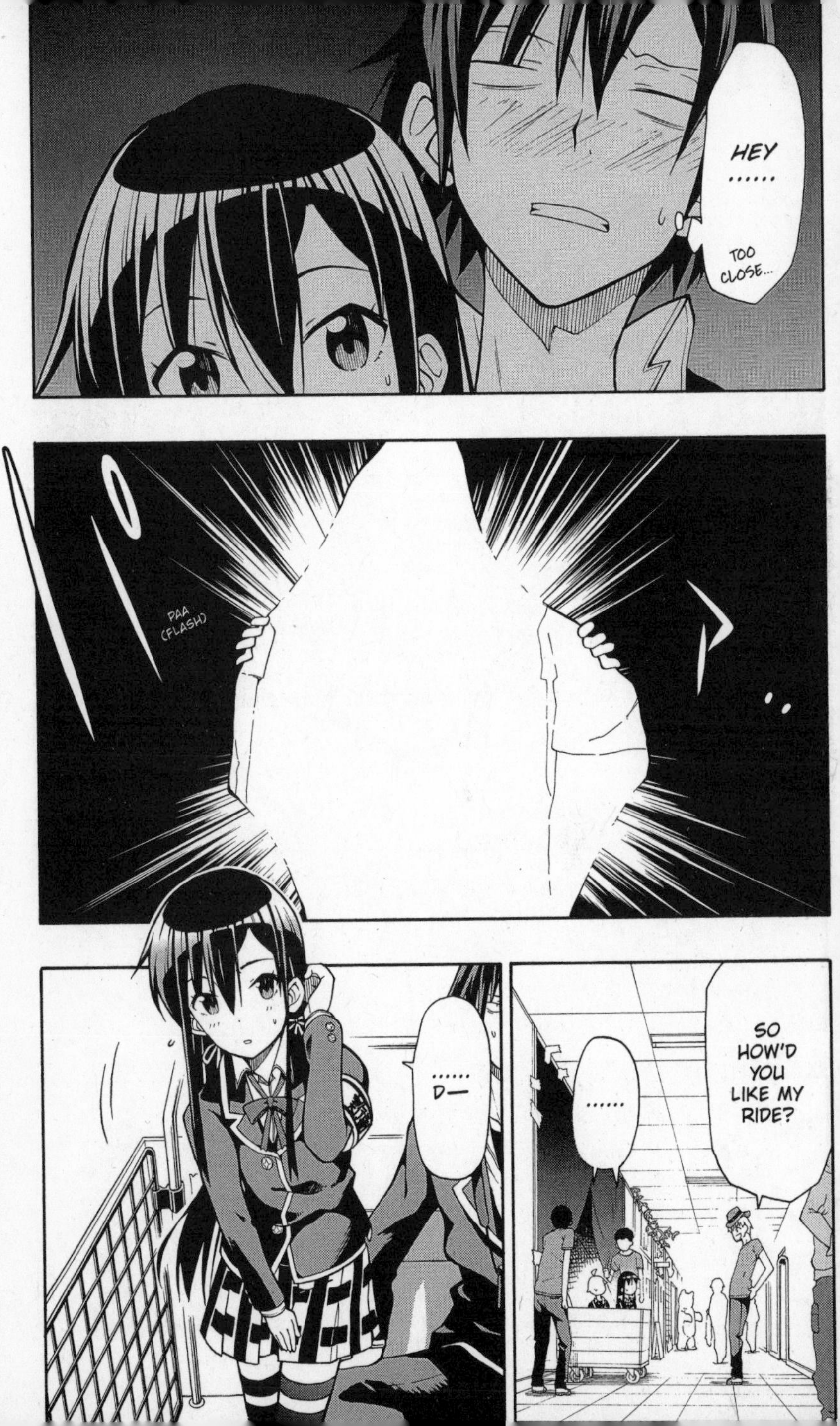
HEY ......
TOO CLOSE...
PAA (FLASH)
SO HOW'D YOU LIKE MY RIDE?
......
...... D—

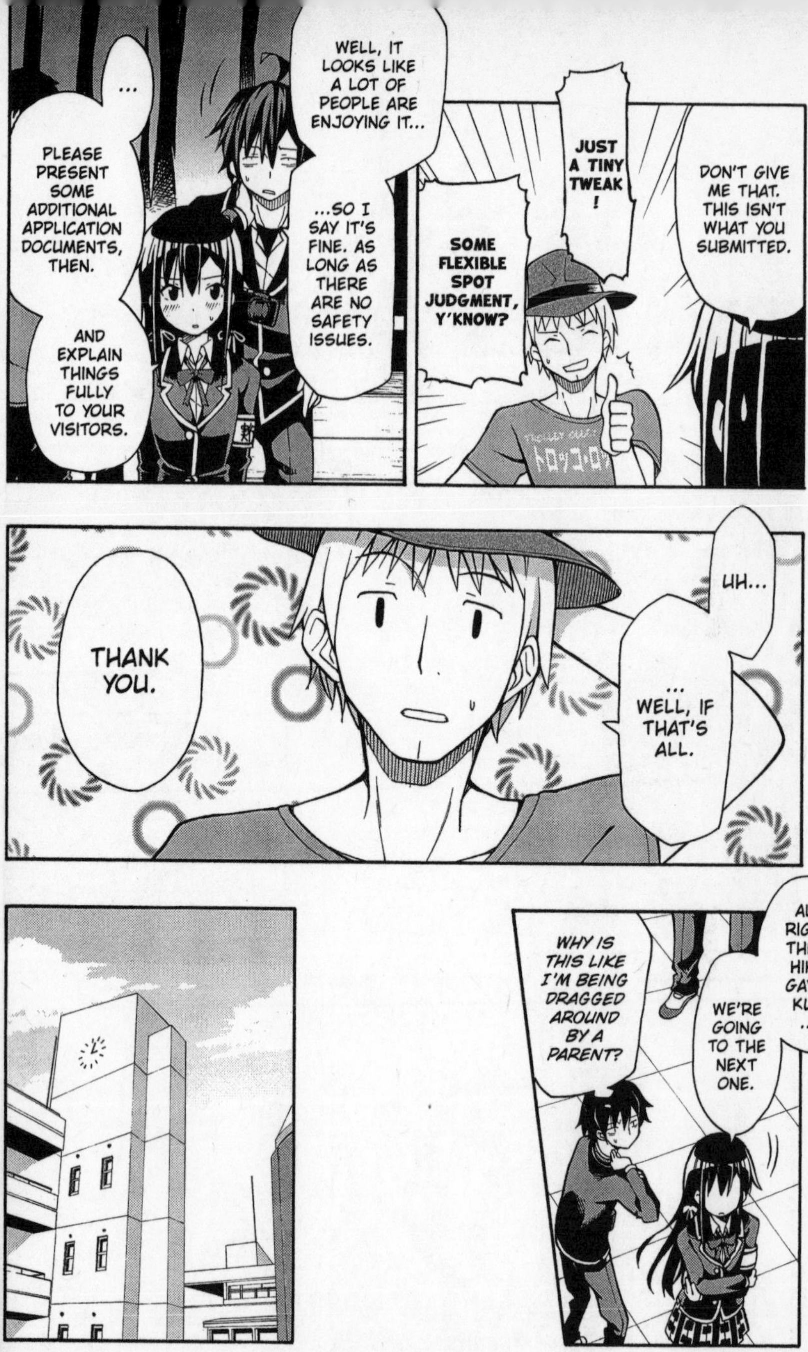
DON'T GIVE ME THAT. THIS ISN'T WHAT YOU SUBMITTED.
JUST A TINY TWEAK!
SOME FLEXIBLE SPOT JUDGMENT, Y'KNOW?
WELL, IT LOOKS LIKE A LOT OF PEOPLE ARE ENJOYING IT...
...SO I SAY IT'S FINE. AS LONG AS THERE ARE NO SAFETY ISSUES.
...
PLEASE PRESENT SOME ADDITIONAL APPLICATION DOCUMENTS, THEN.
AND EXPLAIN THINGS FULLY TO YOUR VISITORS.
UH...
...WELL, IF THAT'S ALL.
THANK YOU.
ALL RIGHT THEN, HIKIGAYA-KUN...
WE'RE GOING TO THE NEXT ONE.
WHY IS THIS LIKE I'M BEING DRAGGED AROUND BY A PARENT?

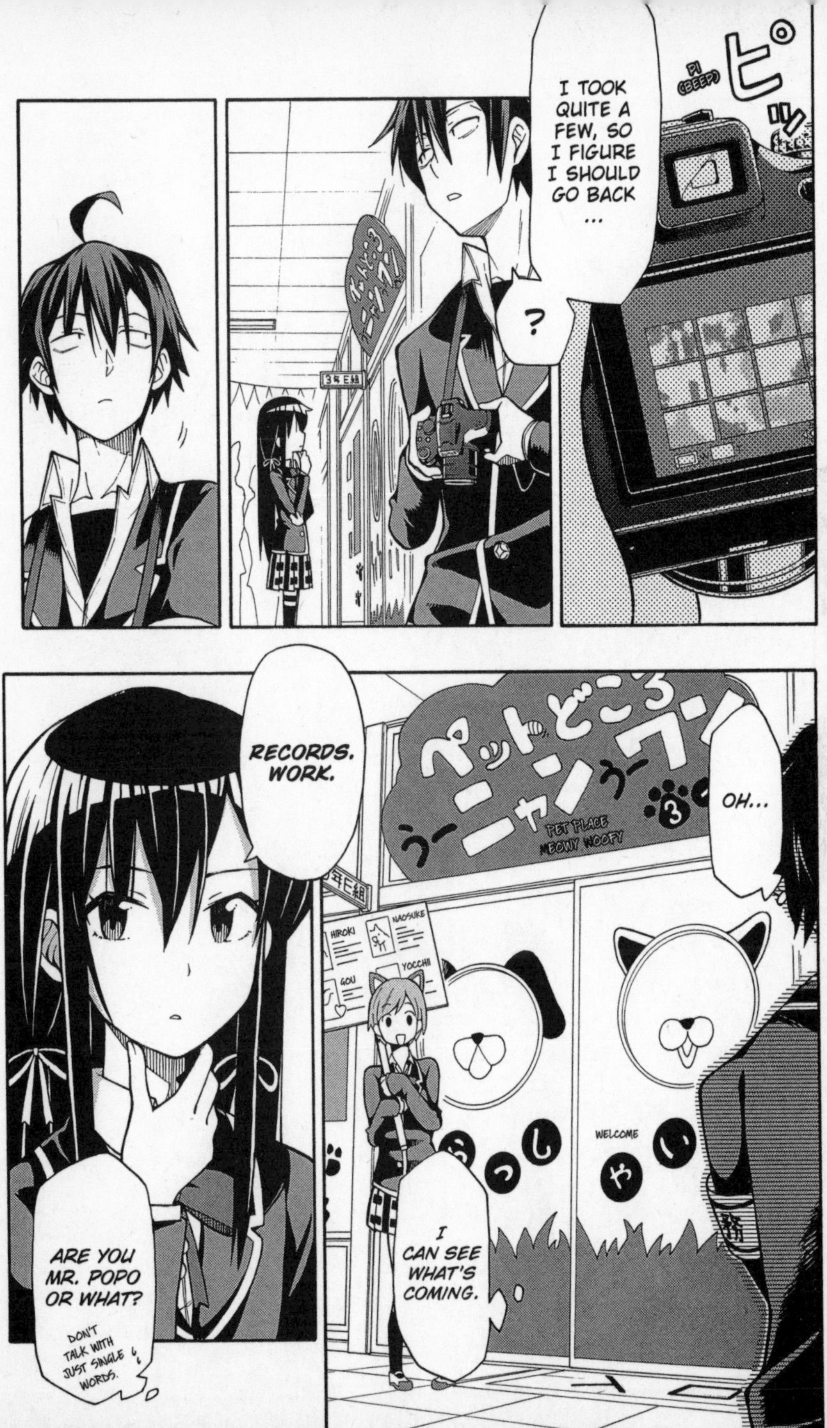
ピッ
PI (BEEP)
I TOOK QUITE A FEW, SO I FIGURE I SHOULD GO BACK ...
?
OH...
RECORDS. WORK.
PET PLACE MEOWY WOOFY
HIROKI
NAOSUKE
GOU
YOCCHII
WELCOME
I CAN SEE WHAT'S COMING.
ARE YOU MR. POPO OR WHAT?
DON'T TALK WITH JUST SINGLE WORDS.

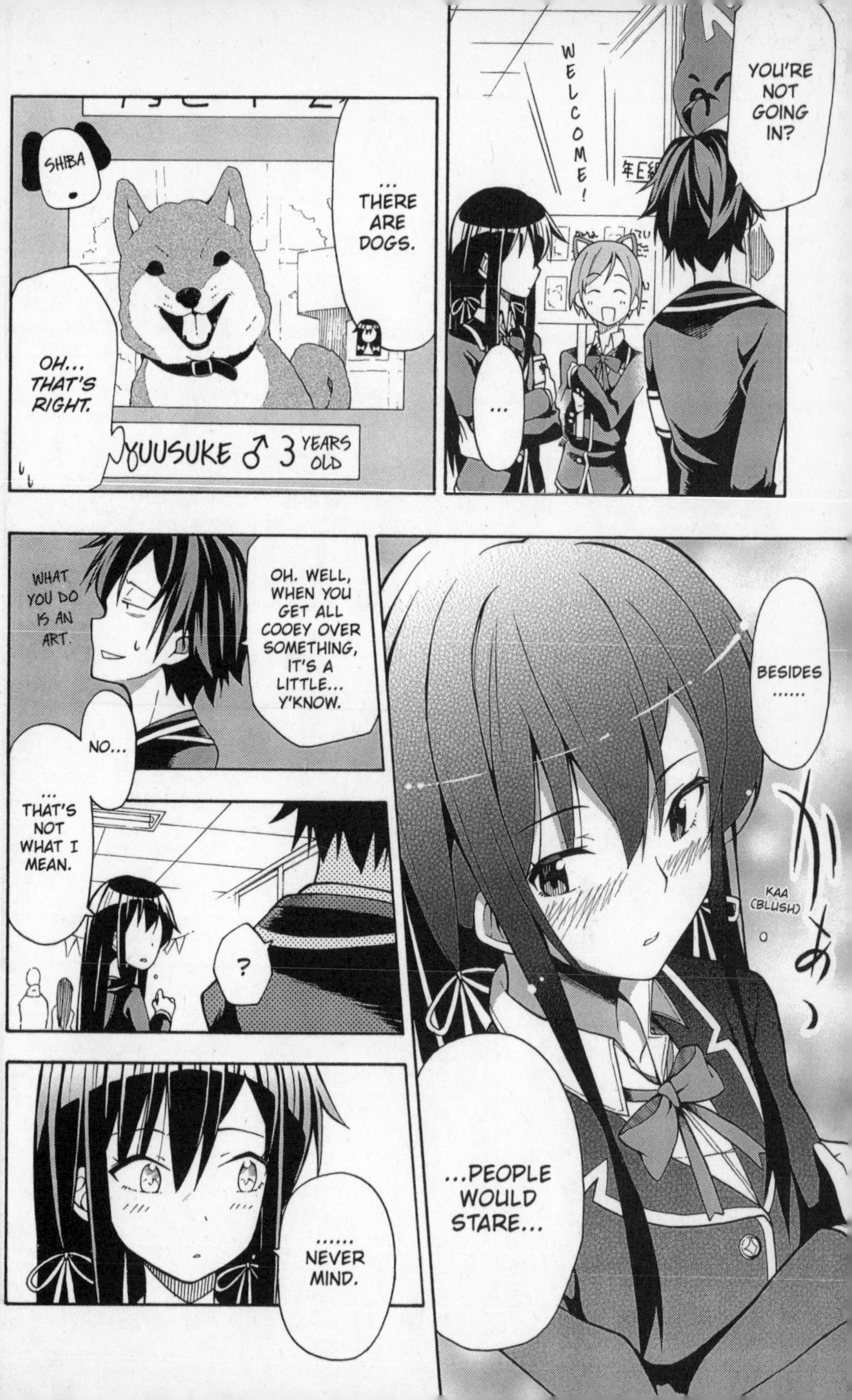
WELCOME!
YOU'RE NOT GOING IN?
...
SHIBA
... THERE ARE DOGS.
OH... THAT'S RIGHT.
YUUSUKE ♂ 3 YEARS OLD
BESIDES ......
KAA (BLUSH)
...PEOPLE WOULD STARE...
OH. WELL, WHEN YOU GET ALL COOEY OVER SOMETHING, IT'S A LITTLE... Y'KNOW.
WHAT YOU DO IS AN ART.
NO...
... THAT'S NOT WHAT I MEAN.
?
...... NEVER MIND.

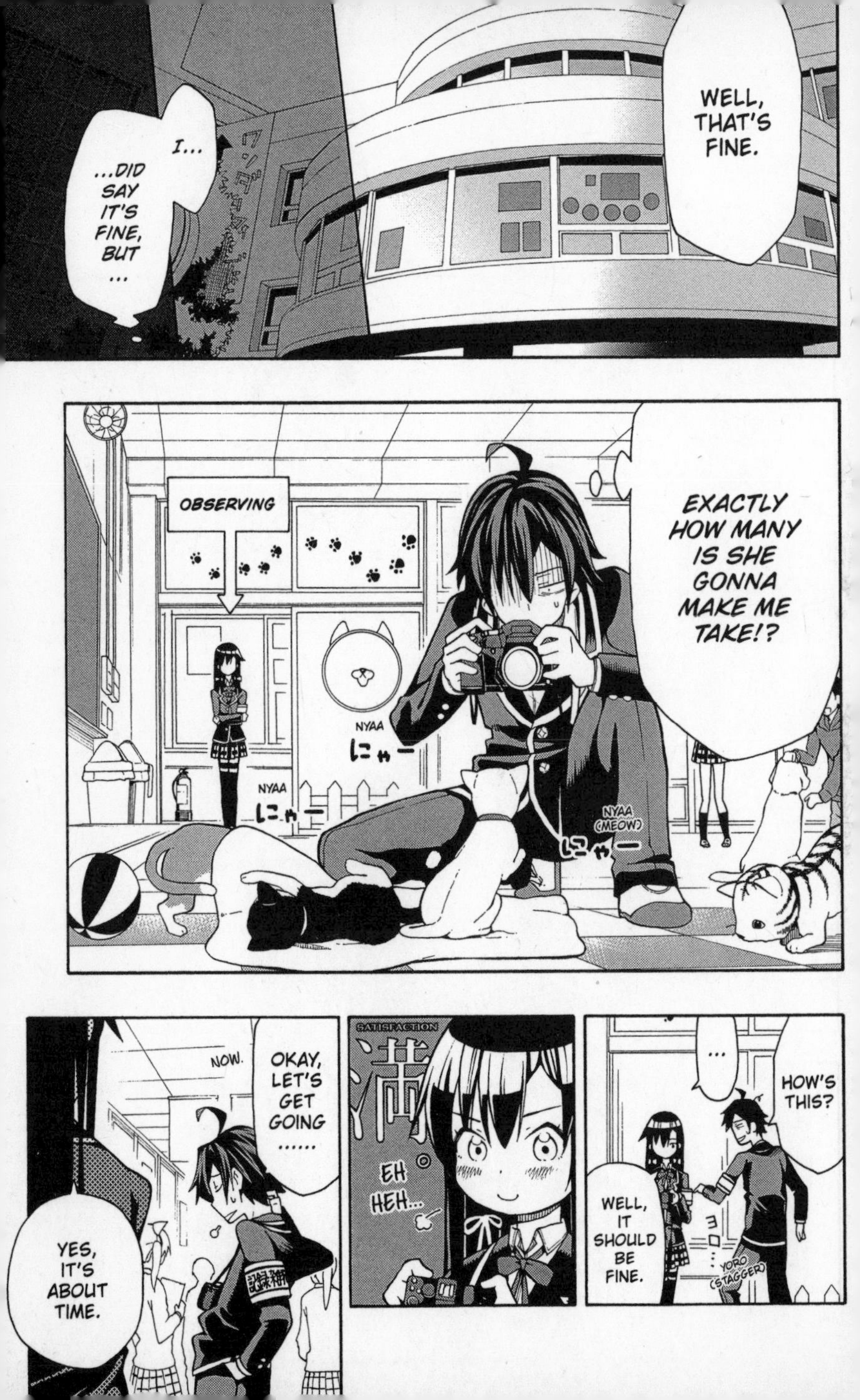
WELL, THAT'S FINE.
I... ...DID SAY IT'S FINE, BUT ...
EXACTLY HOW MANY IS SHE GONNA MAKE ME TAKE!?
OBSERVING
NYAA
にゃー
NYAA
にゃー
NYAA (MEOW)
にゃー
...
HOW'S THIS?
WELL, IT SHOULD BE FINE.
ヨロ...
YORO (STAGGER)
SATISFACTION
満
EH HEH...
NOW.
OKAY, LET'S GET GOING ......
YES, IT'S ABOUT TIME.

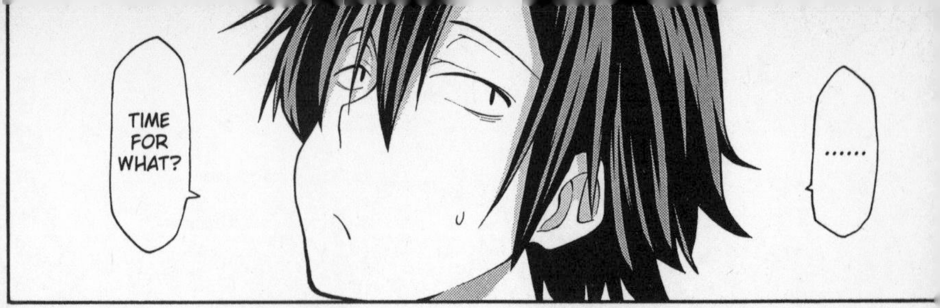
......
TIME FOR WHAT?

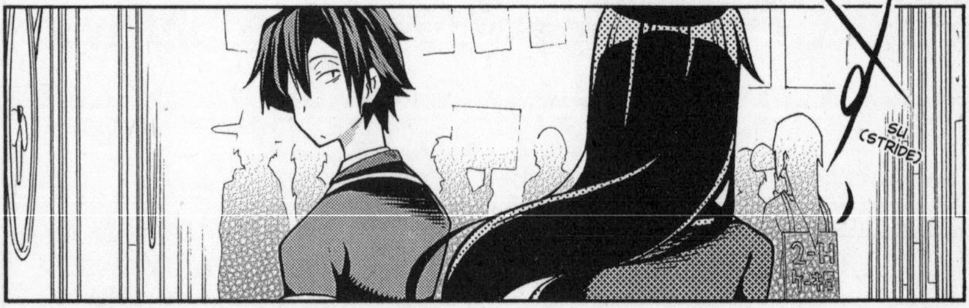
SU (STRIDE)

SIGNS: ENGLISH RESEARCH CLUB SPEECH / —TACOS / VOLLEYBALL CLUB SUPER CREPES / WITCH'S ROOM DOZUE / WELCOME

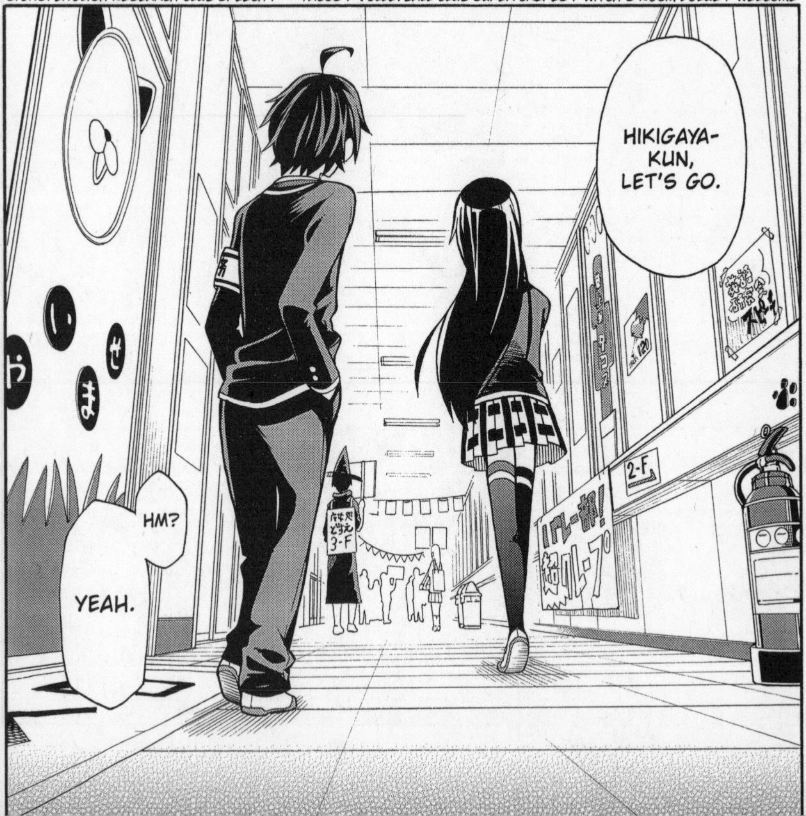
HIKIGAYA-KUN, LET'S GO.
HM?
YEAH.
2-F

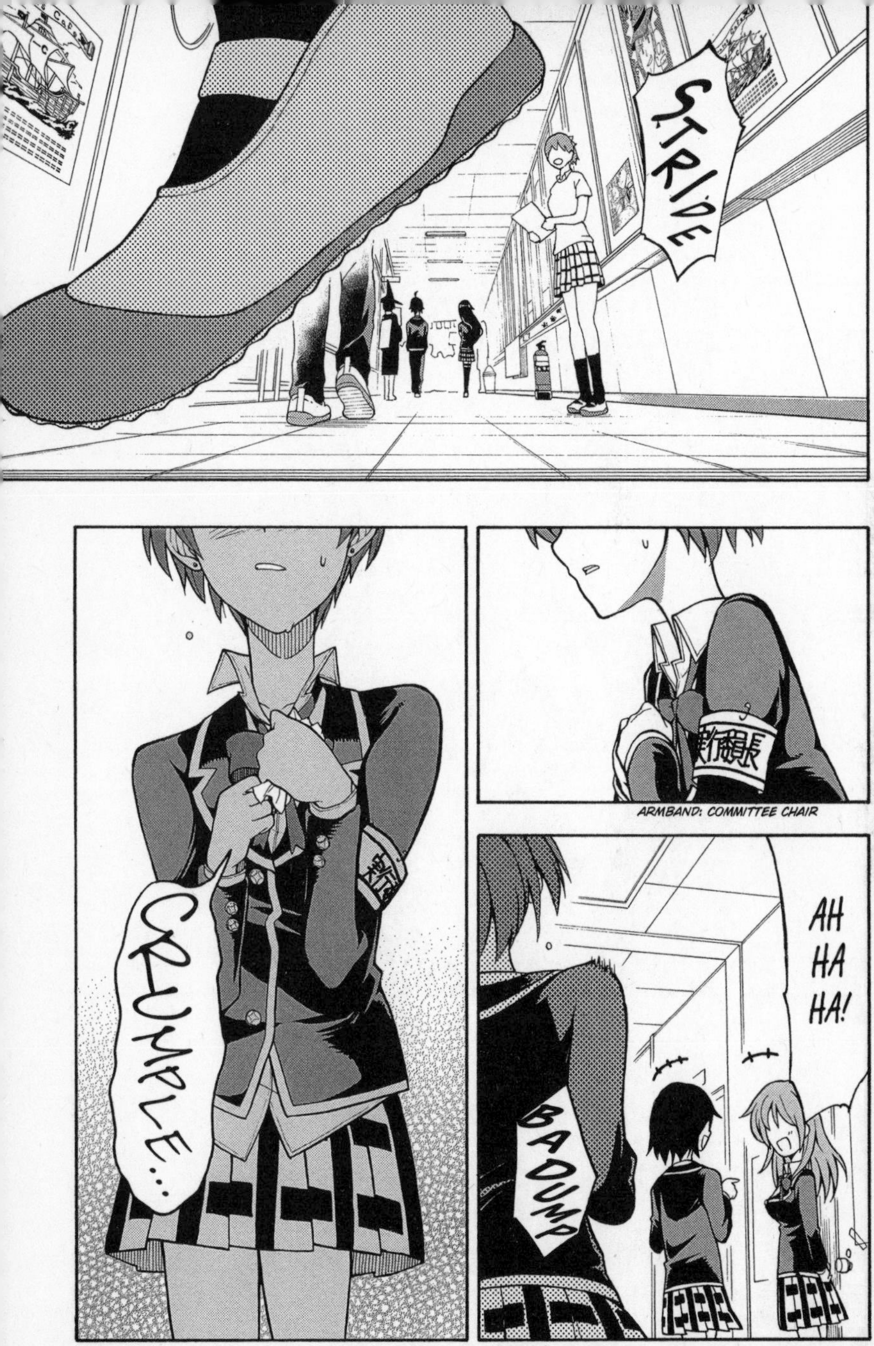
STRIDE
ARMBAND: COMMITTEE CHAIR
AH HA HA!
BADUMP
CRUMPLE...

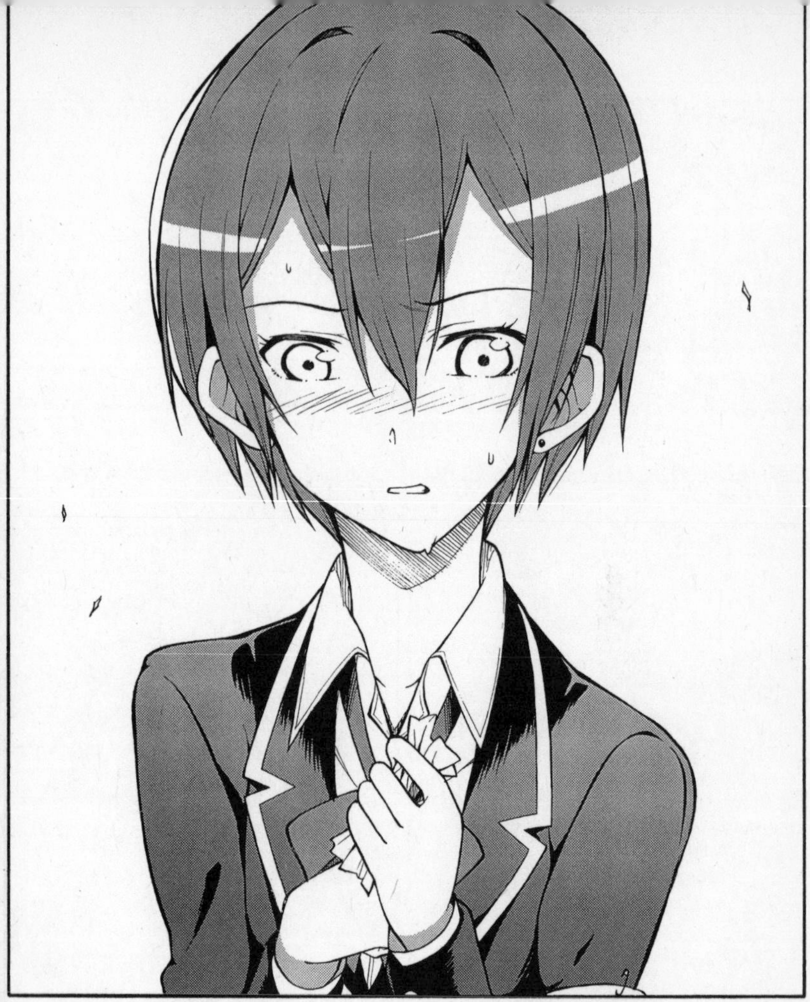

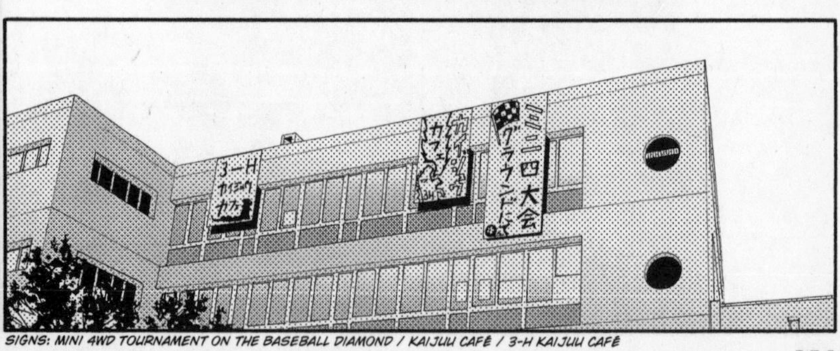
3-H

SIGNS: MINI 4WD TOURNAMENT ON THE BASEBALL DIAMOND / KAIJUU CAFÉ / 3-H KAIJUU CAFÉ

CHAPTER 41

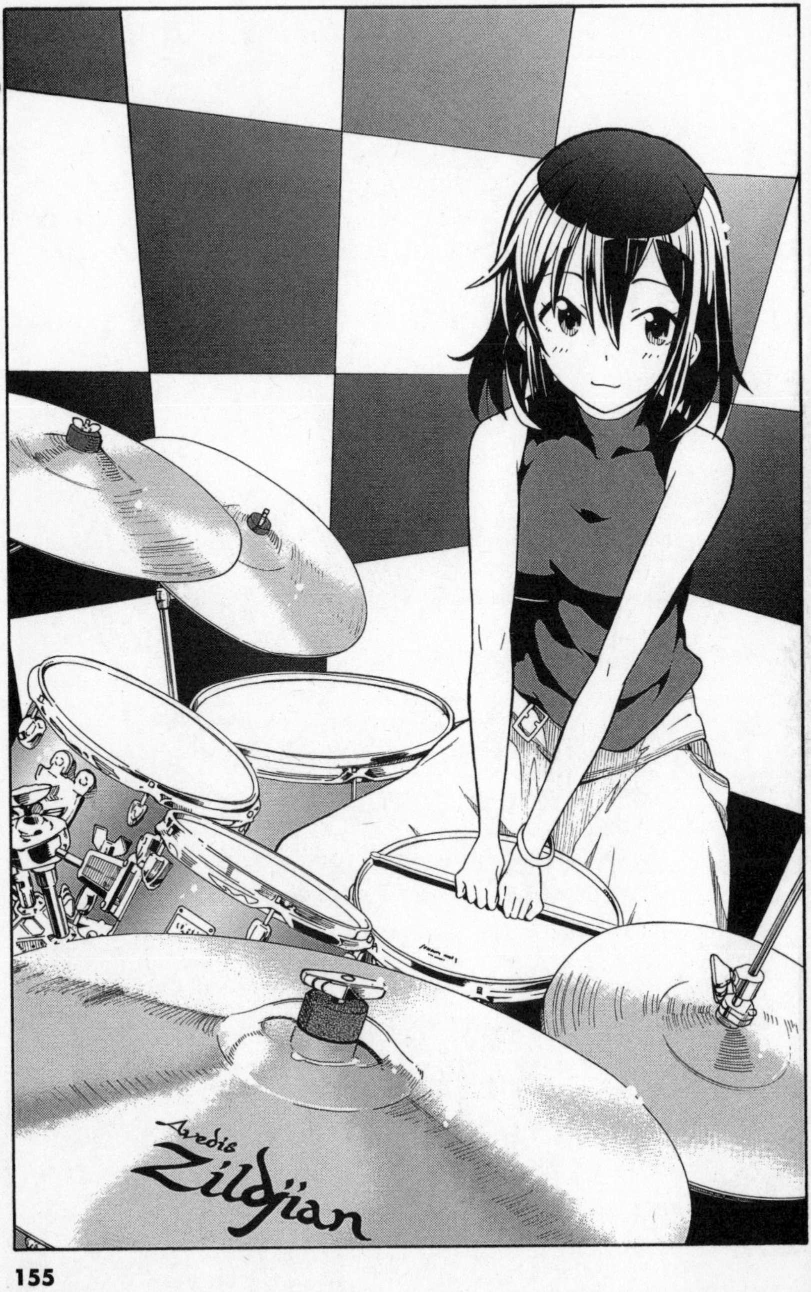
Avedis
Zildjian

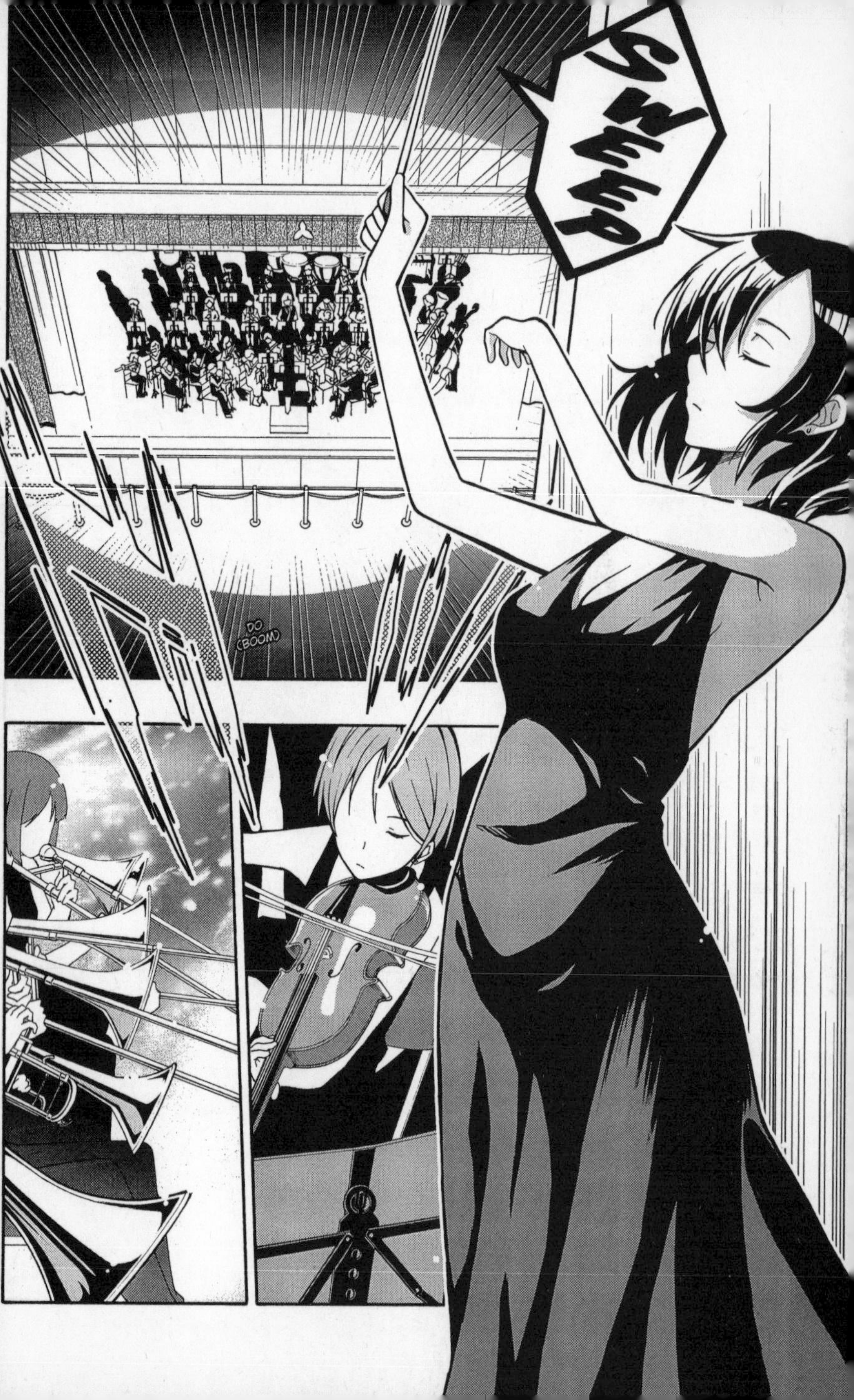
SWEEP
DO
(BOOM)

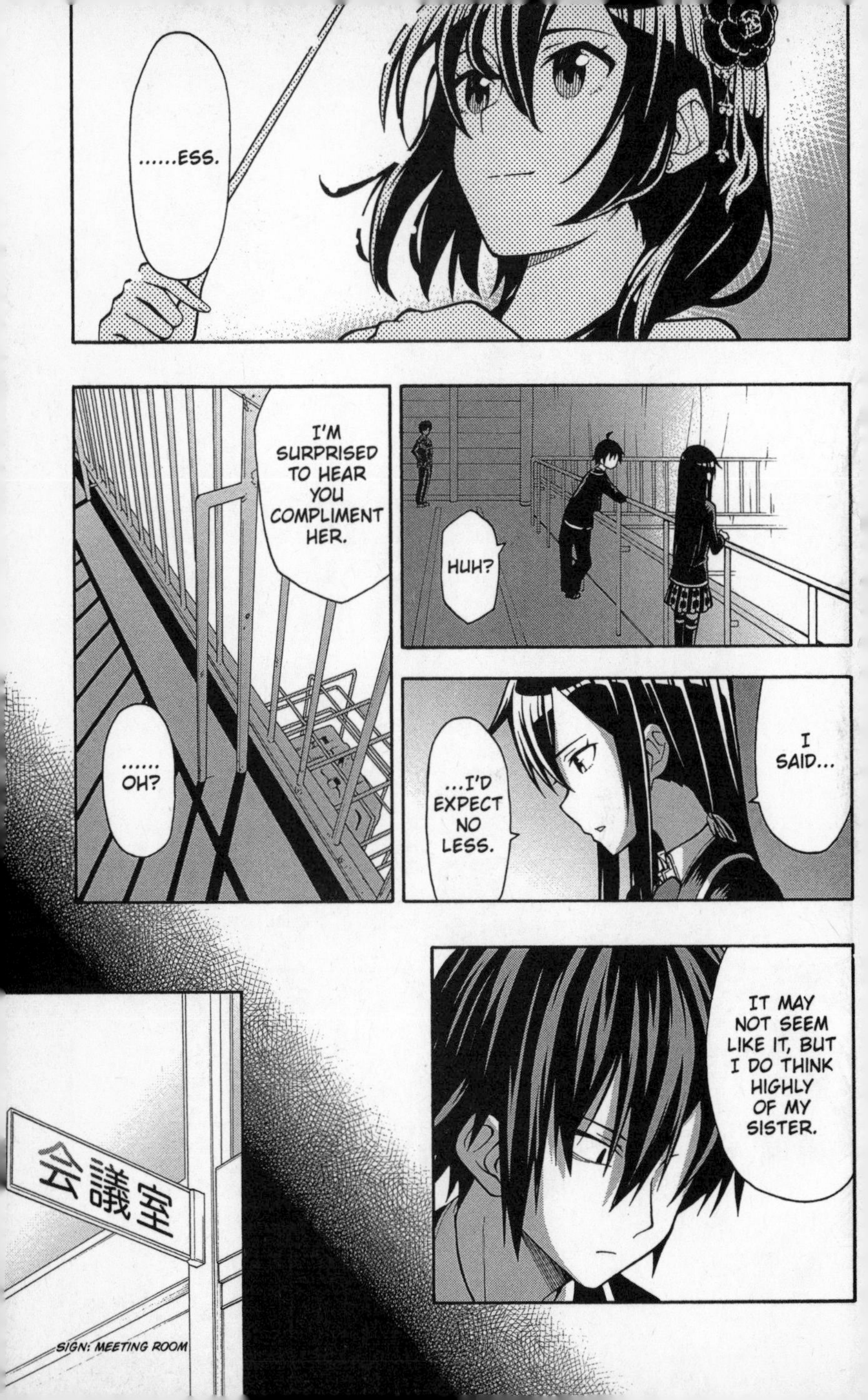
......ESS.
HUH?
I SAID...
...I'D EXPECT NO LESS.
I'M SURPRISED TO HEAR YOU COMPLIMENT HER.
...... OH?
IT MAY NOT SEEM LIKE IT, BUT I DO THINK HIGHLY OF MY SISTER.
会議室
SIGN: MEETING ROOM

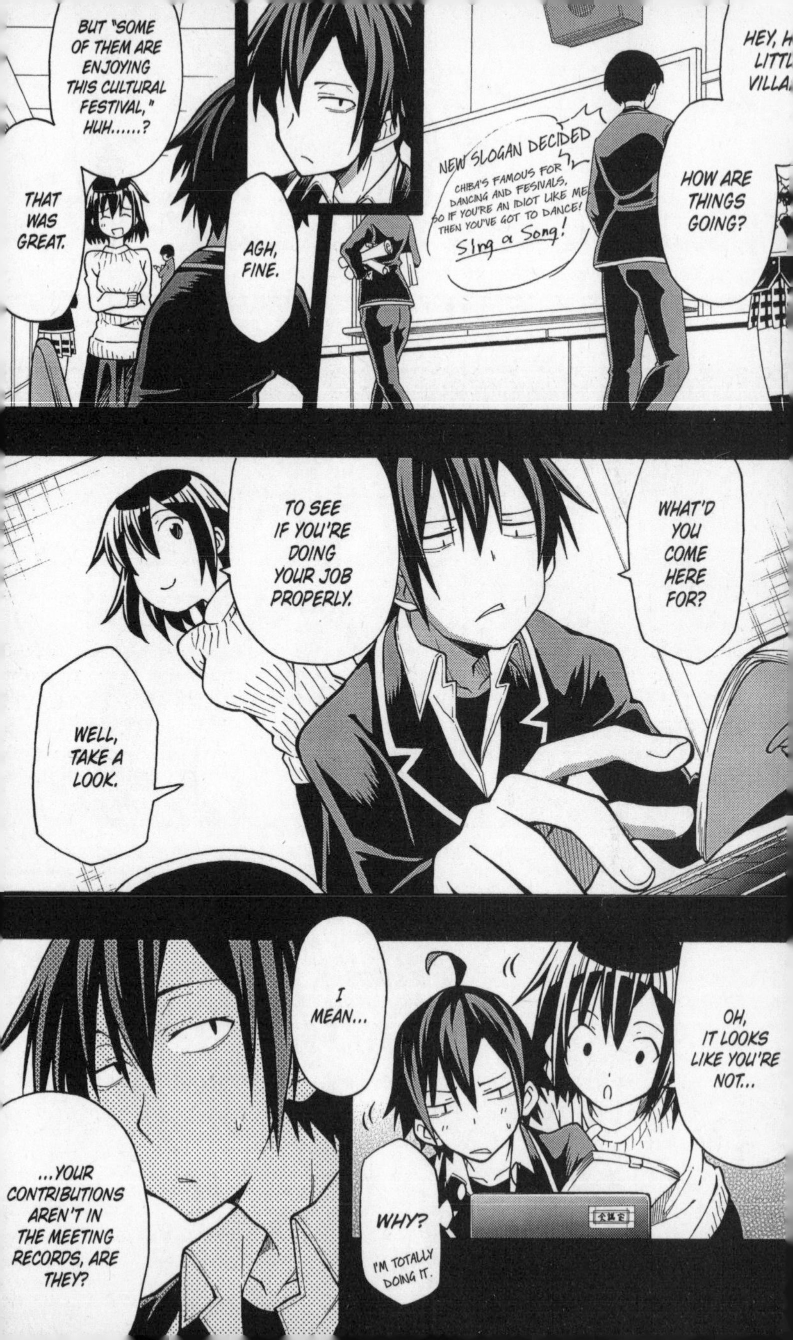
HEY, H
LITTL
VILLA
HOW ARE THINGS GOING?
NEW SLOGAN DECIDED
CHIBA'S FAMOUS FOR DANCING AND FESIVALS, SO IF YOU'RE AN IDIOT LIKE ME THEN YOU'VE GOT TO DANCE! Sing a Song!
AGH, FINE.
BUT "SOME OF THEM ARE ENJOYING THIS CULTURAL FESTIVAL," HUH......?
THAT WAS GREAT.
WHAT'D YOU COME HERE FOR?
TO SEE IF YOU'RE DOING YOUR JOB PROPERLY.
WELL, TAKE A LOOK.
OH, IT LOOKS LIKE YOU'RE NOT...
WHY?
I'M TOTALLY DOING IT.
I MEAN...
...YOUR CONTRIBUTIONS AREN'T IN THE MEETING RECORDS, ARE THEY?

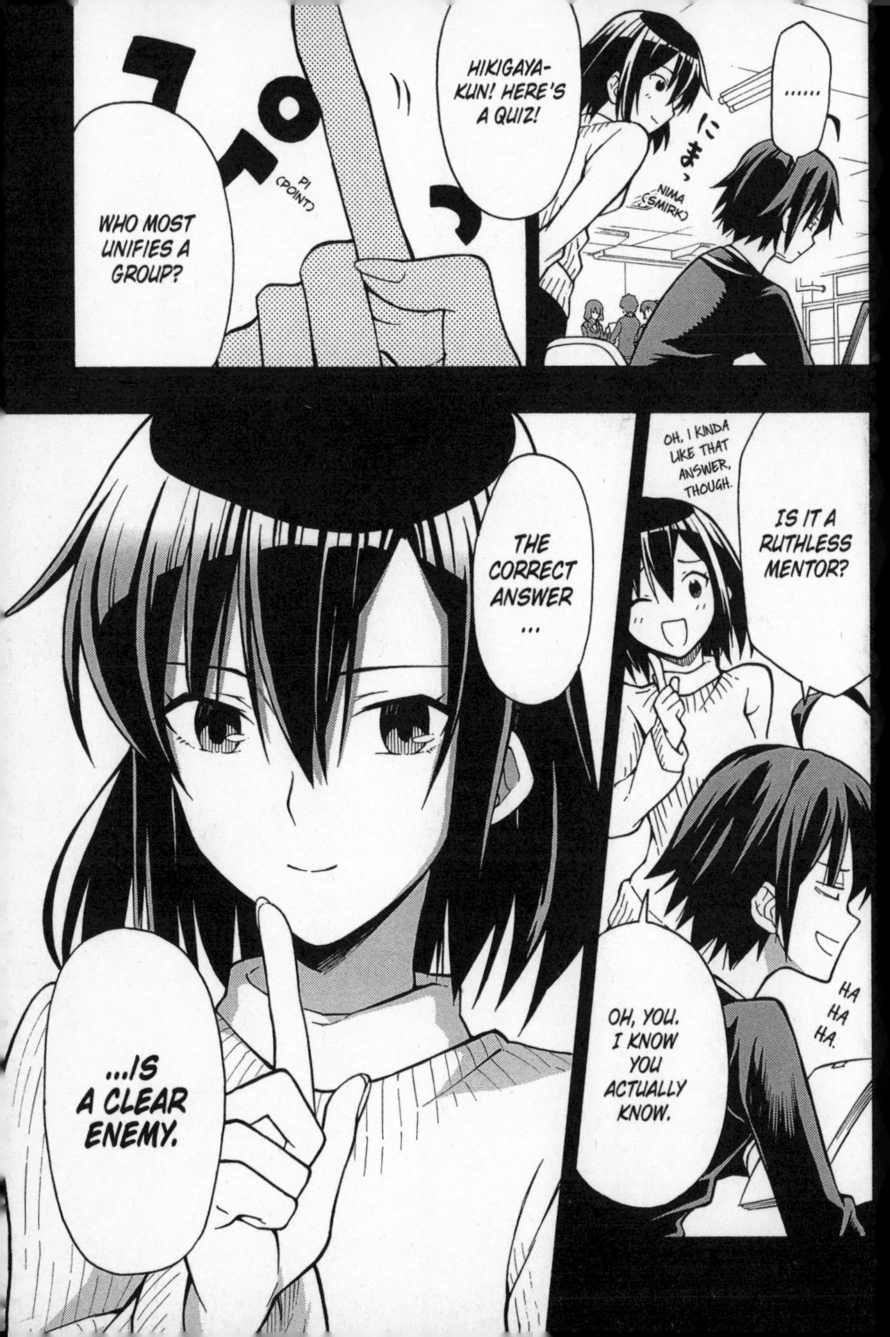
......
にまっ
NIMA (SMIRK)
HIKIGAYA-KUN! HERE'S A QUIZ!
PI (POINT)
WHO MOST UNIFIES A GROUP?
IS IT A RUTHLESS MENTOR?
OH, I KINDA LIKE THAT ANSWER, THOUGH.
HA HA HA.
OH, YOU. I KNOW YOU ACTUALLY KNOW.
THE CORRECT ANSWER ...
...IS A CLEAR ENEMY.

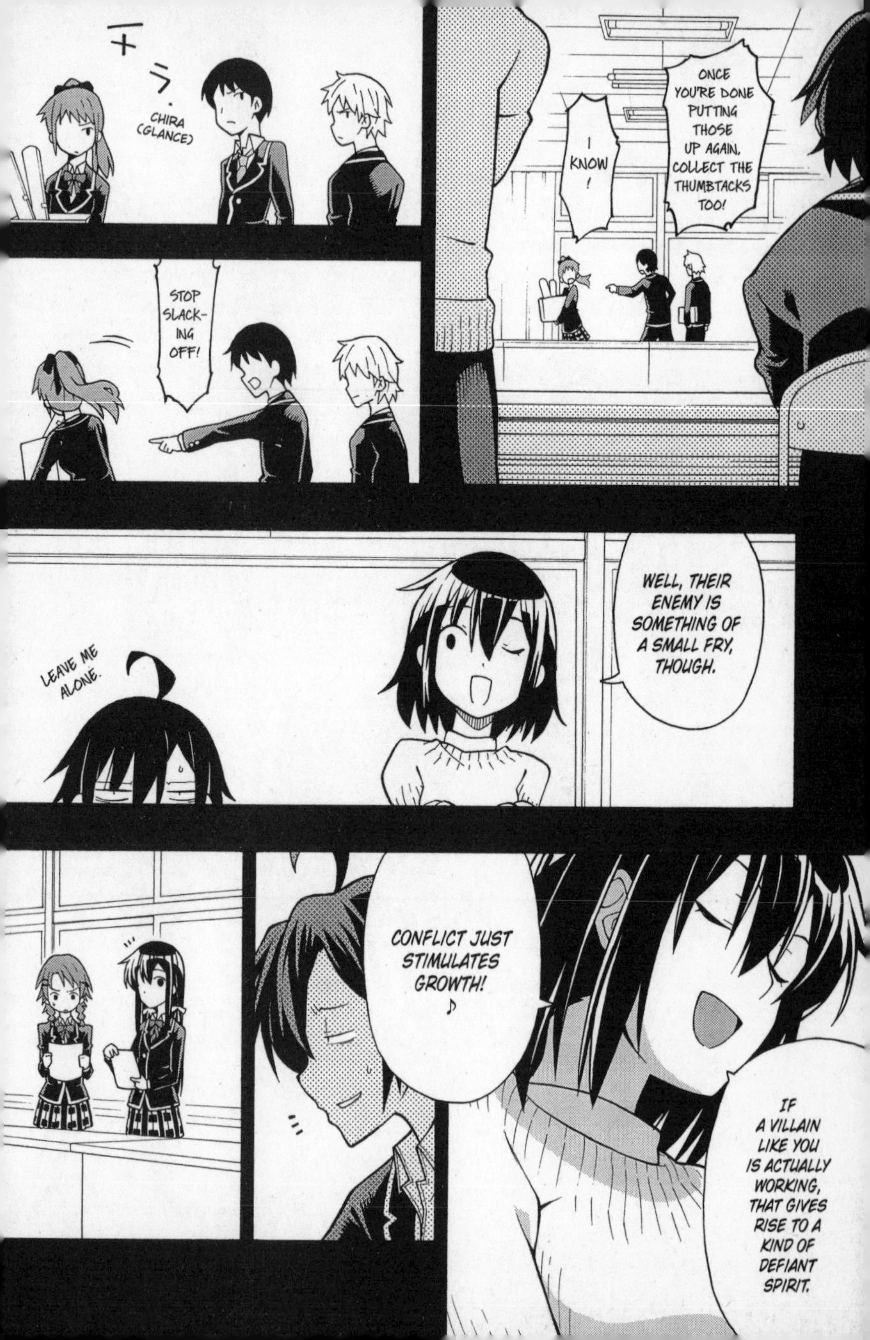
ONCE YOU'RE DONE PUTTING THOSE UP AGAIN, COLLECT THE THUMBTACKS TOO!
I KNOW!
チラ
CHIRA (GLANCE)
STOP SLACKING OFF!
WELL, THEIR ENEMY IS SOMETHING OF A SMALL FRY, THOUGH.
LEAVE ME ALONE.
CONFLICT JUST STIMULATES GROWTH! ♪
IF A VILLAIN LIKE YOU IS ACTUALLY WORKING, THAT GIVES RISE TO A KIND OF DEFIANT SPIRIT.

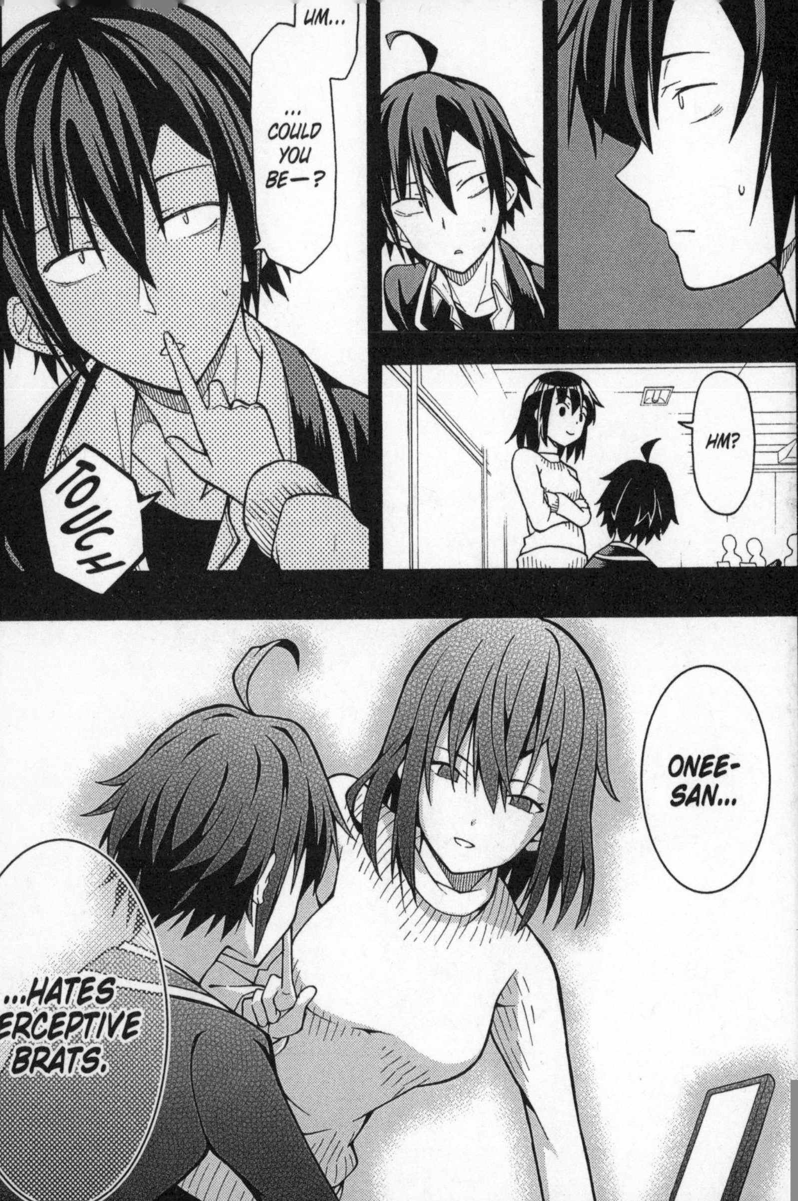
HM?
UM...
...COULD YOU BE—?
TOUCH
ONEE-SAN...
...HATES PERCEPTIVE BRATS.

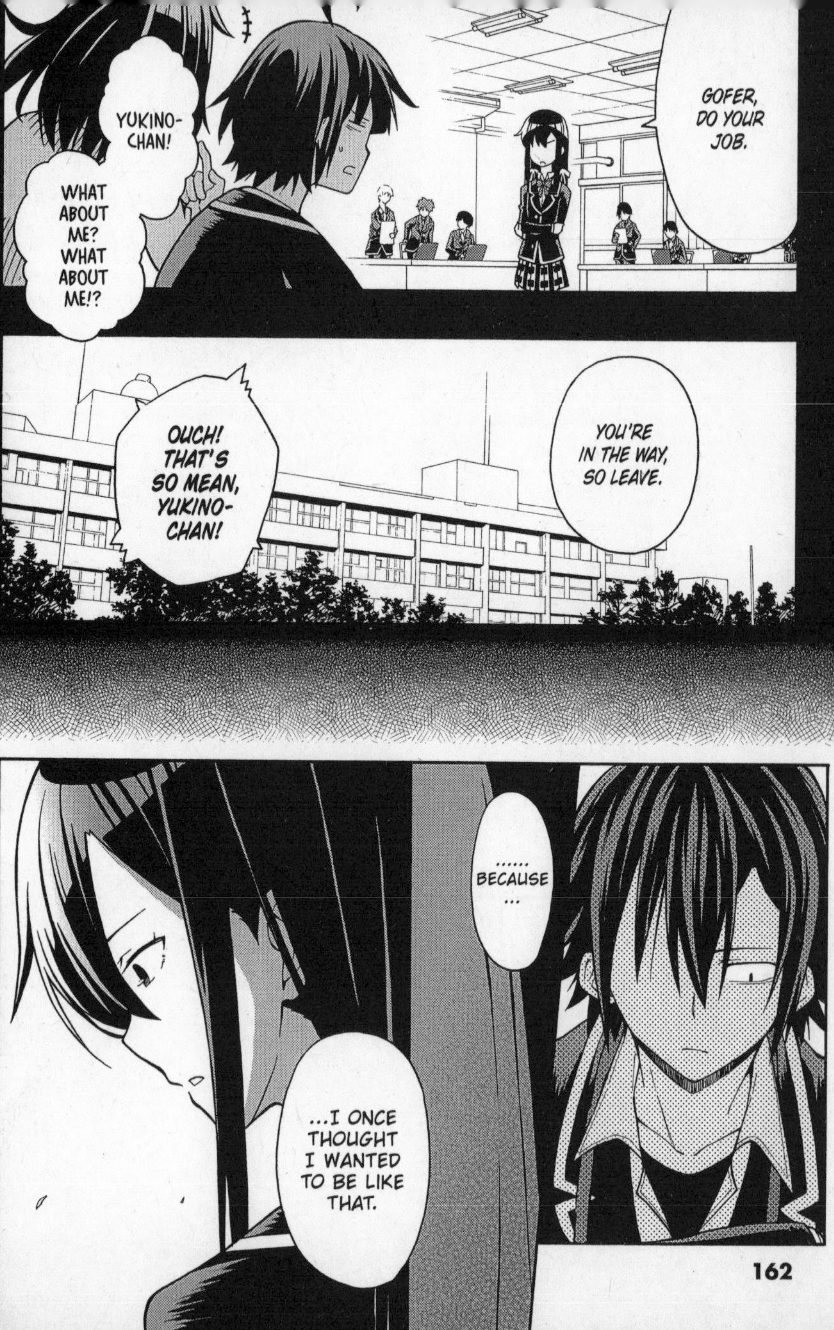
GOFER, DO YOUR JOB.
YUKINO-CHAN!
WHAT ABOUT ME? WHAT ABOUT ME!?
YOU'RE IN THE WAY, SO LEAVE.
OUCH! THAT'S SO MEAN, YUKINO-CHAN!
......BECAUSE...
...I ONCE THOUGHT I WANTED TO BE LIKE THAT.

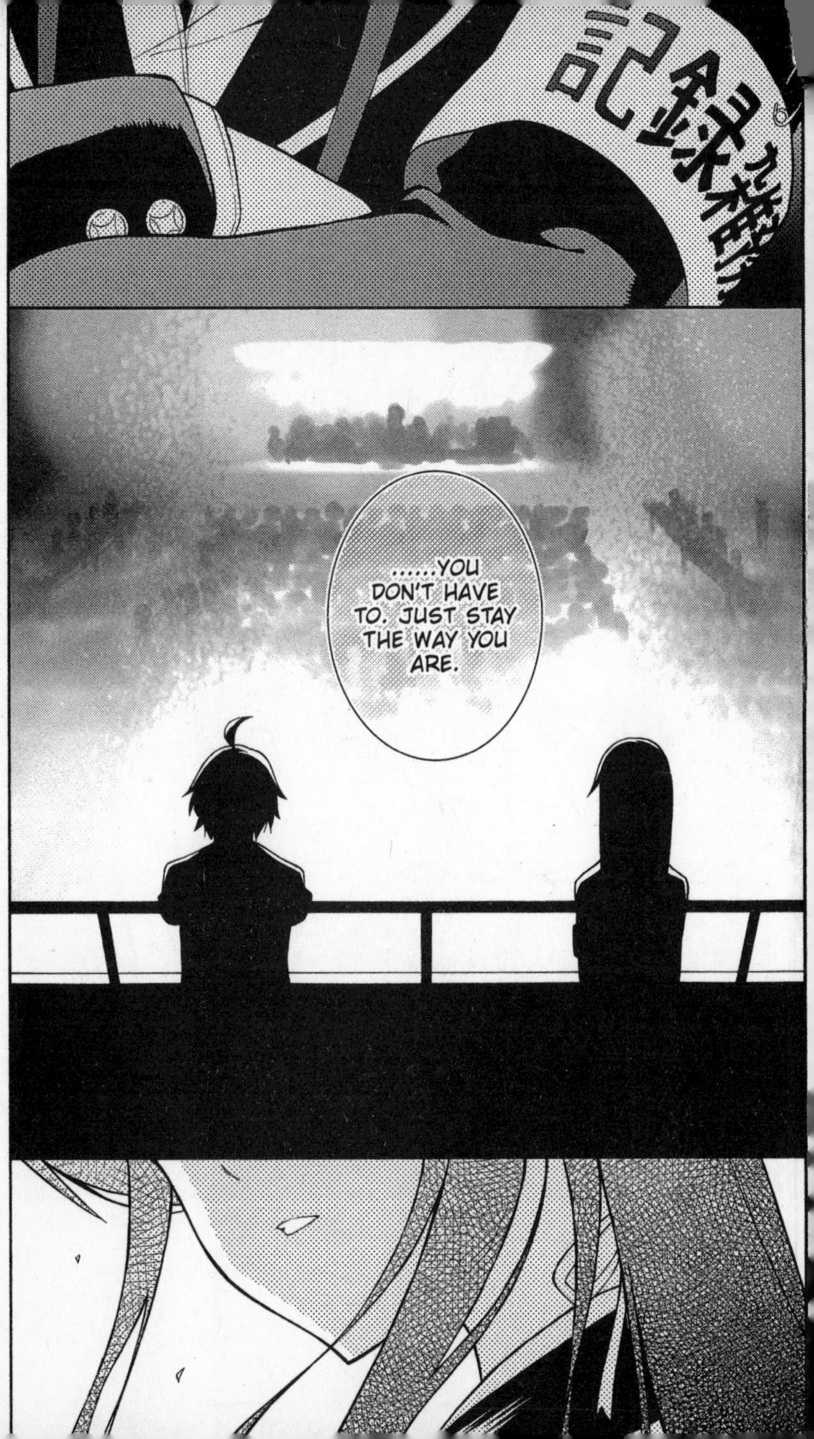
......YOU DON'T HAVE TO. JUST STAY THE WAY YOU ARE.

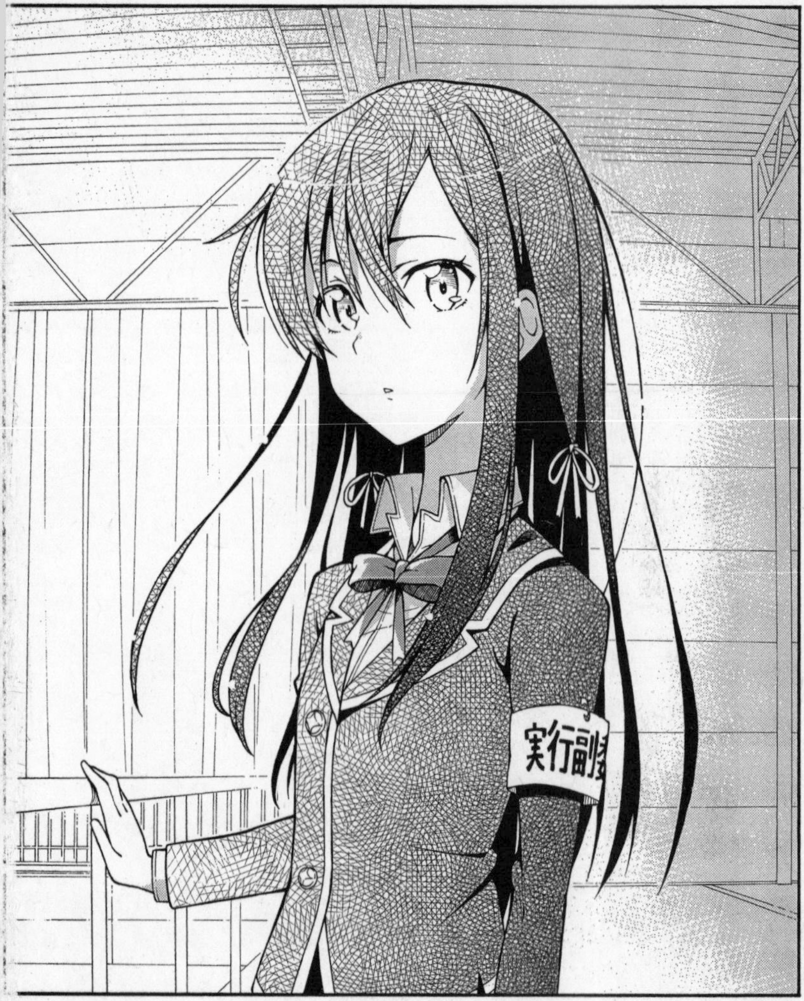
実行副委

CHAPTER 41 ● BEYOND, THERE'S SOMEONE YUKINO YUKINOSHITA IS WATCHING.

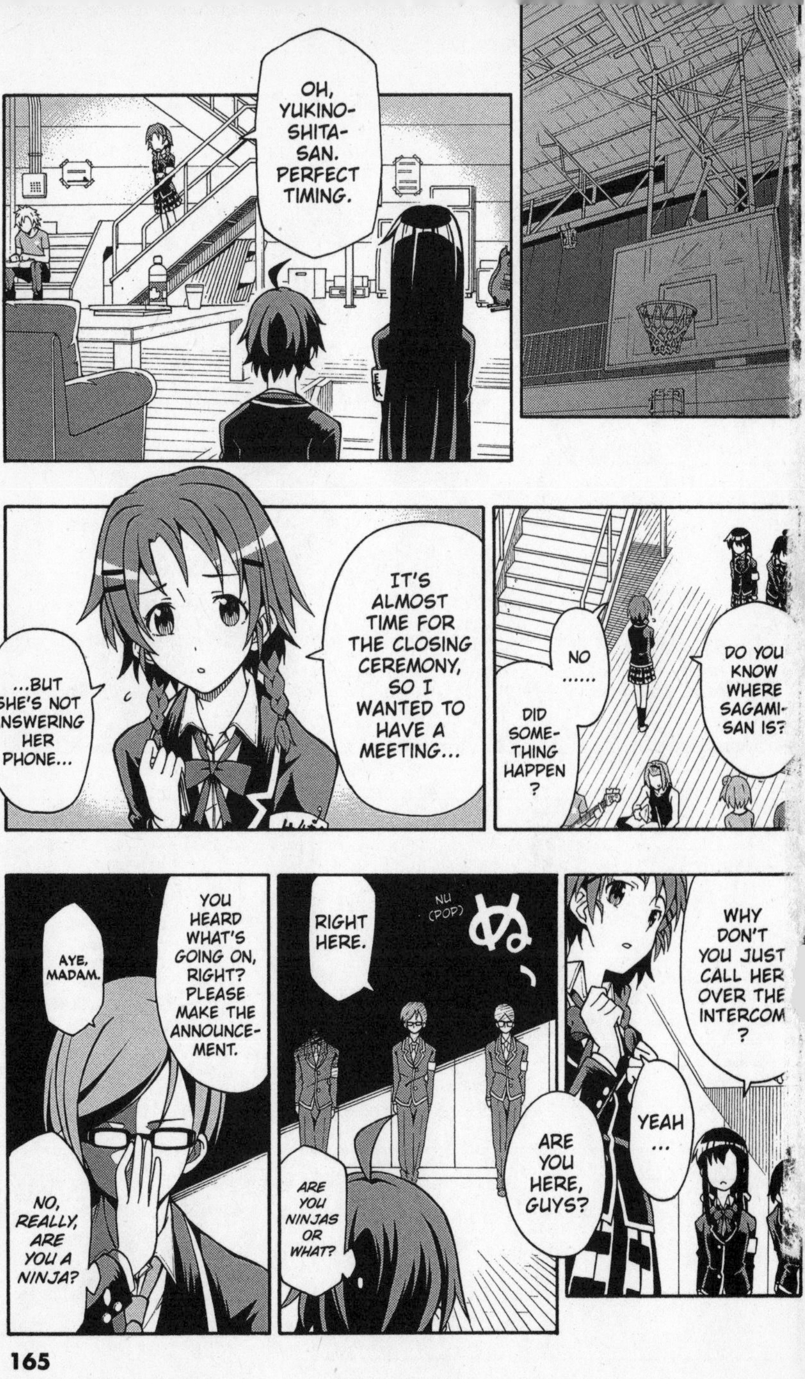
OH, YUKINO-SHITA-SAN. PERFECT TIMING.
DO YOU KNOW WHERE SAGAMI-SAN IS?
NO ......
DID SOME-THING HAPPEN?
IT'S ALMOST TIME FOR THE CLOSING CEREMONY, SO I WANTED TO HAVE A MEETING...
...BUT SHE'S NOT ANSWERING HER PHONE...
WHY DON'T YOU JUST CALL HER OVER THE INTERCOM?
YEAH ...
ARE YOU HERE, GUYS?
ぬ
NU (POP)
RIGHT HERE.
ARE YOU NINJAS OR WHAT?
YOU HEARD WHAT'S GOING ON, RIGHT? PLEASE MAKE THE ANNOUNCE-MENT.
AYE, MADAM.
NO, REALLY, ARE YOU A NINJA?

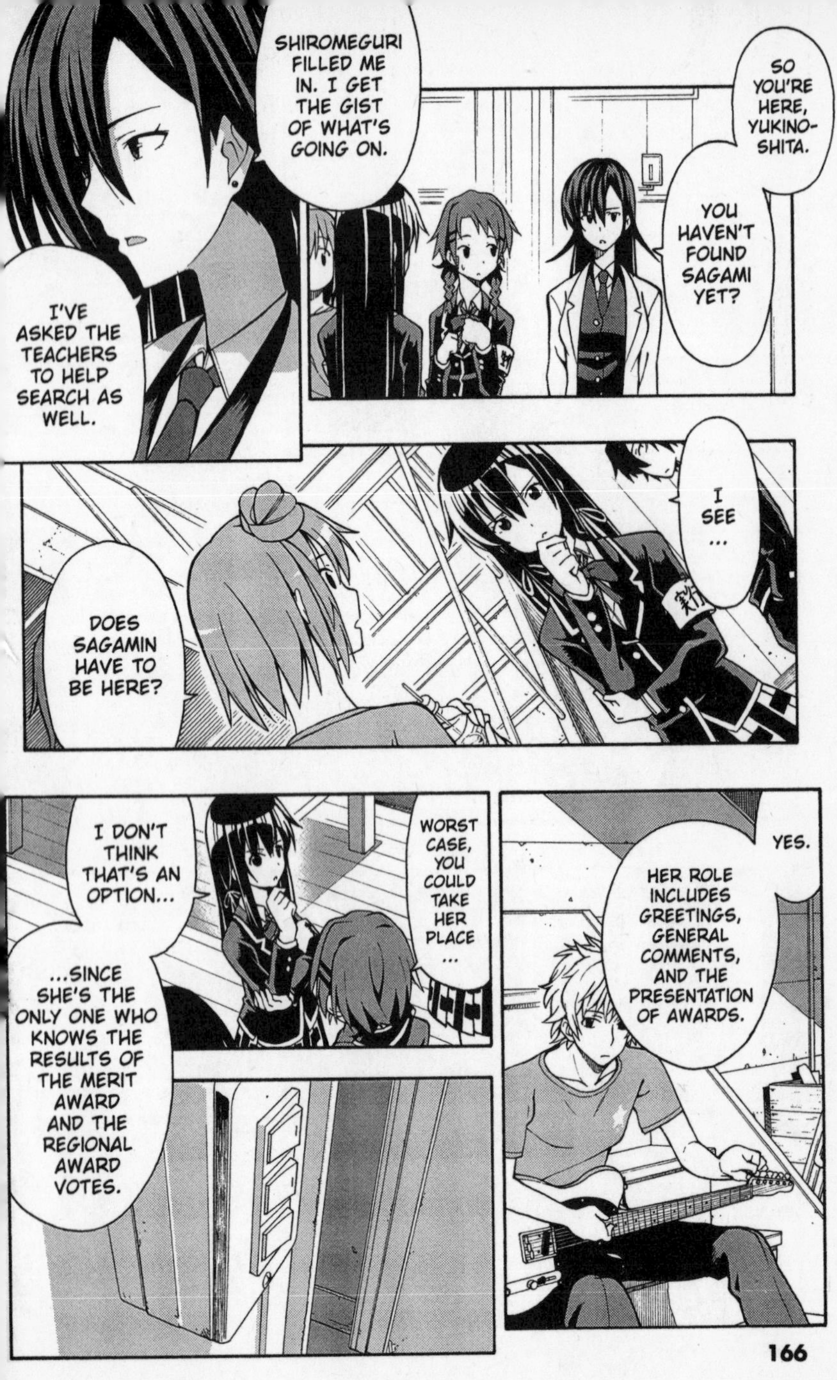
SO YOU'RE HERE, YUKINOSHITA.
YOU HAVEN'T FOUND SAGAMI YET?
SHIROMEGURI FILLED ME IN. I GET THE GIST OF WHAT'S GOING ON.
I'VE ASKED THE TEACHERS TO HELP SEARCH AS WELL.
I SEE...
DOES SAGAMIN HAVE TO BE HERE?
YES.
HER ROLE INCLUDES GREETINGS, GENERAL COMMENTS, AND THE PRESENTATION OF AWARDS.
WORST CASE, YOU COULD TAKE HER PLACE...
I DON'T THINK THAT'S AN OPTION...
...SINCE SHE'S THE ONLY ONE WHO KNOWS THE RESULTS OF THE MERIT AWARD AND THE REGIONAL AWARD VOTES.

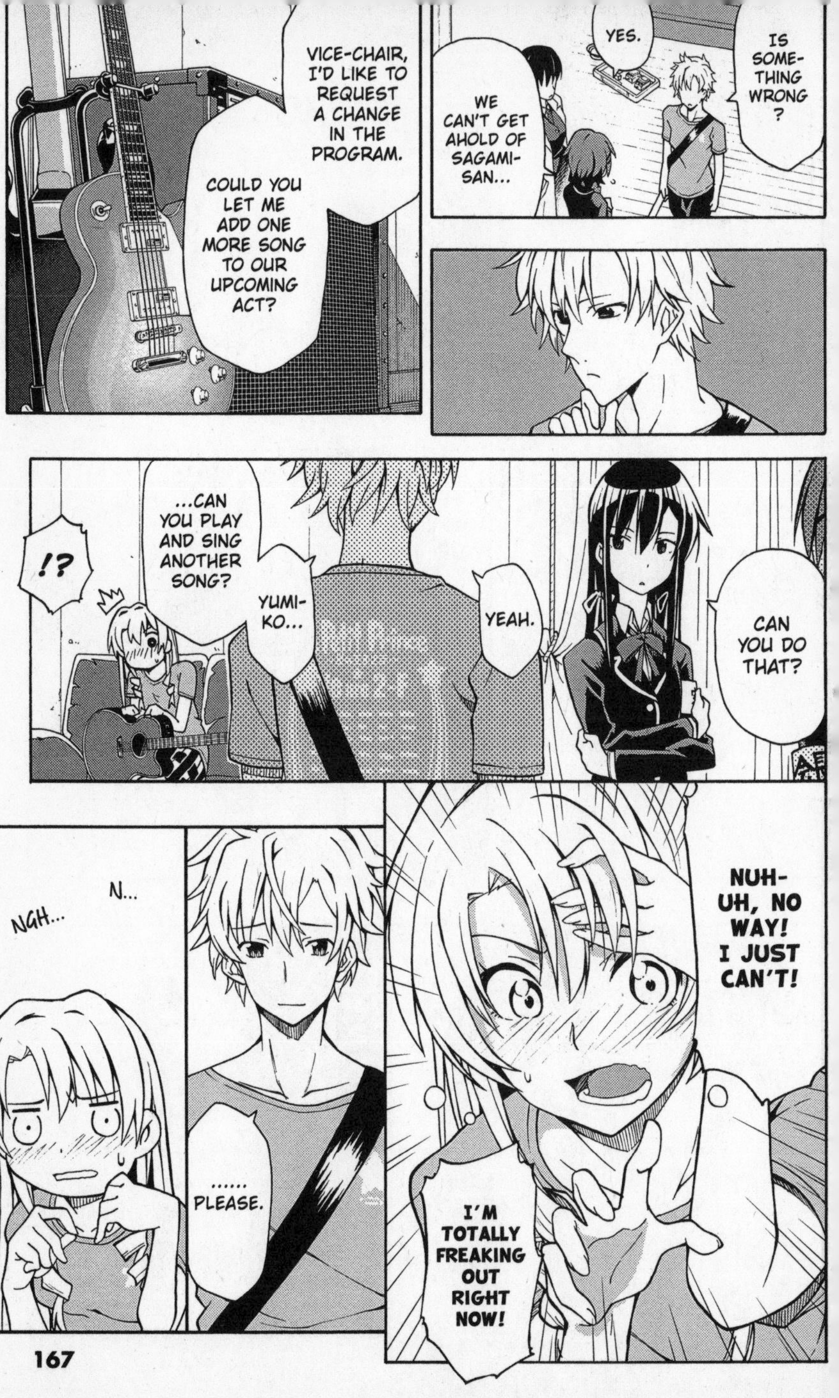
IS SOMETHING WRONG?
YES.
WE CAN'T GET AHOLD OF SAGAMI-SAN...
VICE-CHAIR, I'D LIKE TO REQUEST A CHANGE IN THE PROGRAM.
COULD YOU LET ME ADD ONE MORE SONG TO OUR UPCOMING ACT?
CAN YOU DO THAT?
YEAH.
YUMIKO...
...CAN YOU PLAY AND SING ANOTHER SONG?
!?
NUH-UH, NO WAY! I JUST CAN'T!
I'M TOTALLY FREAKING OUT RIGHT NOW!
......PLEASE.
N...
NGH...

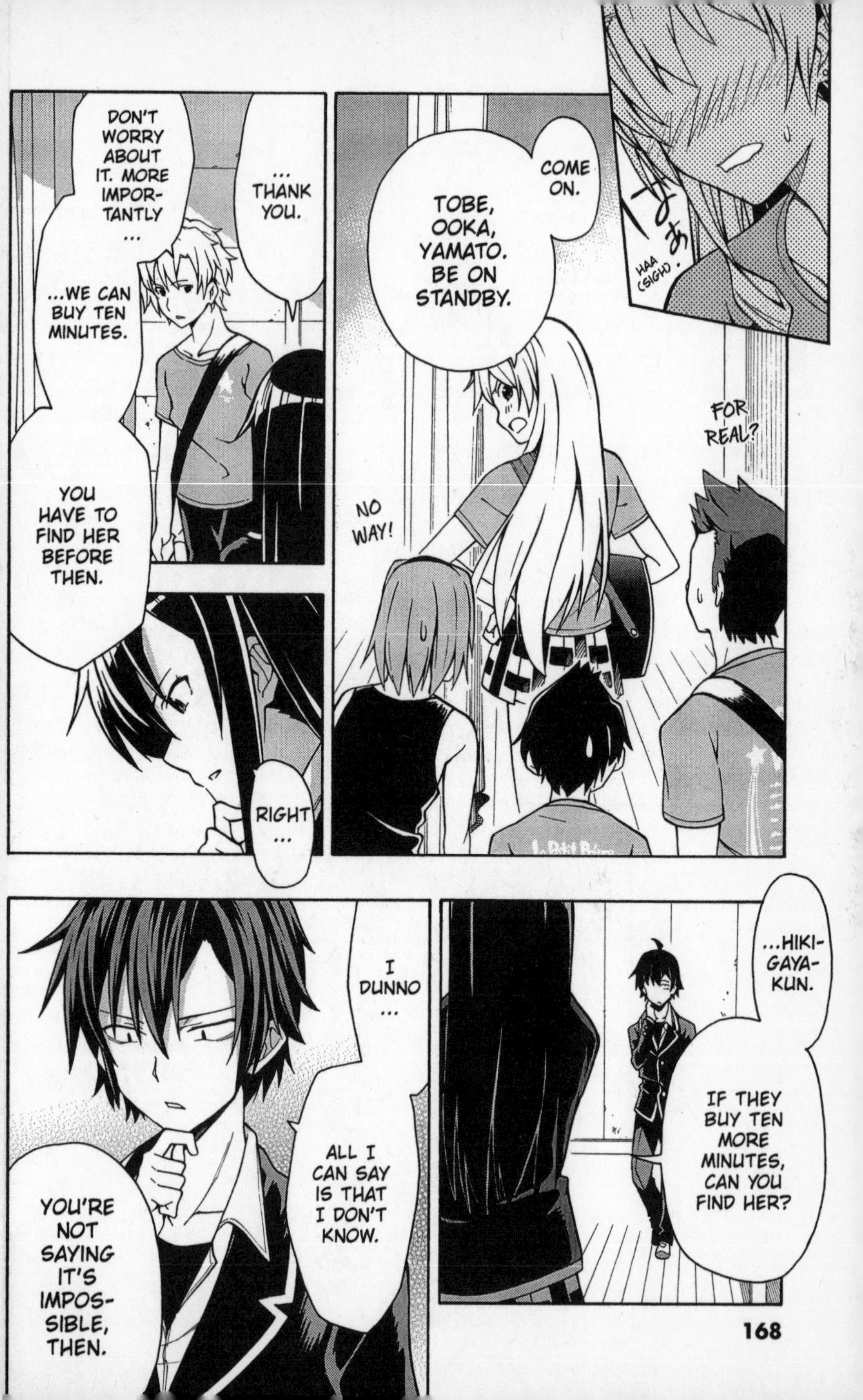
HAA (SIGH)
COME ON.
TOBE, OOKA, YAMATO. BE ON STANDBY.
FOR REAL?
NO WAY!
... THANK YOU.
DON'T WORRY ABOUT IT. MORE IMPOR-TANTLY ...
...WE CAN BUY TEN MINUTES.
YOU HAVE TO FIND HER BEFORE THEN.
RIGHT ...
...HIKI-GAYA-KUN.
IF THEY BUY TEN MORE MINUTES, CAN YOU FIND HER?
I DUNNO ...
ALL I CAN SAY IS THAT I DON'T KNOW.
YOU'RE NOT SAYING IT'S IMPOS-SIBLE, THEN.

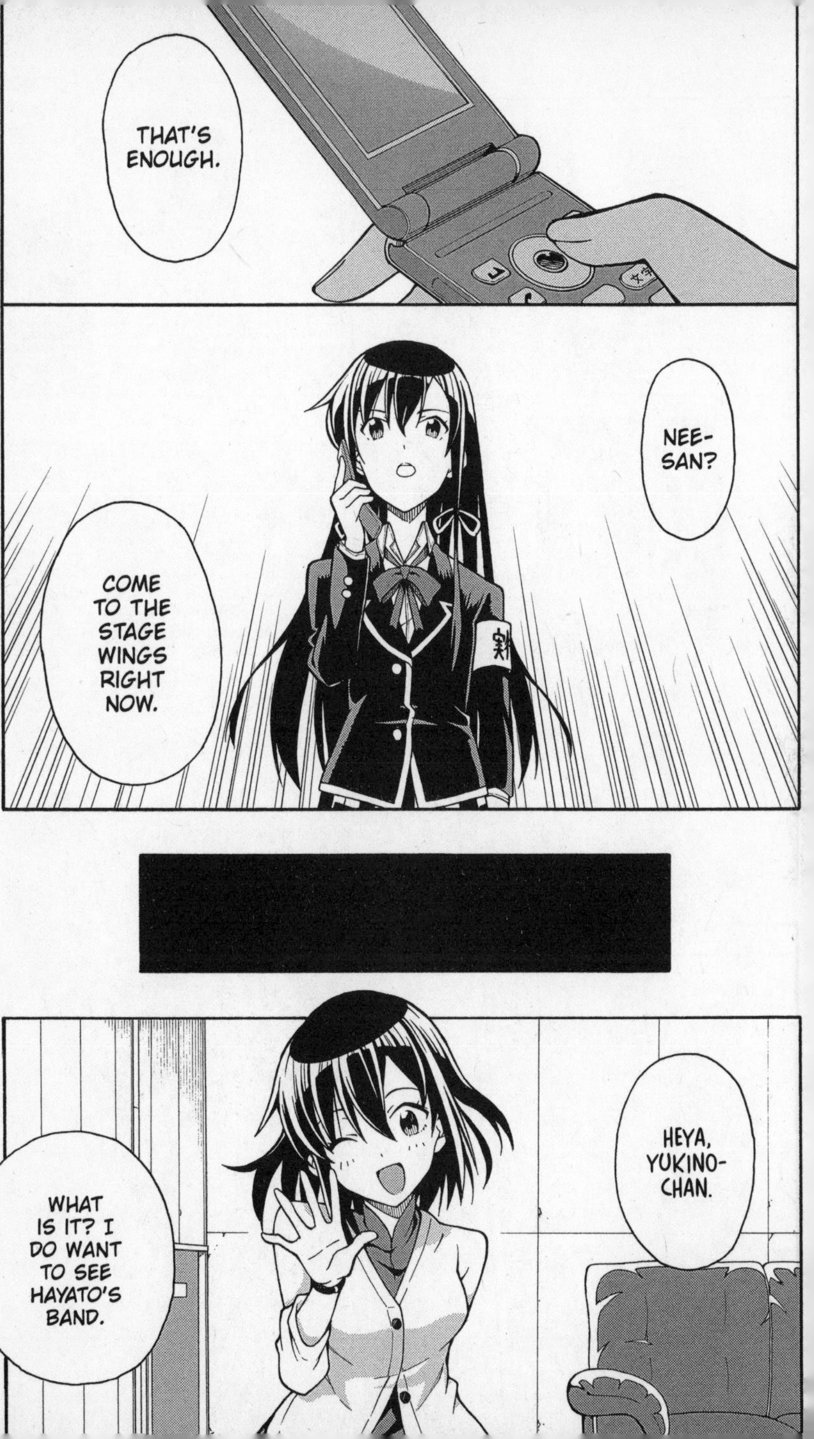
THAT'S ENOUGH.
NEE-SAN?
COME TO THE STAGE WINGS RIGHT NOW.
HEYA, YUKINO-CHAN.
WHAT IS IT? I DO WANT TO SEE HAYATO'S BAND.

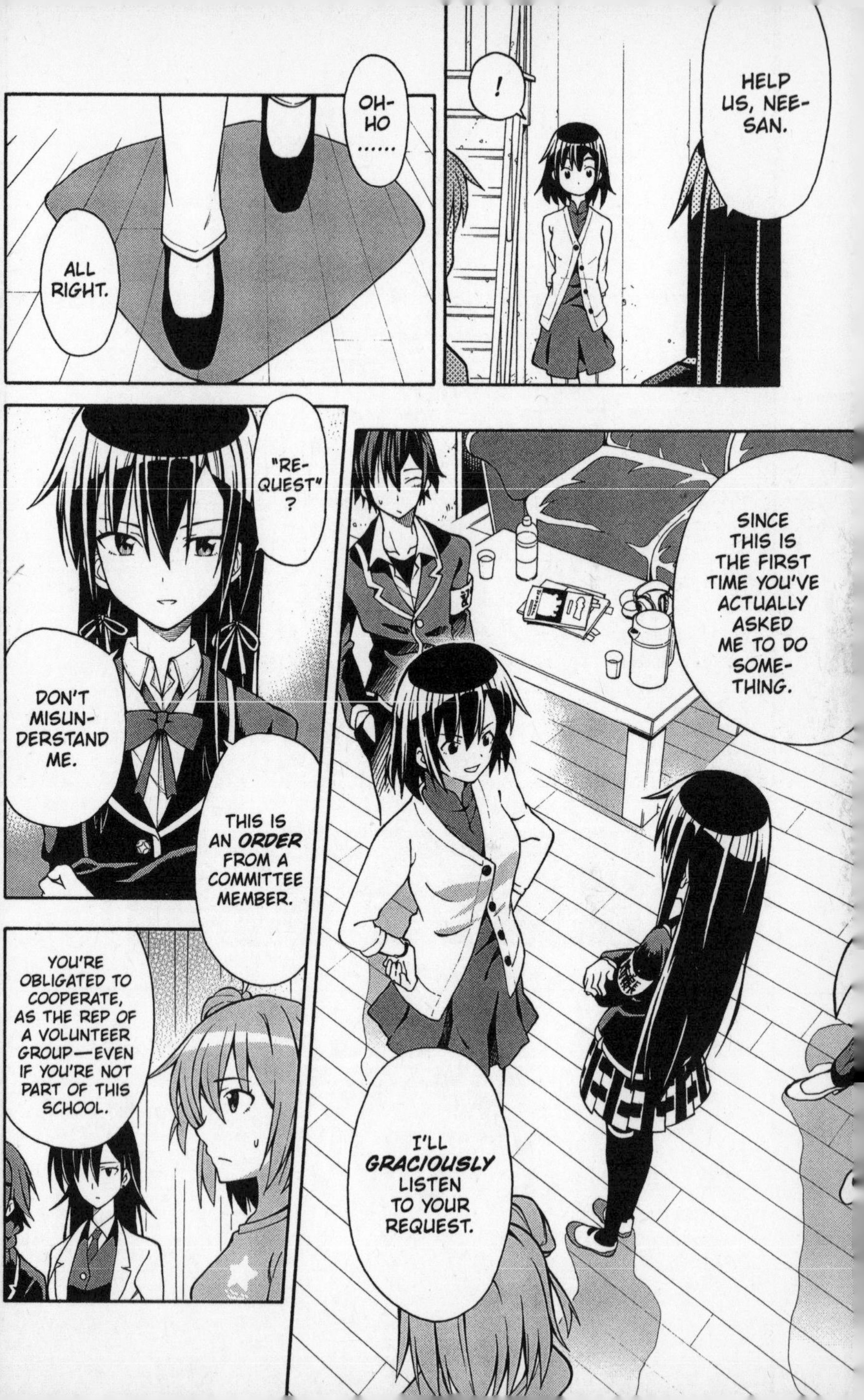
HELP US, NEE-SAN.
!
OH-HO ......
ALL RIGHT.
SINCE THIS IS THE FIRST TIME YOU'VE ACTUALLY ASKED ME TO DO SOME-THING.
I'LL *GRACIOUSLY* LISTEN TO YOUR REQUEST.
"RE-QUEST"?
DON'T MISUN-DERSTAND ME.
THIS IS AN *ORDER* FROM A COMMITTEE MEMBER.
YOU'RE OBLIGATED TO COOPERATE, AS THE REP OF A VOLUNTEER GROUP—EVEN IF YOU'RE NOT PART OF THIS SCHOOL.

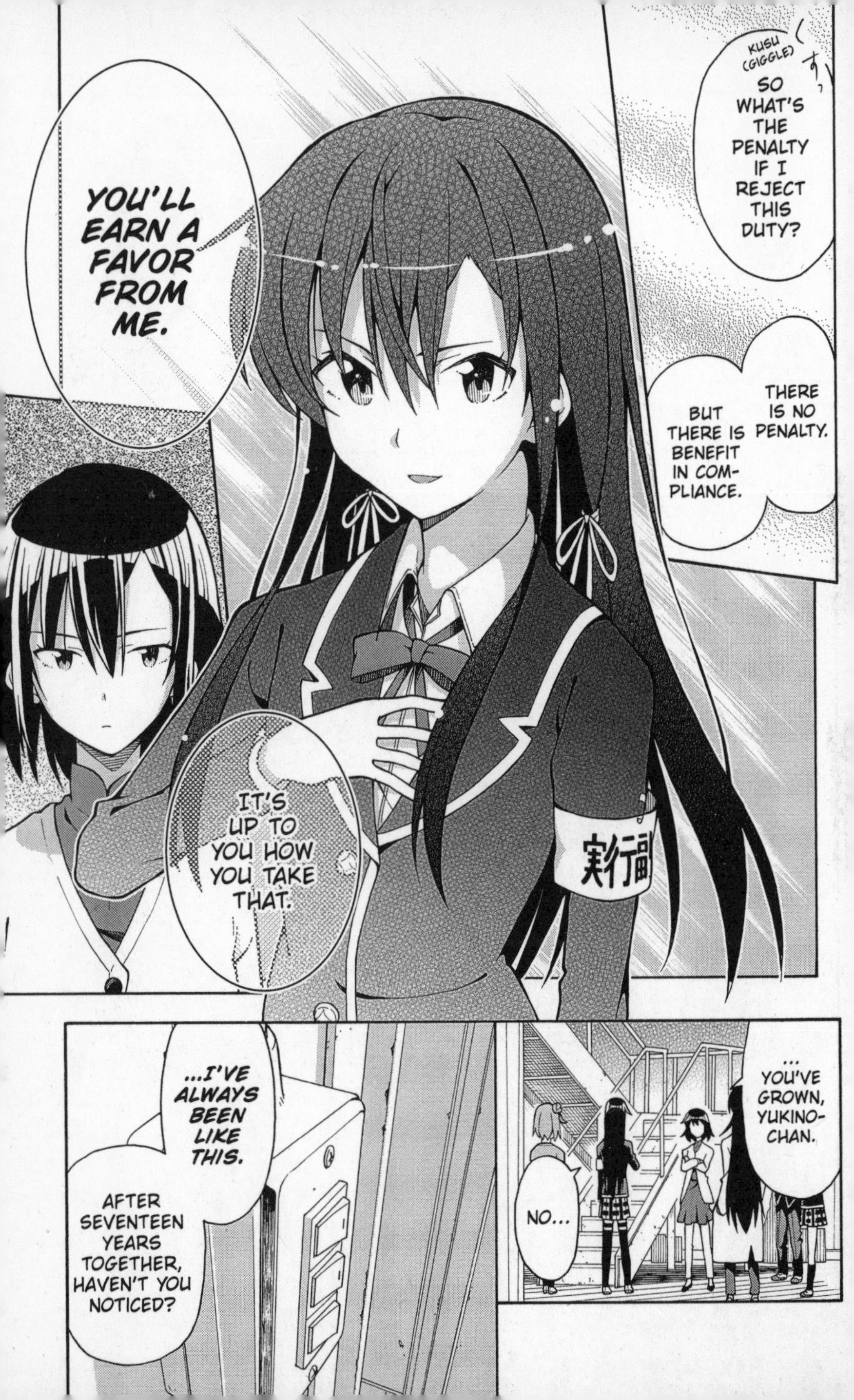
KUSU (GIGGLE)
SO WHAT'S THE PENALTY IF I REJECT THIS DUTY?
THERE IS NO PENALTY.
BUT THERE IS BENEFIT IN COMPLIANCE.
YOU'LL EARN A FAVOR FROM ME.
IT'S UP TO YOU HOW YOU TAKE THAT.
実行副
... YOU'VE GROWN, YUKINO-CHAN.
NO...
...I'VE ALWAYS BEEN LIKE THIS.
AFTER SEVENTEEN YEARS TOGETHER, HAVEN'T YOU NOTICED?

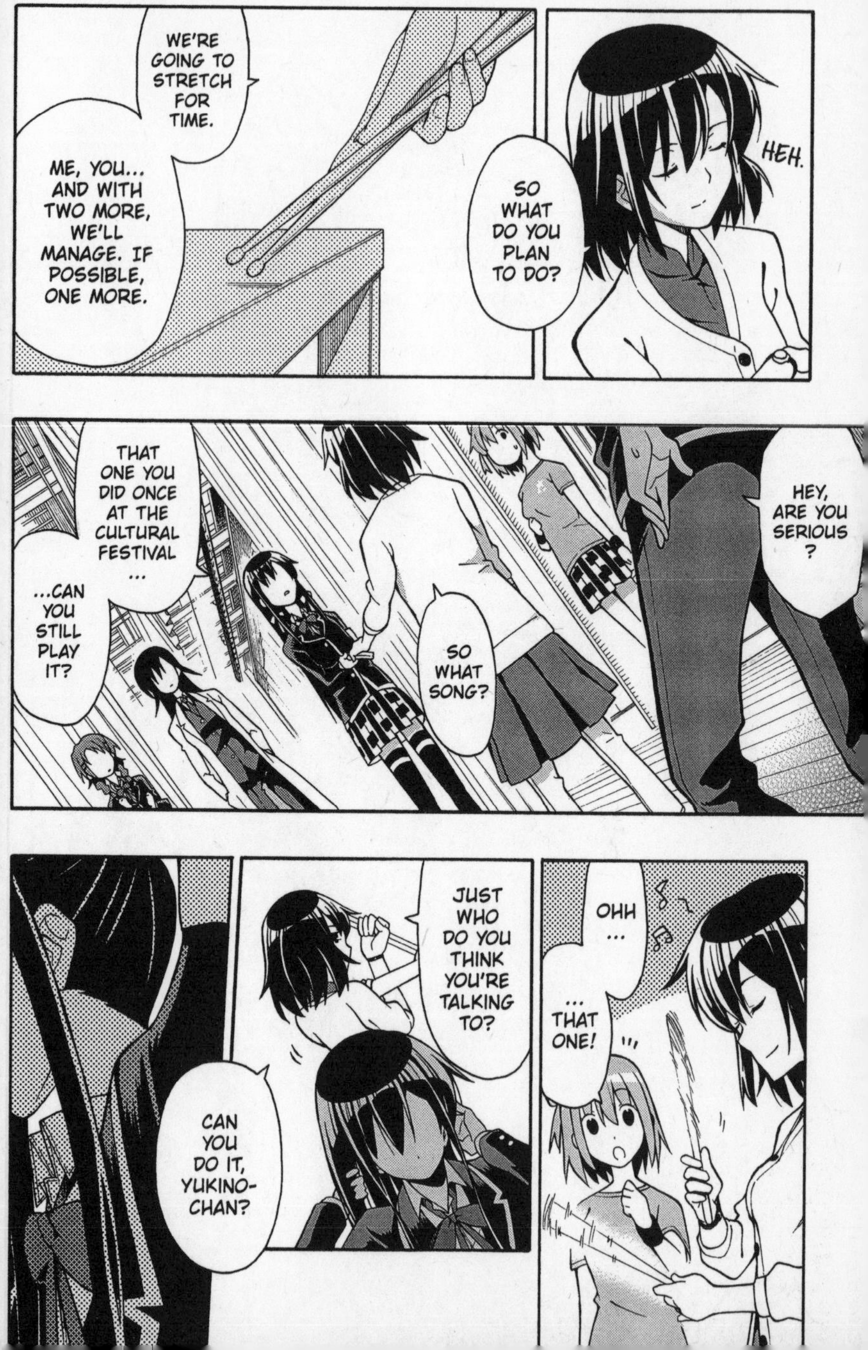
HEH.
SO WHAT DO YOU PLAN TO DO?
WE'RE GOING TO STRETCH FOR TIME.
ME, YOU... AND WITH TWO MORE, WE'LL MANAGE. IF POSSIBLE, ONE MORE.
HEY, ARE YOU SERIOUS?
SO WHAT SONG?
THAT ONE YOU DID ONCE AT THE CULTURAL FESTIVAL...
...CAN YOU STILL PLAY IT?
OHH...
...THAT ONE!
JUST WHO DO YOU THINK YOU'RE TALKING TO?
CAN YOU DO IT, YUKINO-CHAN?

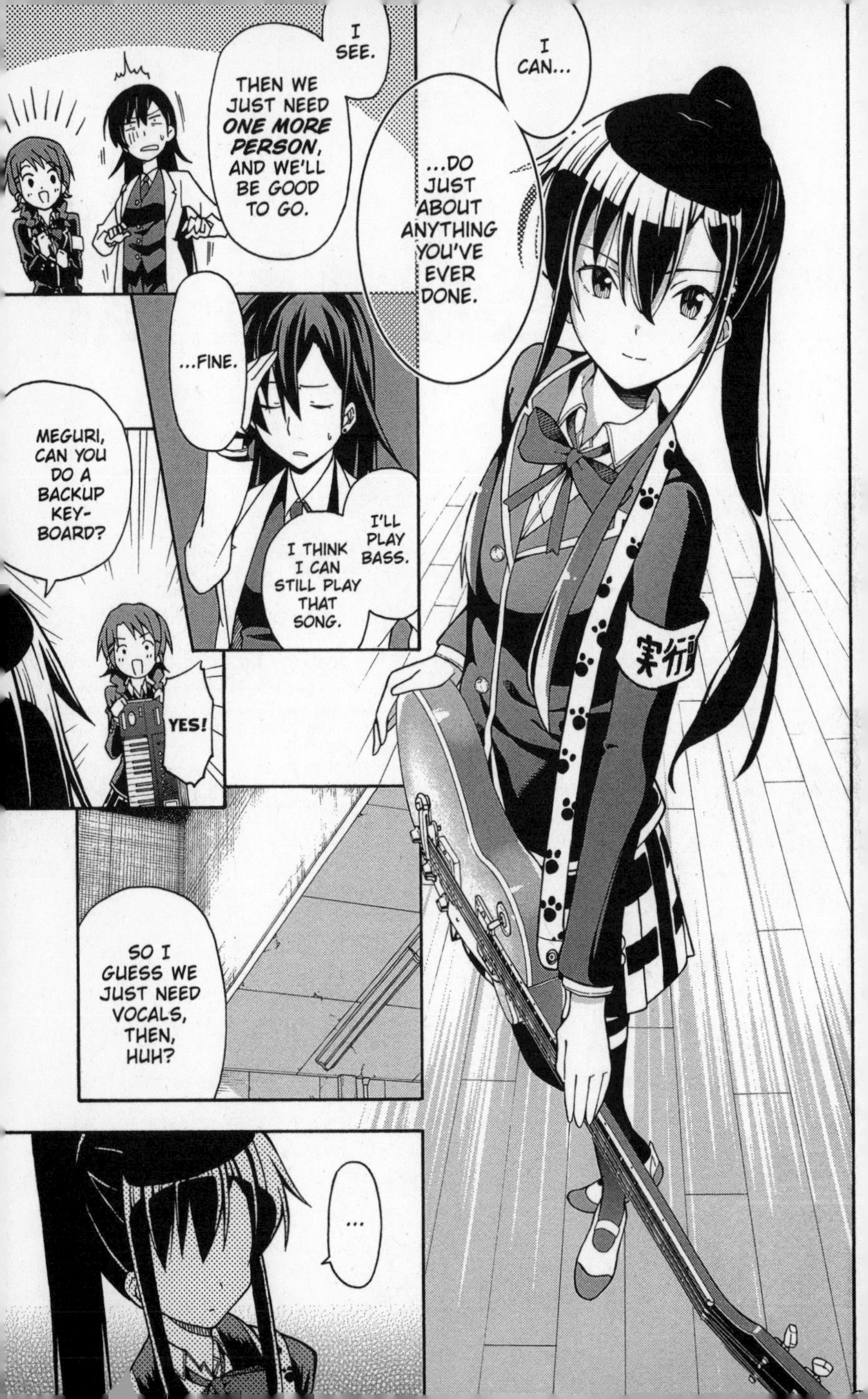
I CAN...
...DO JUST ABOUT ANYTHING YOU'VE EVER DONE.
I SEE.
THEN WE JUST NEED ONE MORE PERSON, AND WE'LL BE GOOD TO GO.
...FINE.
I'LL PLAY BASS.
I THINK I CAN STILL PLAY THAT SONG.
MEGURI, CAN YOU DO A BACKUP KEY-BOARD?
YES!
SO I GUESS WE JUST NEED VOCALS, THEN, HUH?
...

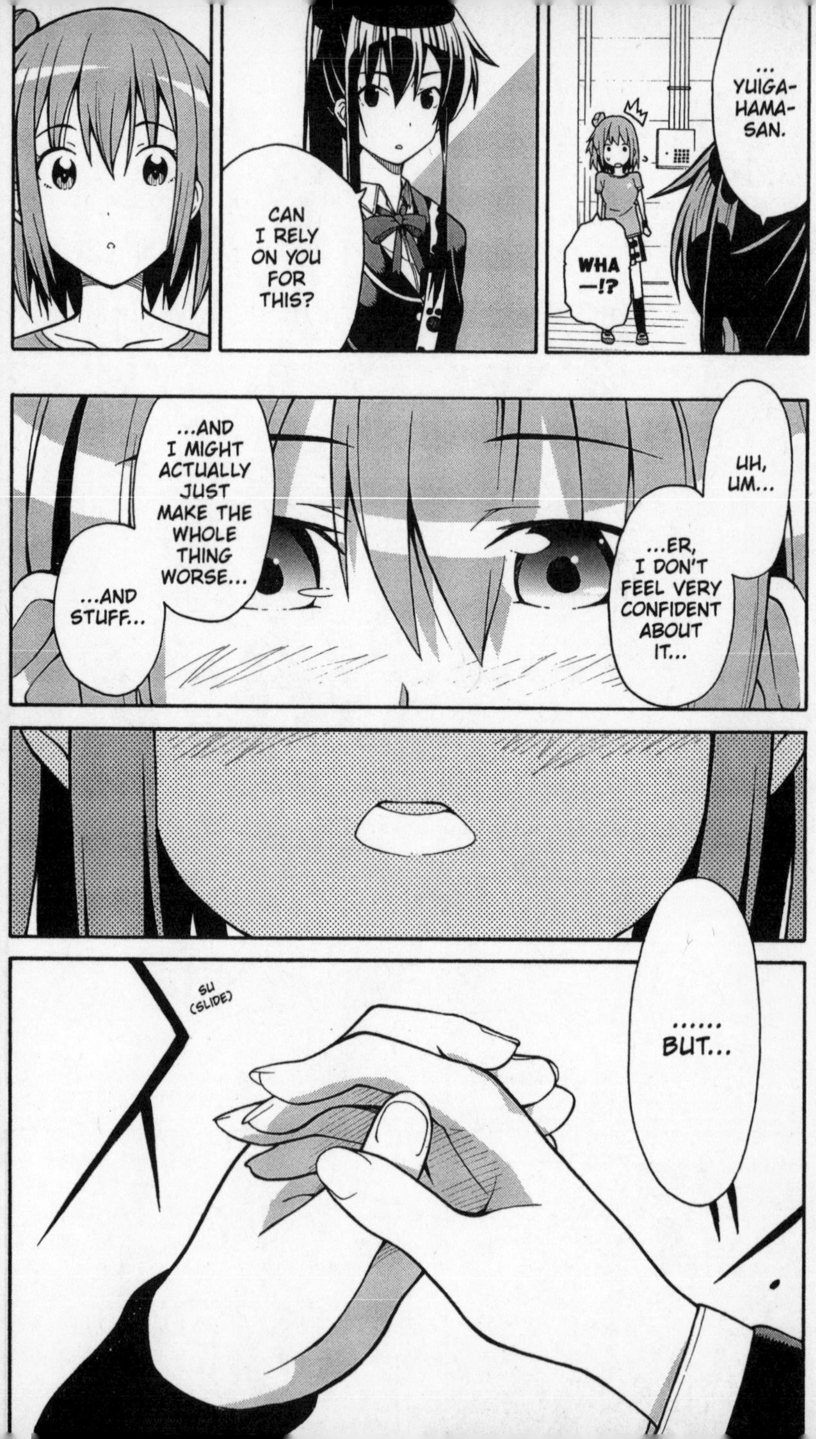
...YUIGA-HAMA-SAN.
WHA—!?
CAN I RELY ON YOU FOR THIS?
UH, UM...
...ER, I DON'T FEEL VERY CONFIDENT ABOUT IT...
...AND I MIGHT ACTUALLY JUST MAKE THE WHOLE THING WORSE...
...AND STUFF...
...... BUT...
SU (SLIDE)

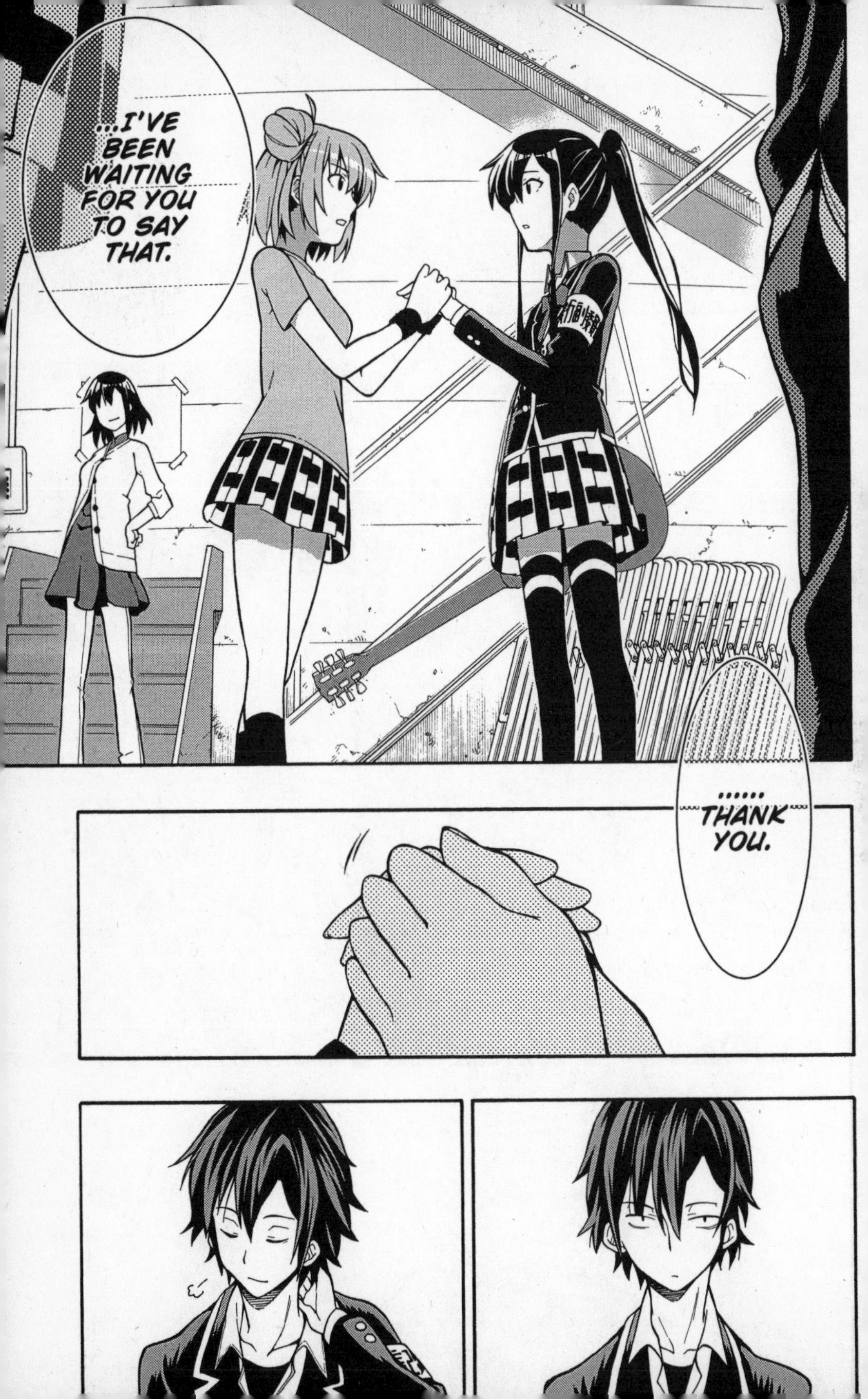
...I'VE BEEN WAITING FOR YOU TO SAY THAT.
...... THANK YOU.

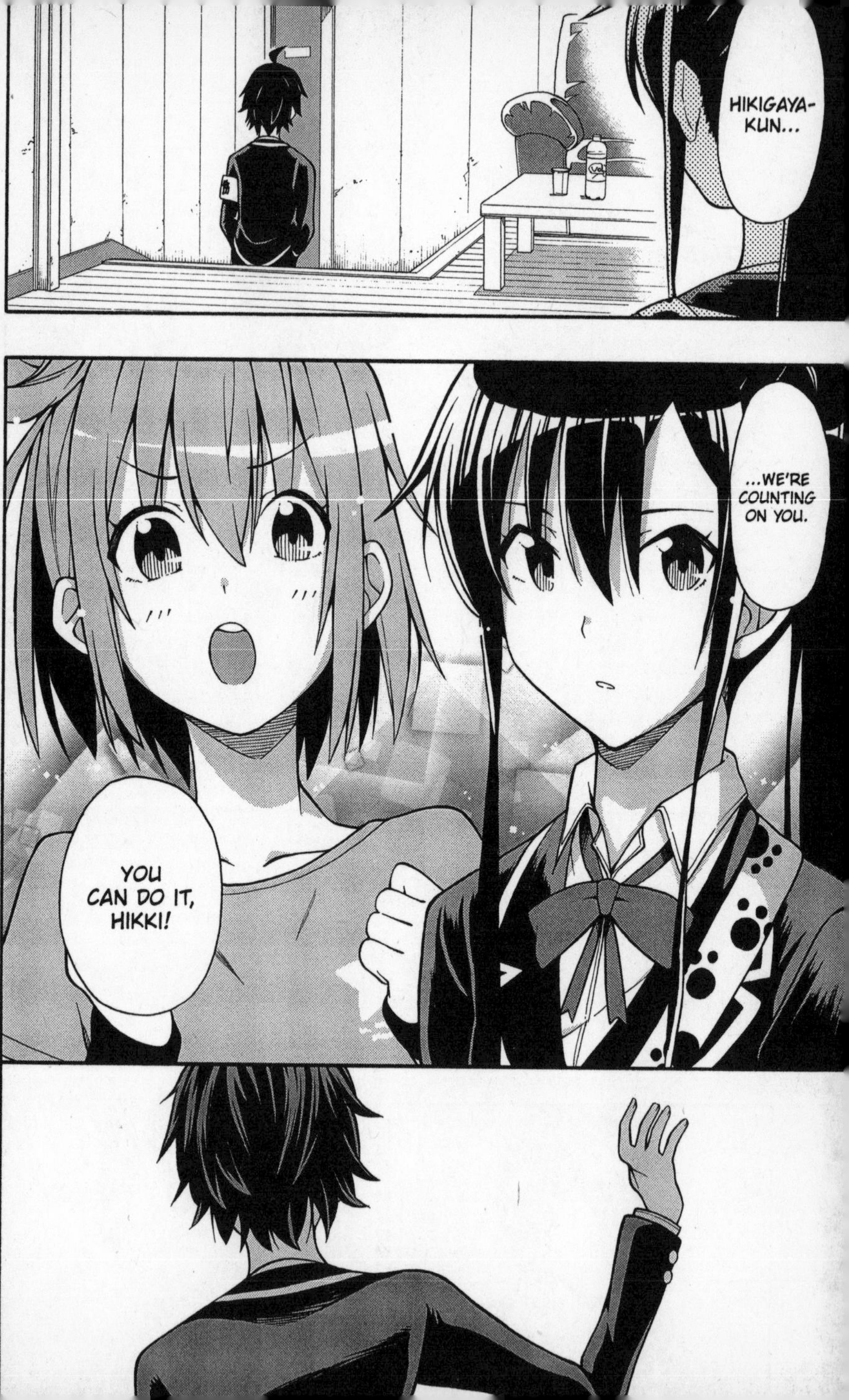
HIKIGAYA-KUN...
...WE'RE COUNTING ON YOU.
YOU CAN DO IT, HIKKI!

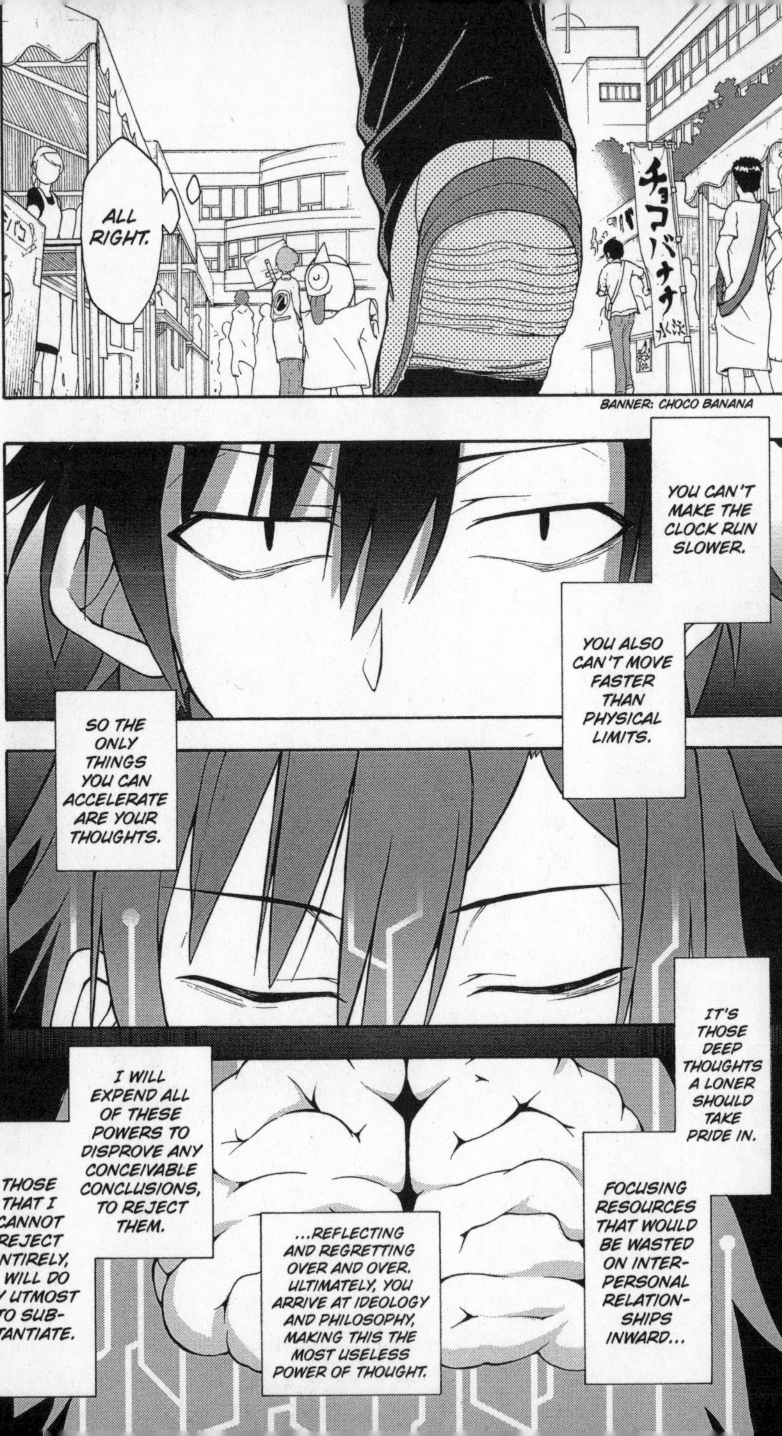
チョコバナナ
ALL RIGHT.
BANNER: CHOCO BANANA
YOU CAN'T MAKE THE CLOCK RUN SLOWER.
YOU ALSO CAN'T MOVE FASTER THAN PHYSICAL LIMITS.
SO THE ONLY THINGS YOU CAN ACCELERATE ARE YOUR THOUGHTS.
IT'S THOSE DEEP THOUGHTS A LONER SHOULD TAKE PRIDE IN.
FOCUSING RESOURCES THAT WOULD BE WASTED ON INTER-PERSONAL RELATION-SHIPS INWARD...
...REFLECTING AND REGRETTING OVER AND OVER. ULTIMATELY, YOU ARRIVE AT IDEOLOGY AND PHILOSOPHY, MAKING THIS THE MOST USELESS POWER OF THOUGHT.
I WILL EXPEND ALL OF THESE POWERS TO DISPROVE ANY CONCEIVABLE CONCLUSIONS, TO REJECT THEM.
THOSE THAT I CANNOT REJECT ENTIRELY, I WILL DO MY UTMOST TO SUB-STANTIATE.

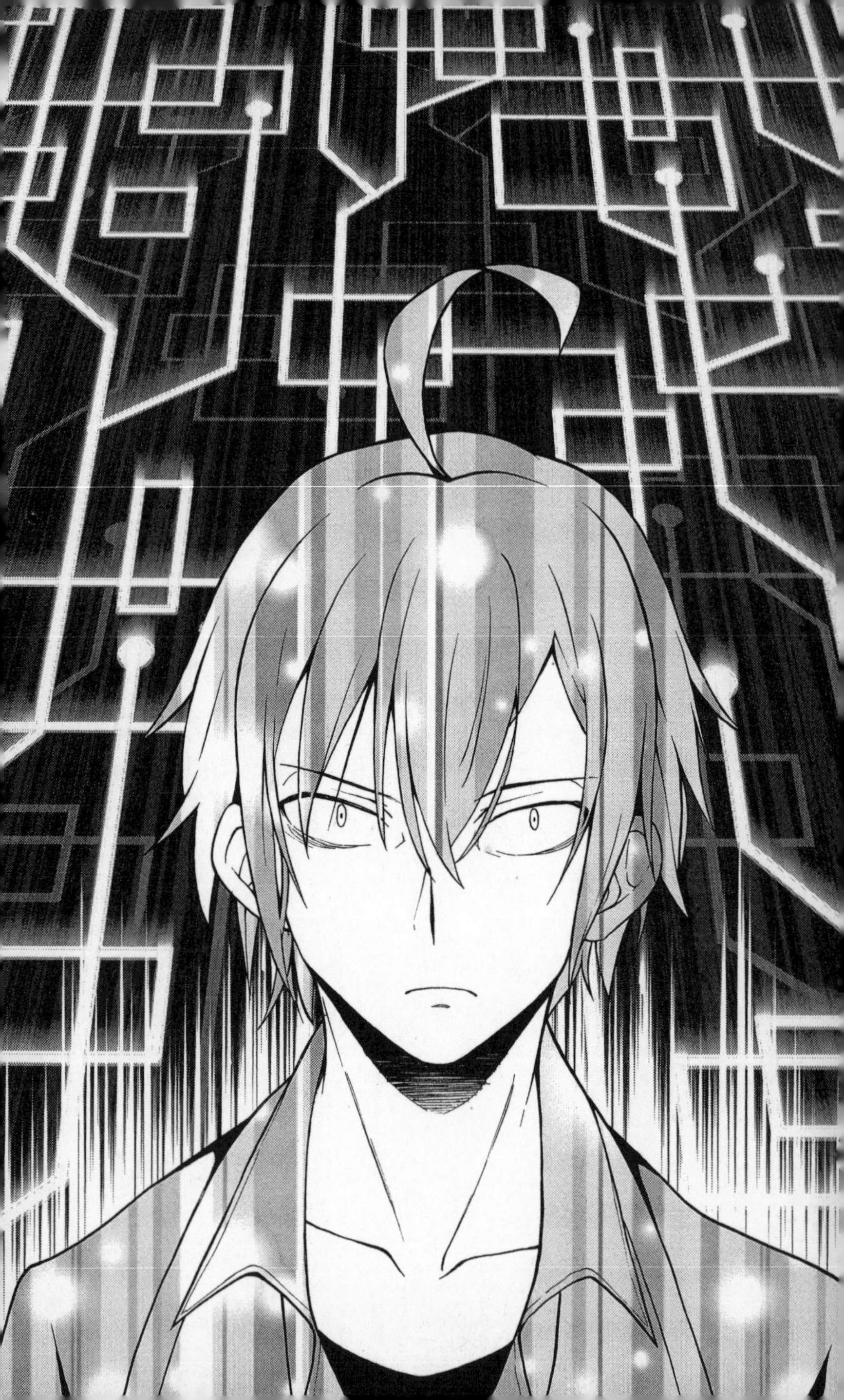

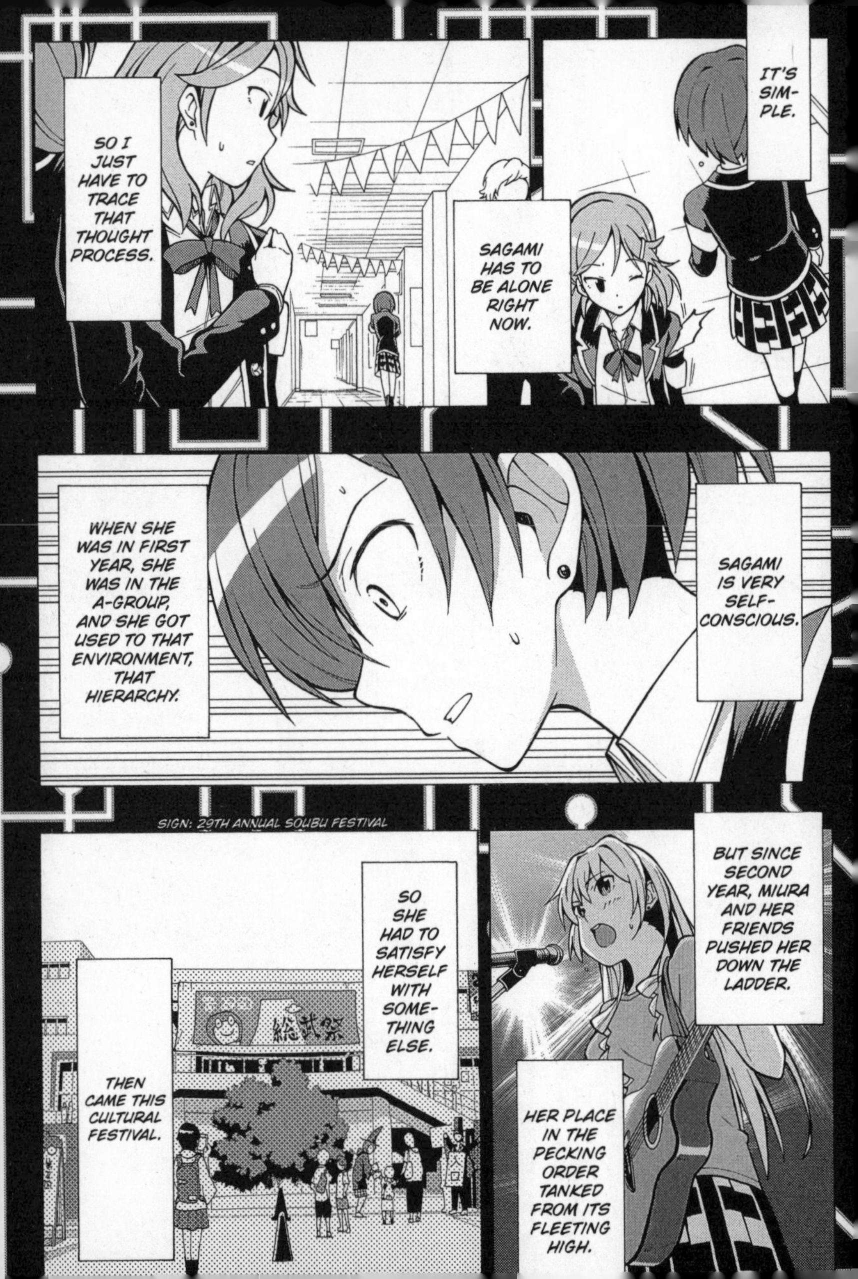
IT'S SIMPLE.
SAGAMI HAS TO BE ALONE RIGHT NOW.
SO I JUST HAVE TO TRACE THAT THOUGHT PROCESS.
SAGAMI IS VERY SELF-CONSCIOUS.
WHEN SHE WAS IN FIRST YEAR, SHE WAS IN THE A-GROUP, AND SHE GOT USED TO THAT ENVIRONMENT, THAT HIERARCHY.
BUT SINCE SECOND YEAR, MIURA AND HER FRIENDS PUSHED HER DOWN THE LADDER.
HER PLACE IN THE PECKING ORDER TANKED FROM ITS FLEETING HIGH.
SIGN: 29TH ANNUAL SOUBU FESTIVAL
SO SHE HAD TO SATISFY HERSELF WITH SOMETHING ELSE.
THEN CAME THIS CULTURAL FESTIVAL.

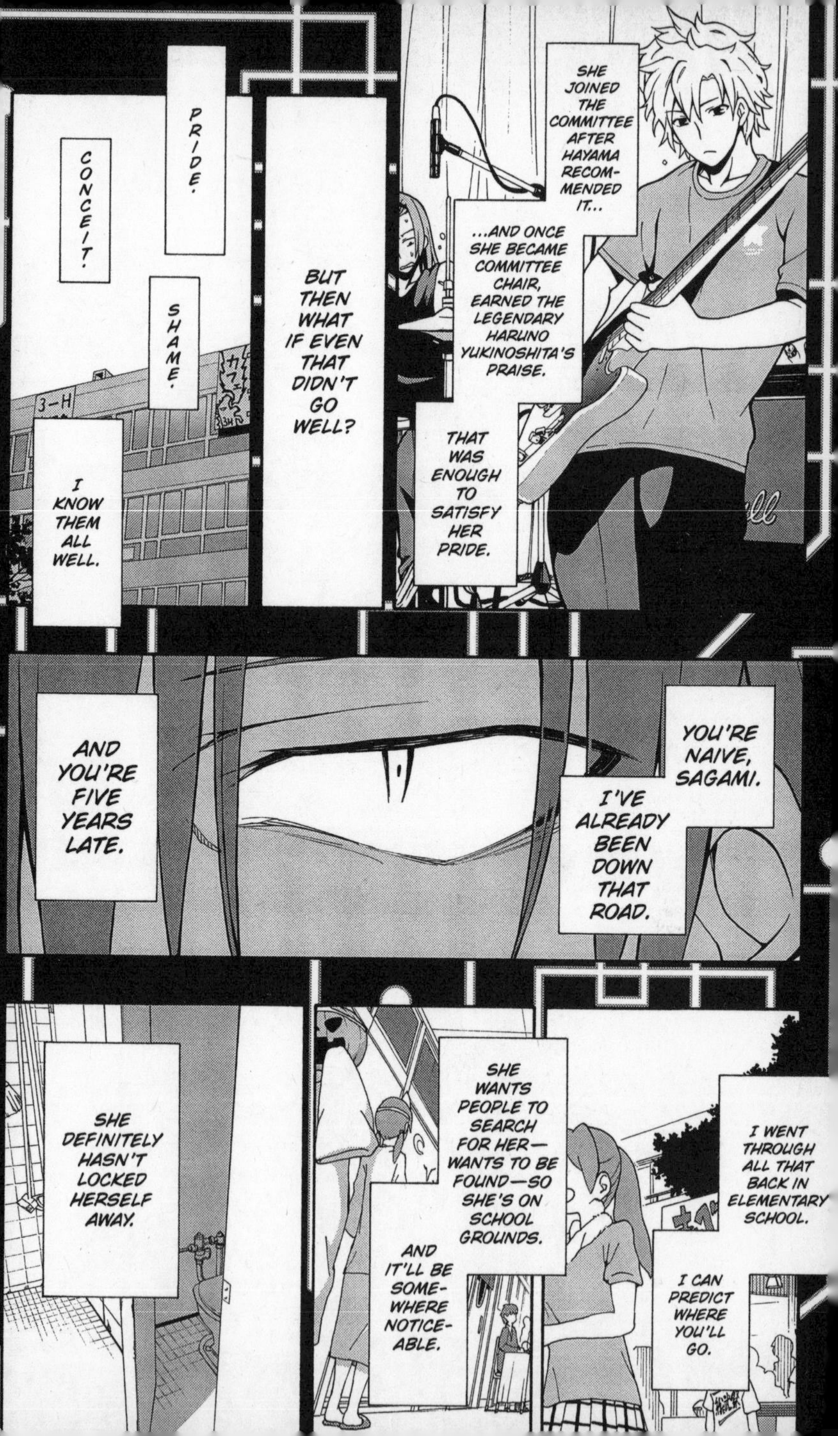
SHE JOINED THE COMMITTEE AFTER HAYAMA RECOMMENDED IT...
...AND ONCE SHE BECAME COMMITTEE CHAIR, EARNED THE LEGENDARY HARUNO YUKINOSHITA'S PRAISE.
THAT WAS ENOUGH TO SATISFY HER PRIDE.
BUT THEN WHAT IF EVEN THAT DIDN'T GO WELL?
PRIDE.
CONCEIT.
SHAME.
I KNOW THEM ALL WELL.
YOU'RE NAIVE, SAGAMI.
I'VE ALREADY BEEN DOWN THAT ROAD.
AND YOU'RE FIVE YEARS LATE.
I WENT THROUGH ALL THAT BACK IN ELEMENTARY SCHOOL.
I CAN PREDICT WHERE YOU'LL GO.
SHE WANTS PEOPLE TO SEARCH FOR HER—WANTS TO BE FOUND—SO SHE'S ON SCHOOL GROUNDS.
AND IT'LL BE SOMEWHERE NOTICEABLE.
SHE DEFINITELY HASN'T LOCKED HERSELF AWAY.

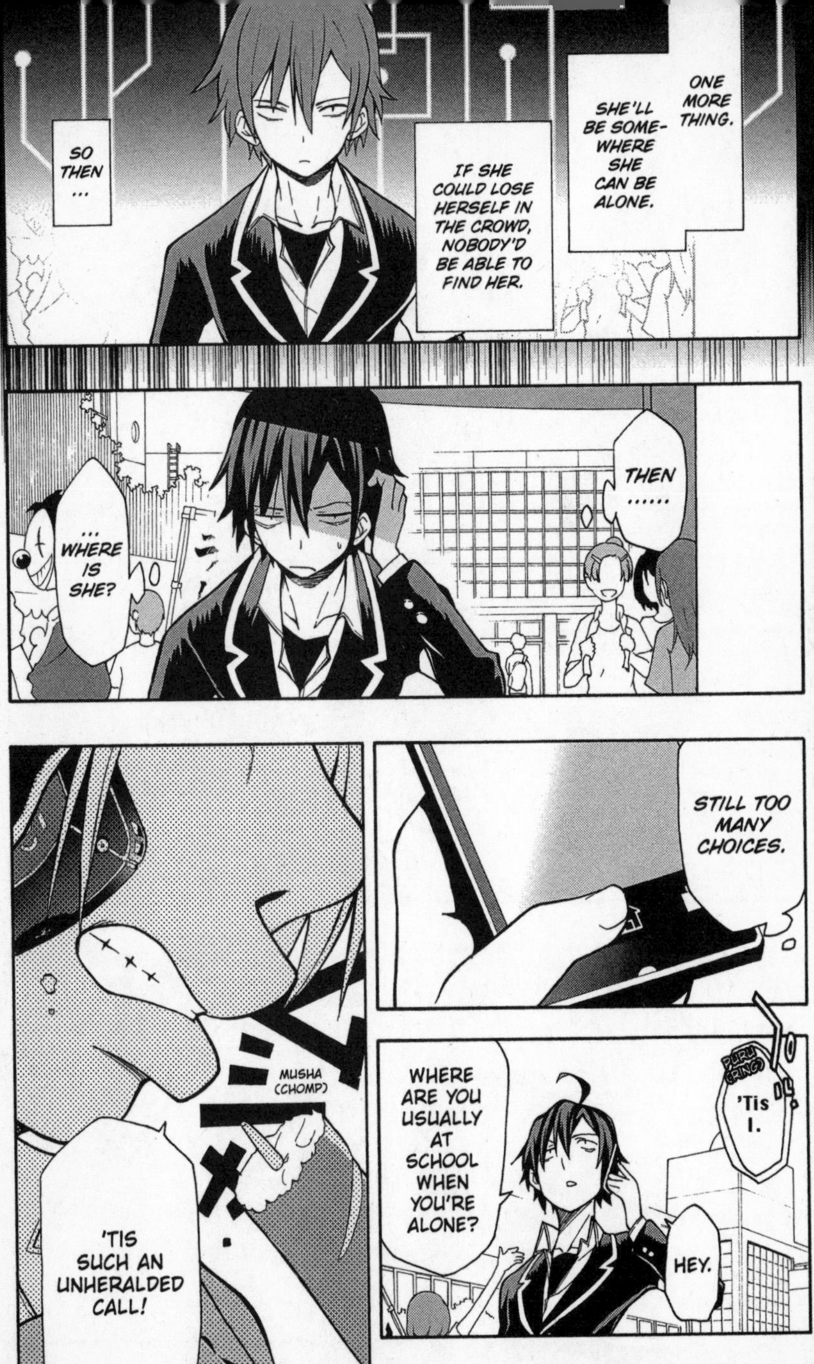
ONE MORE THING.
SHE'LL BE SOME-WHERE SHE CAN BE ALONE.
IF SHE COULD LOSE HERSELF IN THE CROWD, NOBODY'D BE ABLE TO FIND HER.
SO THEN ...
THEN ......
... WHERE IS SHE?
STILL TOO MANY CHOICES.
PURU (RING)
'Tis I.
HEY.
WHERE ARE YOU USUALLY AT SCHOOL WHEN YOU'RE ALONE?
MUSHA (CHOMP)
'TIS SUCH AN UNHERALDED CALL!

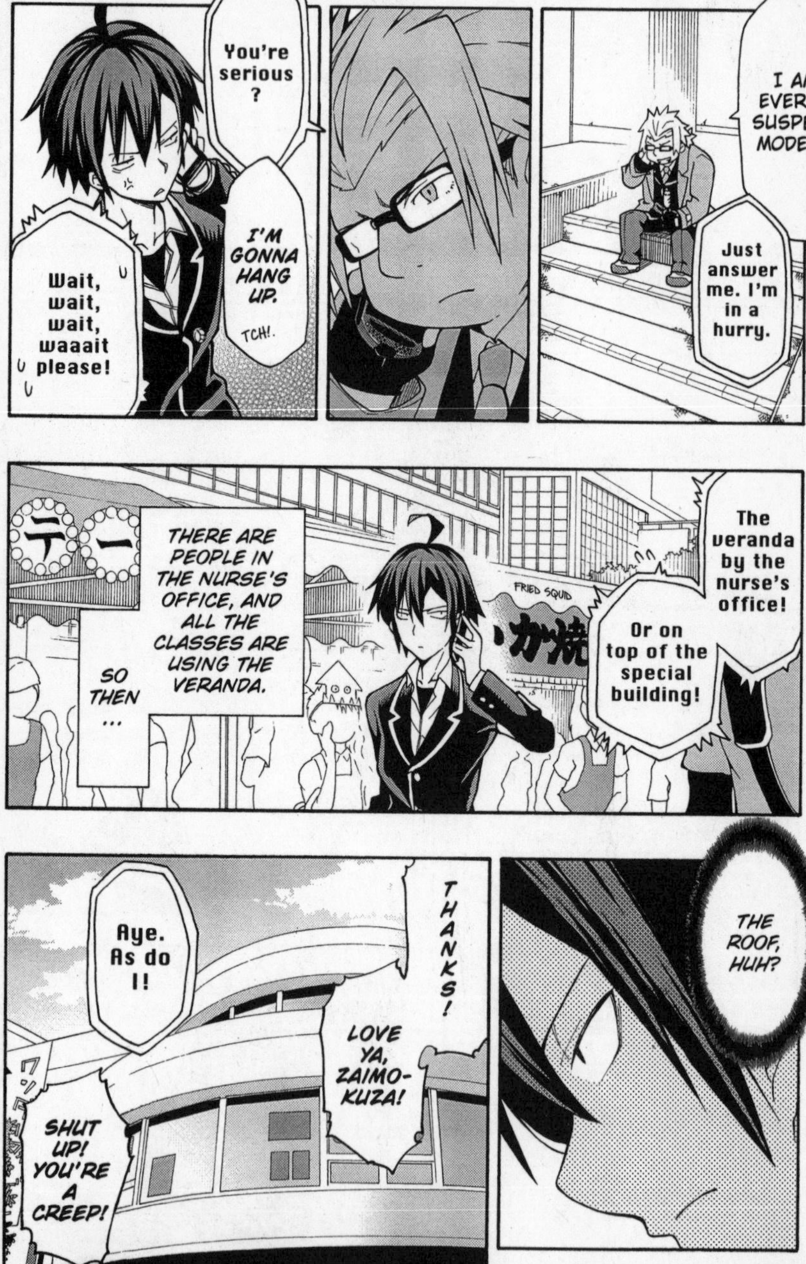

I AM EVER IN SUSPEND MODE—
Just answer me. I'm in a hurry.
You're serious?
I'M GONNA HANG UP.
TCH!.
Wait, wait, wait, waaait please!
The veranda by the nurse's office!
Or on top of the special building!
FRIED SQUID
THERE ARE PEOPLE IN THE NURSE'S OFFICE, AND ALL THE CLASSES ARE USING THE VERANDA.
SO THEN ...
THE ROOF, HUH?
THANKS!
LOVE YA, ZAIMOKUZA!
Aye. As do I!
SHUT UP! YOU'RE A CREEP!

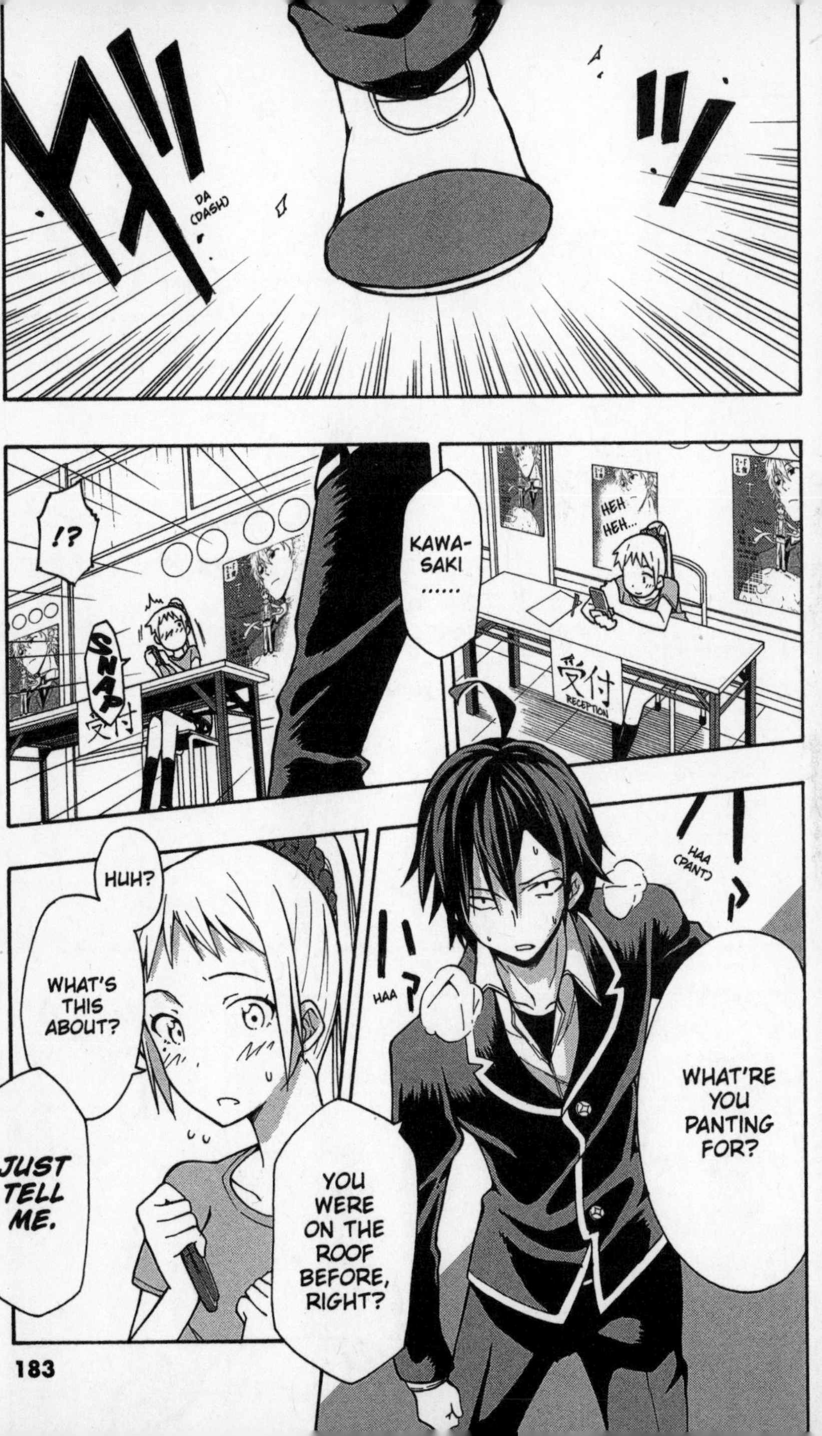
DA (DASH)
KAWA-SAKI......
HEH HEH...
受付
RECEPTION
!?
SNAP
受付
HAA (PANT)
HAA
WHAT'RE YOU PANTING FOR?
YOU WERE ON THE ROOF BEFORE, RIGHT?
HUH?
WHAT'S THIS ABOUT?
JUST TELL ME.

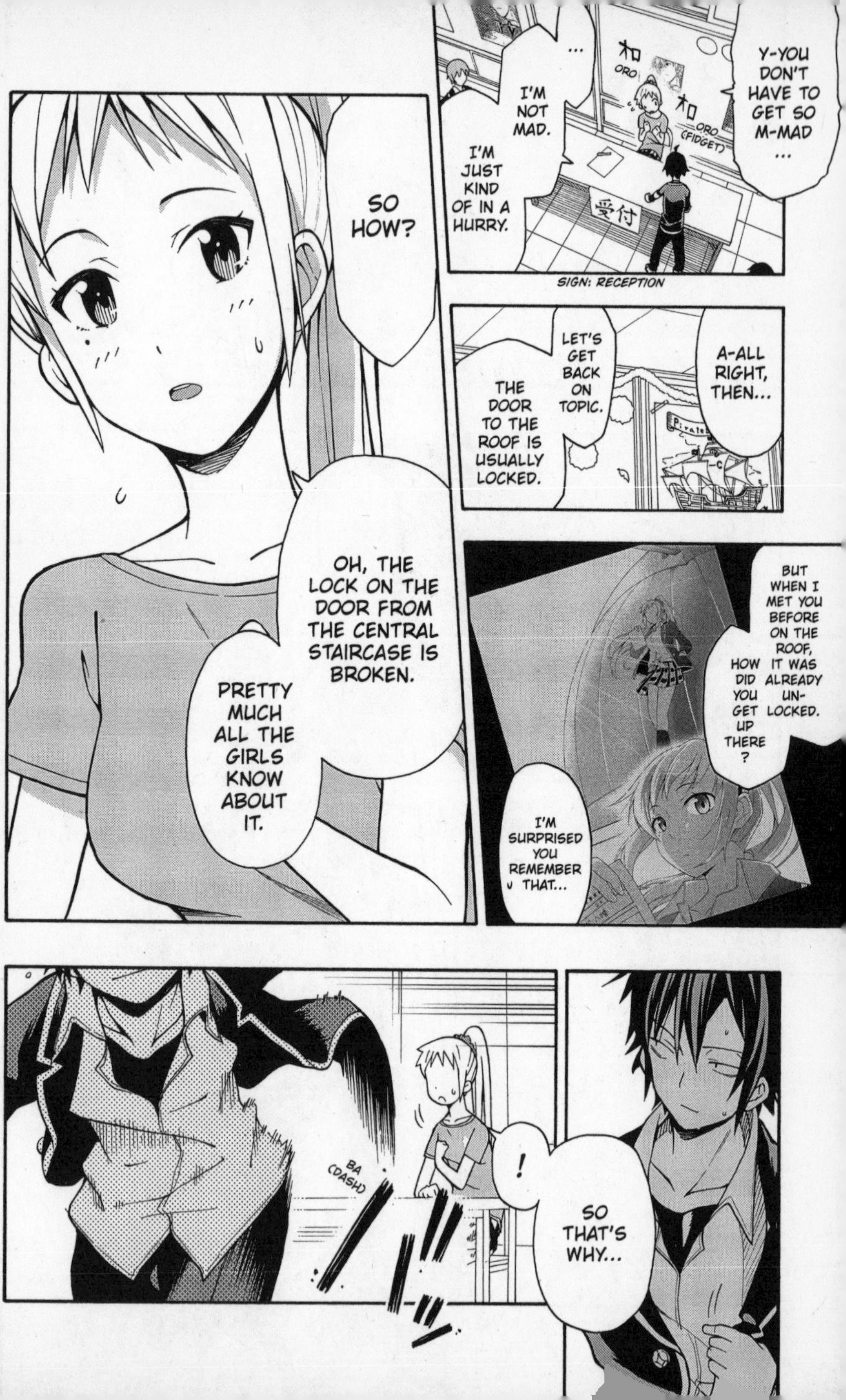
Y-YOU DON'T HAVE TO GET SO M-MAD ...
ORO
ORO (FIDGET)
受付
...
I'M NOT MAD.
I'M JUST KIND OF IN A HURRY.
SIGN: RECEPTION
A-ALL RIGHT, THEN...
LET'S GET BACK ON TOPIC.
THE DOOR TO THE ROOF IS USUALLY LOCKED.
SO HOW?
BUT WHEN I MET YOU BEFORE ON THE ROOF, IT WAS ALREADY UN-LOCKED.
HOW DID YOU GET UP THERE ?
I'M SURPRISED YOU REMEMBER THAT...
OH, THE LOCK ON THE DOOR FROM THE CENTRAL STAIRCASE IS BROKEN.
PRETTY MUCH ALL THE GIRLS KNOW ABOUT IT.
!
SO THAT'S WHY...
BA (DASH)

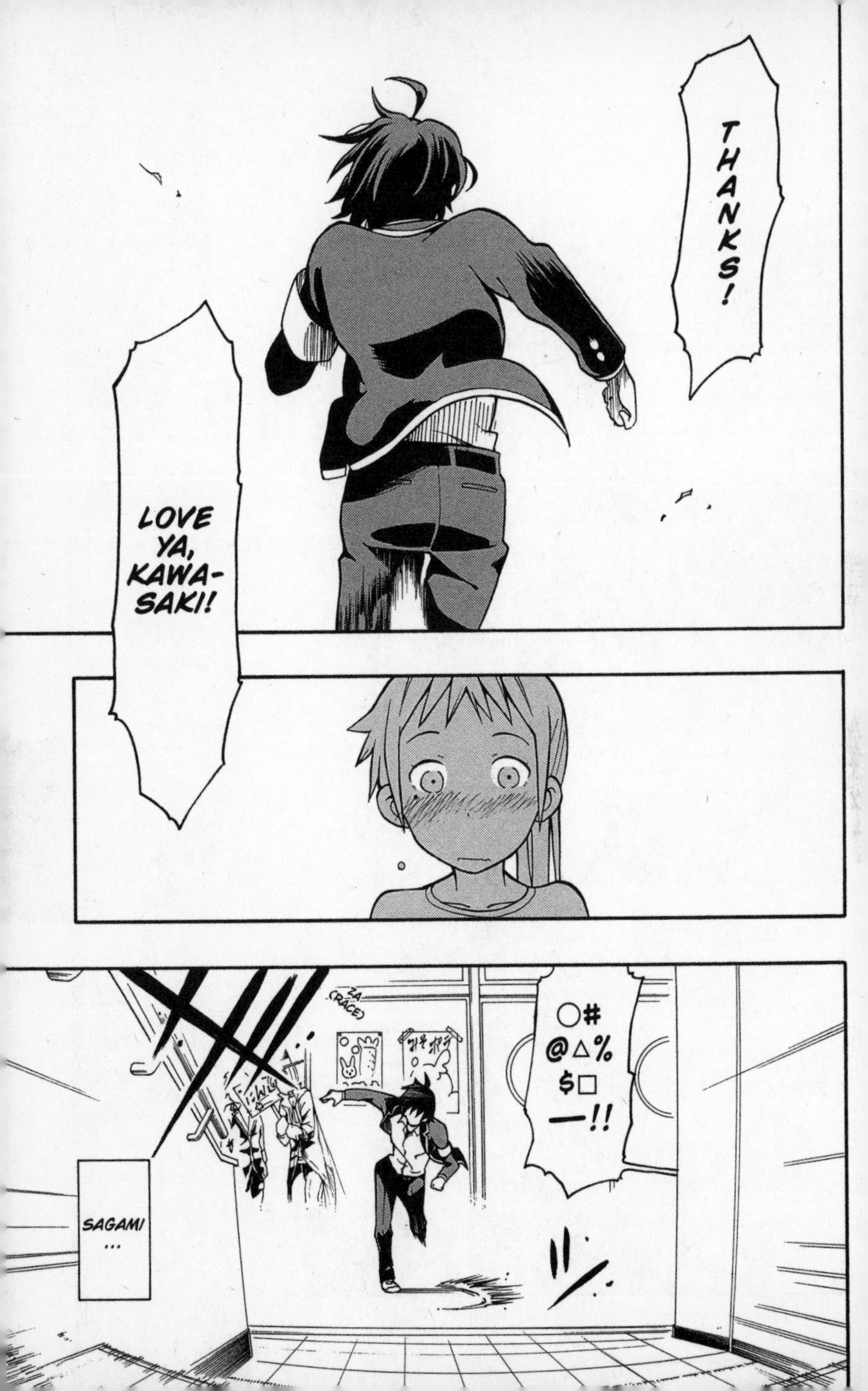
THANKS!
LOVE YA, KAWASAKI!
ZA (RACE)
○# @△% $□ —!!
SAGAMI ...

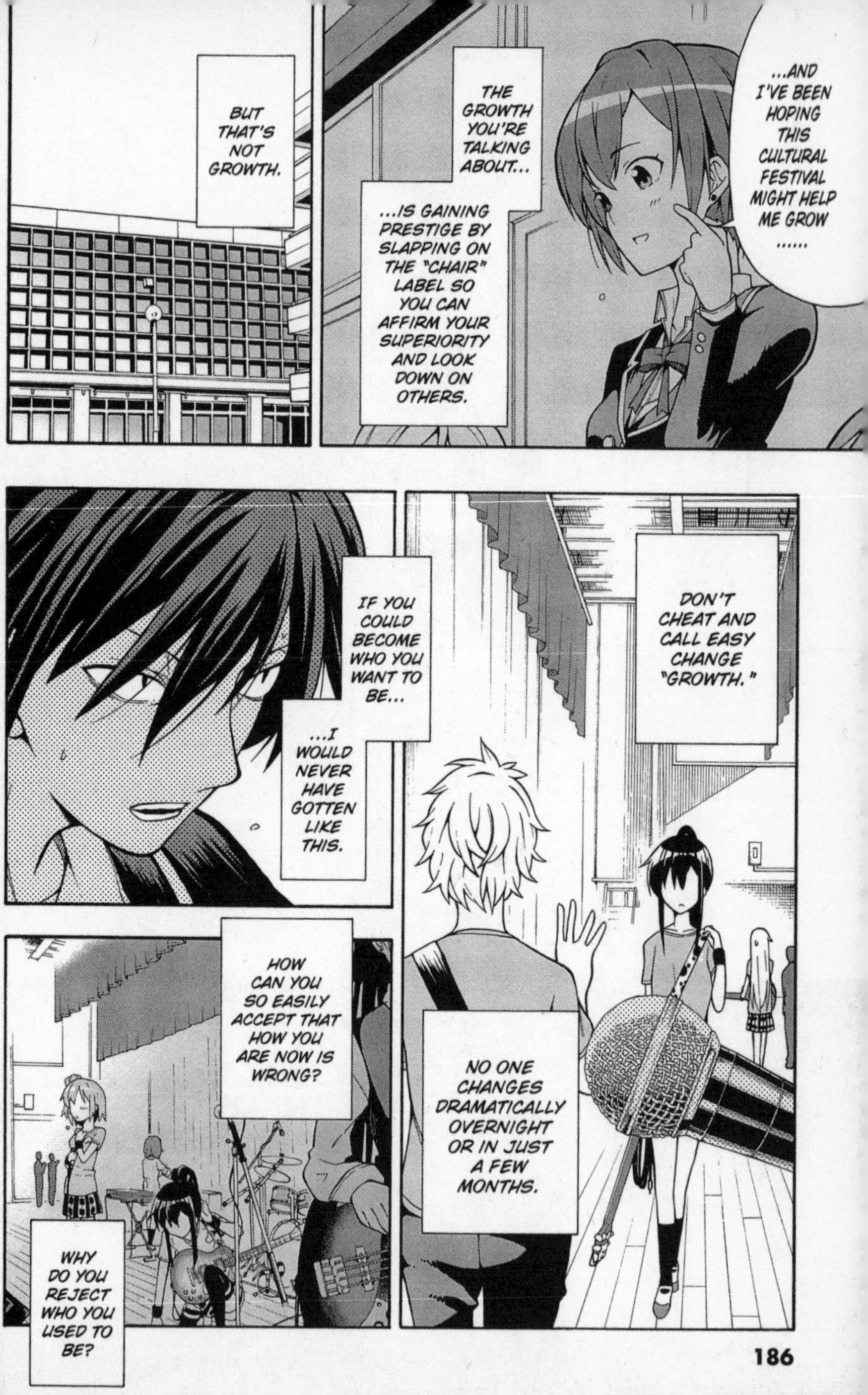
...AND I'VE BEEN HOPING THIS CULTURAL FESTIVAL MIGHT HELP ME GROW ......
THE GROWTH YOU'RE TALKING ABOUT...
...IS GAINING PRESTIGE BY SLAPPING ON THE "CHAIR" LABEL SO YOU CAN AFFIRM YOUR SUPERIORITY AND LOOK DOWN ON OTHERS.
BUT THAT'S NOT GROWTH.
DON'T CHEAT AND CALL EASY CHANGE "GROWTH."
NO ONE CHANGES DRAMATICALLY OVERNIGHT OR IN JUST A FEW MONTHS.
IF YOU COULD BECOME WHO YOU WANT TO BE...
...I WOULD NEVER HAVE GOTTEN LIKE THIS.
HOW CAN YOU SO EASILY ACCEPT THAT HOW YOU ARE NOW IS WRONG?
WHY DO YOU REJECT WHO YOU USED TO BE?

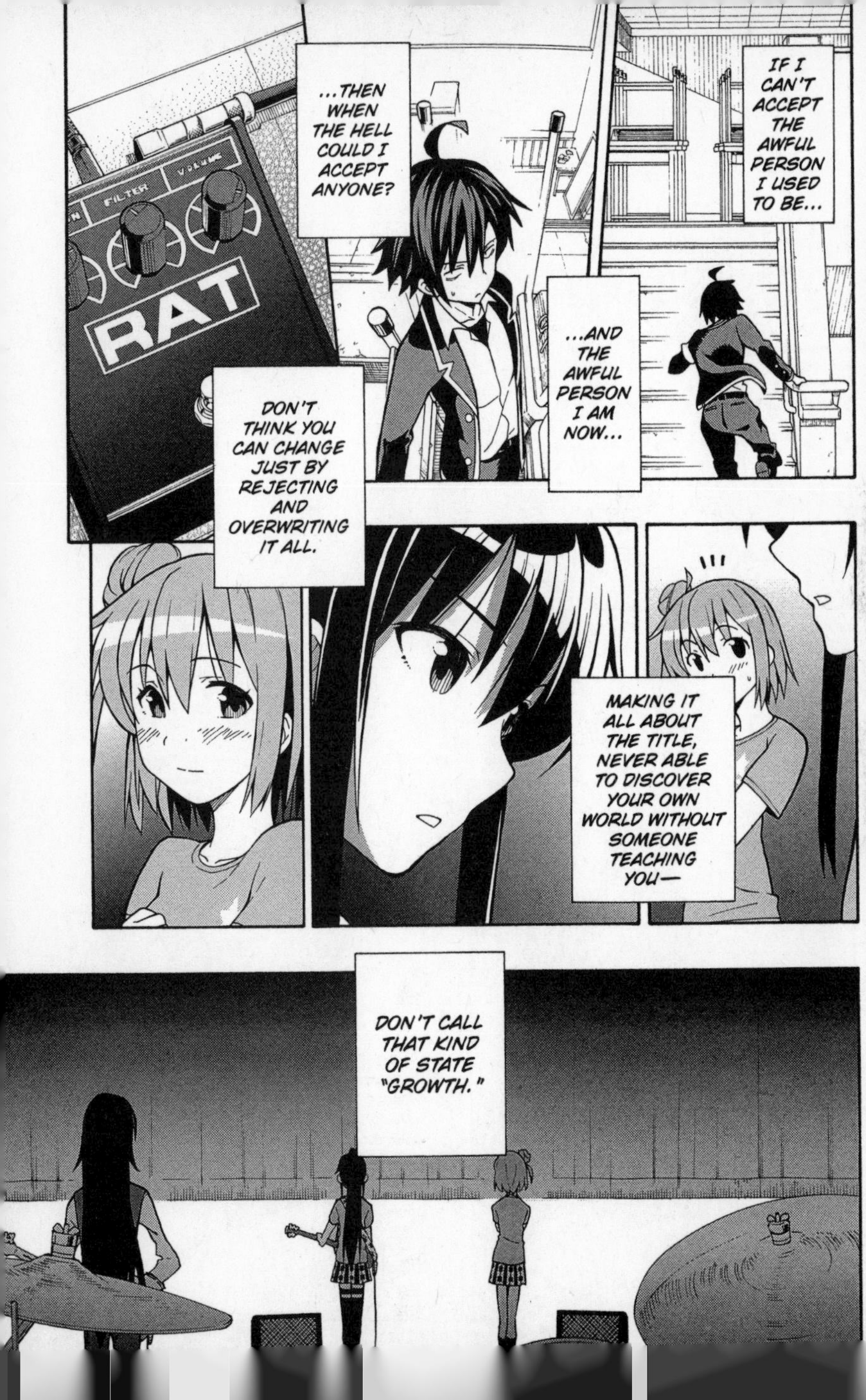
IF I CAN'T ACCEPT THE AWFUL PERSON I USED TO BE...
...AND THE AWFUL PERSON I AM NOW...
...THEN WHEN THE HELL COULD I ACCEPT ANYONE?
RAT
DON'T THINK YOU CAN CHANGE JUST BY REJECTING AND OVERWRITING IT ALL.
MAKING IT ALL ABOUT THE TITLE, NEVER ABLE TO DISCOVER YOUR OWN WORLD WITHOUT SOMEONE TEACHING YOU—
DON'T CALL THAT KIND OF STATE "GROWTH."

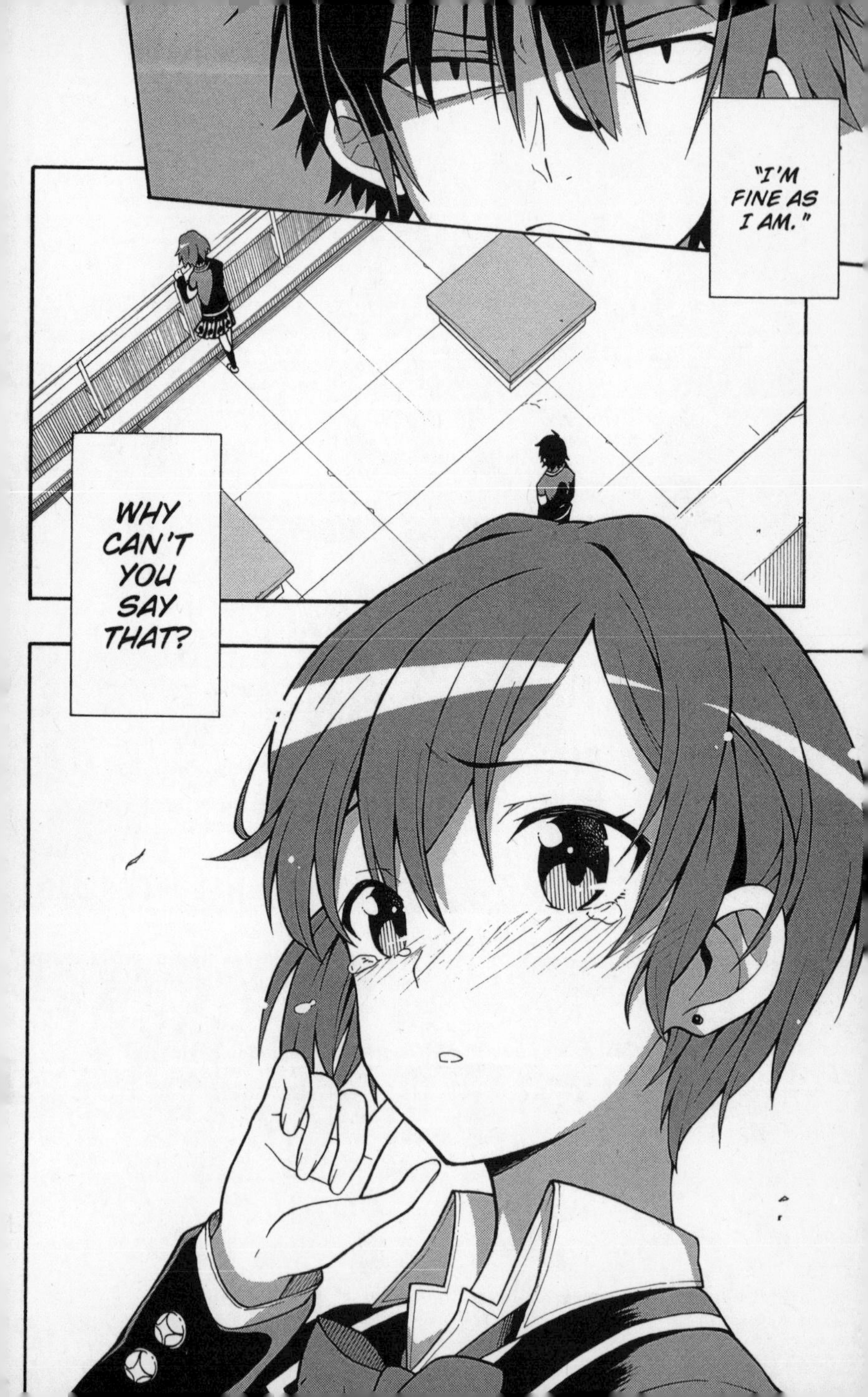
"I'M FINE AS I AM."
WHY CAN'T YOU SAY THAT?

MY YOUTH ROMANTIC COMEDY IS WRONG, AS I EXPECTE

...To Be Continued

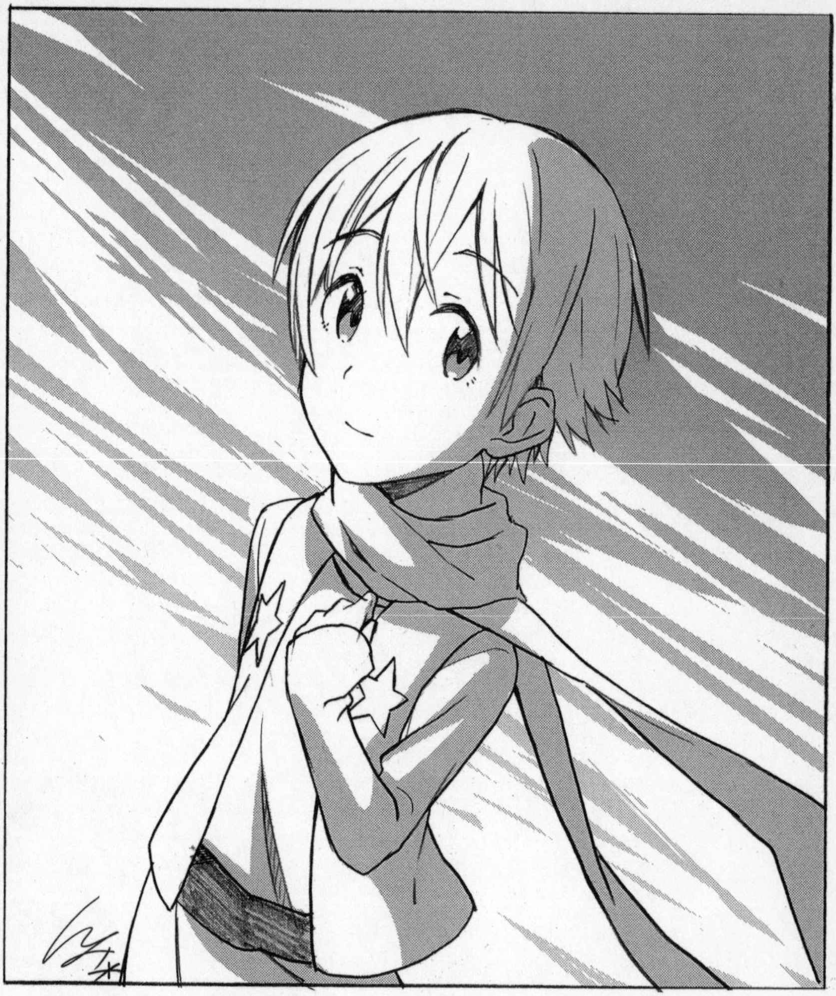

Hello, this is Naomichi Io. This is my first afterword since Volume 2.

Now then, *Youth Romantic Comedy @comic* has finally hit the cultural festival arc, and behind the dazzling show, it's a disaster zone. This sort of thing is realistic, and it happens a lot. When I was in university, it really was just like this. So I couldn't help but get particularly psyched up about this volume of *Youth Romantic Comedy*—the details in Soubu High School during the cultural festival, especially. My idea here is, the fancier the festival gets, the more Hachiman's blandness as he works in the background stands out. So consulting my assistants, we added different ideas and created this. This meant we packed a heck of a lot of images in the book. Well, it was fun, so nothing lost and nothing gained, really!

Anyway, little by little, *@comic* is accelerating toward some sheer excitement!
I hope you'll stay with us for the next volume!

Special thanks: Wataru Watari-sensei, Ponkan⑧-sensei, the Gagaga Bunko editorial department, the *Monthly Sunday GX* editorial department, Chiba city location services, and my assistants, Yamada-kun and Takahashi-kun.

MY YOUTH
R♥MANTIC COMEDY
is WRØNG, AS I EXPECTED
@ comic

CHAPTER 43.5 ··· YET AGAIN, SHIZUKA HIRATSUKA GIVES NEW ORDERS ①

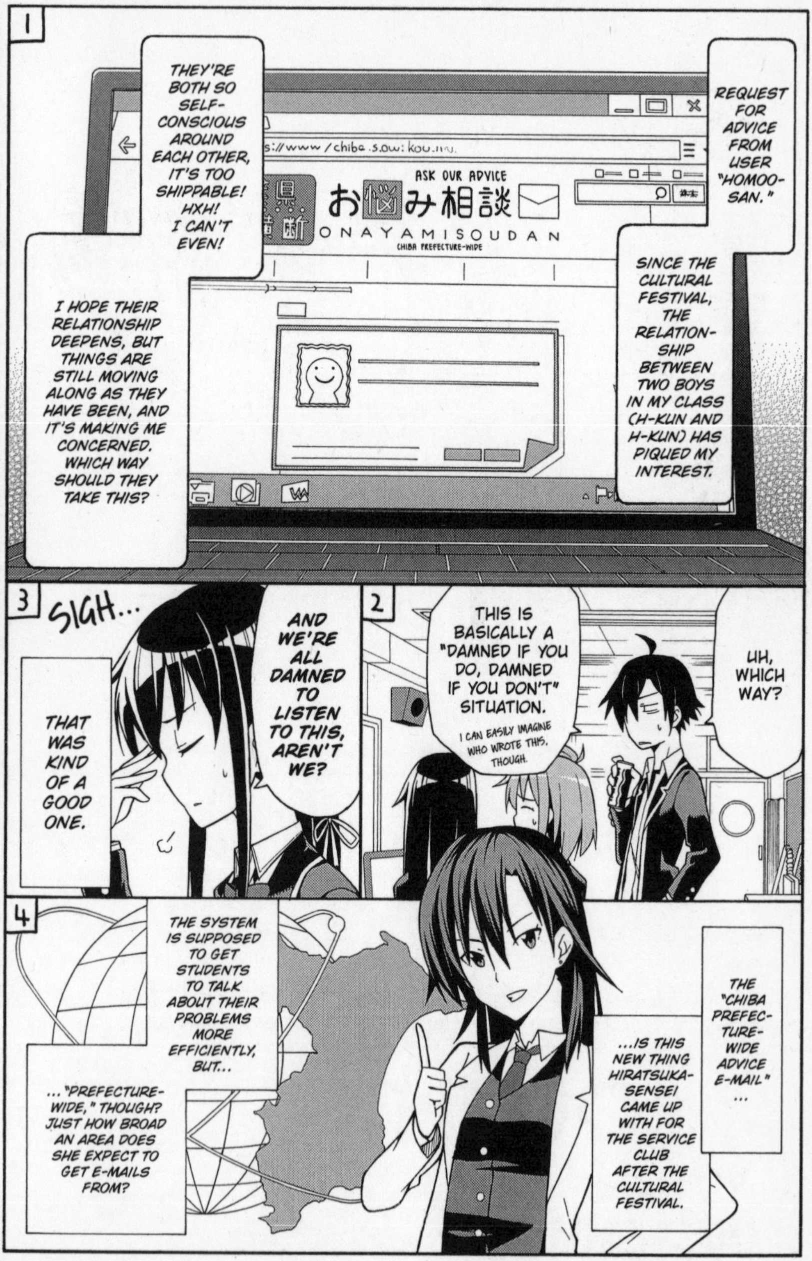
REQUEST FOR ADVICE FROM USER "HOMOO-SAN."
SINCE THE CULTURAL FESTIVAL, THE RELATIONSHIP BETWEEN TWO BOYS IN MY CLASS (H-KUN AND H-KUN) HAS PIQUED MY INTEREST.
ASK OUR ADVICE
お悩み相談
ONAYAMISOUDAN
CHIBA PREFECTURE-WIDE
THEY'RE BOTH SO SELF-CONSCIOUS AROUND EACH OTHER, IT'S TOO SHIPPABLE! HXH! I CAN'T EVEN!
I HOPE THEIR RELATIONSHIP DEEPENS, BUT THINGS ARE STILL MOVING ALONG AS THEY HAVE BEEN, AND IT'S MAKING ME CONCERNED. WHICH WAY SHOULD THEY TAKE THIS?
UH, WHICH WAY?
THIS IS BASICALLY A "DAMNED IF YOU DO, DAMNED IF YOU DON'T" SITUATION.
I CAN EASILY IMAGINE WHO WROTE THIS, THOUGH.
AND WE'RE ALL DAMNED TO LISTEN TO THIS, AREN'T WE?
SIGH...
THAT WAS KIND OF A GOOD ONE.
THE "CHIBA PREFECTURE-WIDE ADVICE E-MAIL"...
...IS THIS NEW THING HIRATSUKA-SENSEI CAME UP WITH FOR THE SERVICE CLUB AFTER THE CULTURAL FESTIVAL.
THE SYSTEM IS SUPPOSED TO GET STUDENTS TO TALK ABOUT THEIR PROBLEMS MORE EFFICIENTLY, BUT...
..."PREFECTURE-WIDE," THOUGH? JUST HOW BROAD AN AREA DOES SHE EXPECT TO GET E-MAILS FROM?

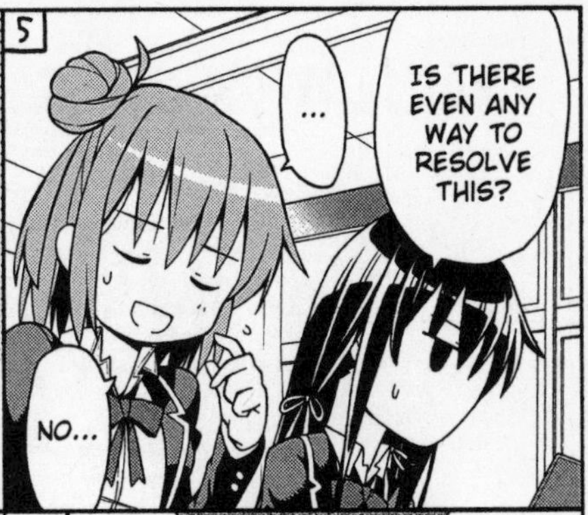
IS THERE EVEN ANY WAY TO RESOLVE THIS?
...
NO...

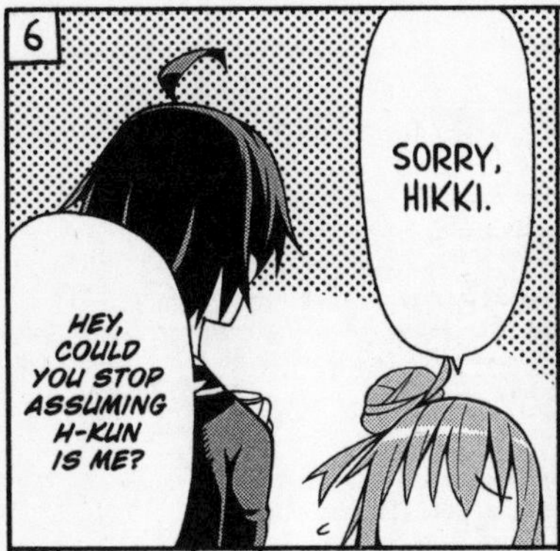
SORRY, HIKKI.
HEY, COULD YOU STOP ASSUMING H-KUN IS ME?

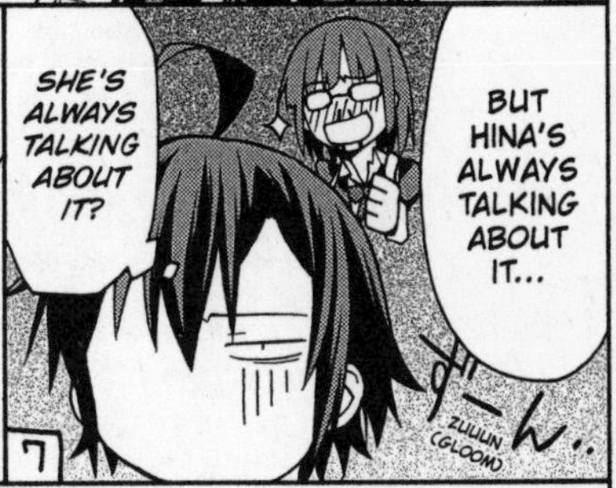
BUT HINA'S ALWAYS TALKING ABOUT IT...
SHE'S ALWAYS TALKING ABOUT IT?
ZUUUN (GLOOM)

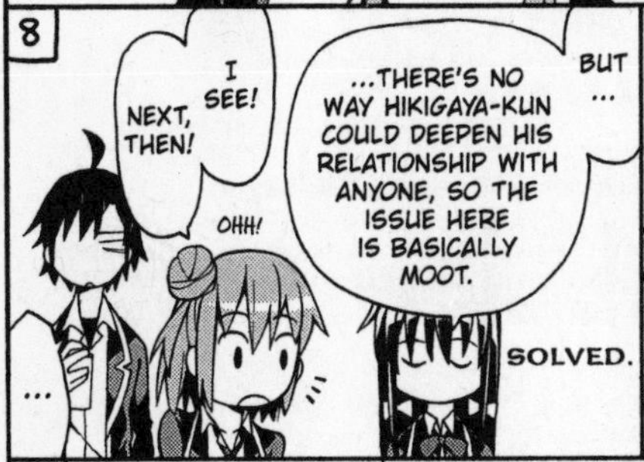
BUT ...
...THERE'S NO WAY HIKIGAYA-KUN COULD DEEPEN HIS RELATIONSHIP WITH ANYONE, SO THE ISSUE HERE IS BASICALLY MOOT.
SOLVED.
I SEE!
NEXT, THEN!
OHH!
...

9

RESPONSE FROM THE SERVICE CLUB—

THOUGH I BELIEVE THIS MAY BE UNLIKELY, COULD IT BE THAT PERHAPS "HXH" IS ENTIRELY A FIGMENT OF YOUR IMAGINATION?

WELL, THIS MIGHT BE WHOLLY OFF THE MARK, BUT ALLOW ME TO SUGGEST THE POSSIBILITY.

THE CHIBA PREFECTURE-WIDE ADVICE E-MAIL CAN ONLY CONVEY INFORMATION VIA TEXT, SO PLEASE CONSIDER THIS THE LIMITS OF THE MEDIUM.

TO BE CONTINUED

TRANSLATION NOTES

Page 21
"No, no, that's the King of Muay Thai" was "No, no, that's Edmond" in Japanese. Meguri originally tries to write the Japanese characters in Sagami's name but accidentally writes them as the similar-looking characters for *sumo*. Edmond Honda (aka E. Honda) is a character from the *Street Fighter* video game series and a sumo wrestler. For the English version, Meguri's sloppy writing turns *Sagami* into *Sagat*, a Muay Thai fighter from *Street Fighter*.

Page 49
Little-Myu is a referencce to how *myu* is often used as short for *musical* in Japanese. Little-Myu is particularly evocative of Tenimyu, the *Prince of Tennis* musicals, of which there have been over a dozen. Unlike the *Prince of Tennis* manga, which was ostensibly a sport series for boys, *Tenimyu* is unabashedly *fujoshi* bait. The Japanese title for *The Little Prince* is *Hoshi no Oujisama* (*Prince of the Stars*), so *Little-Myu* was originally *Hoshimyu*.

Page 51
Hina is indeed using the signature catchphrase from *Pokémon*, **"I choose you."**

Count-count-counting on you was *yoroyoro* in Japanese, a playful version of *yoroshiku* ("counting on you"). The phrase is a verbal quirk from the twin characters Ami and Mami Futami in THE iDOLM@STER.

Page 59
OREGAIRU is short for *Ore no Seishun Love Come wa Machigatteiru*, the Japanese-language title of *My Youth Romantic Comedy Is Wrong, As I Expected*. Long titles commonly have shortened names in Japanese media, and it's a very common practice with light novels.

Page 88
My Teen Romantic Comedy SNAFU is an alternate title for *My Youth Romantic Comedy Is Wrong, As I Expected*, used for the English release of the anime. The text in the background is taken from an old version of the English Wikipedia page for the series and can be found at http://en.wikipedia.org/w/index.php?title=My_Youth_Romantic_Comedy_Is_Wrong,_As_I_Expected&oldid=740438657

Page 106
A Unified World, or *Hakkou Ichiu*, is an Imperial Japanese slogan. The literal meaning in its original context, the *Nihon Shoki*, is roughly, "I shall cover the eight directions and make them my abode" (referring to the emperor). This was later used as justification for imperialist expansion, essentially the Japanese version of "manifest destiny."

Page 110
Hachiman's hands here form the shape of the Japanese character for **person/people**.